Finance Sense

Finance for Non-Finance Executives

FIFTH EDITION

About the Author

Dr Prasanna Chandra, Director of Centre for Financial Management, is an MBA, PhD (Finance). He has over four and a half decades of teaching experience in postgraduate and executive education programmes. He was a professor of finance at Indian Institute of Management, Bangalore, for nearly two decades. He was a visiting professor of finance at Southern Illinois University, USA, for two years. He was appointed as a member of several committees including the Capital Issues Advisory Committee, the High Powered Committee on Insurance Sector Reforms, and the SEBI Committee on Derivatives. He has served on the boards of a number of organisations including Torrent Pharmaceuticals, Power Finance Corporation, UTIIAS, ICFAI, SDMIMD, IFCI, IIM (B), Templeton Mutual Fund, Bangalore Stock Exchange Limited, and Karnataka Soaps and Detergents Limited. He has also been a consultant to many organisations.

Dr Chandra has conducted executive seminars for a number of organisations like TCS, Infosys, Tata Motors, ITC, NIIT, Tata Steel, Sasken Communications, BHEL, Bharat Shell, ANZ Grindlays, HMT, Canara Bank, Vysya Bank, ONGC, Wipro, GAIL, Microsoft, Motorola, and Tata Power.

He has published nine books including *Finance Sense; Strategic Financial Management: Managing for Value Creation; Projects: Planning, Analysis, Financing, Implementation, and Review; Investment Game; Corporate Valuation; Financial Management: Theory and Practice; Fundamentals of Financial Management; Valuation of Equity Shares;* and *Behavioural Finance* and has authored over 70 articles in professional journals and business periodicals. He has been a Fulbright Scholar and a UNDP Fellow. He has received several honours including the Best Teacher Award from the Association of Indian Management Schools.

Finance Sense

Finance for Non-Finance Executives

FIFTH EDITION

Prasanna Chandra
Director
Centre for Financial Management
Bangalore

McGraw Hill Education (India) Private Limited

Published by McGraw Hill Education (India) Private Limited,
Anjana Complex No.: 5/90 A, Butt Road, St. Thomas Mount, Chennai – 600016,
Tamil Nadu, India.

Finance Sense: Finance for Non-Finance Executives, 5e

Seventh reprint 2022

Print Edition
ISBN-13: 978-93-5260-624-5
ISBN-10: 93-5260-624-8

Ebook Edition
ISBN-13: 978-93-5260-625-2
ISBN-10: 93-5260-625-6

08 09 10 11 12 RAJ 26 25 24 23 22

Managing Director: Lalit Singh
General Manager—Production: Rajender P Ghansela
Production Manager: Reji Kumar

Typeset at The Composers, 260, C.A. Apt., Paschim Vihar, New Delhi 110 063 and
Printed and bound in India at Rajkamal Electric Press, Plot No. 2, Phase-IV, Kundli,
Sonepat, Haryana.

Visit us at: www.mheducation.co.in
Toll free in India: **1800 103 5875**
Write to us at: info.india@mheducation.com
CIN: U80302TN2010PTC111532

To

My Brother

Late Prakash Chandra Shrimal

and

My Sister-in-Law

Late Mangala Shrimal

Preface to the Fifth Edition

This book, along with its precusor *Managers' Guide to Accounting and Finance,* is over three decades old. Its longevity and popularity may be attributed to a growing number of readers who have found it useful, relevant, and readable.

Do you know how to do the following:

- Prepare financial statements
- Analyse financial statements
- Prepare financial forecasts
- Estimate the cost of a product
- Conduct break-even analysis
- Evaluate various alternatives relating to an operating decision
- Develop a budget
- Measure business performance
- Evaluate a capital budgeting proposal
- Determine the appropriate financing mix
- Assess the financial impact of changing credit policies
- Monitor the debtors position
- Evaluate an acquisition target
- Manage foreign exchange exposure
- Diagnose the levers of value creation

These are some of the important topics covered in this book. "Almost everything in business eventually boils down to the rupee sign," so the adage goes. Hence, irrespective of what your primary area of work is, you need a basic grounding in finance and accounting.

This book will help you to:

- Understand the financial and accounting reports used in business
- Appreciate the financial implications of your decision, and
- Communicate meaningfully with your colleagues in the language of accounting and finance.

This book will thus hone your finance sense which is essential for your professional or business success. It is divided into five parts which cover key areas of finance and accounting. A brief description of these parts is as follows:

Part One provides a firm grounding in financial statements, financial statement analysis, accounting mechanics, and financial forecasting.

Part Two discusses the key concepts, tools, and systems of cost accounting, budgeting, managerial decision making, and cost management.

Part Three presents an overview of the financial system, dwells on the ideas of compounding and discounting, and introduces the basic risk-return tradeoff in finances.

Part Four covers the key areas of financial management such as capital budgeting, financing strategy, sources of finance, and working capital management.

Part Five explores special topics like mergers, acquisitions, and restructuring, international finance, corporate valuation, risk management, and value-based management. In addition, it provides a primer on macroeconomics.

CHANGES IN THE FIFTH EDITION

Enthused by the encouraging response to the fourth edition, I have added new topics to enrich the book. More specifically, the following enhancements have been made.

- Two new chapters have been added:
  - Chapter 21 : Corporate Valuation
  - Chapter 22: Risk Management
- Four new appendixes have been added:
  - Appendix 8A: Frugal Innovations in Emerging Markets
  - Appendix 10A: Microsoft Excel as a Financial Calculator
  - Appendix 11A: Beta Values for Nifty Junior Stocks
  - Appendix 16A: Supply Chain Management

In addition, a number of revisions have been made in various chapters.

Due to the above enrichments, I believe that this book is an improvement over its predecessor.

I earnestly solicit suggestions and comments from the readers of the book for improving the next edition.

PRASANNA CHANDRA
chandra@cfm-india.com

Acknowledgements

I am grateful to the participants of a numerous executive development programmes for providing the stimulus to write this book. I am indebted to Dr. P. G. Apte for contributing the chapter on Macroeconomics. I am also grateful to Shri Venugopal Unni and Prof. Padmini Srinivasan for their valuable inputs and suggestions. I am deeply thankful to Savita and Pushpalata for their help in preparing the manuscript of the book.

Prasanna Chandra
chandra@cfm-india.com

Contents

PART I

Financial Statements and Financial Accounting

1. Financial Statements
2. Financial Statement Analysis
3. Accounting Mechanics
4. Financial Forecasting

Financial Statements 1

Managers, shareholders, creditors, employees, suppliers, lenders, business partners, tax authorities, regulators, and other interested groups seek answers to the following important questions about a firm:

- *What is the financial position of the firm at a given point of time?*
- *How has the firm performed financially over a given period of time?*
- *What have been the sources and uses of cash over a given period of time?*

To answer the above questions, the accountant prepares three statements, the balance sheet, the profit and loss account, and the cash flow statement. The balance sheet shows the financial position (or condition) of the firm at a given point of time. It provides a snapshot and may be regarded as a static picture. The profit and loss account reflects the performance of the firm over a period of time. Finally, the cash flow statement shows the sources and uses of cash during the period.

Usually a firm has to prepare two sets of statements, one for financial reporting and the other for tax purposes. The statements meant for financial reporting are found in the annual report and are public; the statements for tax purposes are not public. This chapter discusses the former, not the latter.

This chapter provides a primer on financial statements. It is divided into nine sections as follows:

- Overview of business activities
- Basic concepts underlying financial accounting
- How the accounting model works
- Balance sheet
- Statement of profit and loss
- Statement of cash flows
- Other items in annual reports

- Manipulation of the bottom line
- Financial statements in the U.S.

1.1 OVERVIEW OF BUSINESS ACTIVITIES

Financial statements present the results of a firm's business activities. So, before we discuss financial statements, let us look at the business activities they attempt to portray.

The key business activities of a firm are: (a) establishing goals and developing strategies, (b) raising funds, (c) investing in resources, and (d) conducting operations.

The goals of a firm are the end results the firm seeks to achieve and the strategies of the firm are the means for achieving its goals. A firm sets its goals and develops its strategies taking into account the economic, institutional, and cultural environment in which it operates.

To illustrate, the goals of Modern Electronics may be to develop a stream of new electronic products that it can manufacture and market profitably so that the value of the firm is enhanced. To accomplish its goals, Modern Electronics may pursue the following strategies: (a) invest substantially in research and development, (b) manufacture the critical devices internally to ensure quality and protect against imitation by competitors, and (c) market the products through highly qualified and trained technical personnel.

Modern Electronics will need funds for its activities. The two broad sources of finance available to a firm are shareholders' funds (also called equity) and loan funds (also called debt). Shareholders' funds come mainly in the form of equity capital (referred to sometimes as ordinary capital in India) and retained earnings and secondarily in the form of preference capital. Loan funds can be raised through various means or instruments such as debentures, term loans, deferred credit, fixed deposits, and working capital loans.

The finances raised by a firm are invested in a variety of fixed assets such as land, buildings, equipments, and warehouses. These resources provide the capacity to manufacture and distribute products and services for years to come. Apart from fixed assets, the firm also invests in raw materials, receivables, manpower training, research and development, and other things so that it can carry out operating activities.

Operating activities are concerned with the production and delivery of goods and services to customers. Firms seek to charge a price for their goods and services so that they cover all their costs and earn a satisfactory profit margin.

EXHIBIT 1.1 ***Business Activities***

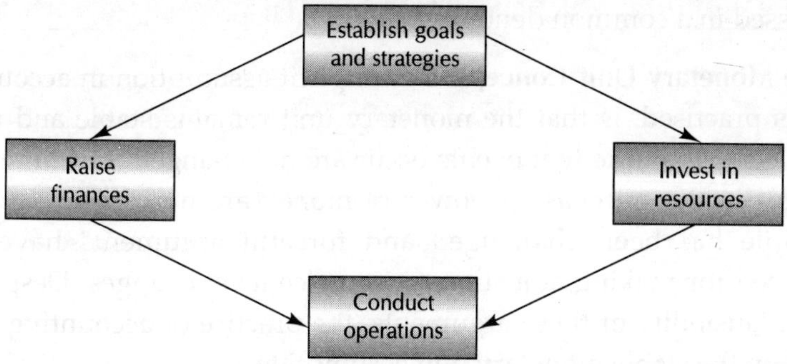

1.2 BASIC CONCEPTS UNDERLYING FINANCIAL ACCOUNTING

A business firm engages in a number of economic transactions. It raises capital, it invests in different kinds of assets, it buys raw materials on credit or cash, it transforms raw materials into finished goods by applying labour and machinery, it sells finished goods on credit, it collects its receivables, it pays interest and taxes, it depreciates its machineries, it repays borrowed money, so on and so forth.

The financial accounting model processes the economic transactions to produce a set of financial statements as shown in Exhibit 1.2.

EXHIBIT 1.2 ***The Accounting Model***

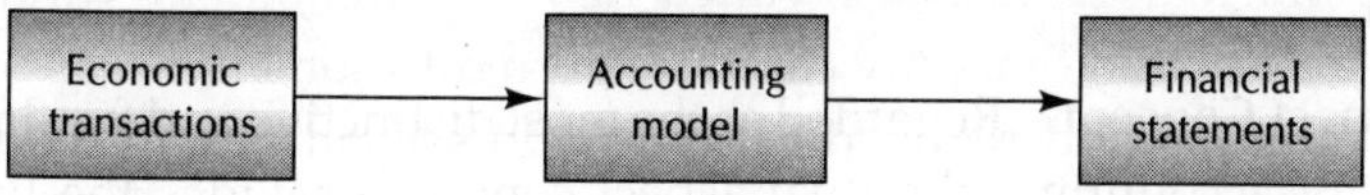

The framework of financial accounting is based on several concepts (also referred to as postulates, conventions and principles) which have received widespread, though not universal, acceptance by accountants. The important concepts are briefly described below:

Entity Concept For purposes of accounting, the business firm is regarded as a separate entity. Accounts are maintained for the entity as distinct from the persons who are connected with it. The accountant records transactions as they affect this entity and regards owners, creditors, suppliers, employees, customers, and the government as parties transacting with this entity.

Money Measurement Concept Accounting is concerned with only those facts which are expressible in monetary terms. The use of a monetary yardstick provides a means by which heterogeneous elements, such as land, plant and equipment, inventories, securities, and goodwill may be expressed in a common denominator.

Stable Monetary Unit Concept An implicit assumption in accounting, as it is practised, is that the monetary unit remains stable and values recorded at the time that events occur are not changed. Put differently, changes in the purchasing power of money are not considered. This principle has been challenged and forceful arguments have been advanced for making adjustments for price level changes. Despite the great plausibility of these arguments, the practice of accounting is still based on the stable monetary unit assumption.

Going Concern Concept According to the going concern concept, accounting is normally based on the premise that the business entity will remain a going concern for an indefinitely long period.

Cost Concept Assets acquired by a business are generally recorded at their cost and this is used for all subsequent accounting purposes. For example, depreciation is charged on the basis of the original cost. It is evident that this concept is related to the stable monetary unit concept.

Conservatism Concept This concept modifies the cost concept in the case of current assets. It is usually stated as follows: "Anticipate no profit but provide for all possible losses". In accordance with this concept, current assets are generally valued at cost or market value, whichever is lower.

Dual Aspect Concept Regarded as the most distinctive and fundamental concept of accounting, the dual aspect concept provides the basis for accounting mechanics. Before explaining this concept, let us define the terms **'assets'**, **'liabilities'**, and **'equity'**.

Assets are what the firm 'owns'. The major assets of a firm are land, buildings, plant and machinery, financial securities, inventories, debtors, bank balances, and advances and loans given to others.

Liabilities are what the firm owes to various parties such as lenders, suppliers, employees, government, and others. Term loans, working capital advances, trade credit, wages payable, and taxes payable are examples of liabilities.

Equity represents the residual interest of the owners in the assets of the firm. Equity is simply the difference between the assets of the firm and its liabilities.

According to the dual aspect principle the assets of the firm are always equal to its liabilities and equity.

Assets = Liabilities + Equity

How come that the above identity always holds? To answer this question let us look at the relationship between the firm (the accounting entity) and the owners.

If the firm makes profits which are ploughed back in the business, reserves and surplus (which represent a part of equity) increase. It is as if the firm were telling the owners: "Since you have created me, the profits that I have retained belong to you. So, I am increasing the reserves and surplus and thereby acknowledging that you have a higher claim on me".

What happens if the firm incurs losses? If the firm incurs losses, reserves and surplus decline. It is as if the firm were telling the owners: "Since you have created me, the losses incurred by me shall be borne by you. So I am reducing the reserves and surplus and thereby reducing your claim on mc".

Thus, the balance in the reserves and surplus account is adjusted to ensure that the balance sheet always balances.

Accounting Period Concept In order to know the results of business operations and financial position of the firm periodically, time is divided into segments referred to as accounting periods. Income is measured for these periods and the financial position is assessed at the end of an accounting period.

Accrual Concept Revenues are recognised when sales are made or services rendered, irrespective of when cash is received. Expenses are matched to sales, regardless of when cash is paid. Net profit of a period is the difference between the revenues earned and expenses incurred in the period.

Realisation Concept According to the realisation concept, revenue is deemed to be earned only when it is realised. When is revenue realised? It is normally deemed to be realised when goods are shipped or delivered to the customer, and not when a sales order is received or a contract signed or goods manufactured.

Matching Concept Once revenues for an accounting period are recognised, expenses incurred in generating these revenues are matched against them. This ensures that sales and cost of goods sold in the income statement refer to the same products. Note that expenses are matched to revenues and not vice versa.

1.3 HOW THE ACCOUNTING MODEL WORKS

At this juncture, it might be instructive to show how the accounting model processes economic transactions. We will use a simple illustration in which all the transactions will be recorded directly on the balance sheet.

Ram sets up a proprietory business called Ram Enterprises. The transactions of the firm for the first quarter are recorded on the balance sheet as follows:

Transaction 1: Ram contributes ₹500,000 as equity capital which is deposited in a bank account opened in the name of Ram Enterprises.

This means that an asset (bank deposit) increases by ₹500,000 and an equity account (share capital) increases by ₹500,000.

The effect of this transaction on the balance sheet of Ram Enterprises is as follows:

Liabilities + Equity		*Assets*	
Share capital	: ₹500,000	Bank deposit	: ₹500,000
Total	: ₹500,000	Total	: ₹500,000

Transaction 2: Ram Enterprises pays ₹100,000 as deposit for hiring office premises - we will call this as 'premise deposit'.

This means that an asset (premise deposit) increases by ₹100,000 and another asset (bank deposit) decreases by ₹100,000.

The effect of this transaction on the balance sheet of Ram Enterprises is as follows:

Liabilities + Equity		*Assets*	
Share capital	: ₹500,000	Bank deposit	: ₹400,000
		Premise deposit	: ₹100,000
Total	: ₹500,000	Total	: ₹5,00,000

Transaction 3: Ram Enterprises buys furniture and fixtures for ₹300,000 in cash.

This means that an asset (furniture and fixtures) increases by ₹300,000 and another asset (bank deposit) decreases by ₹300,000.

The effect of this transaction on the balance sheet of Ram Enterprises is as follows:

Liabilities + Equity		*Assets*	
Capital	₹500,000	Bank deposit	₹100,000
		Premise deposit	₹100,000
		Furniture & fixtures	₹300,000
Total	₹500,000	Total	₹500,000

Transaction 4: Ram Enterprises buys merchandise worth ₹300,000 on credit.

This means that an asset (merchandise) increases by ₹300,000 and an liability account (trade creditors) increases by ₹300,000.

The effect of this transaction on the balance sheet of Ram Enterprises is as follows:

Liabilities + Equity		*Assets*	
Capital	₹500,000	Bank deposit	₹100,000
Trade credit	₹300,000	Premise deposit	₹100,000
		Furniture & fixtures	₹300,000
		Merchandise	₹300,000
Total	₹800,000	Total	₹800,000

Transaction 5: Ram Enterprises sells merchandise costing ₹100,000 for ₹120,000 on cash.

This means that an asset (bank deposit) increases by ₹120,000, another asset (merchandise) decreases by ₹100,000, and an equity account (reserves and surplus) increases by ₹20,000.

The effect of this transaction on the balance sheet of Ram Enterprises is as follows:

Liabilities + Equity		*Assets*	
Capital	₹500,000	Bank deposit	₹220,000
Reserves & surplus	₹20,000	Premise deposit	₹100,000
Trade creditors	₹300,000	Furniture & fixtures	₹300,000
		Merchandise	₹200,000
Total	₹820,000	Total	₹820,000

Note that this transaction generated a profit of ₹20,000 which has been retained in the business. This is shown in the reserves and surplus account.

Transaction 6: Ram Enterprises sells merchandise costing ₹80,000 for ₹100,000 on credit.

This means that an asset (debtors) increases by ₹100,000, another asset (merchandise) decreases by ₹80,000, and an equity account (reserves and surplus) increases by ₹20,000.

The effect of this transaction on the balance sheet of Ram Enterprises is as follows:

Liabilities + Equity		*Assets*	
Capital	₹500,000	Bank deposit	₹220,000
Reserves & surplus	₹40,000	Premise deposit	₹100,000
Trade creditors	₹300,000	Furniture & fixtures	₹300,000
		Merchandise	₹120,000
		Debtors	₹100,000
Total	₹840,000	Total	₹840,000

Transaction 7: Ram Enterprises pays establishment expenses of ₹5,000 in cash.

This means that an asset (bank deposit) decreases by ₹5,000 and an equity account (reserves and surplus) decreases by ₹5,000.

The effect of this transaction on the balance sheet of Ram Enterprises is as follows:

Liabilities + Equity		*Assets*	
Capital	₹500,000	Bank deposit	₹215,000
Reserves & surplus	₹35,000	Premise deposit	₹100,000
Trade credit	₹300,000	Furniture & fixtures	₹300,000
		Merchandise	₹120,000
		Debtors	₹100,000
Total	₹835,000	Total	₹835,000

Transaction 8: Ram Enterprises pays ₹9,000 as rent in cash.

This means that an asset (bank deposit) decreases by ₹9,000 and an equity account (reserves and surplus) decreases by ₹9,000.

The effect of this transaction on the financial position of the firm is as follows:

Liabilities + Equity		*Assets*	
Capital	₹500,000	Bank deposit	₹206,000
Reserves & surplus	₹26,000	Premise deposit	₹100,000
Trade credit	₹300,000	Furniture & fixtures	₹300,000
		Merchandise	₹120,000
		Debtors	₹100,000
Total	₹826,000	Total	₹826,000

Transaction 9: Ram Enterprises depreciates its furnitures and fixtures by ₹10,000.

This means that an asset (furniture and fixtures) decreases by ₹10,000 and an equity account (reserves and surplus) decreases by ₹10,000.

The effect of this transaction on the financial position of the firm is as follows:

Liabilities + Equity		*Assets*	
Capital	₹500,000	Bank deposit	₹206,000
Reserves & surplus	₹16,000	Premise deposit	₹100,000
Trade credit	₹300,000	Furniture & fixtures	₹290,000
		Merchandise	₹120,000
		Debtors	₹100,000
Total	₹816,000	Total	₹816,000

If you compare the above balance sheet with the opening balance sheet you find that 'Reserves and Surplus' which is nil in the opening balance sheet is ₹16,000 in the above balance sheet. This implies that the transactions of the first quarter have resulted in a profit of ₹16,000. Put differently, revenues have exceeded expenses by ₹16,000. The statement showing revenues, expenses, and profit (or loss), which is the profit and loss statement, is given below.

Profit and Loss Statement		
• Revenues		220,000
Cash sales	: 120,000	
Credit sales	: 100,000	
• Expenses		204,000
Merchandise cost	: 180,000	
Establishment expenses	: 5,000	
Rent	: 9,000	
Depreciation	: 10,000	
• Profit		16,000

Accounting Is as Simple as 1-2-3-4

If you carefully review the above illustration, you will find that accounting is as simple as 1-2-3-4. The four rules of accounting are as follows:

Rule 1. Every transaction has a bearing on at least two accounts in the balance sheet. Examples:

- When Ram contributes ₹500,000 toward share capital, the share capital account increases by ₹500,000 and the bank deposit increases by ₹500,000.
- When Ram Enterprises buys furnitures and fixtures for ₹300,000 in cash, the furnitures and fixtures account increases by ₹300,000 and the bank deposit account decreases by ₹300,000.
- When Ram Enterprises sells merchandise costing ₹80,000 for ₹100,000 on credit, the merchandise account decreases by ₹80,000, the debtors account increases by ₹100,000, and the reserves and surplus account increases by ₹20,000.
- When Ram Enterprises pays ₹9,000 as rent in cash, the bank deposit account decreases by ₹9,000 and the reserves and surplus account decreases by ₹9,000.

Rule 2. Irrespective of what the transaction is, the balance sheet identity is always preserved.

Assets = Equity + Liabilities

Rule 3. Transactions which do not result in a revenue or expense, have no bearing on the Reserves and Surplus' account. Examples:

- Ram contributes ₹500,000 toward share capital which is deposited in a bank account.
- Ram Enterprises buys furnitures and fixtures for ₹300,000 in cash.
- Ram Enterprises buys merchandise worth ₹300,000 on credit.

Rule 4. Transactions which result in a revenue or expense have a bearing on the 'Reserves and Surplus' account. Revenues augment 'Reserves and Surplus' whereas expenses decrease 'Reserves and Surplus'. Transactions which result in revenues and expenses are reflected on the Profit and Loss Account.

1.4 BALANCE SHEET

As you have seen, the balance sheet shows the financial condition of a business at a given time. Exhibit 1.3 shows the balance sheet of a hypothetical firm Horizon Limited as at March 31, 20X1, prepared as per the format prescribed under the Companies Act.

EXHIBIT 1.3 ***Balance Sheet of Horizon Limited as at March 31, 20X1***

₹ in crore

ASSETS		
• **Non-current Assets**	600	550
• Property, plant, and equipment	500	450
• Investments	50	40
• Long- term loans and advances	50	60
• **Current Assets**	400	350
• Inventories	160	140
• Investments	20	20
• Trade receivables	140	120
• Cash and cash equivalents	60	50
• Loans	20	20
	1000	900
EQUITY AND LIABILITIES	*20X1*	*20X0*
• **Equity**	500	450
• Equity share capital (Par value ₹10)	100	100
• Other equity	400	350
• **Non-current Liabilities**	300	270
• Borrowings	200	180
• Provisions	50	45
• Deferred tax liabilities (net)	50	45
• **Current Liabilities**	200	180
• Borrowings	40	30
• Trade payables	120	110
• Other current liabilities	30	30
• Short-term provisions	10	10
	1000	900

Before discussing various account categories found on the balance sheet of Horizon Limited note that:

- The balance sheet is prepared for Horizon Limited which is regarded as a separate accounting entity (entity concept).
- The figures in the balance sheet are expressed in monetary terms (monetary concept).
- The balance sheet assumes that Horizon Limited is a going concern (going concern concept).
- The fixed assets are stated at cost less depreciation (cost concept).
- The current assets are stated at cost or market value, whichever is lower (conservatism concept).
- Assets are equal to liabilities + equity (dual aspect concept).

Assets

Assets are resources 'owned' by the firm which are expected to provide the firm with future economic benefits, by way of higher cash inflows or lower cash outflows. Resources are recognised as assets in accounting when (a) the firm acquires rights over them as a result of a past transaction, and (b) the firm can quantify future economic benefits with a fair degree of accuracy.

Assets are classified as follows under the format prescribed by the Companies Act:

- Non-current assets
- Current assets

Non-current Assets Non-current assets are relatively long-lives assets. They are assets other than current assets. The important types of non-current assets are: property, plant, and equipment, capital work-in-progress, goodwill, other intangible assets, and financial assets. **Property, plant, and equipment**, often the most important non-current asset, comprise of land, buildings, plant and equipment, furniture and fixtures, vehicles, office equipment, and so on. They are reported in the balance sheet at their net book value, which is simply the gross value (the cost of acquiring the asset) less accumulated depreciation.

Capital work-in progress reflects the value of plant and equipment which is under construction.

Goodwill arises when a company acquires another company and the purchase consideration is greater than the net book value of assets over liabilities. Goodwill has to be amortised over a period of time.

Other intangible assets include items like brands or trademarks, computer software, mining rights, copyrights, patents and other intellectual property rights, licenses and franchises, and so on.

Financial assets comprise mainly of investments and loans. Investments consists mainly of equity and preference securities of associate companies, joint venture companies, and subsidiary companies. These investments are meant to be held for a long period and are made for the purpose of income and control. They are stated at cost less any diminution of value which is regarded as permanent in the opinion of management. Loans are usually loans and advances to associate companies, subsidiary companies, employees, and others for a period of more than one year.

Current Assets An asset is classified as a current asset when it satisfies any of the following criteria: (a) it is expected to be realised in, or is intended for sale or consumption in, the company's normal operating cycle, (b) it is held primary for the purpose of being traded, (c) it is expected to be realised within twelve months after the reporting date, or (d) it is cash or cash equivalent unless it is restricted from being exchanged or used to settle a liability for at least twelve months after the reporting date. All other assets are classified as non-current.

Current assets include inventories, current investments, trade receivables, cash and cash equivalents, short-term loans and advances, and other currents assets.

Inventories (also called stocks) comprise of raw materials, workin-process, finished goods, packing materials, and stores and spares. Inventories are generally valued at cost or net realisable value, whichever is lower. The cost of inventories includes purchase cost, conversion cost, and other cost incurred to bring them to their respective present location and condition. The cost of raw materials, stores and spares, packing materials, trading and other products is generally determined on weighted average basis. The cost of work-in-process and finished goods is generally determined on absorption costing basis—this means that the cost figure includes allocation of manufacturing overheads.

Current investments mainly represent short-term holdings of units or shares of mutual fund schemes. These investments are made primarily to generate income from short-term cash surpluses of the firm. Current investments are carried at cost or market (fair) value, whichever is lower.

Trade receivables (also called accounts receivable or sundry debtors) represent the amounts owed to the firm by its customers (who have bought goods and services on credit) and others. Trade receivables are classified into two categories viz., debts outstanding for a period exceeding six months and other debts. Further, they are classified as debts considered good and debts considered doubtful. Generally, firms make a provision for doubtful debts which is equal to debts considered doubtful. The net figure of trade receivables is arrived at after deducting the provision for doubtful debts.

Cash and cash equivalents comprise of cash on hand and credit balances with scheduled banks and non-scheduled banks.

Short-term loans and advances comprise of loans and advances given to suppliers, employees, and other companies that are recoverable within a year. The net figure of short-term loans and advances is arrived at after deducting a provision for doubtful advances, if any.

Other current assets comprise of items such as interest accrued on investments, dividends receivable, and fixed assets held for sale (the last item is valued at net book value or estimated net realisable value, whichever is lower).

Equity and Liabilities

Equity and liabilities represent what the firm "owes" others. The format prescribed in the Companies Act classifies equity and liabilities as follows:

- Equity
- Non-current liabilities
- Current liabilities

Equity Equity represents the contributions made by shareholders in some form or the other. It includes equity share capital and other equity.

Equity share capital includes equity capital as well as preference capital.

Other equity, often the most significant item on the balance sheet, represents reserves and surplus (such as, securities premium reserve, retained earnings, capital reserve, and general reserve) and other comprehensive income (such as exchange differences on translating the financial statements of foreign operation and cash flow hedge reserve).

Non-current Liabilities Non-current liabilities are liabilities which are expected to be settled after one year of the reporting date. They include financial liabilities, provisions, deferred tax liabilities (net), and other non-current liabilities.

Financial liabilities are obligations on account of borrowings, trade payable, and other non-current liabilities. *Borrowings* generally comprise of term loans from financial institutions and banks in India and abroad, rupee bonds (debentures) and foreign currency bonds, and public deposits. *Trade payables* are amounts owed to suppliers who have sold goods and services on credit.

Provisions include provisions for employee benefits such as provident fund, gratuity, superannuation, and leave encashment and other provisions.

Deferred tax liabilities (or assets) arise because of the temporary differences between taxable income and accounting profit. A deferred tax liability (asset) is recognised when the charge in the financial statements is less (more) than the amount allowed for tax purposes.

Current Liabilities Current liabilities are liabilities which are due to be settled within 12 months after the reporting date. They include financial liabilities, other current liabilities, provisions, and current tax liabilities (net).

Financial liabilities are obligations on account of borrowings, trade payables, and other financial liabilities. Borrowings are mainly in the form of working capital loans (rupee loans as well as well as foreign currency loans) and other loans and advances. Trade payables are amounts owed to suppliers who have sold goods and services on credit. Other financial liabilities include current maturities of long-term debt, current maturities of finance lease obligation, interest accrued but not yet due, and so on.

Other current liabilities include items like statutory dues and advances from customers.

Provisions include items like provisions for employee benefits.

Current tax liabilities (net) represent items like income tax liabilities (net)

1.5 STATEMENT OF PROFIT AND LOSS

The statement of profit and loss presents a summary of the operating and financial transactions which have contributed to the change in the owners' equity during the accounting period. Revenues are transactions that augment owners' equity and expenses are transactions that diminish owners' equity. Hence, the net change in owners' equity during an accounting period, called as profit after tax, is:

$$\text{Profit after tax} = \text{Revenues} - \text{Expenses}$$

This relationship is the basis for constructing the statement of profit and loss which first reports revenues, then expenses, and finally the profit after tax.

Among the various principles underlying the financial accounting model, two are of particular significance for understanding the profit and loss account, viz., the realisation principle and the matching principle. Though they have been touched upon earlier, they bear reiteration here.

According to the realisation principle, a revenue is recognised when the transaction generating the revenue takes place and not when the cash for the transaction is received. To illustrate this principle, let us consider an example. Suppose a firm sells goods worth ₹10,000 on credit to a customer. The revenue is recognised when the sale takes place even though cash may be received later. When the firm receives cash, it will adjust its balance sheet by decreasing the debtors and increasing the cash.

The matching principle says that the expenses associated with a product are recognised when the product is sold not when the cash payment is made. For example, consider a retail firm that purchases an item from a wholesaler, stocks it, and finally sells it. The expense will be recognised when the item is sold, not when it is purchased or when it is paid for.

Together, the realisation and matching principles form the basis for what is called **accrual accounting**. Thanks to accrual accounting, the profit after tax of a firm is generally different from its net cash flow.

Exhibit 1.4 shows the statement of profit and loss for Horizon Limited for the year ending March 31, 20X1, prepared as per the format prescribed by the Companies Act.

EXHIBIT 1.4 ***Statement of Profit and Loss for Horizon Limited for Year Ending March 31, 20X1***

(₹ in crore)

	Current Period	*Previous Period*
• Revenues from operations	1290	1172
• Other Income	10	8
• Total Income	1300	1180
• Expenses		
• Material expenses	600	560
• Employee benefit expenses	200	180
• Finance costs	30	25
• Depreciation and amortization expenses	50	45
• Other expenses	240	210
• Total Expenses	1120	1020
• Profit before Exceptional Items and Tax	180	160
• Exceptional Items	-	-
• Profit Before Tax	180	160
• Tax Expense	50	40
• Profit (Loss) for the Period from Continuing Operation	130	120

(Contd.)

EXHIBIT 1.4 *(Contd.)*

(₹ in crore)

	Current Period	*Previous Period*
• Profit (Loss) from Discontinued Operations (after Tax)	-	-
• Other Comprehensive Income	-	-
• -Total Comprehensive Income for the Year	130	120
• Earning Per Equity Share		
• Basic	₹ 13	
• Diluted	₹ 13	

Revenues from operations represent revenues from (a) sales of products and services less excise duties, and (b) other operating income. For a finance company, revenues from operations consist of revenues from interest and financial services.

Other income consists of the following: (a) interest income (in case of a company other than a finance company), (b) dividend income, (c) net gain/loss on sale of investments, and (d) other non-operating income (net of expenses directly attributable to such income).

Expenses comprise material expenses, employee benefit expenses, finance costs, depreciation and amortisation expenses, and other expenses. **Material expenses** equal the cost of materials consumed plus purchase of stock-in-trade minus (plus) increase (decrease) in inventories of finished goods, work-in-progress, and stock-in-trade. **Employee benefit expenses** are classified as follows: (a) salaries and wages, (b) contribution to provident and other funds, (c) expenses on employee stock option plan (ESOP) and employee stock purchase plan (ESPP), and (d) staff welfare expenses. **Finance** costs are classified as follows: (a) interest, (b) dividend on redeemable preference shares, (c) exchange differences regarded as an adjustment to borrowing costs, and (d) other borrowings costs. **Depreciation** represents the writeoff of the cost of tangible fixed assets and **amortisation** is the writeoff of the cost of intangible fixed assets. **Other expenses** include advertising and promotion, carriage and freight, royalty, power, fuel, water, rent, travel, repairs, insurance, CSR, and miscellaneous expenses.

Exceptional items are material items which are infrequent, but not unusual, and they have to be disclosed separately by virtue of their size and incidence, for financial statements to present a true and fair view. Schedule III requires the presentations of 'exceptional items' on the face of the statement of profit and loss, without defining that term. Generally, they include items of income such as profit on sale of assets and expenses such as write-down of inventories, litigation settlements, and restructuring.

Tax expense consists of current tax and deferred tax. **Current tax** is computed by multiplying the taxable income, as reported to the tax authorities, by the appropriate tax rate. **Deferred tax**, also called future income tax, is an accounting concept that arises on account of temporary difference (also called timing difference) caused by items which are included for calculating taxable income and accounting profit but in a different manner over time. For example, depreciation is charged as per the written down value for the taxable income but usually as per the straight line method for calculating the accounting profit. As a result, there are differences in the year-to-year depreciation charges under the two methods, but the total depreciation charges over the life of the asset would be the same under both the methods.

Profit (Loss) from discontinued operations (after tax) If during the accounting period, the company has discontinued operations, the profit (loss) from discontinued operations (after tax) has to be shown separately.

Other comprehensive income includes items like changes in revaluation surplus, fair value changes relating to own credit risk of financial liabilities designated at fair value through profit or loss, exchange differences in translating the financial statements of a foreign operation, the effective portion of gains and loss on hedging instruments in a cash loss on hedging instruments in a cash flow hedge, and share of comprehensive income in associates and joint ventures.

Basic earnings per share is the net profit or loss for the period attributable to equity shareholders divided by the weighted average number of equity shares during the period. **Diluted earnings** per share is the net profit or loss for the period attributable to equity shareholders divided by the weighted average number of shares outstanding during the period, adjusted for the potential dilution arising from conversion of debt into equity, exercise of warrants and stock options, and so on.

1.6 STATEMENT OF CASH FLOWS

If a firm spends more cash than it generates, it will eventually court trouble. Many firms have died due to insufficiency of cash, even though their operations have been profitable. So, managers should understand that generating cash over time is essential to a firm's long-term survival.

The balance sheet or the profit and loss account does not focus on cash flows. So, accountants prepare the cash flow statement, the third financial statement.

If we look at the balance sheets of Horizon Limited given in Exhibit 1.3 we find that the amount of current investments plus cash and cash equivalents held by the company increased from ₹70 crores to ₹80 crores between 31.3.20X0 and 31.3.20X1. This means that during 20X0 - 20X1 Horizon Limited generated a positive total cash inflow of ₹ 10 crore.

The total net cash flow reflects the effect of all the transactions of the firm. For analytical purposes it is useful to know how different activities have a bearing on cash flows. A firm's cash position will change as a result of three types of activities, viz., operating activities, investing activities, and financing activities. Exhibit 1.5 shows the components of the cash flows.

Operating activities involve producing and selling goods and services. Cash inflows from operating activities include monies received from customers for sales of goods and services. Cash outflows from operating activities include payments to suppliers for materials, to employees for services, and to the government for taxes.

EXHIBIT 1.5 ***Components of Cash Flows***

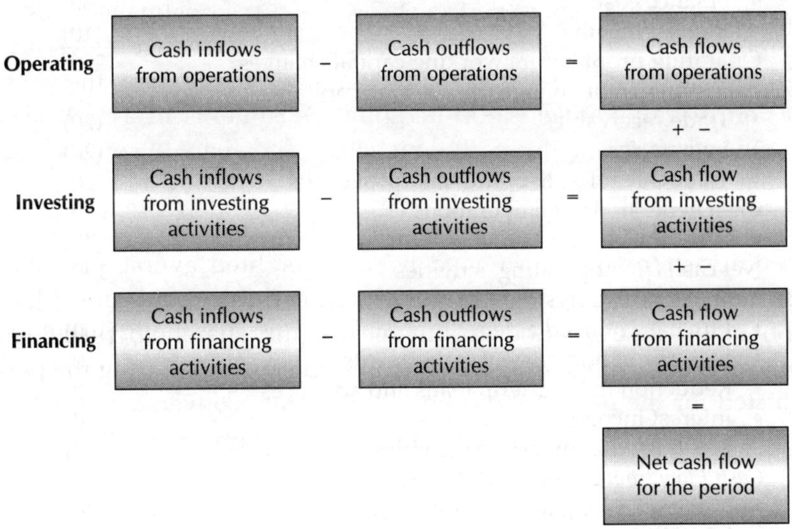

Investing activities involve acquiring and disposing fixed assets, buying and selling financial securities, and disbursing and collecting loans. Cash inflows from investing activities include receipts from the sale of assets (real as well financial), recovery of loans, and collection of dividend and interest. Cash outflows from investing activities include payments for the purchase of assets (real and financial) and disbursement of loans.

Financing activities involve raising money from lenders and shareholders, paying interest and dividend, and redeeming loans and share capital. Cash inflows from financing activities include receipts from issue of securities and from loans and deposits. Cash outflows from financing activities include payment of interest on various forms of borrowings, payment of dividend, retirement of borrowings, and redemption of capital.

Exhibit 1.6 shows the cash flow statement of Horizon Limited for the period 1.4.20X0 to 31.3.20X1 prepared in conformity with the format prescribed by the Accounting Principles Board of the Institute of Chartered Accountants of India.

EXHIBIT 1.6 *Cash Flow Statement*

	(₹ *in crore*)
(A) *Cash Flow from Operating Activities*	
Profit Before Tax	180
Adjustments for	
• Depreciation and amortisation	50
• Finance costs	30
• Interest income*	(10)
Operating profit before working capital changes	250
Adjustments for changes in working capital :	
• Trade receivables	(20)
• Inventories	(20)
• Trade payables, liabilities and provisions	20
Cash generated from operations	230
• Direct taxes paid	(50)
Net cash from operating activities	180
(B) *Cash Flow from Investing Activities*	
• Purchase of fixed assets	(100)
• Increase of non-current investments	(10)
• Reduction in long-term loans and advances	10
• Interest income	10
Net cash used in investing activities	(90)
(C) *Cash Flow from Financing Activities*	
• Increase in long term borrowings	20
• Increase in short-term borrowings	10
• Dividend paid	(80)
• Finance cost paid	(30)
Net cash from financing activities	(80)
Net cash generated (A+B+C)	10
Cash and cash equivalents at beginning of period**	70
Cash and cash equivalents at the end of period	80

* It is assumed that the entire other income is interest income

** This includes two balance sheet items viz, 'Current investments' and 'Cash and cash equivalents'

1.7 OTHER ITEMS IN THE ANNUAL REPORT

The annual report of the company is perhaps the most important source of information about the affairs of the company. In addition to the three financial statements, which form its core, the annual report contains inter alia the following:

Statement of Changes in Equity This statement reconciles the opening and closing balance of shareholders' equity. It summarises the transactions to shareholders' equity over a period of time.

Auditor's Report The financial statements of a joint stock company must be audited by an independent chartered accountant. After examining the accounting records of the company, the auditor renders an opinion as to whether the company's financial statements represent a "true and fair" view of its financial affairs and conform to Generally Accepted Accounting Principles (GAAP).

Notes Forming Part of the Financial Statements The financial statements, stand-alone as well as consolidated, are supported by notes which technically form part of them. These notes provide information on significant accounting policies and details relating to various items in the balance sheet and statement of profit and loss.

Directors' Report The Directors' Report gives a summary of financial performance, recommends a dividend, provides information on appointment of directors, auditors, and cost auditors, and carries a Directors' Responsibility Statement. In addition, it contains information on credit rating, fixed deposits, employee stock option scheme, strategic acquisitions and alliances, human resources development, subsidiary companies, corporate social responsibilities, conservation of energy, technology absorption, and foreign exchange earnings and outgo.

Management Discussion and Analysis The section on Management Discussion and Analysis provides an overview of the industry, spells out the strategy and thrust areas of the company, dwells on the risks faced by the company and its risk mitigation initiatives, presents highlights of the company's financial performance, and gives an idea of its internal control system.

Corporate Governance Report The corporate governance report gives information on the company's philosophy on corporate governance, board of directors, audit committee, shareholders/investors grievance committee, other board committees, remuneration of directors, and general shareholder information.

Business Responsibility and Sustainability Report (BRSR) This report seeks to establish links between the financial results of a business with its ESG performance.

Secretarial Audit Report Given by a practising company secretary, this report comments on whether a company has complied with provisions of all applicable laws, rules, and regulations on the company.

Consolidated Financial Statements

Clause 32 of the listing agreement with the stock exchange(s) requires a company to provide consolidated financial statements (CFS) in addition to the stand-alone financial statements. CFS were not required under the Companies Act, 1956. However, under the Companies Act 2013, all companies, listed or unlisted, are required to prepare CFS. The CFS prepared by consolidating the accounts of the parent company with those of its subsidiaries in accordance with Ind AS 110.

1.8 MANIPULATION OF THE BOTTOM LINE

Financial statements reflect revenues, expenses, assets, and liabilities. Corporate managements have some discretion in influencing the occurrence, measurement, and reporting of these items. They often use this latitude to manipulate the reported profits referred to as the 'bottom line'. The devices commonly employed for this purpose are:

- Inflate the sales for the current year by advancing the sales from the following year.
- Alter the 'other income' figure by playing with non-operational items like sale of fixed assets.
- Fiddle with the method and rate of depreciation. (A switch may be effected from the written down value method to the straight line method or vice versa).
- Capitalise certain expenses like research and development costs and product promotion costs, that are ordinarily written off in the year of incurrence.

- Defer discretionary expenditures (like training, advertising, research and development) to the following year.
- Make inadequate provision for certain known liabilities (gratuity, etc.) and treat certain liabilities as 'contingent liabilities' after getting suitable 'legal opinion' from obliging lawyers.
- Make extra provision during prosperous years and write them back in lean years.
- Revalue assets to create the impression of substantial reserves.
- Lengthen the accounting year in an attempt to cover poor performance.

Why Do Companies Manipulate/ Smoothen Earnings

A variety of motives prompt firms to manipulate/ smoothen earnings. The more common ones are:

- To project an image that the company is a low risk company (It is assumed that financial analysts regard earnings variability as a key factor in risk evaluation).
- To enhance managerial compensation if the same is linked in some way to reported earnings.
- To promote a perception that the management of the firm is competent.
- To communicate more meaningfully about the long-term prospects of the firm.

What Can You Do

What can you do to read in between the lines when corporate managements tend to manage the 'bottom line' by employing a variety of ingenious devices? Our suggestions are as follows:

- Acquire greater knowledge of how accountants prepare financial statements and what are the current financial reporting practices.
- Carefully peruse the notes to financial statements in order to: (a) discover changes in accounting policies; and (b) learn about the nature and magnitude of contingent liabilities.
- Read the auditors' report and understand the implications of the qualifications in that report.
- Look at the performance of the company over a period of time and do not attach much importance to the figures for one year. Remember that while manipulation may pay for a year or two, it tends to be a self-defeating exercise in the long run. This may be a good safeguard against corporate accounting gimmickry.

1.9 FINANCIAL STATEMENTS IN THE U.S.

So far we discussed the format and contents of financial statements as prepared in India. It is instructive to look at how financial statements look in the U.S.

In the U.S., the annual report contains only consolidated financial statements. Exhibits 1.7 and 17.8 show the consolidated financial statements of Procter & Gamble to illustrate how financial statements are presented in the U.S.

EXHIBIT 1.7 ***Consolidated Statements of Earnings of Procter & Gamble***

Amounts in millions except per share amounts: Years ended June 30	*2021*	*2020*	*2019*
NET SALES	$76,118	$70,950	$67,684
Cost of products sold	37,108	35,250	34,768
Selling, general and administrative expense	21,024	19,994	19,084
Goodwill and indefinite-lived intangibles impairment charges	–	–	8,345
OPERATING INCOME	17,986	15,706	5,487
Interest expense	(502)	(465)	(509)
Interest income	45	155	220
Other non-operating income, net	86	438	871
EARNINGS BEFORE INCOME TAXES	17,615	15,834	6,069
Income taxes	3,263	2,731	2,103
NET EARNINGS	$14,352	$13,103	$3,966
Les: Net earning attributable to noncontrolling interests	46	76	69
NET EARNINGS ATRIBUTABLE TO PROCTER & GAMBLE	$ 14,306	$ 13,027	$ 3,897
NET EARNINGS PER COMMON SHARE:(1)			
Basic	$ 5.69	$ 5.13	$ 1.45
Dilute	$ 5.50	$ 4.96	$ 1.43

(1) Basic net earnings per common share and Diluted net earnings per common share are calculated on Net earnings attributable to Procter & Gamble

EXHIBIT 1.8 *Consolidated Balance Sheets of Procter & Gamble*

Amounts in millions except stated values: June 30	*2021*	*2020*
Assets		
CURRENT ASSETS		
Cash and cash equivalents	$ 10,288	$ 16,181
Accounts receivable	4,725	4,178
INVENTORIES		
Materials and supplies	1,645	1,414
Work in process	719	674
Finished goods	3,619	3,410
Total inventories	5,983	5,498
Prepaid expenses and other current assets	2,095	2,130
TOTAL CURRENT ASSETS	23,091	27,987
PROPERTY, PLANT AND EQUIPMENT, NET	21,686	20,692
GOODWILL	40,924	39,901
TRADEMARKS AND OTHER INTANGIBLE ASSETS, NET	23,642	23,792
OTHER NONCURRENT ASSETS	9,964	8,328
TOTAL ASSETS	$ 119,307	$ 120,700
Liabilittes and Shareholders' Equity		
CURRENT LIABLITIES		
Accounts payable	$ 13,720	$ 12,071
Accrued and other liabilities	10,523	9,722
Debt due within one year	8,889	11,183
TOTAL CURRENT LIABILITIES	33,132	32,976
LONG-TERM DEBT	23,099	23,537
DEFERRED INCOME TAXES	6,153	6,199
OTHER NONCURRENT LIABILITIES	10,269	11,110
TOTAL LIABILITIES	72,653	73,822

(Contd.)

EXHIBIT 1.8 *(Contd.)*

Amounts in millions except stated values: June 30	2021	2020
SHAREHOLDERS' EQUITY		
Convertible Class A preferred stock, stated value $1 per share (600 shares authorized)	870	897
Non-Voting Class B preferred stock, stated value $1 per share (200 shares authorized)	—	—
Common stock, stated value $1 per share (10,000 shares authorized; shares issued: 2021 – 4,009.2, 2020 – 4,009.2)	4,009	4,009
Additional paid-in capital	64,848	64,194
Reserve for ESOP debt retirement	(1,006)	(1,080)
Accumulated other comprehensive loss	(13,744)	(16,165)
Treasury stock, at cost (shares held: 2021 – 1,579.5, 2020 – 1,529.5)	(114,973)	(105,573)
Retained earnings	106,374	100,239
Noncontrolling interest	276	357
TOTAL SHAREHOLDERS' EQUITY	46,654	46,878
TOTAL LIABILITIES AND SHAREHOLDERS' EQUITY	$119,307	$120,700

Looking at Exhibit 1.7 and 1.8, we find that:

- The statement of earnings in the U.S. classifies expenses on a functional basis, whereas the statement of profit and loss in India usually lumps together various functional expenses.
- The balance sheet in the U.S. arranges assets in order of decreasing liquidity whereas India the balance sheet arranges assets in order of increasing liquidity. The balance sheet in the U.S. arranges liabilities in order of increasing maturity whereas the balance sheet in India arranges liabilities in order of decreasing maturity.

SUMMARY

- The balance sheet shows the financial position of the firm at a given point of time. The statement of profit and loss reflects the financial performance of the firm over a period of time. The cash flow statement shows the sources and uses of cash during the period.

- The four basic rules of accounting are: (i) Every transaction has a bearing on at least two accounts in the balance sheet. (ii) Irrespective of what the transaction is, the balance sheet identity is always preserved. (iii) Transactions which do not result in a revenue or expense have no bearing on the 'Reserves and Surplus' account. (iv) Transactions which result in a revenue or expense have a bearing on the 'Reserves and Surplus' account.
- The balance sheet identity is :

$$\text{Assets} = \text{Equity} + \text{Liabilities}$$

- Assets are resources which are expected to provide a firm with future economic benefits. Assets are classified as follows under the Companies Act format: non-current assets and current assets. Non-current assets are relatively long-lived assets. Current assets are expected to be converted into cash during the operating cycle of the firm.
- Equity and liabilities are what the firm owes others. The balance sheet format prescribed in the Companies Act classifies equity and liabilities as follows: equity, non-current liabilities, and current liabilities. Equity includes share capital and other equity, non-current liabilities are liabilities which are expected to be settled after one year of the reporting date and current liabilities are liabilities which are due to be settled within twelve months after the reporting date.
- The statement of profit and loss shows revenues,expenses, and the net profit or loss from the operations during the year.
- The statement of cash flows shows the shows the net cash generated by the firm. For analytical purposes, cash flow is broken into three components: cash flow from operations, cash flow from investing activities, and cash flow from financing activities.
- In addition to the three financial statements, the annual report contains the following: Directors' Report, Management Discussion and Analysis, Report on Corporate Governance, and Notes to Financial Statements.
- Corporate managements have some discretion in influencing the occurrence, measurement, and reporting of items reflected in financial statements.

Financial Statement Analysis

2

In the previous chapter, we looked at the contents of the financial statements and pointed towards the limitations of accounting numbers. Yet, financial analysts depend primarily on these statements to diagnose financial performance. Why? It appears that there are three principal reasons: (i) As long as the accounting biases remain more or less the same over time, meaningful inferences can be drawn by examining trends in raw data and in financial ratios. (ii) Since similar biases characterise various firms in the same industry, inter-firm comparisons are useful. (iii) Experience seems to suggest that financial analysis 'works' if one is aware of accounting biases and makes adjustments for the same.

If properly analysed and interpreted, financial statements can provide valuable insights into a firm's performance. Analysis of financial statements is of interest to lenders (short-term as well as long-term), investors, security analysts, managers, and others. Financial statement analysis may be done for a variety of purposes, which may range from a simple analysis of the short-term liquidity position of the firm to a comprehensive assessment of the strengths and weaknesses of the firm in various areas.

This chapter discusses the tools of financial statement analysis. It is divided into six sections:

- Financial ratios
- Comparative analysis
- DuPont analysis
- Percentage-format financial statements
- Problems in financial statement analysis
- Guidelines for financial statement analysis

2.1 FINANCIAL RATIOS

A ratio is an arithmetical relationship between two numbers. Financial ratio analysis is a study of ratios between various items or groups of items in financial statements. Financial ratios have been classified in several ways. For our purposes, we divide them into five broad categories as follows:

- Liquidity ratios
- Leverage ratios
- Turnover ratios
- Profitability ratios
- Valuation ratios

To facilitate the discussion of various ratios, the financial statements of Horizon Limited, shown in Exhibits 2.1 and 2.2 will be used.

EXHIBIT 2.1 *Balance Sheet of Horizon Limited as on March 31, 20X1*

(₹ in crore)

	20X1	*20X0*
ASSETS		
NON-CURRENT ASSETS	600	550
• Property, plant, and equipment	500	450
• Investments	50	40
• Long-term loans and advances	50	60
• **Current Assets**	400	350
• Inventories	20	20
• Investments	160	140
• Trade receivables	140	120
• Cash and cash equivalents	60	50
• Loans	20	20
	1000	900
EQUITY AND LIABILITIES		
• **Equity**	500	450
• Equity share capital (Par value ₹ 10)	100	100
• Other equity	400	350
• **Non-current Liabilities**	300	270
• Borrowngs	200	180
• Provisions	50	45
• Deferred tax liablilites (net)	50	45

(Contd.)

EXHIBIT 2.1 *(Contd.)*

(₹ *in crore)*

	20X1	*20X0*
• **Current Liabilites**	200	180
• Borrowings	40	30
• Trade payables	120	110
• Other current liabilities	30	30
• Short-term provision	10	10
	1,000	900

EXHIBIT 2.2 ***Statement of Profit and Loss for Horizon Limited for the Year Ending March 31, 20X1***

(₹ *in crore)*

	Current Period	*Previous Period*
• Revenues from Operations	1290	1172
• Other Income	10	8
• Total Income	1300	1180
• Expenses		
• Material expenses	600	560
• Employee benefit expenses	200	180
• Finance costs	30	25
• Depreciation and amortisation expenses	50	45
• Other expenses	240	210
• Total Expenses	1120	1020
• Profit before Exceptional and Extraordinary Items and Tax	180	160
• Exceptional Items	—	—
• Profit before Extraordinary Items and Tax	180	160
• Extraordinary Items	—	—
• Profit Before Tax	180	160
• Tax Expense	50	40
• Profit (Loss) for the Period	130	120
• Dividend	80	
• Earning Per Equity Share (in rupees)		
• Basic	13	
• Diluted	13	

Liquidity Ratios

Liquidity refers to the ability of a firm to meet its obligations in the short run, usually one year. Liquidity ratios are generally based on the relationship between current assets (the sources for meeting short-term obligations) and current liabilities. The important liquidity ratios are: current ratio and acid-test ratio.

Current Ratio A very popular ratio, the current ratio is defined as:

$$\frac{\text{Current assets}}{\text{Current liabilities}}$$

Current assets include current investments,inventories, trade receivables, cash and cash equivalents, and short-term loans and advances. *Current liabilities* represent liabilities that are expected to mature in the next twelve months. These comprise of short-term borrowings, trade payables, other current liabilities, and short-term provisions.

Horizon Limited's current ratio for 20X1 is 400/200 = 2.00

The current ratio measures the ability of the firm to meet its current liabilities - current assets get converted into cash during the operating cycle of the firm and provide the funds needed to pay current liabilities. Apparently, the higher the current ratio, the greater the short-term solvency. However, in interpreting the current ratio the composition of current assets must not be overlooked. A firm with a high proportion of current assets in the form of cash and debtors is more liquid than one with a high proportion of current assets in the form of inventories even though both the firms have the same current ratio.

The general norm for current ratio in India is 1.33. Internationally it is 2.

Acid-test Ratio Also called the quick ratio, the acid-test ratio is defined as:

$$\frac{\text{Quick assets}}{\text{Current liabilities}}$$

Quick assets are defined as current assets excluding inventories.

Horizon's acid-test ratio for 20X1 is: (400 – 160)/200 = 1.20

The acid-test ratio is a fairly stringent measure of liquidity. It is based on those current assets which are highly liquid - inventories are excluded from the numerator of this ratio because inventories are deemed to be the least liquid component of current assets.

Leverage Ratios

Financial leverage refers to the use of debt finance. While debt capital is a cheaper source of finance, it is also a riskier source of finance. Leverage ratios help in assessing the risk arising from the use of debt capital.

Two types of ratios are commonly used to analyse financial leverage: structural ratios and coverage ratios. *Structural ratios* are based on the proportions of debt and equity in the financial structure of the firm. The most important structural ratio is the debt-equity ratio. *Coverage ratios* show the relationship between debt servicing commitments and the sources for meeting these burdens. The important coverage ratios are: interest coverage ratio and debt service coverage ratio.

Debt-equity Ratio The debt-equity ratio shows the relative contributions of creditors and owners. It is defined as:

$$\frac{\text{Total liabilities}}{\text{Shareholders' funds}}$$

The numerator of this ratio consists of all liabilities[1], non-current and current, and the denominator consists of share capital and reserves and surplus[2].

Horizon's debt-equity ratio for the 20X1 year-end is:

$$(300 + 200)/500 = 1.0$$

In general, the lower the debt-equity ratio, the higher the degree of protection enjoyed by the creditors. In using this ratio, however, the following points should be borne in mind:

- The book value of equity often understates its market value. This happens because tangible assets are carried at their historical values less depreciation and many highly valuable intangible assets are not recorded on the balance sheet.
- Some forms of debt (like term loans, secured debentures, and secured short-term bank borrowing) are usually protected by charges on specific assets and hence enjoy superior protection.

[1] Alternatively the ratio of long-term debt to equity may be calculated. What is important is that the same ratio is used consistently when comparisons are made.

[2] For the sake of simplicity, preference capital is subsumed under equity. Since preference capital is usually a very minor source of finance, its inclusion or exclusion hardly makes any difference.

Interest Coverage Ratio Also called the times interest earned, the interest coverage ratio is defined as:

$$\frac{\text{Profit before interest and taxes}}{\text{Interest}}$$

Horizon's interest coverage ratio for 20X1 is: 210/30 = 7.0

Note that profit before interest and taxes are used in the numerator of this ratio because the ability of a firm to pay interest is not affected by tax payment, as interest (or finance costs) on debt funds is a tax-deductible expense. A high interest coverage ratio means that the firm can easily meet its interest burden even if earnings before interest and taxes suffer a considerable decline. A low interest coverage ratio may result in financial embarrassment when earnings before interest and taxes decline. This ratio is widely used by lenders to assess a firm's debt capacity. Further, it is a major determinant of bond rating.

Though widely used, this ratio is not a very appropriate measure of interest coverage because the source of interest payment is cash flow before interest and taxes, not profit before interest and taxes. In view of this, we may use a modified interest coverage ratio:

$$\frac{\text{Profit before interest and taxes + Depreciation and amortisation}}{\text{Interest}}$$

For Horizon Limited, this ratio for 20X1 is (210 + 50)/30 = 8.67

This ratio measures debt servicing ability comprehensively because it considers both the interest and the principal repayment obligations. The ratio may be amplified to include other fixed chargers like lease payment and preference dividends.

Debt Service Coverage Ratio Used by financial institutions in India, the debt service coverage ratio is defined as:

$$\frac{\text{Profit after tax + Depreciation + Other non-cash charges + Interest on term loan + Lease rentals}}{\text{Interest on term loan + Lease rentals + Repayment of term loan}}$$

Financial institutions calculate the average debt service coverage ratio for the period during which the term loan for the project is repayable. Normally, financial institutions regard a debt service coverage ratio of 1.5 to 2.0 as satisfactory.

Turnover Ratios

Turnover ratios, also referred to as activity ratios or asset management ratios, measure how efficiently the assets are employed by a firm. These ratios are based on the relationship between the level of activity, represented by revenues or cost of goods sold, and levels of various assets. The important turnover ratios are: inventory turnover, average collection period, receivables turnover, fixed assets turnover, and total assets turnover.

Inventory Turnover The inventory turnover, or stock turnover, measures how fast the inventory is moving through the firm and generating sales. It is defined as:

$$\frac{\text{Revenues from operations}}{\text{Average inventory}}$$

Horizon's inventory turnover for 20X1 is:

$$1290 \div [(160 + 140)/2] = 8.6$$

The inventory turnover reflects the efficiency of inventory management. The higher the ratio, the more efficient the management of inventories and vice versa. However, this may not always be true. A high inventory turnover may be caused by a low level of inventory which may result in frequent stockouts and loss of sales and customer goodwill.

Notice that as inventories tend to change over the year, we use the average of the inventories at the beginning and the end of the year. *In general, averages may be used when a flow figure (such as revenues from operations) is related to a stock figure (such as inventories).*

Debtors' Turnover This ratio shows how many times sundry debtors or trade receivables turn over during the year. It is defined as:

$$\frac{\text{Net credit sales}}{\text{Average trade receivables}}$$

If the figure for net credit sales is not available, one may have to make do with the revenues from operations.

Horizon's debtors' turnover for 20X1 is:

$$1290 \div [(140 + 120)/2] = 9.92$$

Obviously, the higher the debtors' turnover the greater the efficiency of credit management.

Average Collection Period The average collection period represents the number of days' worth of credit sales that is locked in trade receivables. It is defined as:

$$\frac{\text{Average trade receivables}}{\text{Average daily credit sales}}$$

If the figure for credit sales is not available, one may have to make do with the revenue from operations.

Horizon's average collection period for 20X1 is:

$$\frac{[(140 + 120)/2]}{(1290/365)} = 36.8 \text{ days}$$

Note that the average collection period and the debtors' turnover are related as follows:

$$\text{Average collection period} = \frac{365}{\text{Debtors's turnover}}$$

The average collection period may be compared with the firm's credit terms to judge the efficiency of credit management. For example, if the credit terms are 2/10, net 45, an average collection period of 85 days means that the collection is slow and an average collection period of 40 days means that the collection is prompt. An average collection period which is shorter than the credit period allowed by the firm needs to be interpreted carefully. It may mean efficiency of credit management or excessive conservatism in credit granting that may result in the loss of some desirable sales.

Fixed Assets Turnover This ratio measures sales per rupee of investment in fixed assets. It is defined as:

$$\frac{\text{Revenues from operations}}{\text{Average net fixed assets}}$$

Horizon's fixed assets turnover ratio for 20X1 is:

$$1290 \div [(500 + 450)/2] = 2.72$$

This ratio is supposed to measure the efficiency with which fixed assets are employed - a high ratio indicates a high degree of efficiency in asset utilisation and a low ratio reflects inefficient use of assets. However, in interpreting this ratio, one caution should be borne in mind. When the fixed assets of the firm are old and substantially depreciated, the fixed assets turnover ratio tends to be high because the denominator of the ratio is very low.

Total Assets Turnover Akin to the output-capital ratio in economic analysis, the total assets turnover is defined as:

$$\frac{\text{Total revenues}}{\text{Average total assets}}$$

Horizon's total assets turnover ratio for 20X1 is:

$$1300 \div [(1000 + 900)/2] = 1.37$$

This ratio measures how efficiently assets are employed, overall.

Profitability Ratios

Profitability reflects the final result of business operations. There are two types of profitability ratios: profit margins ratios and rate of return ratios. *Profit margin ratios* show the relationship between profit and sales. Since profit can be measured at different stages, there are several measures of profit margin. The most popular profit margin ratios are: gross profit margin ratio and net profit margin ratio. *Rate of return ratios* reflect the relationship between profit and investment. The important rate of return measures are: return on assets, earning power, return on capital employed, and return on equity.

Gross Profit Margin Ratio The gross profit margin ratio is defined as:

$$\frac{\text{Gross profit}}{\text{Revenues from operations}}$$

Gross profit is defined as the difference between revenues from operations and cost of goods sold. Cost of goods sold is the sum of manufacturing costs relating to the operating revenues of the period. Manufacturing costs include material costs, employee benefit costs for manufacturing personnel, and manufacturing expenses. Since the published financial statements lump together employee benefit expenses for manufacturing personnel and non-manufacturing personnel and subsume manufacturing expenses under other expenses (a catch-all category that includes a lot of expenses relating to sales and general administration as well), it is not possible for the external analyst to estimate accurately the cost of goods sold. For our purposes, we will assume that one-half of employee benefit expenses and one-half of other expenses relate to manufacturing—this is indeed a heroic assumption. So, the estimated manufacturing costs are ₹820 crore—material cost (600) + employee benefit cost (100) + other expenses (120). This means that the gross profit for 20X1 is: 1290 – 820 = ₹470 crore. Hence, Horizon's gross profit margin ratio for 20X1 is:

$$470/1290 = 0.36 \text{ or } 36 \text{ percent}$$

This ratio shows the margin left after meeting manufacturing costs. It measures the efficiency of production as well as pricing. To analyse the factors underlying the variation in gross profit margin the proportion of various elements of cost (labour, materials, and manufacturing overheads) to sales may be studied in detail.

Net Profit Margin Ratio The net profit margin ratio is defined as:

$$\frac{\text{Net profit}}{\text{Total revenues}}$$

Horizon's net profit margin ratio for 20X1 is:

$$130/1300 = 0.10 \text{ or } 10 \text{ percent}$$

This ratio shows the earnings left for shareholders (both equity and preference) as a percentage of total revenues. It measures the overall efficiency of production, administration, selling, financing, pricing, treasury, and tax management. Jointly considered, the gross and net profit margin ratios provide a valuable understanding of the cost and profit structure of the firm and enable the analyst to identify the sources of business efficiency/inefficiency.

Return on Assets The return on assets (ROA) is defined as:

$$\text{ROA} = \frac{\text{Profit after tax}}{\text{Average total assets}}$$

Horizon's ROA for the year 20X1 is:

$$130 \div [(1000 + 900)/2] = 13.7 \text{ percent}$$

Though widely used, ROA is an odd measure because its numerator measures the return to shareholders (equity and preference) whereas its denominator represents the contribution of all investors (shareholders as well as lenders).

Earning Power The earning power is defined as:

$$\text{Earning power} = \frac{\text{Profit before interest and tax}}{\text{Average total assets}}$$

Horizon's earning power for the year 20X1 is:

$$210 \div [(1000 + 900)/2] = 22.1 \text{ percent}$$

Earning power is a measure of business performance which is not affected by interest charges and tax burden. It abstracts away the effect of capital structure and tax factor and focuses on operating performance. Hence it is eminently suited for inter - firm comparison. Further, it is internally consistent. The numerator represents a measure of pre-tax earnings belonging to all sources of finance and the denominator represents total financing.

Return on Capital Employed The return on capital employed is defined as:

$$\text{ROCE} = \frac{\text{Profit before interest and tax (1 – Tax rate)}}{\text{Average total assets}}$$

The numerator of this ratio viz., profit before interest and tax (1-tax rate) is also called net operating profit after tax (NOPAT).

Assuming that the tax rate is 30 percent, Horizon's ROCE for the year 20X1 is:

$$210\ (1 - 0.3) \div [(1000 + 900)/2] = 15.5 \text{ percent}$$

ROCE is the post-tax version of earning power. It considers the effect of taxation, but not the capital structure. It is internally consistent. Its merit is that it is defined in such a way that it can be compared directly with the post-tax weighted average cost of capital of the firm.

Return on Equity A measure of great interest to equity shareholders, the return on equity is defined as:

$$\frac{\text{Equity earnings}}{\text{Average equity}}$$

The numerator of this ratio is equal to profit after tax less preference dividends. The denominator includes all contributions made by shareholders (paid-up capital + reserves and surplus). This ratio is also called the return on net worth or return on shareholders' funds. For our purpose equity, net worth, and shareholders' funds are synonymous.

Horizon's return on equity for 20X1 is:

$$130 \div [(500 + 450)/2] = 27.4 \text{ per cent}$$

The return on equity measures the profitability of equity funds invested in the firm. It is regarded as a very important measure because it reflects the productivity of the ownership (or risk) capital employed in the firm. It is influenced by several factors: earning power, debt-equity ratio, average cost of debt funds, and tax rate.

In judging all the profitability measures it should be borne in mind that the historical valuation of assets imparts an upward bias to profitability measures during an inflationary period. This happens because the numerator of these measures represents current values, whereas the denominator represents historical values.

Valuation Ratios

Valuation ratios indicate how the equity stock and the company are assessed in the capital market. Since the market value of equity reflects the combined influence of risk and return, valuation ratios are the most comprehensive measures of a firm's performance. The important valuation ratios are: price-earnings ratio, EV-EBITDA ratio, and market value to book value ratio.

Price-earnings Ratio Perhaps the most popular financial statistic in stock market discussion, the price-earnings ratio is defined as:

$$\frac{\text{Market price per share}}{\text{Earnings per share}}$$

The market price per share may be the price prevailing on a certain day or the average price over a period of time. The market price per share of Horizon as on 31st March 20X1 is ₹200. The earnings per share is simply: profit after tax less preference dividend divided by the number of outstanding equity shares.

Horizon's price-earnings ratio at the end of 20X1 is:

$$200/13 = 15.4$$

The price-earnings ratio (or the price-earnings multiple as it is commonly referred to) is a summary measure which primarily reflects the following factors: growth prospects, risk characteristics, shareholder orientation, corporate image, and degree of liquidity.

EV-EBITDA Ratio A widely used multiple in company valuation, the EV-EBITDA ratio is defined as:

$$\frac{\text{Enterprise value (EV)}}{\text{Earnings before interest, taxes, depreciation, and amortisation (EBITDA)}}$$

EV is the sum of the market value of equity and the market value of debt. The market value of equity is simply the number of outstanding equity shares times the price per share. As far as debt is concerned, its market value has to be imputed. Generally, a rupee of loan is deemed to have a rupee of market value.

Horizon's EV-EBITDA ratio for 20X1 is:

$$\frac{10 \times 200 + 500}{260} = \frac{2500}{260} = 9.62$$

EV-EBITDA is supposed to reflect profitability, growth, risk, liquidity, and corporate image.

Market Value to Book Value Ratio Another popular stock market statistic, the market value to book value is defined as:

$$\frac{\text{Market value per share}}{\text{Book value per share}}$$

Horizon's market value to book value ratio at the end of 20X1 was:

$$200/50 = 4.00$$

In a way, this ratio reflects the contribution of a firm to the wealth of society. When this ratio exceeds 1 it means that the firm has contributed to the creation of wealth in the society - if this ratio is, say, 2, the firm has created a wealth of one rupee for every rupee invested in it. When this ratio is equal to 1, it implies that the firm has neither contributed to nor detracted from the wealth of society.

It may be emphasised here that if the market value to book value ratio is equal to 1, all the three ratios, namely, return on equity, earnings-price ratio (which is the inverse of the price-earnings ratio), and total yield, are equal.

2.2 COMPARATIVE ANALYSIS

We have discussed a long list of financial ratios. For judging whether the ratios are high or low, one has to make a comparative analysis such as a cross-section analysis (in which the industry averages may be used as benchmarks) or time series analysis (in which the ratios of the firm are compared over time).

Comparison with Industry Averages

Exhibit 2.3 shows the ratios of Horizon Limited along with industry averages. The industry averages often provide useful benchmarks for comparisons. Sometimes the ratios of a few competitor firms may be used as benchmarks.

Comparing the ratios of Horizon Limited with industry averages we find that:

- Horizon Limited has a favourable liquidity position. All the liquidity ratios of Horizon Limited are higher than the industry average.
- Leverage ratios of Horizon Limited are a shade better than the industry average.
- Turnover ratios of Horizon Limited are more or less comparable with the industry average.
- Profit margin ratios of Horizon Limited are somewhat higher than the industry average. The rate of return measures of Horizon Limited is also higher than the industry average.
- The valuation ratios of Horizon Limited compare favourably in relation to industry average.

PROFIT AFTER TAX	5.21	3.15

Total		5.30	4.50
		35.51	29.50
APPLICATION OF FUNDS:			
FIXED ASSETS			
GROSS BLOCK	20.0		20.0
LESS: DEPRECIATION	6.0		3.0
Net		14.00	17.0
CURRENT ASSETS			
INVENTORY	3.80		2.0
TRADE RECEIVABLES	5.20		2.5
CASH AND BANK BALANCES	6.00		4.0
OTHER CURRENT ASSETS	6.51		4.0
Total	total	21.51	12.5

GLANZA PRIVATE LIMITED

BALANCE SHEET AS AT 31st MARCH

		2021 Rs.Lakhs	**2020** Rs.Lakhs
SOURCES OF FUNDS:	(inner col)		
Capital		15.00	15.00
RESERVES AND SURPLUS(Retained Earnings)			
Opening Balance	5.00		1.85
Profit and Loss (balance)	5.21	10.21	3.15
Total		25.21	20.00
LOAN FUNDS			
Borrowings			
From bank and others		5.00	5.00
Total		5.00	5.00
CURRENT LIABILITY			
Trade Paybles		2.10	1.50

GLANZA PRIVATE LIMITED

PROFIT AND LOSS ACCOUNT FOR THE YEAR ENDED 31st March

-	2021 Rs.Lakhs	2020 Rs.Lakhs
INCOME		
Sales	33.00	20.00
Total	33.00	20.00
DIRECT EXPENSES		
Material Consumption	13.00	7.00
Direct Labor	1.10	0.50
Manufacturing expenses	4.80	2.50
Total Direct Expenses	18.90	10.00
GROSS PROFIT	**14.10**	**10.00**
INDIRECT EXPENSES		
Administrative expenses	1.10	0.50
Marketing Expenses	2.00	1.00
Depreciation	3.00	3.00
Total Indirect Expenses	6.10	4.50
OPERATING PROFIT (PBIT)	**8.00**	**5.50**

Exhibit 2.3 ***Comparison of Ratios of Horizon Limited with Industry Average***

Ratios	*Formula*	*Horizon Limited*	*Industry Average*
Liquidity			
• Current ratio	$\frac{\text{Current assets}}{\text{Current liabilities}}$	2.00	1.80
• Acid-test ratio	$\frac{\text{Quick assets}}{\text{Current liabilities}}$	1.20	1.05
Leverage			
• Debt-equity ratio	$\frac{\text{Total liabilities}}{\text{Shareholders' funds}}$	1.00	1.10
• Interest coverage ratio	$\frac{\text{PBIT}}{\text{Interest}}$	7.0	5.0
Turnover			
• Inventory turnover	$\frac{\text{Revenues from operations}}{\text{Average inventory}}$	8.6	8.4
• Debtors' turnover	$\frac{\text{Net credit sales}}{\text{Average trade receivables}}$	9.92	10.1
• Fixed assets turnover	$\frac{\text{Revenues from operations}}{\text{Average net fixed assets}}$	2.72	2.75
• Total assets turnover	$\frac{\text{Total revenues}}{\text{Average total assets}}$	1.37	1.40
Profitability			
• Gross profit margin ratio	$\frac{\text{Gross profit}}{\text{Revenues from operations}}$	29.0%	25.0%
• Net profit margin ratio	$\frac{\text{Net profit}}{\text{Total revenues}}$	10.0%	8.5%
• Return on assets	$\frac{\text{Profit after tax}}{\text{Average total assets}}$	13.7%	12.5%
• Earning power	$\frac{\text{PBIT}}{\text{Average total assets}}$	22.1%	19.3%
• Return on capital employed	$\frac{\text{PBIT (1 – T)}}{\text{Average total assets}}$	15.5%	13.8%
• Return on equity	$\frac{\text{Equity earnings}}{\text{Average equity}}$	27.4%	23.2%

(*Contd.*)

EXHIBIT 2.3 ***(Contd.)***

Ratios	*Formula*	*Horizon Limited*	*Industry Average*
Valuation			
• Price earnings ratio	$\frac{\text{Market price per share}}{\text{Earnings per share}}$	15.4	12.00
• EV-EBITDA	$\frac{\text{Enterprise Value}}{\text{Earnings before interest, taxes, deprecation, and amortisation}}$	9.92	8.35
• Market value to book value ratio	$\frac{\text{Market price per share}}{\text{Book value per share}}$	4.00	3.2

Time Series of Financial Ratios

Besides looking at the ratios for one year, one would like to look at the ratios for several years. This will help in the detection of secular changes and avoidance of the bias introduced by transitory forces. Exhibit 2.4 presents certain selected ratios for Horizon Limited for a period of five years (year 5 corresponds to 20X1). Looking at this exhibit we find that:

- The debt-equity ratio improved steadily for three years and increased slightly in the last year.
- The total assets turnover ratio remained more or less flat with minor fluctuations.
- The net profit margin improved steadily for three years but dipped marginally in the last year.
- The return on equity followed the pattern of the net profit margin.
- The price-earnings ratio improved steadily over time.

EXHIBIT 2.4 ***Time Series of Certain Financial Ratios***

	1	*2*	*3*	*4*	*5*
Debt-equity ratio	1.3	1.2	1.0	0.9	1.0
Total assets turnover	1.34	1.41	1.35	1.39	1.37
Net profit margin(%)	8.0	9.0	10.2	10.5	10.0
Return on equity(%)	20.1	22.0	26.0	27.6	27.4
Price-earnings ratio	12.5	13.2	13.8	14.9	15.4

2.3 DuPont ANALYSIS

The DuPont Company of the US pioneered a system of financial analysis which has received widespread recognition and acceptance. A useful system of analysis, which considers important interrelationships based on information found in financial statements, it has been adopted by many firms in some form or the other. Exhibit 2.5 shows the DuPont chart as applied to Horizon Limited.

On the left hand side of the DuPont chart is the return on assets (ROA), defined as the product of net profit margin (NPM) and the total assets turnover ratio (TAT):

$$\underbrace{\frac{\text{Net profit}}{\text{Average total assets}}}_{\text{ROA}} = \underbrace{\frac{\text{Net profit}}{\text{Total revenues}}}_{\text{NPM}} \times \underbrace{\frac{\text{Total revenues}}{\text{Average total assets}}}_{\text{TAT}} \tag{2.1}$$

Such decomposition helps in understanding how return on assets is influenced by the net profit margin and the total assets turnover.

The upper right hand side of the DuPont chart shows the details underlying the net profit margin ratio. An examination of this side may indicate areas where cost reductions may be effected to improve the net profit margin. If this is supplemented by comparative common size analysis, it becomes relatively easier to understand where cost control efforts should be directed.

The lower right hand side of the DuPont chart throws light on the determinants of the assets turnover ratio. If this is supplemented by a study of component turnover ratios (inventory turnover, debtors' turnover, and fixed assets turnover), a deeper insight can be gained into efficiencies/inefficiencies of asset utilisation.

The basic DuPont analysis may be extended to explore the determinants of return on equity (ROE).

$$\underbrace{\frac{\text{Net profit}}{\text{Average Equity}}}_{\text{ROE}} = \underbrace{\frac{\text{Net profit}}{\text{Total revenue}}}_{\text{NPM}} \times \underbrace{\frac{\text{Total revenues}}{\text{Average total assets}}}_{\text{TAT}} \times \underbrace{\frac{\text{Average total assets}}{\text{Average equity}}}_{\text{LM}} \tag{2.2}$$

Note that the third component on the right hand side of Eq (2.2) is referred to as the leverage multiplier (LM).

The extension of DuPont chart as applied to Horizon Limited is shown in Exhibit 2.6.

EXHIBIT 2.5 ***DuPont Chart Applied to Horizon Limited***

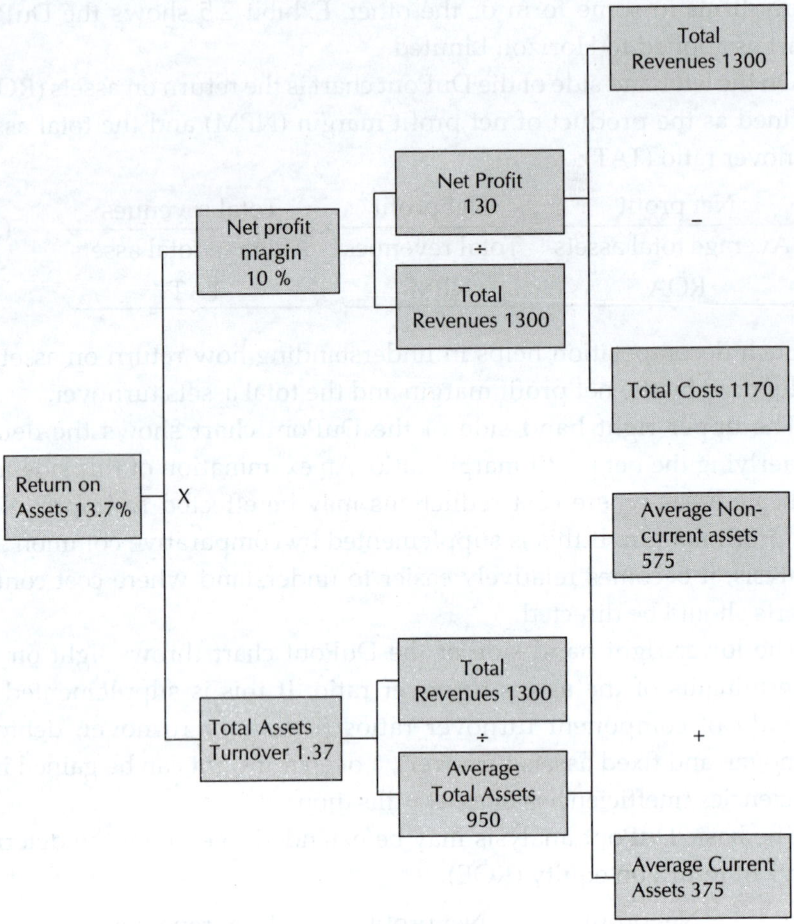

EXHIBIT 2.6 ***Extension of DuPont Chart***

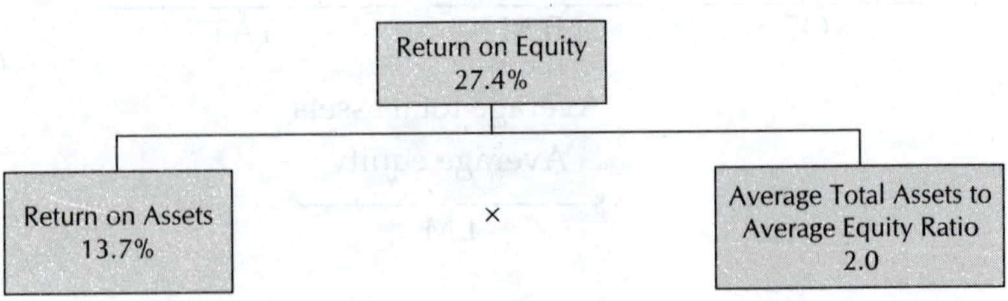

2.4 PERCENTAGE-FORMAT FINANCIAL STATEMENTS

To understand better a firm's changing financial position and performance over time, and to compare one firm with another, it is helpful to prepare the balance sheet and profit and loss account in a percentage format. In a percentage-format balance sheet, each asset and liability amount is expressed as a percentage of total assets. Likewise in a percentage-format profit and loss statement, each item is expressed as a percentage of total revenues. Exhibit 2.7 shows the percentage-format financial statements of Horizon Limited.

EXHIBIT 2.7 ***Regular and Percentage Financial Statements of Horizon Limited***

Part A: Balance Sheet

	Regular (in crore)		*Percentage (%)*	
	20X0	*20X1*	*20X0*	*20X1*
• Shareholders' funds	450	500	50	50
• Loan funds	270	300	30	30
• Deferred tax liability	180	200	20	20
Total	900	1000	100	100
• Fixed assets	550	600	61	60
• Current assets	350	400	39	40
Total	900	1000	100	100

Part B: Statement of Profit and Loss

	Regular (in crore)		*Percentage (%)*	
	20X0	*20X1*	*20X0*	*20X1*
A. Revenues from operations	1100	1200	93	92
B. Other income	80	100	7	8
C. Total revenues	1180	1300	100	100
D. Total expenses	1020	1120	86	86
E. Profit before exceptional and extraordinary items	160	180	14	14
F. Exceptional and extraordinary items	-	-	-	-
G. Profit before tax	160	180	14	14
H. Tax expense	40	50	3	4
I. Profit(loss) for the period	120	130	10	10

Percentage format balance sheet and profit and loss statements enable the analyst to assess the changes in the financial position and performance of a firm over time and make inter-firm comparisons more easily. You can answer questions like the following:

- How has the debt to total assets percentage of the firm behaved over time? Is the debt to total assets percentage of the firm higher or lower than its peers?
- Which firm has the greatest amount of receivables relative to total assets?
- How has the cost of goods sold as a percentage of sales behaved over time?
- Which firm has the highest percentage spend on R & D?

2.5 PROBLEMS IN FINANCIAL STATEMENT ANALYSIS

Financial statement analysis can be a very useful tool for understanding a firm's performance and condition. However, there are certain problems and issues encountered in such analysis which call for care, circumspection, and judgement.

Heuristic and Intuitive Character Most of the ratios found in the traditional literature on financial statement analysis have been proposed in a somewhat heuristic or intuitive fashion. The ratios are often not related logically to a well-defined theoretical framework. Instead they have been suggested in a somewhat impressionistic manner. In the absence of a well defined theoretical underpinning, the traditional approach to financial statement analysis seems to be lacking in direction. It appears ad hoc, informal, subjective, and somewhat disjointed.

Development of Benchmarks Many firms, particularly the larger ones, have operations spanning a wide range of industries. Given the diversity of their product lines, it is difficult to find suitable benchmarks for evaluating their financial performance and condition. Hence, it appears that meaningful benchmarks may be available only for firms which have a well defined industry classification.

Window Dressing Firms may resort to window dressing to project a favourable financial picture. For example, a firm may prepare its balance sheet at a point when its inventory level is very low. As a result, it may appear that the firm has a very comfortable liquidity position and a high turnover of inventories. When window dressing of this kind is suspected, the financial analyst should look at the average level of inventory over a period of time and the not the level of inventory at just one point of time.

Price Level Changes Financial accounting, as it is currently practiced in India and most other countries, does not take into account price level changes. As a result, balance sheet figures are distorted and profits misreported. Hence, financial statement analysis can be vitiated.

Variations in Accounting Policies Business firms have some latitude in the accounting treatment of items like depreciation, valuation of stocks, research and development expenses, foreign exchange transactions, installment sales, preliminary and pre-operative expenses, provision of reserves, and revaluation of assets. Due to diversity of accounting policies found in practice, comparative financial statement analysis may be vitiated.

Interpretation of Results Though industry averages and other yardsticks are commonly used in financial ratios, it is somewhat difficult to judge whether a certain ratio is 'good' or 'bad'. A high current ratio, for example, may indicate a strong liquidity position (something good) or excessive inventories (something bad). Likewise, a high turnover of fixed assets may mean efficient utilisation of plant and machinery or continued flogging of more or less fully depreciated, worn out, and inefficient plant and machinery.

Another problem in interpretation arises when a firm has some favourable ratios and some unfavourable ratios - and this is rather common. In such a situation, it may be somewhat difficult to form an overall judgement about its financial strength or weakness. Multiple discriminant analysis, a statistical tool, may be employed to sort out the net effect of several ratios pointing in different directions.

Potential Red Flags

As an analyst, you should learn to identify potential red flags. Here is a list of common red flags.

- A qualified audit opinion.
- A change in accounting policy that is not satisfactorily explained.
- An unusual increase in accruals.
- A widening gap between reported income and cash flow from operations.
- Large adjustments in the fourth quarter.
- An abrupt change in external or internal auditor.
- An increase in transactions with related parties.

2.6 GUIDELINES FOR FINANCIAL STATEMENT ANALYSIS

From the foregoing discussion, it is clear that financial statement analysis cannot be treated as a simple, structured exercise. When you analyse financial statements bear in mind the following guidelines.

1. **Use ratios to get clues to ask the right questions:** By themselves ratios rarely provide answers, but they definitely help you to raise the right questions.
2. **Be selective in the choice of ratios:** You can compute scores of different ratios and easily drown yourself into confusion. For most purposes a small set of ratios—three to seven—would suffice. Few ratios, aptly chosen, would capture most of the information that you can derive from financial statements.
3. **Employ proper benchmarks:** It is a common practice to compare the ratios (calculated from a set of financial statements) against some benchmarks. These benchmarks may be the average ratios of the industry or the ratios of the industry leaders or the historic ratios of the firm itself.
4. **Know the tricks used by accountants:** Since firms tend to manipulate the reported income, you should learn about the devices employed by them.
5. **Read the notes:** The notes to financial statements contain valuable information. They may reveal things that management may try to hide. The more difficult it is to read a note, the more information-laden it may be.
6. **Remember that financial statement analysis is an odd mixture of art and science:** Financial statement analysis cannot be regarded as a simple, structured exercise. It is a process requiring care, thought, common sense, and business judgement—a process for which there are no mechanical substitutes.

SUMMARY

- Financial statements contain a wealth of information which, if properly analysed and interpreted, can provide valuable insights into a firm's performance and position. Analysis of financial statements is of interest to several groups interested in a variety of purposes.

- The principal tool of financial statement analysis is financial ratio analysis which essentially involves a study of ratios between various items or groups of items in financial statements. Financial ratios may be divided into five broad types: liquidity ratios, leverages ratios, turnover ratios, profitability ratios, and valuation ratios.
- Liquidity refers to the ability of the firm to meet its obligations in the short run, usually one year. Liquidity ratios are generally based on the relationship between current assets and current liabilities. The important liquidity ratios are: current ratios and acid test ratio.
- Leverage refers to the use of debt finance. Leverage ratios reflect the ratio of debt to equity and the ability of the firm to meet its debt-related commitments. The important leverage ratios are: debt-equity ratio, times interest earned ratio, and debt service coverage ratio.
- Turnover ratios, also referred to as activity ratios or asset management ratios, measure how efficiently the assets are employed by the firm. These ratios are based on the relationship between the level of activity and the level for various assets. The important turnover ratios are: inventory turnover ratio, debtors turnover ratio, fixed assets turnover ratio, and total assets turnover ratio.
- Profitability ratios reflect the final results of business operations. There are two types of profitability ratios: profit margin ratios and rate of return ratios. Profit margin ratios show the relationship between profit and sales. The two popular profit margin ratios are: gross profit margin ratio and net profit margin ratio. Rate of return ratios reflect the relationship between profit and investment. The important rate of return ratios are: return on assets, return on capital employed, and return on equity.
- Valuation ratios indicate how the equity stock and the company are assessed in the capital market. Since the market value of equity reflects the combined influence of risk and return, valuation ratios are the most comprehensive measures of a firm's performance. The important valuation ratios are: price earnings ratio, EV-EBITDA ratio, and market value to book value ratio.
- Generally, the financial ratios of a company are compared with some benchmark ratios. Industry averages often serve as benchmark ratios. Sometimes the ratios of a firm which is deemed to be representative may be used as benchmarks.
- While analysis based on a single set of financial statements is helpful, it may often have to be supplemented with time series analysis

which provides insight into a firm's performance and condition over a period of time. In this context, an analysis of time series of financial ratios is helpful.

- The DuPont chart is a popular tool of financial analysis. A useful diagnostic tool, it provides insights into the two determinants of return on total assets: net profit margin and total assets turnover ratio. By including the financial leverage multiplier, the DuPont analysis may be extended to explore the determinants of the return on equity.
- In percentage-format financial statements, the items in the balance sheet are stated as percentages of total assets and the items in the profit and loss account are stated as percentages of total income.
- While financial statement analysis can be a very useful tool, there are certain problems and issues encountered in such analysis that call for care, circumspection, and judgement.

Accounting Mechanics 3

In the preceding chapters, we studied the contents of financial statements and discussed certain tools for analysing these statements. We now look at the accounting mechanics to learn how financial transactions are analysed, recorded, and summarised in order to generate the financial statements of a firm. While we are not concerned with detailed book-keeping procedures as such, a basic knowledge of accounting mechanics is useful towards a better understanding of financial statements and appreciation of the accounting implications of certain decisions.

Our discussion of accounting mechanics is divided into three sections. The first section deals with the fundamental accounting model and the device of accounts for efficiently handling the analysis of transactions; the second section discusses the series of steps involved in the information-processing cycle which culminates in the preparation of financial statements; the third section presents a comprehensive illustration of accounting information processing.

3.1 ACCOUNTING MODEL AND THE DEVICE OF ACCOUNT

Accounting is concerned with transactions which have an economic impact on the firm. These transactions generally involve an exchange of assets and/or obligations between the firm (the accounting entity) and outside parties. Examples of this can be purchase of materials, sale of goods, and raising of a loan from a commercial bank. Sometimes the transactions may not involve an external party and yet have an effect on the accounting entity, as in the case of a loss due to fire or depreciation of an asset.

The basic characteristic of any transaction is that it has a dual economic effect on the accounting entity. For example, when a firm sells merchandise for cash, it gives up a resource (merchandise) in return for another resource (cash). To reflect this dual economic effect of each transaction, we will work with the fundamental accounting model:

Assets = Liabilities + Owners' equity

However, we have also learnt that the owners' equity increases by investments and revenue but decreases by withdrawals and expenses. Hence, the fundamental accounting model may be expanded as follows:

Assets = Liabilities + Owners' equity

Increases by:	Decreases by:
• Investments	• Withdrawals
• Revenues	• Expenses

This model facilitates the recording of the dual economic effect of each transaction. To elucidate how these are recorded in terms of this accounting model, let us look at an illustration.

Illustration

Prakash and seven friends set up a cold storage unit called Subzero Private Limited on January 1, 20X1. Each of them subscribed to 1,000 equity shares of ₹100 each issued at par. Exhibit 3.1 enumerates a series of transactions for the business entity Subzero Private Limited during the year and the effect of these transactions. On the basis of the information given in Exhibit 3.1, the profit and loss account and the balance sheet for Subzero Private Limited have been prepared as shown in Exhibit 3.2.

EXHIBIT 3.1 *Subzero Private Limited Transaction Analysis*

Transactions	*Assets*		*Liabilities*	*+ Owners' Equity*
a. Received ₹800,000 on issue of equity shares	Cash	+ 800,000		Equity capital + 800,000
b. Purchased building for ₹600,000	Cash	– 600,000		
Bldg.		+ 600,000		

(*Contd.*)

EXHIBIT 3.1 *(Contd.)*

Transactions	*Assets*		*Liabilities*	*+ Owners' Equity*
c. Borrowed ₹500,000 at 15 percent from a commercial bank by signing notes payable	Cash	+ 500,000	Notes payable + 500,000	
d. Bought cold-storage plant for ₹400,000	Cash Plant	– 400,000 + 400,000		
e. Bought delivery trucks for ₹200,000	Cash Delivery trucks	– 200,000 + 200,000		
f. Operating expenses paid in cash, ₹30,000	Cash	– 30,000		Operating expenses expenses – 30,000
g. Operating expenses accrued but not yet paid, ₹60,000			Creditors + 60,000	Operating expenses – 60,000
h. Collected cold-storage charges, ₹150,000	Cash	+ 150,000		Operating revenues + 150,000
i. Cold-storage charges earned but not yet collected, ₹350,000	Debtors	+ 350,000		Operating revenues + 350,000
j. Interest paid on bank borrowings, ₹75,000	Cash	– 75,000		Interest expenses – 75,000
k. Depreciation charged for building, ₹30,000	Bldg.	– 30,000		Depr'n. expenses – 30,000
l. Depreciation charged for cold-storage plant, ₹100,000	Plant	– 100,000		Depr'n. expenses – 100,000

(Contd.)

EXHIBIT 3.1 *(Contd.)*

Transactions	*Assets*		*Liabilities*	*+ Owners' Equity*
m. Depreciation charged for delivery trucks, ₹50,000	Delivery trucks	– 50,000		Depr'n. expenses – 50,000
n. Dividend paid, ₹80,000	Cash	– 80,000		Dividend paid – 80,000

EXHIBIT 3.2 ***Financial Statements of Subzero Private Limited***

Profit and Loss Account for the Year Ended on 31st December, 20X1

Operating revenues		₹500,000
Expenses		
Operating expenses	90,000	
Interest expenses	75,000	
Depreciation expenses	180,000	345,000
Net profit		155,000

Balance Sheet as on 31st December, 20X1

Owners' Equity and Liabilities		*Assets*	
Share capital	₹8,00,000	Fixed assets	
Reserves & surplus	75,000	• Building	570,000
(Net income, 155,000		• Cold-storage plant	300,000
–dividends paid, 80,000)		• Delivery trucks	150,000
Secured loans	5,00,000	Investments	—
Unsecured loans	—	Current assets, loans advances	
Current liabilities & provisions	60,000	• Debtors	350,000
		• Cash	65,000
	1,435,000		1,435,000

The illustration in Exhibit 3.1 shows that: (i) the dual effect of each transaction is recorded separately, and (ii) the integrity of the accounting model (assets = liabilities + owners' equity) is maintained in recording each transaction.

Handling Data Processing Problems

Recording transactions as we have done in Exhibit 3.1 may pose two problems:

- It is difficult to keep track of the amount of each kind of asset, liability, and owners' equity.
- There is scope for making errors in recording the increases and decreases in various accounts.

To cope with these problems, we require (i) an efficient method for keeping track of the amount of each kind of asset, liability, and owners' equity, and (ii) a systematic approach for recording the increases and decreases in them.

For these purposes, accountants have developed the device of the account and a system of debits and credits.

The Account

An account represents a standardised arrangement for recording data. In a typical accounting system, there exists a separate account for each asset (such as land, building, equipment, inventory, cash), each liability (such as notes payable, creditors), each category of owners' equity (such as share capital, general reserve, investment allowance reserve), each item of revenue, and each item of expense.

Every account has two sides, the debit side and the credit side. In the arrangement known as the 'T-account' format, the left side is the debit side and the right side is the credit side. As an example, the Cash Account of Subzero Private Limited is shown in Exhibit 3.3. The left or debit side of the cash account totals to ₹14,50,000 and the right or credit side totals to ₹13,85,000. The difference between the total on the left side and the total on the right side represents the cash balance at the end of the period. This is the amount shown in the balance sheet presented in Exhibit 3.2.

Although the T-account format is used for pedagogic convenience, the format used commonly in manual accounting systems is as shown in Exhibit 3.4.

EXHIBIT 3.3 *Ledger Account (T - Account Form)*

Cash

Left or Debit side (Increases)	₹	*Right or Credit Side (Decreases)*	₹
Investment by owners	800,000	Purchase of building	600,000
Loan from bank	500,000	Purchase of cold-storage plant	400,000

(Contd.)

Exhibit 3.3 *(Contd.)*

Left or Debit side (Increases)	₹	*Right or Credit Side (Decreases)*	₹
Cold-storage charges	150,000	Purchase of delivery trucks	200,000
		Operating expenses	30,000
		Interest expenses	75,000
		Dividend payment	80,000
	1,450,000		1,385,000

Exhibit 3.4 *Ledger Account (Account Form)*

Account Title : Cash		*Account Number : 11*		
Date	*Explanation*	*Debit*	*Credit*	*Balance*
	Investment by owners	800,000		800,000
	Purchase of building		600,000	200,000
	Loan from bank	500,000		700,000
	Purchase of cold-storage plant		400,000	300,000
	Purchase of delivery trucks		200,000	100,000
	Operating expenses		30,000	70,000
	Cold-storage charges	150,000		220,000
	Interest expenses		75,000	145,000
	Dividend payment		80,000	65,000

System of Debits and Credits

The fundamental accounting model and the T-account were designed and developed by Pacioli, the father of modern accounting. For systematic recording of increases and decreases in accounts, he added another algebraic balance feature:

Assets		=	Liabilities		+	Owners' Equities	
Debit	*Credit*		*Debit*	*Credit*		*Debit*	*Credit*
+	–		–	+		–	+

Thanks to the addition of this balance feature, we have the rules "debits are always equal to credits", and "assets are always equal to liabilities and owners' equities."

The system used for recording increases and decreases in accounts, according to this second balancing feature, may be stated as follows:

	Increases	*Decreases*
Assets	Debit	Credit
Liabilities	Credit	Debit
Owners' equity	Credit	Debit

From this, it is clear that the owners' equity is increased by credits and decreased by debits. Since revenues increase owners' equity and expenses decrease, we get the following rules:

(i) revenues are recorded as credits, and
(ii) expenses are recorded as debits.

Illustration

To clarify the use of the device of accounts and the system of debits and credits, let us look at some of the transactions of Subzero Private Limited discussed earlier.

(a) Received ₹800,000 from the owners on issue of equity shares.
Transaction analysis: The cash of the company increases by ₹800,000 and equity capital by ₹800,000. Cash account is debited (increased) and equity capital account is credited (increased).

Cash (asset)		*Equity Capital (Owners' equity)*	
Debit	Credit	Debit	Credit
(a) 8,00,000			(a) 8,00,000

(b) Purchased building for ₹600,000, paid in cash.
Transaction analysis: This increases the asset, building, by ₹600,000 and decreases another asset, cash, by ₹600,000. Buildings account is debited (increased) and cash account is credited (decreased).

Buildings (asset)		*Cash (asset)*	
Debit	Credit	Debit	Credit
(b) 600,000			(b) 600,000

(c) Operating expenses paid in cash, ₹30,000.
Transaction analysis: Cash decreases by ₹30,000 and owners' equity by ₹30,000. Cash account is credited (decreased) and operating expenses (owners' equity) account is debited (decreased) by ₹30,000.

Cash (asset)		*Operating Expenses (Owners' equity)*	
Debit	Credit	Debit	Credit
	(c) 30,000	(c) 30,000	

(d) Operating expenses accrued, but not yet paid, ₹60,000.
Transaction analysis: This increases the company's liabilities and operating expenses by ₹60,000. Accounts payable, a liability account, is credited (increased) and operating expenses (owners' equity) account is debited (decreased) by ₹60,000.

Account Payable (Liability)		*Operating Expenses (Owners' equity)*	
Debit	Credit	Debit	Credit
	(d) 60,000	(d) 60,000	

3.2 INFORMATION PROCESSING CYCLE

Having discussed the conceptual foundations of financial accounting, let us look at the steps involved in the accounting information processing cycle which culminates in the preparation of financial statements. The steps involved in this cycle are as follows:

- Collection of raw data
- Analysis of transactions
- Recording of transactions in the journal
- Transfer of information to the ledger
- Preparation of trial balance
- Passing of adjustment entries
- Preparation of financial statements

Collection of Raw Data

This is the first step in the cycle and is concerned with the collection of data relating to transactions affecting the accounting entity. Transactions with external parties are reflected in documents like sales invoices, purchase invoices, receipts, etc., which provide the data required for accounting purposes. For economic events which do not involve external parties as in the consumption of materials, documents are usually generated by the operating functions of the business.

Analysis of Transactions

This is a mental process concerned with determining the effects of a transaction on the business entity. Transaction analysis, as we have learnt, is done in terms of the basic accounting model. It shows the accounts which have to be debited and credited.

Recording the Transactions in the Journal

Once the economic effects of a transaction have been determined, it is recorded in the journal. The journal is an accounting record which lists chronologically the transactions of the business and their impact on various accounts in terms of debits and credits. To illustrate this, Exhibit 3.5 shows the journal for the first three transactions of Subzero Private Limited. With reference to this exhibit, it may be noted that

(i) the debit entry relating to a transaction is listed first and the amount of debit is shown in the first of the two money columns, and
(ii) the credit entry relating to a transaction is listed next (with indentation) and the amount of credit is shown in the second money column. The ledger folio column of the journal shows where the concerned account is maintained, that is, which folio of the ledger.

EXHIBIT 3.5 ***Journal***

Date	*Transaction*	*LF*	*Debit*	*Credit*
	Cash		800,000	
	Equity capital			800,000
	(Capital contributed by the owners in cash)			
	Buildings		600,000	
	Cash			600,000
	(Buildings purchased for cash)			
	Cash		500,000	
	Notes payable			500,000
	(Cash borrowed by signing notes payable)			

Posting to the Ledger

A ledger represents a group of accounts. It may be in the form of a bound book, a set of loose-leaf pages, or a more commonly in electronic form. Irrespective of its form, the rules for making entries into the accounts of the ledger remain the same.

Transactions entered in the journal are posted, or transferred, to the ledger. While the journal is usually written each day, ledger posting may be done less frequently, say once a week. The frequency of these information-processing activities may vary from one firm to another. In Exhibit 3.6, the ledger of Subzero Private Limited is shown.

Exhibit 3.6 ***Ledger of Subzero Private Limited***

Assets	=	*Liabilities* +	*Owners' Equity*	
Cash		*Notes Payable*	*Equity Capital*	
(a) 800,000	(b) 600,000			
(c) 500,000	(d) 400,000	(c) 500,000		(a) 800,000
(h) 150,000	(e) 200,000			
	(f) 30,000	Accounts Payable	Dividends Paid	
	(j) 75,000			
	(n) 80,000	(g) 60,000	(n) 80,000	
Buildings			Operating Expenses	
(b) 6,00,000	(k) 30,000		(f) 30,000	
			(g) 60,000	
Cold Storage Plant			Operating Revenues	
(d) 400,000	(l) 100,000			(h) 150,000
				(l) 350,000
Delivery Truck			Interest Expenses	
(e) 200,000	(m) 50,000		(j) 75,000	
Accounts Receivable			Depreciation Expenses	
(i) 350,000			(k) 30,000	
			(l) 100,000	
			(m) 50,000	

Preparation of Trial Balance

A trial balance is a listing of the ledger accounts, along with their net debit or credit balances. It is prepared at the end of the accounting period. Exhibit 3.7 shows the trial balance of Subzero Private Limited.

The trial balance serves two functions:

(i) It provides a check on the equality of debits and credits.
(ii) It arranges data in a convenient form for preparing the financial statements.

Exhibit 3.7 ***Trial Balance of Subzero Private Limited***

Account	*Debit*	*Credit*
Cash	65,000	
Buildings	570,000	
Cold-storage plant	300,000	
Delivery truck	150,000	

(Contd.)

EXHIBIT 3.7 *(Contd.)*

Account	*Debit*	*Credit*
Accounts receivable	350,000	
Notes payable		500,000
Accounts payable		60,000
Equity capital		800,000
Dividends paid	80,000	
Opening expenses	90,000	
Operative revenues		500,000
Interest expenses	75,000	
Depreciation expenses	180,000	
Total	1,860,000	1,860,000

Passing of Adjustment Entries

At the end of the year, after the trial balance has been prepared, several adjustment entries have to be passed. These are meant to reflect economic events relating to the period but not recorded earlier. Adjustments usually relate to the following: (i) recording of accrued expenses and accrued revenues, (ii) allocation of revenues received in advance and expenses incurred in advance, (iii) adjustment for cost of goods sold during the accounting period, (iv) provision for bad debts, (v) writing off of bad debts, (vi) provision for depreciation, (vii) provision for income taxes, (viii) provision for dividends, and (ix) creation of reserves. It is necessary to prepare journal entries for these adjustments and post them to the ledger.

Preparation of Financial Statements

After the adjustment entries are made in the journal and posted to the ledger, the balances in ledger accounts have to be determined afresh. Then, a modified trial balance is drawn. This forms the basis for preparing the financial statements.

All revenue and expense items are taken to the profit and loss account. This may be viewed as a clearing account through which the impact of revenues and expenses is transmitted to owners' equity. The net profit (if there is a loss, the net profit figure obviously would be negative), less dividends, represents increase in owners' equity which may be maintained in one or more reserve accounts. All asset, liability, and owners' equity account balances are shown on the balance sheet.

3.3 ACCOUNTING INFORMATION PROCESSING: A COMPREHENSIVE ILLUSTRATION

On November 1, 20X1, Prakash and Gautam set up an advertising agency called Space Age Advertisers, as a partnership concern. During the period November 1, 20X1 to March 31, 20X2, several transactions occurred. The partners decided to use the fiscal year, April 1 through March 31, for their business purposes. The ledger balances as on March 31, 20X2, are shown below:

Space Age Advertisers
Ledger Balances, March 31, 20X2

Account No.	Account Title	Balance ₹ Debit	Credit
101	Cash	10,000	
102	Debtors	25,000	
103	Deposits	50,000	
104	Furniture and fixtures	200,000	
105	Equipments	150,000	
106	Stationery	30,000	
107	Prepaid insurance	—	
108	Capital of partners		200,000
109	Retained earnings (accumulated earnings up to March 31, 2002)		15,000
110	Bank borrowings		180,000
111	Income tax payable		5,000
112	Creditors		40,000
113	Accumulated depreciation on furniture and fixtures		10,000
114	Accumulated depreciation on equipments		15,000
115	Advertising revenues		—
116	Salary and wage expenses		—
117	Telephone and telex expenses		—
118	Stationery expense		—
119	Interest expense		—
120	Miscellaneous expense		—
121	Depreciation expense		—
122	Insurance expense		—

The summarised transactions for the 12-month period, April 1, 20X2 through March 31, 20X3, are as follows (a letter notation is used at the left of each transaction to facilitate tracing):

(a) On April 5, 20X2, ₹2,000 was paid toward a two-year insurance premium covering furniture, fixture, and equipments.
(b) Advertising revenues earned were ₹300,000. Out of this, ₹225,000 were collected and ₹75,000 remained uncollected.
(c) Operating expenses incurred and paid in cash were: telephone and telex expenses, ₹30,000; salary and wage expenses, ₹80,000.
(d) Interest expense incurred and paid in cash was ₹27,000.
(e) At the end of the accounting year (March 31, 20X3), the following bills for expenses incurred had not been recorded or paid: telephone bill for March and April, ₹1,500; miscellaneous expenses, ₹2,500.
(f) ₹20,000 was collected from debtors outstanding at the beginning of the year.
(g) Depreciation was estimated to be ₹10,000 for furniture and fixtures and ₹15,000 for equipments.
(h) ₹30,000 was paid to creditors outstanding at the beginning of the year.
(i) Out of ₹2,000 paid toward insurance premium, ₹1,000 represented the insurance expense for the year 20X2-20X3.
(j) At the end of the year, ₹20,000 was paid to the bank on account of the principal.
(k) Stationery worth ₹20,000 was consumed during the year.
(l) Income tax payable at the beginning of the year was paid.
(m) Income tax expense for the year ending on March 31, 20X3 was estimated to be ₹15,000. This amount will be paid in the following year.

Required

1. Analyse and journalise each transaction listed above.
2. Set up a ledger with T-accounts that includes all of the accounts listed above. Enter the April 1, 20X2 balances in each account wherever applicable.
3. Post all entries from the journal to the ledger; utilise the folio columns.
4. Prepare the trial balance at March 31, 20X3.
5. Prepare the income statement for the year ending March 31, 20X3.
6. Prepare the balance sheet as on March 31, 20X3.

Requirement 1
Space Age Advertisers
(Entries for the year ended March 31, 20X3) Journal

Account Titles and Explanation	F	Debit	Credit
a. Prepaid insurance	107	2,000	
Cash	101		2,000
(Payment of insurance premium for two years in advance)			
b. Cash	101	225,000	
Debtors	102	75,000	
Advertising revenues			300,000
(To record advertising revenues earned for the year, of which ₹75,000 has not yet been collected)			
c. Telephone and telex expenses	117	30,000	
Salary and wage expenses	116	80,000	
Cash	101		110,000
(Payment of expenses)			
d. Interest expense	119	27,000	
Cash	101		27,000
(Payment of expenses)			
e. Telephone and telex expenses	117	1,500	
Miscellaneous expenses	120	2,500	
Creditors	112		4,000
(Expenses for the year not yet paid)			
f. Cash	101	20,000	
Debtors	102		20,000
(Receipt of dues carried over from the previous year)			
g. Depreciation expense	121	25,000	
Accumulated depreciation on furniture and fixtures	113		10,000
Accumulated depreciation on equipments	114		15,000
(Depreciation expense for the year)			
h. Creditors	112	30,000	
Cash	101		30,000
(Paid obligations carried forward from the previous year)			

(Contd.)

(*Contd.*)

Account Titles and Explanation	*F*	*Debit*	*Credit*
i. Insurance expense	122	1,000	
Prepaid insurance	107		1,000
(To record as an expense the cost of the insurance that expired)			
j. Bank borrowings	110	20,000	
Cash	101		20,000
(Repayment of a portion of bank borrowings)			
k. Stationery expense	118	20,000	
Stationery	106		20,000
(Stationery expense for the year)			
l. Income tax payable	111	5,000	
Cash	101		5,000
(Payment of tax obligation carried forward from the previous year)			
m. Income tax expense	123	15,000	
Income tax payable	111		15,000
(To record the income tax expense that has not been paid)			

Requirements 2 and 3
Space Age Advertisers Ledger (As on March 31, 20X3)

Cash (101)				*Debtors (102)*			
	Amount		*Amount*		*Amount*		*Amount*
Balance	10,000	(a)	2,000	Balance	25,000	(f)	20,000
(b)	225,000	(c)	110,000	(b)	75,000		
(f)	20,000	(d)	27,000				
		(h)	30,000				
		(j)	20,000	*Deposits* (103)			
		(l)	5,000	Balance	50,000		
Equipments (105)				*Furniture and fixtures* (104)			
Balance	150,000			Balance	200,000		
Prepaid insurance (107)				*Stationery* (106)			
(a)	2,000	(i)	1,000	Balance	30,000	(k)	20,000
Capital of partners (108)				*Retained earnings* (109)			
		Balance	200,000			Balance	15,000
Bank borrowings (110)				*Income tax payable* (111)			
(j)	20,000	Balance	180,000	(l)	5,000	Balance	5,000
						(m)	15,000

(*Contd.*)

(*Contd.*)

Cash (101)				*Debtors (102)*			
Creditors (112)							
(h)	30,000	Balance	40,000	*Accumulated depreciation on furniture & fixtures (113)*			
		(c)	4,000			Balance	10,000
Accumulated depreciation on equipment (114)						(g)	10,000
		Balance	15,000	*Advertising revenues (115)*			
		(g)	15,000			(b)	300,000
Salary and wage expense (116)				*Telephone and telex expense (117)*			
(c)	80,000			(c)	30,000		
Stationery expense (118)				(e)	1,500		
(k)	20,000			*Interest expense (119)*			
Miscellaneous expense (12)				(d)	27,000		
(e)	2,500			*Depreciation expense (121)*			
Insurance expense (122)				(g)	25,000		
(i)	1,000			*Income tax expense (123)*			
				(m)	15,000		

Requirement 4

Space Age Advertisers Trial Balance as on March 31,20X3

		Balance	
Account No.	*Account Titles*	*Debit*	*Credit*
101	Cash	61,000	
102	Debtors	80,000	
103	Deposits	50,000	
104	Furniture & fixtures	200,000	
105	Equipments	150,000	
106	Stationery	10,000	
107	Pre-paid insurance	1,000	
108	Capital of partners		200,000
109	Retained earnings		15,000
110	Bank borrowings		160,000
111	Income tax payable		15,000
112	Creditors		14,000
113	Accumulated depreciation on furniture and fixtures		20,000
114	Accumulated depreciation on equipments		30,000

(*Contd.*)

(Contd.)

Account No.	Account Titles	Balance Debit	Balance Credit
115	Advertising revenues		300,000
116	Salary and wage expense	80,000	
117	Telephone and telex expense	31,500	
118	Stationery expense	20,000	
119	Interest expense	27,000	
120	Miscellaneous expenses	2,500	
121	Depreciation expense	25,000	
122	Insurance expense	1,000	
123	Income tax expense	15,000	
		754,000	754,000

Requirement 5

Statement of Profit and Loss for the year Ended March 31, 20X3

Revenue:			300,000
Advertising revenue	300,000		
Operating expenses			160,000
Salary and wage expenses		80,000	
Telephone and telex expenses		31,500	
Stationery expense		20,000	
Depreciation expense		25,000	
Insurance expense		1,000	
Miscellaneous expenses		2,500	
		160,000	
Operating profit			140,000
Financial expenses			27,000
Interest expense	27,000		
Pre-tax profit			113,000
Income tax expense			15,000
Net profit			98,000

Requirement 6
Space Age Advertisers Balance Sheet As on March 31, 20X3

Liabilities		Assets		
Capital of partners	200,000	Furniture and fixtures	200,000	
Retained earnings (beginning balance, 15,000 plus net profit, 98,000)	113,000	Less: accumulated depreciation	20,000	180,000
Bank borrowings	160,000	Equipments	150,000	
Creditors	14,000	Less: accumulated depreciation	30,000	
Income tax payable	15,000			120,000
		Stationery		10,000
		Debtors		80,000
		Deposits		50,000
		Pre-paid insurance		1,000
		Cash		61,000
	502,000			502,000

SUMMARY

- The basic characteristic of any transaction is that it has a dual economic effect on the accounting entity. To reflect this, we work with the fundamental accounting model:

Assets = Liabilities + Owners' Equity

Increased by:	Decreased by:
• Investments	• Withdrawals
• Revenues	• Expenses

- An account represents a standardised arrangement for recording data. In a typical accounting system, there exists a separate account for each asset (such as land, building, equipment, inventory, and cash), each liability (such as notes payable, creditors, and tax provision), each category of owners' equity (such as share capital, general reserves, and dividend equalisation reserve), each item of revenue (such as sales, dividend, and commission), and each item of expense (such as wages, rent, and interest).

- Every account has two sides, the debit side and the credit side. In the arrangement known as the 'T-account' format, the left side is the debit side and the right side the credit side.
- The system used for recording increases and decreases in accounts is as follows:

	Increases	Decreases
Assets	Debit	Credit
Liabilities	Credit	Debit
Owner's equity	Credit	Debit

- The principal steps involved in the accounting information processing cycle which culminates in the preparation of financial statements are: (i) collection of raw data, (ii) analysis of transactions, (iii) recording of transactions in the journal, (iv) transfer of information to the ledger, (v) preparation of the trial balance, (vi) passing of adjustment entries, and (vii) preparation of financial statements.

Financial Forecasting 4

Chapters 1 and 2 described what financial statements are and showed how you can analyse them to assess a firm's financial performance. In addition to knowing what happened in the past, you would like to anticipate the future. So you need to understand how to prepare *pro forma* or *projected financial statements*. These statements help you to:

- Assess whether the firm's anticipated performance is in line with its own targets and with the expectations of investors.
- Estimate the effect of proposed changes as they can be used to do "what if" analysis.
- Determine the future financing needs of the firm.

This chapter discusses the basics of financial planning and forecasting. It is organised into eight sections as follows:

- Strategic plan
- Components of a financial plan
- Sales forecast
- Pro forma profit and loss account
- Pro forma balance sheet
- Computerised financial planning system
- Additional funds needed
- Sustainable growth rate

4.1 STRATEGIC PLAN

In the liberalised business environment, characterised by expanding opportunities and swiftly changing market conditions, strategic planning has assumed greater significance not only for growth but for survival as well.

The strategic plan of a firm spells out its corporate purpose, corporate scope, corporate objectives, and corporate strategies. The **corporate purpose** defines the mission of the firm. Put differently, it states the **raison d'etre** of the firm. For example, a pharmaceutical company has expressed its purpose as "To provide quality health care for the masses". The **corporate scope** delineates the lines of business in which the firm wishes to engage in and the geographic spread of its operations. For example, Nucor Corporation, a firm listed on the New York Stock Exchange, has defined its scope as follows: "We are a manufacturing company, producing primarily steel products." While the corporate purpose and scope reflect the broad philosophy and nature of the firm's activities, **corporate objectives** spell out the specific goals sought by the firm. Some goals are stated in quantitative terms such as achieving a market share of 30 percent, a growth rate of 25 percent, and a return on equity of 20 percent. Other goals are stated in qualitative terms such as "attaining a measure of stability". **Corporate strategies** or policies are the instruments for achieving corporate objectives. A firm may, for example, follow the policy of vertical integration to achieve growth and stability.

4.2 COMPONENTS OF A FINANCIAL PLAN

Pro forma statements are part of a financial plan. While there is considerable variation in the scope, degree of formality, and level of sophistication in financial planning across firms, most of the financial plans have certain common elements. These are:

1. **Economic assumptions** The financial plan is based on certain assumptions about the economic environment (interest rate, inflation rate, growth rate, exchange rate, and so on).
2. **Sales forecast** The sales forecast is typically the starting point of the financial forecasting exercise. Most financial variables are related to the sales figure.
3. **Pro forma statements** The heart of a financial plan are the *pro forma* (forecast) profit and loss accounts and balance sheets.
4. **Asset requirements** Firms need to invest in plant and equipment and working capital. The financial plan spells out the projected capital investments and working capital requirements over time.
5. **Financing plan** Suitable sources of financing have to be thought of for supporting the investment in capital expenditure and working

capital. The financing plan delineates the proposed means of financing.

6. **Cash budget** The cash budget shows the cash inflows and outflows expected in the budget period.

4.3 SALES FORECAST

The sales forecast is typically the starting point of the financial forecasting exercise. Most of the financial variables are projected in relation to the estimated level of sales. Hence, the accuracy of the financial forecast depends critically on the accuracy of the sales forecast.

Although the financial manager may participate in the process of developing the sales forecast, the primary responsibility for it typically vests with the marketing department or the planning group.

Sales forecasts may be prepared for varying planning horizons to serve different purposes. A sales forecast for a period of 3–5 years, or even longer durations, may be developed mainly to aid investment planning. A sales forecast for a period of one year (and in some cases two years) is the primary basis for the financial forecasting exercise discussed in this chapter. Sales forecasts for shorter durations (six months, three months, one month) may be prepared for facilitating working capital planning and cash budgeting.

A wide range of sales forecasting techniques and methods are available. They may be divided into three broad categories:

- **Qualitative Techniques** These techniques rely essentially on the judgement of experts to translate qualitative information into quantitative estimates.
- **Time Series Projection Methods** These methods generate forecasts on the basis of an analysis of the past behaviour of time series.
- **Causal Models** These techniques seek to develop forecasts based on cause-effect relationships expressed in explicit, quantitative manner.

Each technique has its own advantages and limitations. Often, exclusive reliance on a single technique is somewhat dangerous. Practical wisdom suggests that at least two techniques, which seem to make sense in the specific circumstances of the firm, may be employed to hammer out the sales forecast.

4.4 PRO FORMA PROFIT AND LOSS ACCOUNT

These are two commonly used methods for preparing the *pro forma* profit and loss account—the percent of sales method and the budgeted expense method.

Percent of Sales Method

The percent of sales method for preparing the *pro forma* profit and loss account is fairly simple. Basically this method assumes that the future relationship between various elements of costs to sales will be similar to their historical relationship. When using this method, a decision has to be taken about which historical cost ratios to be used: Should these ratios pertain to the previous year, or the average of two or more previous years?

Exhibit 4.1 illustrates the application of the percent of sales method of preparing the *pro forma* profit and loss account to Spaceage Electronics for the year 20X3. In this table historical data are given for two previous years, 20X1 and 20X2. For projection purposes, a ratio based on the average of two previous years has been used. The forecast value of each item is obtained as the product of the estimated sales and the average percent of sales ratio applicable to that item. For example, the average percent of sales ratio for cost of goods sold is 65.0 percent. Multiplying the estimated sales of 1400 by 65.0 percent, the projected value of cost of goods sold has been calculated. Likewise, the projected values of other items in the profit and loss statement have been calculated. Although in practice some deviation from a mechanical application of this method is unavoidable, for the sake of illustration the projections shown in Exhibit 4.1 are based on a strict application of this method, except for dividends and retained earnings. Remember that the distribution of earnings between dividends are retained earnings reflects a managerial policy which is not easily expressible in mechanistic terms.

Budgeted Expense Method

The percent of sales method, though simple, is too rigid and mechanistic. For deriving the *pro forma* profit and loss account shown in Exhibit 4.1, we assumed that all elements of costs and expenses bore a strictly proportional relationship to sales. The budgeted expense method, on the other hand, calls for estimating the value of each item on the basis of expected developments in the future period for which the *pro forma* profit and loss account is being prepared. Obviously,

EXHIBIT 4.1 ***Pro Forma Profit and Loss Account for Spaceage Electronics for 20X3 Based on Percent of Sales Method***

	Historical Data			*Pro forma profit and loss account of 20X3 assuming sales of 1400*
	20X1	*20X2*	*Average percent of sales*	
Net sales	1200	1280	100.0	1400.0
Cost of goods sold	775	837	65.0	910.0
Gross profit	425	443	35.0	490.0
Selling expenses	25	27	2.1	29.4
General and administration expenses	53	54	4.3	60.2
Depreciation	75	80	6.3	88.2
Operating profit	272	282	22.3	312.2
Non-operating surplus/deficit	30	32	2.5	35.0
Profit before interest and tax	302	314	24.8	347.2
Interest on bank borrowings	60	65	5.0	70.0
Interest on debentures	58	60	4.8	67.2
Profit before tax	184	189	15.0	210.0
Tax	82	90	6.9	96.6
Profit after tax	102	99	8.1	113.4
Dividends	60	63		
Retained earnings	42	36		

this method requires greater effort on the part of management because it calls for defining likely developments.

A Combination Method

It appears that a combination of the two methods described above often works best. For certain items, which have a fairly stable relationship with sales the percent of sales method is quite adequate. For other items, where future is likely to be very different from the past, the budgeted expense method, which calls for managerial assessment of expected future developments, is eminently suitable. A combination method of this kind is neither overly simplistic as the percent of sales method nor unduly onerous as the budgeted expense method.

Exhibit 4.2 presents the 20X3 *pro forma* profit and loss account for Spaceage Electronics, constructed by using a combination of the percent of sales and the budgeted expense methods. Cost of goods sold, selling expenses, and interest on bank borrowings are assumed to change proportionally with sales, the proportions being

EXHIBIT 4.2 ***Pro Forma Profit and Loss Account for Spaceage Electronics for 20X3 Using the Combination Method***

	Historical Data			*Pro forma profit and loss account of for 20X3*
	20X1	*20X2*	*Average percent of sales*	
Net sales	1200	1280	100.0	1400.0
Cost of goods sold	775	837	65.0	910.0
Gross profit	425	443	35.0	490.0
Selling expenses	25	27	2.1	29.4
General and administration	53	54	Budgeted	56.0
Depreciation	75	80	Budgeted	85.0
Operating profit	272	282	@	319.6
Non-operating surplus/deficit	30	32	2.5	35.0
Profit before interest and tax	302	314	@	354.6
Interest on bank borrowings	60	65	5.0	70.0
Interest on debentures	58	60	Budgeted	65.0
Profit before tax	184	189	@	219.0
Tax	82	90	Budgeted	90.0
Profit after tax	102	99	@	129.6
Dividends	60	63	Budgeted	70.0
Retained earnings	42	36	@	59.6

@ These items are obtained using accounting identities.

the average of the two preceding years. All the remaining items have been budgeted on some specific basis.

4.5 PRO FORMA BALANCE SHEET

The projections of various items on the assets side and liabilities side of the balance sheet may be derived as follows:

1. Employ the percent of sales method to project the items on the assets side, except 'investments' and 'miscellaneous expenditures and losses'.
2. Estimate the expected values for 'investments' and 'miscellaneous expenditures and losses' using specific information applicable to them.
3. Use the percent of sales method to derive the projected values of current liabilities and provisions (referred to as spontaneous liabilities).

4. Obtain the projected value of reserves and surplus by adding the projected retained earnings (from the *pro forma* profit and loss statement) to the reserves and surplus figure of the previous period.
5. Set the projected values for equity and preference capital to be tentatively equal to their previous values.
6. Assume that the projected values for loan funds will be tentatively equal to their previous levels less repayments or retirements as per terms and conditions applicable to them.
7. Compare the total of the assets side with that of the liabilities side and determine the balancing item (If assets exceed liabilities, the balancing item represents the 'additional funds needed'. If the liabilities exceed assets, the balancing item represents the 'surplus available funds').

EXHIBIT 4.3 ***Pro Forma Balance Sheet of Spaceage Electronics for December 31, 20X3***

	Historical Data			*Projection for*
	March 31, 20X1	*March 31, 20X2*	*Average of per cent of sales or some other basis*	*March 31, 20X3 based on a forecast sales of 1400*
Net sales	1200	1280	100.0	1400.0
Assets				
Fixed assets (net)	800	850	66.5	931.0
Investments	30	30	No change	30
Current assets, loans and advances				
• Cash and bank	25	28	2.1	29.4
• Receivables	200	212	16.6	232.4
• Inventories	375	380	30.4	425.6
• Pre-paid expenses	50	55	4.2	58.8
Miscellaneous expenditures and losses	20	20	No change	20
Total	1500	1575		1727.2
Liabilities				
Share capital				
• Equity	250	250	No change	250.0
• Preference	50	50	No change	50.0

(*Contd.*)

EXHIBIT 4.3 (Contd.)

	Historical Data			*Projection for March 31, 20X3 based on a forecast sales of 1400*
	March 31, 20X1	*March 31, 20X2*	*Average of per cent of sales or some other basis*	
Reserves and surplus	250	286	Proforma profit and loss account	345.6
Secured loans				
• Debentures	400	400	No change	400
• Bank borrowings	300	305	24.4	341.6
Unsecured loans				
• Bank borrowings	100	125	9.1	127.4
Current liabilities and provisions				
• Trade creditors	100	112	8.5	119.0
• Provisions	50	47	3.9	54.6
Additional funds needed			Balancing figure	39.0
Total	1500	1575		1727.2

Illustration

To illustrate the preparation of the *pro forma* balance sheet, let us continue the example of Spaceage Electronics. Exhibit 4.3 shows the balance sheets of Spaceage for 20X1 and 20X2.

The pro forma balance sheet for 20X3, shown in the last column of Exhibit 4.3, is derived as follows:

Items	*Basis of Projection*
• Current assets	• Percent of sales method wherein the proportions are based on the average for the previous two years.
• Fixed assets	• -do-
• Investments	• Assumption of no change
• Miscellaneous expenditures and losses	• -do-
• Current liabilities and provisions	• Percent of sales method wherein the proportions are based on the average for the previous two years.
• Equity and preference capital	• Previous values

- Reserves and surplus
- Loan funds
- Additional funds needed
- *Pro forma* profit and loss account
- Previous values
- Balancing item

Circularity Problem

A circularity problem arises when the *pro forma* financial statements are prepared because the income statement and the balance sheet are interrelated. The *pro forma* balance sheet cannot be prepared unless the *pro forma* profit and loss account, showing the amount of retained earnings to be carried to the balance sheet, is ready. At the same time, without the *pro forma* balance sheet, we cannot figure out the interest expense associated with the amount of external financing, an item required to prepare the *pro forma* profit and loss account.

4.6 COMPUTERISED FINANCIAL PLANNING SYSTEM

Computerised financial planning systems are gaining in popularity. At the heart of a computerised financial planning system is a model which specifies the relationships relevant to the firm. The model defines relationships like the following:

Cost of goods sold = 65 percent of sales
Selling expenses = ₹100,000 + 5 percent of sales
Inventories = 15 percent of sales
• •
• •
• •
• •

A computerised financial planning system helps in preparing *pro forma* financial statements, estimating the additional funds needed, and calculating a variety of ratios. Such a system naturally offers a number of advantages: (i) Once the model has been developed, the tedium of manual computations is eliminated. (ii) The circularity problem mentioned earlier is easily tackled as the computer can quickly perform the required iterations. (iii) The model can be employed very conveniently to perform sensitivity analysis.

Thanks to the above advantages, the computerised financial planning system strengthens considerably the firm's planning ability. However, there is a potential disadvantage associated with it which may be overlooked. The ease with which computations can be performed and forecasts generated may result in misdirected efforts. A large quantity of low-quality predictions may be churned out creating confusion and bewilderment on the part of management. Quality may be sacrificed at the altar of quantity. To guard against this danger, greater thought should be given to the kinds of scenarios evaluated and the quality of analysis.

4.7 ADDITIONAL FUNDS NEEDED

Most firms forecast their additional funds needed by constructing pro forma financial statements as described above. However, if the financial ratios of the firm remain constant, then the additional funds needed can be forecast using the following formula:

Additional funds needed	=	Required increase in assets	–	Spontaneous increase in liabilities	–	Increase in retained earnings
AFN	=	$(A^*/S_0)\,\Delta S$	–	$(L^*/S_0)\,\Delta S$	–	$m\,S_1\,r$

where A^* are the assets that increase when sales increase, S_0 is the sales during the last year, ΔS is the expected change in sales, L^* are the liabilities that increase spontaneously with sales, r is the retention ratio, S_1 is the sales expected during the next year, and m is the net profit margin ratio

Example The following holds for Pioneer Chemicals: $A^*/S_0 = 0.9$, S_0 = ₹400 million, $L^*/S_0 = 0.40$, $m = 0.05$, S_1 = ₹460 million, and $r = 0.4$. What are the additional funds needed for Pioneer Chemicals for the forthcoming year? The additional funds needed for Pioneer Chemicals are:

$$\text{AFN} = (0.90)(60) - (0.40)(60) - (0.05)(460)(0.4)$$
$$= ₹20.8 \text{ million}$$

4.8 SUSTAINABLE GROWTH RATE

Growth is often the central theme of corporate planning. Firms generally state corporate goals in terms of growth rates.

While firms are interested in growth, they may be reluctant to raise external equity capital for the following reasons: (i) There may be a significant degree of underpricing when external equity is raised. (ii) The cost of issue tends to the unreasonably high. (iii) The dilution of control, consequent to the external issue, may not be acceptable to the existing controlling interest.

Given managerial disinclination to raise external equity capital, the following question is often raised in corporate financial planning: What rate of growth can be sustained with internally available equity?

The sustainable growth rate is simply:

$$\text{Return on equity} \times \text{Retention ratio}$$

Since the return on equity is a product of net profit margin, asset turnover, and equity multiplier, the sustainable growth rate may be expressed as follows:

$$\text{Sustainable growth rate} = \text{Net profit margin} \times \text{Asset turnover} \times \text{Equity multiplier} \times \text{Retention ratio}$$

Example The following information is available for Astra Infotech Limited:

Net profit margin	: 20%
Asset turnover	: 1.2
Equity multiplier	: 1.1
Retention rate	: 0.80

What is the sustainable growth rate for Astra Infotech Limited? The sustainable growth rate is:

$$20\% \times 1.2 \times 1.1 \times 0.80 = 21.1\%$$

This means that Astra Infotech Limited can grow at a rate of 21.1 percent without resorting to external equity issue.

SUMMARY

- The strategic plan of a firm spells out its corporate purpose, corporate scope, corporate objectives, and corporate strategies. The corporate purpose defines the mission of the firm; the corporate scope delineates the lines of business in which the firm wishes to engage in and the geographic spread of its operations; corporate objectives spell out the specific goals sought by the firm; corporate strategies are the instruments for achieving corporate objectives.
- The long-term financial plan represents a blueprint of what the firm proposes to do in the future. Most corporate financial plans have the following elements: economic assumptions, sales forecast, pro forma financial statements, asset requirements, financing plan, and cash budget.
- The sales forecast is typically the starting point of the financial forecasting exercise as most of the financial variables are projected in relation to the estimated level of sales.

- A wide range of sales forecasting methods are available. They may be divided into three broad categories: qualitative techniques, time series projections methods, and causal models.
- There are two commonly used methods for preparing the pro forma profit and loss account: the per cent of sales methods and the budgeted expense method.
- The per cent of sales methods assumes that the future relationship between various elements of costs to sales will be similar to their historical relationship. The budgeted expense method calls for estimating the value of each item on the basis of expected developments in the future period. It appears that a combination of the two methods often works best.
- Computerised financial planning systems are gaining in popularity. At the heart of a computerised financial planning system is a model which specifies the relationships relevant to the firm.
- If the financial ratios of the firm remain constant, then the additional funds needed can be forecast using a simple formula.
- The rate of growth that can be sustained with internally available equity is equal to: return on equity × retention ratio.

Part II

Cost and Management Accounting

Cost Systems and Methods 5

The accounting system of an organisation is the most important segment of its information system. It broadly serves three functions, which are:

- To provide information to external parties (shareholders, creditors, regulatory bodies, and others).
- To estimate the costs of goods and services produced by the organisation.
- To provide information useful for planning, decision making, and control.

Financial accounting caters to external information needs in conformity with generally accepted accounting principles. **Cost accounting** generates information on costs which is required for financial accounting as well as management accounting purposes. **Management accounting** seeks to provide information useful for planning, decision making, and control. Exhibit 5.1 shows the relationship between financial accounting, cost accounting, and management accounting.

Exhibit 5.1 ***Relationship Between Financial, Cost and Management Accounting***

While the first part of this book was devoted to financial accounting, the second part (this part) will focus on cost and management accounting.

This chapter discusses the basic concepts, systems, and methods of cost accounting. Since the cost accounting system in a manufacturing firm encompasses production, marketing, and service functions, it tends to be the most general one. Hence, we will focus on cost accounting in a manufacturing firm. Remember that the framework discussed here can be applied to any setting. This chapter is divided into five sections, which are as follows:

- Cost concepts and classifications
- Costing process
- Cost systems
- Standard costing
- Activity based costing

5.1 COST CONCEPTS AND CLASSIFICATIONS

Cost information is used in a variety of contexts. Managers ask questions such as: At what cost should inventories be valued? How do costs behave with changes in volume? What is the cost of accepting a special order?

Costs are classified in accounting in different ways to meet different purposes. Exhibit 5.2 shows the cost classifications commonly used in practice. As a manager, you should understand these classifications and how they are used.

Exhibit 5.2 *Common Cost Classifications*

1. **Relationship to the Cost Object**
   - Direct cost
   - Indirect cost
2. **Cost Behaviour Pattern**
   - Variable cost
   - Fixed cost
3. **Manufacturing Costs**
   - Direct material
   - Direct labour
   - Factory overhead
4. **Non-manufacturing Costs**
   - Selling and distribution cost
   - Research and development cost
   - Administrative cost
   - Financial cost

(Contd.)

EXHIBIT 5.2 *(Contd.)*

5. **Service Costs**
   - Service labour
   - Materials and supplies
   - Occupancy costs
   - Technology costs
   - Other service overheads
6. **Timing of Recognition**
   - Product cost
   - Period cost
7. **Decision Analysis**
   - Relevant cost
   - Sunk cost
   - Opportunity cost

Relationship to the Cost Object

Accountants distinguish between direct and indirect costs. **Direct costs** are costs that can be traced economically to a cost object. For example, the cost of wood used to make a sofa set in a furniture factory is a direct cost as it is fairly easy to trace the amount of wood required for the sofa set.

Indirect costs are costs that are related to a cost object but not traceable to it in a cost-effective manner. For example, the cost of power in the furniture factory where the sofa set is made is an indirect cost of sofa set, as it may not be feasible to determine in a cost-effective way how much power is consumed for the manufacture of the sofa set. Indirect costs are allocated to the cost object using some reasonable basis.

Notice that direct and indirect costs are defined with respect to a given cost object for which the manager wishes to measure cost. The cost object may be a product, department, programme, service, customer, or whatever. The cost object defines the context for classifying a cost as direct or indirect.

Cost Behaviour Pattern

In terms of their behaviour, costs may be classified as fixed or variable. A **fixed cost** is a cost that does not vary in total with the changes in output or volume. For example, if Maruti Motors pays ₹10 million per year toward the insurance of its Zen car plant, the total insurance cost remains at ₹10 million, irrespective of the number of Zen cars produced.

A **variable cost**, on the other hand, changes in total, proportionately to changes in output or volume. For example, if Maruti Motors buys a steering wheel for ₹1,000 for its Zen car, the total cost of steering wheels will be ₹1000 times the number of Zen cars assembled.

Costs are regarded as fixed only in the short run, a brief period of time, usually one to two years, during which the quantities of the available resources cannot be changed. In the long run, however, all costs are variable because equipment can be sold, plant can be shut down, employees can be laid off, and branches can be closed.

Often the terms **direct** and **variable** are used interchangeably; so are the terms **indirect** and **fixed**. This is not correct because these classifications have different bases.

A direct cost may be fixed or variable, likewise an indirect most may be fixed or variable. Exhibit 5.3 illustrates these possibilities when the cost object is a unit produced.

EXHIBIT 5.3 ***Cost Classification Along Two Dimensions***

	Direct	*Indirect*
Fixed	Labour*	Depreciation
Variable	Material	Power

*It is assumed that labour is paid a fixed compensation irrespective of changes in output

Manufacturing Costs

The process of manufacture involves transforming materials into finished goods by applying labour and capital employed in plant and equipment. As shown in Exhibit 5.4, manufacturing costs comprise of three elements, viz., direct material, direct labour, and manufacturing overhead. The sum of direct material cost and direct labour cost is referred to as **prime cost** whereas the sum of direct labour cost and manufacturing overhead is referred to as **conversion cost**.

EXHIBIT 5.4 ***Components of Manufacturing Cost***

Prime cost { Direct material
+ Direct labour } Conversion cost
+ Manufacturing overhead }

Direct material cost includes the cost of all materials that become part of the finished product. Examples: iron ore to make steel, wood to make furniture, plastic to make toys, and microprocessors to make computers. The cost typically includes the purchase price of materials plus other costs such as freight, insurance, taxes, and duties.

Direct labour cost represents the cost of workers directly involved in producing the product. Examples: carpenters who make furniture, masons who build houses, and workers who assemble cars. Direct labour cost includes wages, fringe benefits, payroll taxes, bonus, and other types of compensation.

Manufacturing overhead comprises of all other manufacturing costs besides direct material cost and direct labour cost. The important components of manufacturing overhead are:

- *Indirect materials* like glue, screws, and tape.
- *Indirect labour* like supervisory, maintenance, and support personnel.
- *Depreciation* of plant, equipment, and other assets.
- *Utilities* like electricity, gas, water, telephone, and Internet.
- *Rent* for factory and warehouse.
- *Maintenance and repair* costs for production facilities and warehouse.
- *Allocated costs* of service departments like purchasing, material handling, and quality control.

Non-manufacturing Costs

Non-manufacturing costs consist of selling and distribution cost, administration cost, financial cost, and research and development cost. **Selling and distribution cost** includes the salaries and commission of sales personnel, transportation cost, warehousing cost, sales promotion cost, advertising cost, and so on. **Research and development cost** represents the cost incurred for developing new products or processes, improving existing products or processes, and searching for new knowledge. Representing outlays on research and development efforts—not for production and marketing activities—these costs are assuming greater significance with rapid changes in technology. **Financial cost** includes interest on different kinds of borrowing, commitment fee, guarantee fee, and so on. **Administration cost** includes the cost of general administration and other costs which do not fit into any other category.

Service Costs

Service costs are the costs of rendering a service to the customers. Service organisations (hotels, hospitals, audit firms, educational establishments, software service firms, and so on) like their manufacturing counterparts, incur material cost, labour cost, and overhead costs. However, there are some difficulties in applying manufacturing cost concepts to a service environment. Unlike manufacturing costs, service costs are not inventoriable and hence cannot be carried as inventory on the balance sheet or reported as cost of goods sold on the profit and loss account. Further, raw material costs loom large for manufacturing firms but tend to be insignificant for service organisations.

In view of these differences, service costs are broken up in a somewhat different manner. They are usually divided into five major components viz., service labour, materials and supplies, technology costs, occupancy costs, and other service overheads.

Service labour represents the cost of employees engaged in rendering services to the customer. It includes wages, perquisites, bonus, and other types of compensation. Service labour may be divided into frontline labour and support labour. Frontline labour refers to employees who are directly involved in providing service to the customers. Support labour refers to supervisory, administrative, and maintenance personnel who do not directly service the customer but provide support services to frontline labour.

Materials and supplies represent the cost of materials and supplies used for providing service. Examples: food ingredients in a restaurant; medicines and hospital supplies in a hospital; books and journals in a college; pen drives and computer stationery in a software services firm.

Occupancy costs are the cost for using and maintaining the premises. They include rent, maintenance and repair, depreciation, utilities, security, insurance, property taxes, and so on.

Technology costs are costs relating to the use of technology. They include items such as depreciation, maintenance, software packages, leased lines, and so on.

Other service overheads consist of all other costs that have not been included under service labour, materials and supplies, occupancy costs, and technology costs.

Timing of Recognition

Eventually, all the costs incurred by a firm are expensed. If a cost is not expensed immediately, it is added to an inventory account on the balance sheet until the goods are sold. Such a cost is deemed to be "inventoriable". Inventoriable costs are called **product costs**. Costs that are not inventoriable are called **period costs** as they are expensed in the period which they are incurred.

Income tax regulations as well as the generally accepted accounting principles require that all manufacturing costs are treated as product costs for external financial reporting using absorption costing. Under **absorption costing** (sometimes called full absorption costing), all the costs incurred in manufacturing, irrespective of their behaviour with respect to volume are regarded as product costs.

By contrast, under **variable costing**, also called **direct costing**, manufacturing overheads are segregated into two components, namely variable manufacturing overheads and fixed manufacturing overheads (such as depreciation). The former is treated as a product cost and the latter as a period cost.

Non-manufacturing costs are generally treated as period costs. Hence they are not inventoriable under either method.

Decision Anlaysis

In the context of decision making, three concepts are commonly considered: relevant costs, opportunity cost, and sunk cost.

Relevant costs, also called incremental costs or differential costs, are costs that are expected to differ between the alternatives in future. Suppose you are considering buying a car for your office. You are looking at two cars, A and B. The following cost information has been gathered.

	A	*B*
• Purchase cost	₹800,000	₹1000,000
• Annual fuel cost	₹50,000	₹40,000
• Annual maintenance cost	₹30,000	₹30,000
• Annual insurance cost	₹10,000	₹12,000
• Annual compensation for the driver	₹100,000	₹100,000

Purchase cost, annual fuel cost, and annual insurance cost differ between the alternatives in future. So they are relevant costs. Annual maintenance cost and annual compensation for the driver do not differ between the alternatives in future. So they are not relevant costs.

Cost represents a sacrifice of resources. This leads to the concept of opportunity cost. If a resource is used for some purpose, the **opportunity cost** of using it for that purpose is the benefit foregone by not putting that resource to its best alternative use. For example, the opportunity cost of using a plant to manufacture a certain product is the profit foregone by not putting the plant to manufacture some other product which represents its best alternative use.

A **sunk cost** is an outlay already incurred in the past or already committed irrevocably. So it should not have any bearing on present decision. Suppose you are debating whether your company should supply goods to a certain customer. Your company has already spent ₹100,000 in preliminary work and negotiation. Is this ₹100,000 relevant for decision making? Clearly not. ₹100,000 represents a sunk cost as it cannot be recovered irrespective of what your decision is. Bygones are bygones and hence are not relevant for decision making.

5.2 COSTING PROCESS

If a firm manufactures just one product (or provides a single service), determining the unit cost of production is a fairly simple exercise. It merely involves adding up all the manufacturing costs (such as material cost, labour cost, power, rent, depreciation, and so on) incurred in the period and dividing this total by the number of units produced during the period.

Most of the firms, however, manufacture multiple products which pass through different departments or processes. In such a case, the process of costing is more complex. It involves the following steps:

1. Define the cost object
2. Accumulate costs
3. Determine the direct costs
4. Allocate indirect costs
5. Calculate the total cost of production

Define the Cost Object

The definition of the cost object is an important first step in the costing exercise. The cost object can be almost anything. The commonly chosen cost objects are:

Cost Object	*Example*
Product	An 800 cc diesel car
Service	An air journey from Chennai to Delhi
Programme	A one-week top management executive development programme
Department	The purchase department of a company
Customer	All the vehicles purchased by MSRTC from Tata Motors

In the rest of the discussion we will assume that the cost object is some product.

Accumulate Costs

Cost accumulation refers to the collection of costs in natural categories like materials, labour, power, transport, rent, depreciation, insurance, and so on. Typically, these costs are collected department-wise. The departments are treated as cost centres. Some cost centres are product centres and some cost centres are service centres. A product centre is a centre where some work is done on a product. Examples: machining department and assembly department. A service centre represents a centre which renders some service but does not work directly on the product. Examples: maintenance department, security department.

Determine the Direct Costs

Direct costs are costs that can be traced in a cost-effective manner to the cost object. Direct costs consist of direct material costs and direct labour costs. When a product passes through two or more product centres, the direct costs of the product is the sum of the direct costs incurred in all the product centres.

Allocate Indirect Costs

Indirect costs, also called manufacturing overhead, are costs that cannot be traced to the cost object economically. So they have to be allocated to the product (cost object) in some reasonable manner. The procedure for allocating indirect costs is as follows:

- Estimate indirect costs for various product centres.
- Estimate costs of various service centres.
- Transfer the estimated service centre costs to product centres by a direct charge or by allocation.[1]

---

[1] The costs of certain service centres may be charged to product centres directly on the basis of the actual service provided. For example, the costs of maintenance department (a service centre) may be charged to operating departments (product centres) on the basis of the actual maintenance services provided. The costs of other service centres are allocated to product centres on some basis which appears reasonable or fair. The numerous possible bases for such allocation may be divided into the following broad categories:

- Labour-related basis (example: personnel department costs may be allocated on the basis of the number of employees or total direct labour cost in product centres).
- Material-related basis (example: store department costs may be allocated on the basis of the volume or cost of material used in product centres).

- Divide the total cost accumulated in each product centre by a measure of activity such as direct labour hours or machine hours, or total direct cost, to get the overhead application rate.
- Apply the overhead application rate to the product passing through the product centres.

Remember that the process of accumulation and allocation of indirect costs has the following characteristics:

- The entire process is based on subjective judgement of what an equitable overhead rate is. Hence, there is an inescapable element of arbitrariness in it.
- The overhead application rate is based on an overhead budget and a projected level of activity.
- The total amount of overhead application may, and often does, differ from the actual overhead expenditure incurred.

Calculate the Total Cost of Production

The total cost of producing a unit is simply the sum of its direct costs (which are traced to it) and indirect costs (which are allocated to it).

5.3 COST SYSTEMS

There are two basic forms of production viz., job order production and process (or continuous) production. The cost systems used for them are the job cost system and the process cost system.

Job Cost System

The job cost system is normally used in industries where individual jobs, lots or batches are identifiable. It is applicable to industries such as ship building, housing, construction, book publication, and manufacture of special purpose machines.

The cost object in a job cost system is the individual job. Every job (a single unit or a specified lot) is given a number and a separate job cost sheet is maintained for it. As the job progresses through various departments, various elements of production cost, namely, direct material cost, direct labour cost, and manufacturing overhead cost are recorded on the job cost sheet. Direct material cost and direct labour cost are recorded on the basis

---

- Space-related basis (example: occupancy costs such as rent may be allocated on the basis of floor area occupied by various product centres).
- Activity-related basis (example: utility department costs may be allocated on the basis of overall volume of acitivity).

of material and labour directly employed on the job. Factory overhead element, an allocated charge, is entered as per a pre-determined rate. For example, if the pre-determined basis of overhead allocation is ₹2 per direct labour hour, a job for which 10 direct labour hours have been spent will be charged with ₹20 of factory overhead. When the job is completed, the total cost can be ascertained from the job cost sheet. A specimen job cost sheet for a book entitled **Guide to Costing** is shown in Exhibit 5.5.

All costs charged to production during a given period must appear on some job cost sheet or the other. Hence, the total of charges to all the job cost sheets in a given period must equal the total debit to the work in process accounts. Similarly, the sum of all costs charged to job cost sheets of completed jobs corresponds to the debit to the finished goods account (and credit to the work in process account). Finally, the cost of finished goods which are sold during the period represents debit to the cost of goods sold account and credit to the finished goods account.

EXHIBIT 5.5 ***A Specimen Job Cost Sheet***

Job No.102	Product: Guide to Costing		
Date started 1/1/20X0	Units required : 1,000		
Date required 1/4/20X0	Purpose : For inventory		
Date completed 25/3/20X0	Job authorised : MNV		
	Job Costs		
Direct material:	*Requisition Number*	*Cost* ₹	
Printing department			
Paper	12	40,000	
Ink	15	9,000	
Binding department			
Glue	17	4,000	
Cardboard	19	7,000	60,000
Direct labour:			
Printing department —300 hours @ ₹30.00		9,000	
Binding department —200 hours @ ₹30.00		6,000	
			15,000
Manufacturing overhead:			
Printing department—300 hours @ ₹30.00		9,000	
Binding department—200 hours @ ₹25.00		5,000	
			14,000
	Total job cost		₹89,000

Process Cost System

In a process cost system, production is viewed as a continuous flow rather than as a series of identifiable jobs or lots. This kind of system is applied to industries such as steel, cement, glass, and petrochemicals, where production processes are of a continuous and repetitive nature.

Basically, in a process cost system, cost is accumulated by processes (departments) rather than by jobs. For each process, the unit cost of production is calculated. To get the total unit cost of a product, the unit cost of each process through which the product passes is summated.

The unit cost of a process is defined as:

$$\frac{\text{Total cost of the process}}{\text{Number of units produced in the process}}$$

The total cost of the process consists of direct material, direct labour, and manufacturing overhead (applied). The number of units produced in the process is necessarily defined as an average because both at the beginning and at the end of a period partially complete inventories generally exist in the process.

Calculation of Average Units Produced The average units (equivalent units) produced during a given period is equal to:

Number of units completed and transferred to finished goods

+ Ending work-in-process inventory, expressed in terms of equivalent units
– Opening work-in-process inventory, expressed in terms of equivalent units

An illustration of this calculation is given below:

Basic Data

Beginning work-in-process: 10,000 units, 40% complete
Ending work-in-process: 15,000 units, 60% complete
Completed and transferred to finished goods: 100,000 units

Average Units Produced Calculation

Number of units completed and transferred to finished goods:	100,000
Ending work-in-process in terms of equivalent units (15,000 × 0.6)	9,000
Less : Beginning inventory in terms of equivalent units (10,000 × 0.4)	4,000
Average units completed during the period	105,000

Choice of Cost System

How should one choose between the job order cost system and the process cost system? If there are wide differences between individual jobs/lots/batches, the job order cost system is appropriate because it is desirable to determine the varying costs of different jobs for pricing, inventory valuation, and control purposes. On the other hand, if the products are identical, the process cost system is preferable because it is economical and yet accurate.

In the intermediate cases, where there are some differences among products/jobs/lots, the choice is not very obvious. It depends on considerations of accuracy and cost. If accuracy is the dominant criterion, the job order cost system is preferable; conversely, if economy is the main consideration, the process cost system is preferable.

5.4 STANDARD COSTING

In the early stages of the development of cost accounting, historical costing was used for ascertaining costs for planning and control purposes. This kind of costing suffers from certain drawbacks: (i) cost data becomes available rather late for planning and decision making and (ii) past actuals, without a yardstick for comparison, are not very useful for control purposes.

To overcome the limitations of historical costing, standard costing was developed. Designed initially as a tool of cost control, standard costing has been found useful for several inter-related purposes: (i) control over cost, (ii) costing of inventories, (iii) planning and budgeting, and (iv) pricing of present or prospective products.

Under a system of standard costing (i) standards are developed for various elements of manufacturing cost, namely, material, labour, and overhead, (ii) actual costs are compared with standard costs and variances are determined, and (iii) variances are analysed for their causes to identify corrective action.

Development of Standards

Development of standards is the most difficult part of standard costing. Standards may be ideal, normal, or expected. The ideal standard is based on the assumption that perfect conditions prevail-no wastage, no idleness, no breakdowns, no rest. A normal standard makes allowances for normal wastages, idleness, breakdowns, and rest period. An expected standard is based upon the most likely outcome. This is, strictly speaking, not a standard because it indicates what will happen and not what should happen. Hence, it has no inherent efficiency requirement. In practice, a normal (or average) standard is widely used. However, in developing this standard there may be disagreement about what is normal in terms of wastage, idle time, rest period, and so on.

Once the standards are developed for material requirement, material prices, direct labour hours, direct labour rates, factory overhead hours, and factory overhead rates, the standard cost sheet is prepared. An illustrative standard cost sheet is given in Exhibit 5.6.

EXHIBIT 5.6 ***Standard Cost Sheet***

	Code	*Quantity*	*Standard Unit Price*	*Department* 1	2	3	4	*Totals*
Direct Material	2-469	3	40 per pc		120			
	3-235	4	30 per pc			120		
	4-871	24	10 per doz				20	
	Total Material Cost							260
Direct Labour	Operation Number	Standard Hours	Standard Rate per Hour					
	2-476	2	25		50			
	3-581	$1\frac{1}{2}$	24			36		
	3-218	3	26				78	
	Total Labour Cost							164
Factory Overhead	Standard Hours		Rate per Direct Labour Hour					
	2		18		36			
	$1\frac{1}{2}$		16			24		
	3		14				42	
	Total Factory Overhead							102
	Total Manufacturing Cost Per Unit							526

Variance Analysis

Variance analysis examines the differences between actual and standard costs to find the causative factors and identify areas for improvement. Variances are divided into three broad categories viz., material variances, labour variances, and overhead variances. To illustrate the calculation of these variances the information furnished in Exhibit 5.7 will be used.

EXHIBIT 5.7 ***Standard and Actual Cost Data, Modern Electronics Company***

Standard Cost		
Materials	2 units @ ₹200 per unit	₹400
Labour	4 hours @ ₹25 per hour	₹100
Overhead	1 unit @ ₹300 per unit	₹300
		₹800
Actual Costs Incurred		
Materials used	1100 units	
Materials purchased	1200 units @ ₹220	₹264,000
Labour	2500 hours @ ₹24	₹60,000
Overheads costs	₹200,000	
Other Information		
Budgeted volume	500	
Actual volume produced	600	

Materials Variances The material cost variance, which represents the difference between the standard cost of material for the output during the period and the actual cost of material, is defined as:

Standard quantity for the output × Standard price – Actual quantity × Actual price

The material cost variance is usually broken down into a price variance and a usage variance, which are defined as follows.

Material price variance = (Standard unit price – Actual unit price) × Actual quantity

Material usage variance = (Standard quantity – Actual quantity) × Standard price

The material cost variance, material price variance, and material usage variance for Modern Electronics Company are calculated as follows:

Material cost variance = 1200 × ₹200 – 1100 × ₹220
= – ₹2000

Material price variance = (₹200 – ₹220) × 1100 = – ₹22,000

Material usage variance = (1200 – 1100) × ₹200 = ₹20,000

Labour Variances The labour cost variance is the difference between the standard labour cost for the actual production and the actual labour cost incurred during the period. It is defined as:

(Standard hours for actual output × Standard rate) – (Actual hours × Actual rate)

The labour cost variance is usually broken down into two components, reflecting rate and efficiency, which are defined as follows:

Labour rate variance = (Standard rate – Actual rate) × Actual hours

Labour efficiency variance = (Standard hours – Actual hours) × Standard rate

The labour cost variance, labour rate variance, and labour efficiency variance for Modern Electronics Company are calculated as follows:

Labour cost variance = 2400 × ₹25 – 2500 × ₹24 = 0

Labour rate variance = (₹25 – ₹24) × 2500 = ₹2500

Labour efficiency variance = (2400 – 2500) × ₹25 = – ₹2500

Overhead Variances The overhead cost variance is the difference between the standard overhead costs charged to the product and the actual overhead cost incurred:

Overhead cost variance = Standard overhead costs charged to the the product – Actual overhead costs incurred

In theory, variances are calculated separately for variable and fixed overhead. There are two variable overhead variances namely a spending variance and an efficiency variance, and two fixed overhead variances namely a budget variance and a volume variance. This type of analysis, called a four-way variance analysis, is not widely used. In practice, companies generally compute only two variances, namely the spending variance and the volume variance, which are defined below. The **spending variance** shows how much of the overhead cost variance was on account of spending more or less than what was budgeted for. The **volume variance** shows how much of the overhead cost variance was on account of operating at more or less than at the budgeted activity level. The spending variance and volume variance are defined below.

Spending variance = Budgeted overhead costs – Actual overhead cost incurred

Volume variance = Standard overhead costs – Budgeted overhead costs charged to the product

The overhead cost variance, spending variance, and volume variance for Modern Electronics Company are calculated as follows:

Overhead cost variance = 180,000 – 200,000 = – 20,000

Spending variance = 150,000 – 200,000 = – 50,000
Volume variance = 180,000 – 150,000 = 30,000

Sources of Variances

Variances may be caused by the following:

- The operations may be inefficient due to labour absenteesim, power failure, machine breakdown, transport delay, or other difficulties.
- The standards may be incorrect due to errors in estimating material requirement, labour time, material prices, and labour rates.
- The costs may not be recorded correctly. For example, the accountant may charge utilities to the wrong department or the production manager may put a wrong account number on a purchase order.
- There may be an implementation breakdown because of a delay in installing a machine.

Pre-requisites for Standard Costing

For the successful operation of a standard costing system, the following conditions should be satisfied:

- The operation for which standard costs are defined are standardised.
- A system of responsibility accounting is used.
- A well designed communication and reporting system exists.
- A group of qualified personnel with continuing responsibility monitors the system.

Standard Costing and Budgeting

Standard costing and budgeting are two important techniques in the armoury of management accounting. A comparison of these techniques is given below:

- As techniques of management control, both of them involve target (or standard) setting, performance measurement, comparison of actuals with the targets (or standards), and analysis and reporting of performance.
- Budgeting is broad in scope. It focuses on the entire organisation and covers both revenues and costs. Standard costing is somewhat narrow in scope: Its focus is mainly on manufacturing costs.
- While budgeting and standard costing may be introduced independently, the two are complementary in nature. Standard costs provide a firmer basis for budgeting. Similarly, the budgets developed for factory overhead costs help in setting standard overhead rates for standard costing purposes.

Evaluation

Standard costing has gained importance in practice because of the following advantages associated with it:

- Standard costing system establishes benchmarks for performance measurement. This promotes cost consciousness and checks inefficiencies.
- The spadework done before setting standards often results in simplification and standardisation of products, methods, and operations.
- The procedure and paperwork relating to costing is simplified.
- Cost estimates are readily available for pricing, product planning, and other decisions.

Though a useful tool, standard costing suffers from the following limitations in practice:

- Establishment of standards poses problems. Further, however well determined the standards are, they may become outdated soon.
- Due to the interaction of various factors, variances may not be readily explained. It becomes difficult to distinguish between controllable and uncontrollable variances.
- Standards may have undesirable psychological effects—they may breed frustration.

The Future of Standard Costing

The standard costing system serves well when the cost accounting system is used to control the production floor. As computer technology shifts the control process to operations personnel, managers get information on a real-time basis. They do not have to wait till the end of the period to get feedback on their operations. In such a situation, standard costing does not serve much purpose.

Thanks to advances in computerisation and automation, it appears that companies would move from the standard cost system to the actual cost system in the years to come. This trend may be accelerated if the business environment becomes more volatile.

5.5 ACTIVITY-BASED COSTING

Traditional costing systems assign indirect costs to products using drivers like direct labour hours, machine hours, or units produced. This is acceptable if activities are performed in proportion to physical production volumes. This may be the case in a business environment characterised by limited product variety, low indirect costs, simple production methods, and local competition.

However, in today's business environment marked by wide product range, high indirect costs, complex production methods, and intense global competition, the traditional costing systems provide inaccurate information about the drivers of cost and profitability that can lead to wrong decisions. As Robert Kaplan says, this can lead managers to make poor decisions about pricing, product design, product mix, and so on.

To cope with the challenges of today's business environment, activity based costing has been developed.

What Is Activity Based Costing

Activity based costing identifies the key activities that consume a firm's resources, accumulates overhead costs for each of these activities, determines the drivers of these activities, and finally assigns the cost of these activities to the ultimate cost objects (products, services, or whatever).

Activity based costing may be viewed as an amplification and refinement of the traditional costing system. The key differences between traditional costing and activity based costing are :

- In traditional costing, overhead costs are usually accumulated in a single cost pool; in activity based costing, overhead costs are broken into several cost pools, each corresponding to a key activity.
- In traditional costing, the single overhead cost pool is assigned to cost objects (products or whatever) using a gross cost driver like direct labour hours, or machine hours, or units produced; in activity based costing, the cost driver of each activity is identified and then used as the basis for assigning the cost pool associated with it.

Exhibit 5.8 contrasts traditional costing with activity based costing. Note that in traditional costing, the total overhead cost is allocated to a product on the basis of total direct labour hours. In activity based costing important overhead activities (designing, machining, assembling, quality control, etc.) and their costs are separately identified and later assigned to (traced to) products using appropriate cost drivers like design time, machine hours, number of parts, number of inspections, etc.

EXHIBIT 5.8 ***Traditional Cost System vs. Activity Based Cost System***

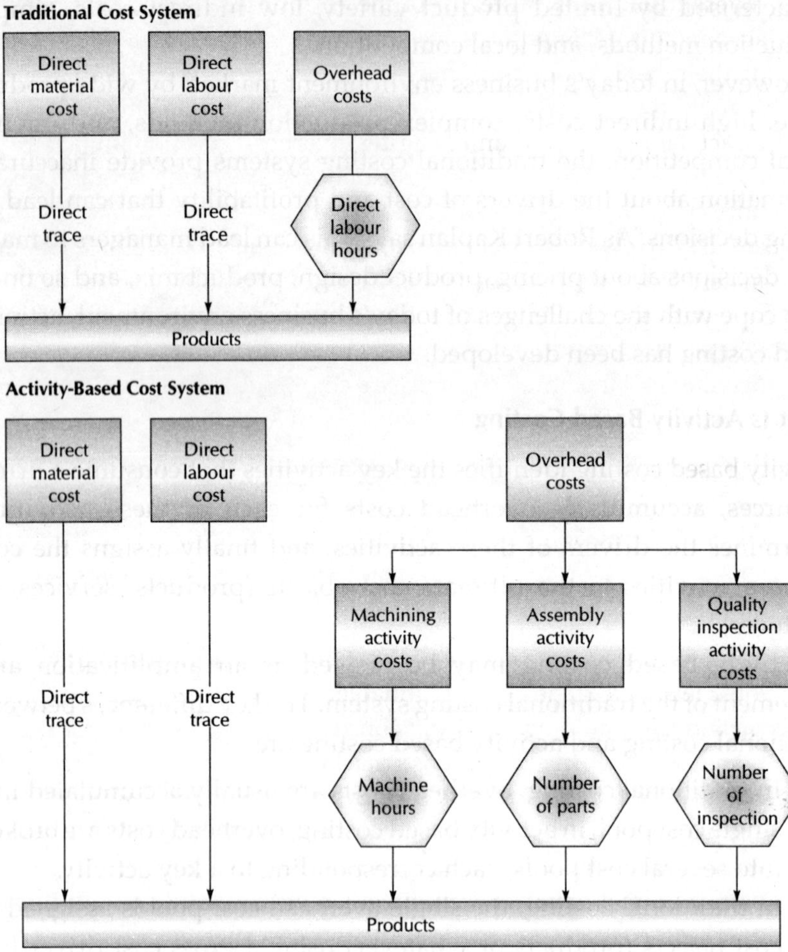

SUMMARY

- The accounting system of an organisation is the most important segment of its information system. It comprises of financial accounting, cost accounting, and management accounting.
- Financial accounting caters to external information needs in conformity with generally accepted accounting principles. Cost accounting generates information on costs. Management accounting seeks to provide information useful for planning, decision making, and control.

- Costs are classified in accounting in different ways to meet different purposes. In terms of the relationship to the cost object, accountants distinguish between direct and indirect costs. In terms of their behaviour, costs may be classified as fixed or variable. Manufacturing costs comprise of three elements, viz., direct material, direct labour, and manufacturing overhead. Non-manufacturing costs consist of selling and distribution cost, administration cost, financial cost, and research and development cost. Service costs are usually divided into five major components, viz., service labour, materials and supplies, occupancy costs, technology costs, and other service overheads. Inventoriable costs are called product costs. Costs that are not inventoriable are called period costs. In the context of decision making, three concepts are commonly considered: relevant costs, opportunity cost, and sunk cost.
- The process of costing involves five broad steps: (i) Define the cost object. (ii) Accumulate costs. (iii) Determine the direct costs. (iv) Allocate indirect costs. (v) Calculate the total cost of production.
- There are two systems of product costing : job order cost system and process cost system.
- The job cost system is normally used in industries where individual jobs, lots, or batches are identifiable. It is applicable to industries such as ship building, housing, construction, book publication, and manufacture of special purpose machines. The cost object in a job cost system is the individual job. Every job is given a number and a separate job cost sheet is maintained for it. As the job progresses through different departments, various elements of production cost, namely, direct material cost, direct labour cost, and manufacturing overhead cost are recorded on the job cost sheet.
- In a process cost system, production is viewed as a continuous flow rather than as a series of identifiable jobs or lots. This kind of system is applied to industries such as steel, cement, glass, and petrochemicals, where the production process is of a continuous and repetitive nature.
- In a process cost system, cost is accumulated by processes (departments) rather than by jobs. For each process, the unit cost of production is calculated. To get the total unit cost of a product, the unit cost of each process through which the product passes is summated.
- For determining the product cost, two problems have to be solved : (i) measurement of direct costs, and (ii) accumulation and allocation of indirect costs.

- In the early stages of the development of cost accounting, historical costing was used. This kind of costing suffers from certain drawbacks. To overcome these shortcomings, standard costing was developed. Under a system of standard costing (i) standards are developed for various elements of manufacturing costs, namely, material, labour and overhead, (ii) actual costs are compared with standard costs and variances are determined, and (iii) variances are analysed for their causes to identify corrective action.
- Activity based costing identifies the key activities that consume a firm's resources, accumulates overhead costs of each of these activities, determines the drivers of these activities and finally assigns the costs of these activities to the ultimate cost objects (products, services, or whatever). Activity based costing may be viewed as an amplification and refinement of the traditional costing system.

Managerial Decision Making

6

Managers have to often choose among alternative courses of action and decide about allocation of resources. What products should the firm make? Should the firm make or buy a given part? Should the firm accept or reject a special order? What price should the firm bid on a contract?

So far we discussed the systems and process of costing using the full cost approach. Full costs represent the total resources consumed by the organisation in providing a product or service. In the short run, many organisational costs are fixed as they do not vary with changes in volume or activity levels. While an organisation must recover all its costs in the long run to be viable, fixed costs may not be relevant for short-term decisions.

The contribution margin approach and relevant cost analysis are useful decision tools for certain business situations. This chapter discusses how these tools may be used to address specific business situations. It is divided into five sections as follows:

- Steps in decision making
- Contribution margin
- Break-even analysis
- Cost behaviour
- Application to decision situations

6.1 STEPS IN DECISION MAKING

Before discussing the relevant information useful for decision making, it is helpful to look at the process of decision making itself. While this process is complex and not amenable to standardisation, the following steps seem useful for most problems:

- Define the problem
- Develop alternative solutions
- Evaluate the alternatives
- Arrive at a decision

Define the Problem

Identifying the problem is the first and often a very critical step in the process of decision making. While this may be fairly easy in some cases, it might be more difficult in others. Perceptive analysis and insight may be required to articulate the problem. The real problem may have to be distinguished from the apparent one.

Develop Alternative Solutions

Once the nature of the problem is understood, alternative courses of action for solving it have to be developed. This requires a sound understanding of the factors causing the problem and imaginative thinking about ways and means that can solve it. In the initial stages of developing alternative solutions, several possibilities may arise. The analyst should eliminate those which are clearly unattractive and narrow his choice down to a few, perhaps two or three. This will prevent the analysis from becoming complex and unwieldy. Of course, there must be at least two alternatives. If only one course of action is available, then there is no choice and hence no decision making problem. Often one of the alternatives is to continue what is being currently done. Other alternatives may be compared against this.

Evaluate the Alternatives

The alternative solutions developed in the preceding step have to be carefully evaluated. Each solution may have several advantages and disadvantages that have to be weighed and balanced for judging its overall desirability.

If the advantages and disadvantages of an alternative solution are stated in qualitative terms only, evaluation may be difficult. Consider, for example, the following statement: The proposed change in the manufacturing method will reduce material costs but enhance labour costs, maintenance charges and electricity costs. Clearly, such a qualitative expression of costs and benefits does not facilitate overall evaluation.

On the other hand, if it is stated that the material costs will be reduced by ₹10,000, whereas labour costs, maintenance charges, and electricity costs will increase by ₹6,000, ₹1,000, and ₹2,000 respectively, the net advantage of the proposed change in the manufacturing method can be easily figured out.

While efforts should not be spared to quantify costs and benefits, it may be difficult, or even impossible, to measure certain consequences. How, for instance, can we measure consequences such as improvement in morale, greater customer satisfaction, increased vulnerability to competition, and higher threat of technological obsolescence. Such effects, though difficult to measure, are important in overall evaluation and have to be duly considered. Evaluation of non-measurable consequences is essentially a judgmental process.

Arrive at a Decision

Once the alternative courses of action are evaluated in terms of their measurable and non-measurable effects, the decision maker may be in a position to select one of the alternatives finally. Of course, he may decide to gather further information in order to sharpen his assessment before arriving at a decision. This, however, requires additional effort, cost, and time. So, the act of decision cannot be delayed beyond reason. At some point, the decision maker would do well to reach a decision rather than defer it till more information is gathered.

6.2 COST BEHAVIOUR

For purposes of planning, it is helpful to analyse the behaviour of costs in relation to volume. In this context, three types of cost patterns may be distinguished: fixed costs, variable costs, and semi-variable costs.

Fixed Costs

Almost every business incurs certain costs which are fixed in nature, that is, they remain constant irrespective of changes in the volume of output. They may represent depreciation charges, property tax, insurance, and rent which arise because the firm owns plant and equipment and hires factory premises; they may consist of salaries paid to managerial and supervisory staff or interest burden on a long term debt. Fixed costs arise as a result of capacity creation and are invariant with respect to changes of activity (capacity utilisation). They are a function essentially of time.

Part A of Exhibit 6.1 shows the behaviour of total fixed costs with respect to output, while the behaviour of unit fixed costs with respect to output is shown in Part B.

EXHIBIT 6.1 ***Fixed Costs***

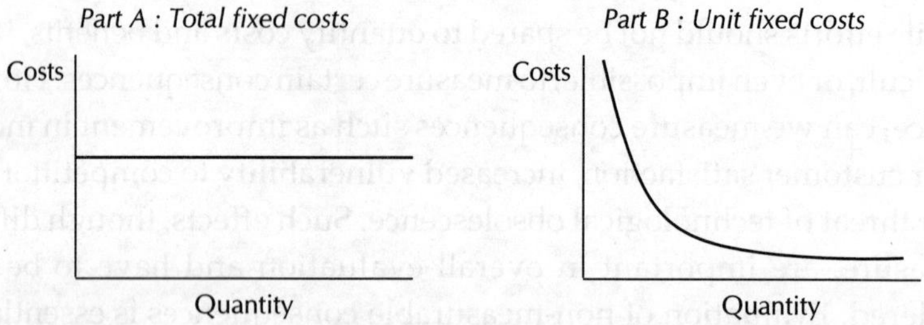

Variable Costs

There are several important elements of cost that vary directly with the output. For example, the total material cost varies linearly with output as does the cost of power and other utilities. All such costs which vary directly (or proportionately) with output are referred to as variable costs.

Part A of Exhibit 6.2 shows the behaviour of total variable costs in relation to output, and Part B the behaviour of unit variable costs in relation to output. Two points may be noted here: (a) Total fixed costs remain fixed whereas unit fixed costs decline as the output increases. (b) Total variable costs vary linearly with output whereas unit variable costs remain fixed irrespective of the output level.

EXHIBIT 6.2 ***Variable Costs***

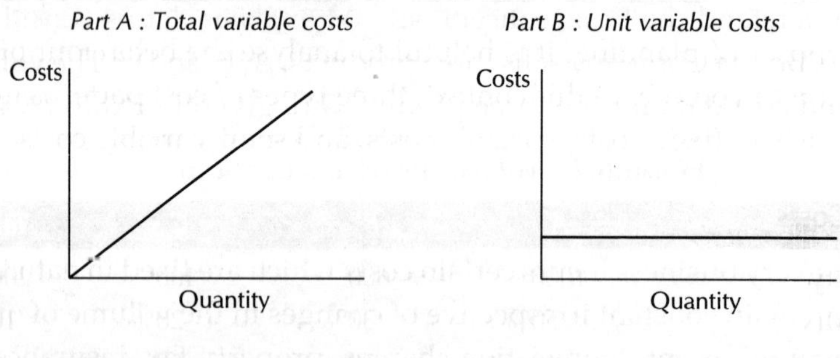

Semi Variable Costs

Many cost items do not conform to the pattern of fixed or variable costs. Such costs are known as semi-variable costs. For example, the cost of telephone calls consists of a fixed tariff plus a variable tariff which becomes applicable only beyond a certain number of calls. There is a family of such semi-variable costs. Some commonly occurring semi-variable cost patterns are shown in Exhibit 6.3.

EXHIBIT 6.3 ***Semi-Variable Cost Patterns***

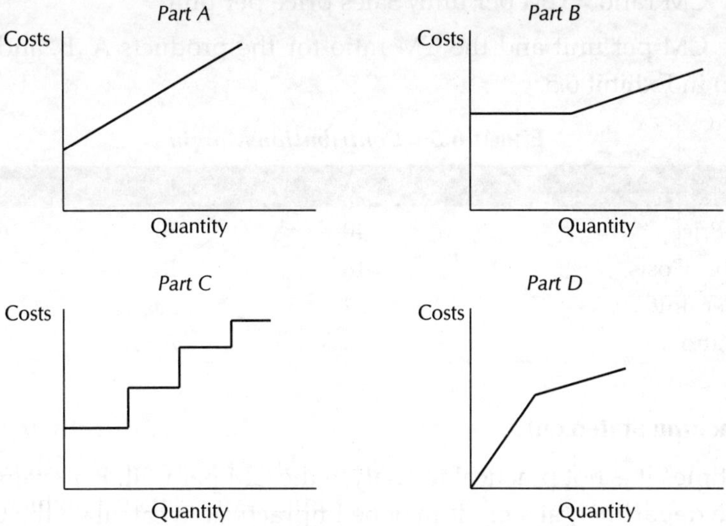

6.3 CONTRIBUTION MARGIN

The contribution margin (CM) of a product or service is the difference between its sales and variable costs. It represents the surplus available after covering the variable costs to meet fixed costs and generate a profit. You can calculate the CM in total, per unit, or as a percentage of sales depending on the purpose of analysis.

To understand the basic concepts in CM analysis, let us consider an example. Bravia Company sells three products, A, B, and C. The volume, price, and cost data for the three products are given in Exhibit 6.4

EXHIBIT 6.4 ***Volume, Price, and Cost Data***

	A	*B*	*C*	*Total*
Quantity	1000	600	400	2000
Sales Mix	50%	30%	20%	100%
Sales Price	40	50	60	
Variable Costs	16	15	30	
Fixed Costs	8	15	12	
Full Costs	24	30	42	

You can calculate the CM per unit and CM ratio using the following formulae:

CM per unit = Sales price per unit—Variable costs per unit
CM ratio = CM per unit/Sales price per unit

The CM per unit and the CM ratio for the products A, B, and C are shown in Exhibit 6.5.

EXHIBIT 6.5 ***Contribution Margin***

	A	*B*	*C*
Sales Price	40	50	60
Variable Costs	16	15	30
CM per unit	24	35	30
CM Ratio	60%	70%	50%

CM Income Statement

Sometimes it is not practical to analyse the CM per unit. For example, in a large departmental store it may be impractical to calculate the CM on a product by product basis. However, it may be feasible and worthwhile to evaluate the performance of an entire product family (as against an individual product). The format for such a CM statement is given in Exhibit 6.6

EXHIBIT 6.6 ***Format for a CM Statement***

Sales	xx
Less: Variable Costs	xx
Contribution Margin	xx
Less: Fixed Costs	xx
Operating Income	xx

6.4 BREAK-EVEN ANALYSIS

Cost-volume-profit analysis, popularly referred to as break-even analysis, examines the relationship between volume, costs, revenues, and profits. It throws light on how changes in price, volume, or costs impact profitability.

The break-even point represents the volume where total revenues and total costs are equal.

Basic Assumptions

A simple tool for profit planning and analysis, cost-volume-profit analysis is based on some assumptions. Effective use of such analysis calls for an understanding of these assumptions which are discussed below:

Predictability of Costs The cost-volume-profit model is based on the assumption that the costs of the firm are divisible into two components: fixed costs and variable costs. Fixed costs remain unchanged for all ranges of output and variable costs vary proportionately to volume. Hence, the behaviour of costs is predictable. For practical purposes, however, it is not necessary for these assumptions to be valid over the entire range of volume. If they are valid over the range of output within which the firm is most likely to operate, referred to as the relevant range, cost-volume-profit analysis, is a useful tool.

Constancy of Unit Selling Price This implies that the total revenue of the firm is a linear function of the output. For firms which have a strong market for their products, this assumption is quite valid. For other firms, however, it may not be so. Price reductions might be necessary to achieve a higher level of sales. On the whole, however, this is a reasonable assumption and not unrealistic enough to impair the validity of the cost-volume-profit model, particularly in the relevant range of output.

Stability of Product Mix In the case of a multi product firm, the cost-volume-profit model assumes that the product mix of the firm remains stable. Without this premise, it is not possible to define the average variable profit ratio when different products have different variable profit ratios. While it is necessary to make this assumption, it must be borne in mind that the actual mix of products may differ from the planned one. Where this discrepancy is likely to be significant, cost-volume-profit model has limited applicability.

No Change in Inventory A final assumption underlying the conventional cost-volume-profit model is that the volume of sales is equal to the volume of production during an accounting period. Put differently, inventory changes are assumed to be nil. This is required because in cost-volume-profit analysis, we match total costs and total revenues for a particular period.

Graphic Analysis

Cost-volume-profit analysis may be carried out graphically or algebraically. We first deal with the graphic analysis and then with the algebraic. For our discussion, the following example will be used. The Smoothflow Company manufactures a certain ball pen. The fixed costs of the company are ₹300,000 per year. The unit selling price (net) is ₹8 and the unit variable cost is ₹5. At present, the firm manufactures and sells 140,000 ball pens.

Given the basic assumptions of cost-volume-profit analysis, the relationship between volume and costs, and volume and revenues for the Smoothflow Company are shown in Exhibit 6.7. From this exhibit, we find that: (i) total revenues are less than total costs so long as the volume is less than 100,000 units, (ii) total revenues and total costs are equal when the volume is 100,000 units, and (iii) total revenues exceed total costs when the volume exceeds 100,000 units. The volume of 100,000 units, thus, represent the break-even point.

EXHIBIT 6.7 ***Cost-Volume-Profit Graph***

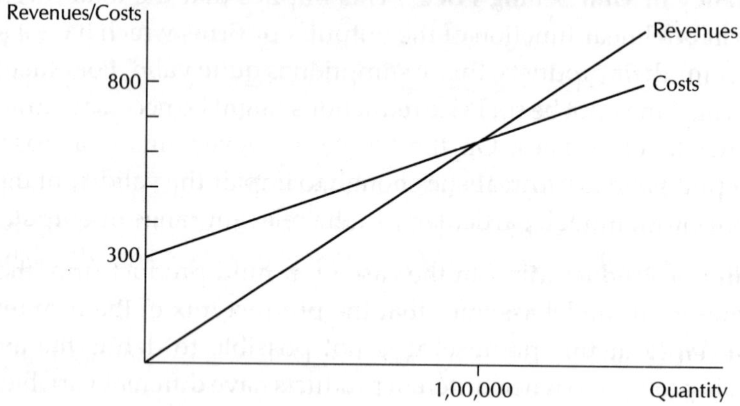

The level of profit for a given level of volume is the difference between the total revenues and total costs corresponding to that volume. The relationship between profit and volume can, however, be studied more easily with the help of the profit-volume graph shown in Exhibit 6.8. Derived from the cost-volume-profit graph, the profit-volume graph plots the difference between the heights of the total revenue line and the total cost line of the cost-volume profit graph. The slope of the profit-volume line is simply the difference between the slopes of the total revenue line and the total cost line of the cost-volume-profit graph.

Algebraic Analysis

The cost-volume-profit (C-V-P) model shows the relationship among revenues, cost, volumes, and profits. In equation form, this model is:

EXHIBIT 6.8 ***Profit-Volume Graph***

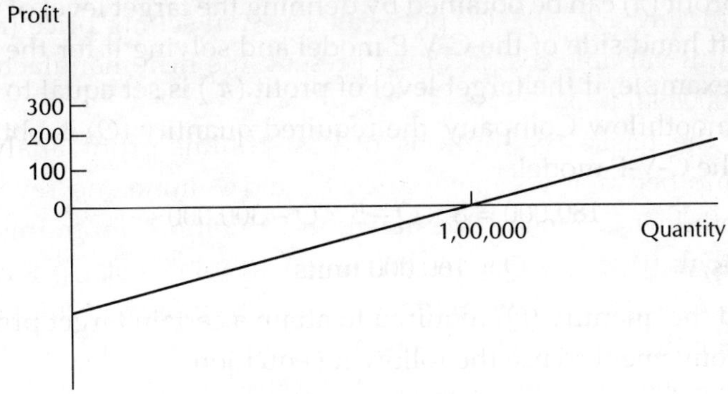

$$\pi = TR - TC$$
$$= PQ - (VQ + F)$$
$$= Q(P - V) - F$$

where π is the operating profit, TR the total revenues, TC the total costs, P the unit selling price, V the unit variable cost, F the fixed costs of the period, Q the quantity produced and sold, and $(P - V)$ the unit contribution margin.

The C-V-P model may be used, among other things, to find: (a) the break even quantity; (b) the profit for a given quantity level; (c) the quantity required for attaining a given level of profit; and (d) the break-even sales in rupees.

Break-even Quantity The break even quantity is the value of quantity (Q) for which the profit (π) is zero. Setting profit equal to zero in the C-V-P model, we get:

$$Q = \frac{F}{P - V}$$

In the above equation, $(P - V)$, which represents the difference between unit selling price and unit variable cost, is called the contribution margin.

The break-even quantity for the Smoothflow Company is:

$$Q = \frac{3,00,000}{8 - 5} = 1,00,000 \text{ units}$$

Profit for a Given Quantity The profit (π) for a given quantity level is obtained by putting the value of quantity (Q) on the right hand side of the C-V-P model. For example, when the quantity is 140,000 units, the profit for the Smoothflow Company is:

$$\pi = 3 \times 140,000 - 300,000$$
$$\pi = ₹120,000$$

Quantity for a Given Profit The quantity (Q) required to attain a target level of profit (π) can be obtained by defining the target level of profit (π) on the left hand side of the C-V-P model and solving it for the quantity (Q). For example, if the target level of profit (π^t) is set equal to ₹180,000 by the Smoothflow Company, the required quantity (Q) is obtained by solving the C-V-P model:

$$180{,}000 = 8 \times Q - 5 \times Q - 300{,}000$$

This gives, $Q = 160{,}000$ units

To find the quantity (Q) required to attain a certain target profit (π^t) it is more convenient to use the following equation:

$$Q = \frac{\pi^t + F}{P - V}$$

Break- even Sales in Rupees Break-even sales in rupees is simply :

Break even quantity × unit selling price

The following equation can be employed to calculate more directly the break even sales in rupees:

$$\text{Break even sales in rupees} = \frac{F}{1 - (V/P)}$$

Applying the above equation to the Smoothflow Company, we find that the break-even sales in rupees are:

$$\frac{300{,}000}{1 - 5/8} = ₹800{,}000$$

Limitations of Cost-Volume-Profit Analysis

Cost-volume-profit analysis is a useful tool of profit planning. However, it suffers from several limitations arising out of the following:

- *Complex Cost Structures* Many firms have cost structures that include items which cannot be classified as fixed or variable costs. Naturally, such costs structures are not easily amenable to the application of break-even analysis.
- *Multiple Products* Most of our analysis was focussed on a single product firm. In the multi-product firm case, we assumed a standard product mix to obtain a representative 'unit of production'. This, however, presents difficulties in cost allocation.
- *Varying Temporal Incidences* In its basic formulation, break-even analysis ignores the time value of money. This is acceptable if costs and revenues occur more or less simultaneously. If they occur at different points of time and there are systematic differences in their

temporal incidences (for example, fixed costs occur before variable costs and these two costs precede revenue generation), costs and revenues must be expressed in present value terms.

- *Non-linear Relationships* The basic break-even analysis postulates a linear relationship. Put differently, the unit variable cost (V) and the unit selling price (P) are assumed to remain constant per unit of output. Since P and V are likely to change with output (because of factors like intensification of competition and realisation of economies of scale), the results of break-even analysis may provide somewhat misleading indication. To overcome this limitation, break-even analysis which captures non-linearities in relationships may be attempted. Although more realistic, such an exercise becomes more complex and deprives break-even analysis of an important practical appeal, viz. its simplicity.

To sum up, break-even analysis is a useful tool for profit planning in relatively simple situations. Its utility, however, is impaired in situations of even moderate complexity where it has to be refined and/or supplemented with more elaborate tools of analysis.

6.5 RELEVANT INFORMATION AND DECISION MAKING: PRODUCTION DECISIONS

One of the purposes of management accounting is to provide information relevant to decision making. Very broadly, **costs and revenues that are expected to differ between the alternatives in future** only are relevant for decision making. In other words, we have to apply the differential analysis model, displayed in Exhibit 6.9, which is an extension of the cost-volume-profit model discussed earlier. In Exhibit 6.9, the first column represents the alternative being evaluated, the second the status quo (or baseline), and the third the difference between the alternative being considered and the status quo.

EXHIBIT 6.9 ***Differential Analysis Model***

	Alternative	*Status Quo*	*Difference*
Revenue	R_1	R_0	ΔR
Less: Variable Costs	V_1	V_0	ΔV
Contribution	$R_1 - V_1$	$R_0 - V_0$	$\Delta R - \Delta V$
Less: Fixed Costs	F_1	F_0	ΔF
Operating profit	Π_1	Π_0	$\Delta \Pi$

We now examine and analyse various production decisions. The principal focus of this analysis is on determining the incremental operating profit. Non-financial considerations which are difficult to quantify have also been briefly touched upon.

Extent of Processing a Product

The Advance Company manufactures a product which it sells to other firms, who process it further and sell it to industrial users. The normal monthly production of the company is 50,000 units. The unit selling price and standard cost per unit are as follows:

Selling price		₹60.00
Standard costs		45.00
Direct materials	₹20.00	
Direct labour	7.00	
Variable manufacturing overhead	8.00	
Fixed manufacturing overhead	4.00	
Variable selling expenses	4.00	
Fixed selling expense	2.00	
Unit profit before tax		15.00

The management of the company is considering a proposal to process the product further so that it can sell the finished product directly to the industrial users at ₹80.00 per unit. Further processing does not require any capital investment but does entail the following additional costs:

Direct labour	₹8.00 per unit
Variable manufacturing overhead	₹3.00 per unit
Variable selling expenses	₹2.00 per unit
Fixed manufacturing overhead	₹100,000 per month
Fixed selling expenses	₹50,000 per month

The question to be answered is, should the company process the product further?

Incremental Profit Analysis Before analysing the alternatives, the current fixed costs in standard amounts per unit of product, are stated in total terms. This is because stating fixed costs per unit of volume can be misleading. The fixed manufacturing overhead cost is ₹200,000 and the fixed selling expense is ₹100,000.

The differential analysis of further processing is shown in Exhibit 6.10. Since further processing enhances the operating profit, it is the preferable alternative.

EXHIBIT 6.10 ***Differential Analysis of Further Processing***

	Alternative (Further processing)	*Status Quo*	*Difference*
Revenue	4,000,000	3,000,000	1,000,000
Variable costs			
Direct material	1,000,000	1,000,000	
Direct labour	750,000	350,000	
Manufacturing overhead	550,000	400,000	
Selling expense	300,000	200,000	
Total variable costs	2,600,000	1,950,000	650,000
Contribution	1,400,000	1,050,000	350,000
Fixed costs			
Manufacturing overhead	300,000	200,000	
Selling expense	150,000	100,000	
Total fixed costs	450,000	300,000	150,000
Operating profit	950,000	750,000	200,000

Other Aspects Certain other aspects that may be looked into in this decision-making situation are:

- Technical know-how and skill of the firm to process the product further.
- Additional working capital requirement as a consequence of further processing.
- Flexibility in hiring and retrenching people.
- Marketing set-up for distributing the finished product.

While these aspects do not lend themselves to precise financial measurement, they cannot be overlooked before a decision is taken.

Accepting or Rejecting a Special Offer

Premier Corporation manufactures and sells 1 million units of a certain electrical fitting at a price of ₹50 each. The income statement of Premier Corporation is shown below:

Sales (1 million units at ₹50 per unit)	₹50,000,000
Variable costs	
Manufacturing	32,500,000
Selling and administration	2,500,000
Total variable costs	35,000,000

Contribution margin	15,000,000
Fixed costs	
Manufacturing	6,000,000
Selling and administration	4,000,000
Total fixed costs	10,000,000
Operating profit	5,000,000

Toward the year end, Premier Corporation receives a special order to supply 100,000 units at a concessional price of ₹35 per unit. Now, Premier does have capacity to execute this order. If Premier Corporation accepts this order, it will incur only variable manufacturing costs. All other costs will remain unchanged. In such a situation, should Premier Corporation accept the special order?

Incremental Profit Analysis Exhibit 6.11 shows how the acceptance of the special order impacts on the operating profit of Premier Corporation. Since the special order is expected to increase the operating profit, Premier Corporation would do well to accept the same.

EXHIBIT 6.11 ***Differential Analysis of a Special Order***

	Alternative (Acceptance of special order)	*Status Quo*	*Difference*
Revenue	₹53,500,000	50,000,000	3,500,000
Variable costs			
Manufacturing	35,750,000	32,500,000	
Selling	2,500,000	2,500,000	
Total variable cost	38,250,000	35,000,000	3,250,000
Fixed costs			
Manufacturing	6,000,000	6,000,000	
Selling	4,000,000	4,000,000	
Total fixed costs	10,000,000	10,000,000	
Operating profit	5,250,000	5,000,000	250,000

Other Aspects While looking at a special order at a concessional price, the firm should take into account the following:

- Impact of the order on the regular sales of the firm.
- Possibility of such requests coming up in the future.
- Physical wear and tear of machinery on account of such an order.

Continuing or Dropping a Product

Sameekha Limited makes three products viz. Bips, Nips, and Dips, that uses common facilities for manufacture and sales. The relevant data for these products are given below:

	Product			
	Bips	*Nips*	*Dips*	*Total*
Sales volume	120,000	100,000	50,000	
Unit selling price	₹25	₹16	₹18	
Revenue	₹3,000,000	₹1,600,000	₹900,000	₹5,500,000
Unit variable cost	₹16	₹12	₹15	
Fixed costs				₹1,100,000

To evaluate how well each product is doing, the management has asked the accountant to allocate fixed costs to each product. Since the total fixed costs are 20 percent of revenues, the accountant charged fixed costs at the rate of 20 percent of the product revenues. The effect of such allocation on product line income statement is shown on the top panel of Exhibit 6.12. Based on the income statement analysis of various products a senior executive of Sameekha argued that Dips should be dropped as it was losing money. Another executive, however, suggested that a differential analysis be done to assess the costs saved and the revenues foregone. The bottom panel of Exhibit 6.12 presents differential analysis. It shows that dropping Dips is not profitable.

EXHIBIT 6.12 ***Analysis of Dropping a Product***

Income Statement Analysis

	Product			
	Bips	*Nips*	*Dips*	*Total*
Sales	₹3,000,000	₹1,600,000	₹900,000	₹5,500,000
Less: Variable costs	1,920,000	1,200,000	750,000	3,870,000
Total Contribution margin	1,080,000	400,000	150,000	1,630,000
Less: Fixed costs allocation	600,000	320,000	180,000	1,100,000
Operating profit(loss)	480,000	80,000	(30,000)	530,000

(Contd.)

Exhibit 6.12 (Contd.)

Differential Analysis

	Alternative: Drop Dips		*Status Quo*		*Difference*
Sales	₹4,600,000	–	₹5,500,000	=	₹(900,000)
Less: Variable costs	(3,120,000)	–	(3,870,000)	=	750,000
Total contribution margin	1,480,000	–	1,630,000	=	(150,000)
Less: fixed costs	(1,100,000)	–	(1,100,000)	=	0
Operating profit (loss)	380,000	–	530,000	=	(150,000)

Other Aspects A decision to discontinue a product should also take into account the following:

- Complementary or competitive nature of the products of the company.
- Impact on the image of the company.
- Effect on the motivation of employees.
- Value of resources released on discontinuation.

Making or Buying a Part

Zenith Automobiles Limited is engaged in the manufacture of automobiles. The company manufactures a wide range of parts and also buys many parts from external suppliers. One of the parts that it manufactures is Part No.101. The monthly requirement of this part is 1,000 units and the standard cost for one unit is:

Direct material	₹40.00
Direct labour	20.00
Variable manufacturing overhead	20.00
Fixed manufacturing overhead	35.00
	₹115.00

At a monthly budget meeting, the materials manager suggested that the company could save money if Part No.101 were purchased from an outside supplier willing to supply the quantity required by Zenith at ₹100 per unit. He estimated that if the part is bought from outside, the fixed clerical costs would increase by ₹1,500 and the variable handling cost would be ₹5 per unit. The plant manager reported that if the manufacture of Part No.101 were discontinued, there would be no change in total fixed manufacturing overheads.

Incremental Profit Analysis A cursory look at the alternatives may suggest that the company saves money if Part No.101 is bought from outside because the cost of manufacture is higher than the cost of purchase. Closer examination, however, reveals a different picture. A portion of the standard cost of ₹115 represents the allocation of fixed manufacturing overhead. For purposes of inventory valuation, this allocation is proper if the system of absorption costing and a reasonable overhead allocation method are used. However, for purposes of decision making, such a cost is irrelevant because the fixed manufacturing overheads would not change if the firm decides to discontinue the manufacture of Part No.101. Only variable manufacturing costs (direct material, direct labour, and variable manufacturing overhead) are relevant in this case. Hence, the decision to make or buy the part would be analysed as follows:

Make		
Variable manufacturing cost (1,000 units @ 80 per unit)	=	₹80,000
Buy		
Purchase cost (1,000 units @ ₹100)	=	₹100,000
Handling cost (1,000 units @ ₹5)	=	5,000
Clerical cost	=	1,500
		₹106,500

Since it costs less to make than to buy it, the company should continue to manufacture Part No.101.

Other Aspects Other aspects that should be taken into account while making a decision of this kind are:

- Value of facilities that would be released if the part is not manufactured.
- Reliability of the external supplier.
- Control over the quality of the external supplier.
- Difficulty in retrenching or using labour for some other purpose if manufacture of the part is discontinued.

Again, while these aspects cannot be easily quantified, they cannot be ignored too.

6.6 RELEVANT INFORMATION AND DECISION MAKING: MARKETING DECISIONS

Pricing, a major decision that managers face, can take many forms: What price should be set for a new product? How should we respond to a new price of a competitor? What price should be quoted in a sealed/open bidding situation?

The pricing decision is extensively covered in economics and marketing. We will focus on few important points relating to the role of costs in pricing.

Economic Theory and Pricing

The characteristics of the market has a bearing on the pricing decision. In a **perfect competition**, a firm can sell any quantity at the given market price. If it charges more, it can't sell; if it charges less, it foregoes profits. Therefore, in a perfectly competitive market, the firm has no latitude in pricing. It has to only decide on how much to produce.

While costs do not influence prices in a perfectly competitive market, they have a bearing on the production decision. To appreciate this, consider Exhibit 6.13, which shows the marginal cost curve and the marginal revenue curve. The *marginal cost* is the incremental cost resulting from producing and selling one additional unit. Typically, the marginal cost declines as production increases up to a certain point, because the firm enjoys economies of scale. Thereafter, the marginal cost tends to increase on account of diseconomies of scale.

EXHIBIT 6.13 ***Marginal Revenue and Cost in Perfect Competition***

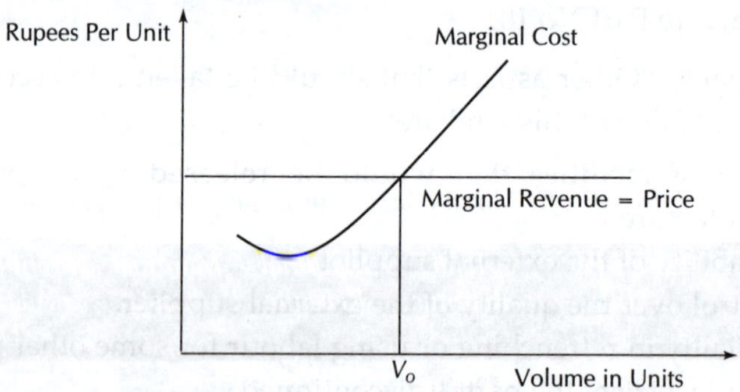

The *marginal revenue* is the incremental revenue arising from the sale of an additional unit. In a perfectly competitive market, the marginal revenue curve is a horizontal line as the price per unit remains the same for all volumes of sale.

From Exhibit 6.13 it is clear that as long as the marginal cost is less than the price, incremental production and sales are profitable. When the marginal cost exceeds marginal revenue, it is unprofitable to increase production. Hence, profit is maximised when marginal cost equals price. In Exhibit 6.13, profit is maximised when the firm produces V_o units.

In an **imperfectly competitive market**, a firm's price has a bearing on the quantity it sells. Generally, price reductions generate additional sales. Exhibit 6.14 depicts a typical demand curve (or the average revenue curve) for imperfect competition. It reflects the volume of sales at each possible price. To sell additional units, the price of all units sold has to be lowered. So, the marginal revenue curve, also shown in Exhibit 6.14, lies below the demand curve. This means that the marginal revenue for selling one more unit is less than the price at which it is sold because the price of all units sold has to be reduced as well. For example, suppose 20 units can be sold for ₹100 per unit. To sell 21 units, the price must be dropped to ₹99; to sell 22 units the price must be dropped to ₹98; and to sell 23 units the price must be dropped to ₹97. The fourth column of Exhibit 6.15 shows the marginal revenue for units 21 through 23.

EXHIBIT 6.14 ***Marginal Revenue and Cost in Imperfect Competition***

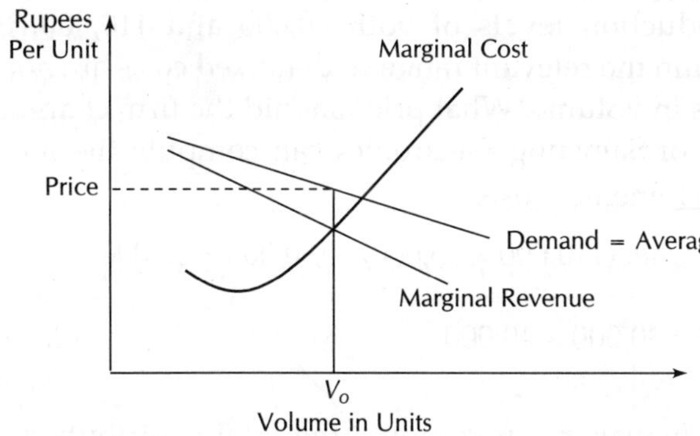

EXHIBIT 6.15 ***Profit Maximisation in Imperfect Competition***

Units Sold	*Price Per Unit*	*Total Revenue*	*Marginal Revenue*	*Marginal Cost*	*Profit from the Additional Unit*
20	₹100	₹2000			
21	99	2079	₹79	₹75	79 – 75 = 4
22	98	2159	77	76	77 – 76 = 1
23	97	2231	75	77	75 – 77 = (2)

If the marginal cost is as shown in the fifth column of Exhibit 6.15, the optimal output would be 22 units. This is clear from the numbers in the last column of Exhibit 6.15: the 21st unit adds ₹4 to profit, the 22nd unit adds ₹1, but the 23rd unit decreases profit by ₹2.

What is the difference between *marginal cost* (a concept relevant for pricing decisions in economic theory) and *variable cost* (a concept used in management accounting)? While marginal cost may change with each unit of production, variable cost is assumed to be constant within a relevant range of output. Since changes in marginal cost are often small within wide ranges of output, variable cost may be a reasonable approximation for marginal cost in many situations.

Maximisation of Total Contribution

In practice, managers rarely compute marginal revenue curves and marginal cost curves. Instead, they examine selected volumes, not the whole range of possible volumes, and use judgemental estimates to predict the effects of additional production and sales on profit.

Consider a division of Samsung Electronics that makes LED television. Suppose market researchers estimate that 80,000 units can be sold if the price is 60,000 per unit and 110,000 units can be sold if the price is ₹55,000 per unit. The variable cost is ₹40,000 per unit at production levels of both 80,000 and 110,000. Both the volumes are within the relevant range so that fixed costs are not affected by the variations in volume. What price should the firm charge?

The manager of Samsung Electronics can compute the incremental revenues and incremental costs.

Incremental revenue: (110,000 × 55,000) – (80,000 × 60,000)

= 1250,000,000

Incremental costs: 30,000 × 40,000 = 1200,000,000

₹50,000,000

Alternately, the manager can compute the total contribution for each alternative:

Contribution at ₹55,000

(₹55,000 – ₹40,000) × 110,000 = ₹1650,000,000

Contribution at ₹60,000

(₹60,000 – ₹40,000) × 80,000 = ₹1600,000,000

₹50,000,000

Target Pricing

Target prices are often fixed on a cost plus basis. The size of the "plus" depends the target operating income which is generally based on a target return on investment. For this discussion, we will assume a target operating income.

There are different ways to arrive at the same target price. They represent different markups on different definitions of cost. Exhibit 6.16 shows the relationships of costs to target selling prices, assuming a target operating income of ₹15 million on a volume of 1 million (or a target operating income of ₹15 per unit). The percentage there represent four popular markups based on different definitions of cost: (a) a percentage of variable manufacturing costs, (b) a percentage of total variable costs, (c) a percentage of total manufacturing costs, and (d) a percentage of full costs.

EXHIBIT 6.16 ***Relationships of Costs to Same Target Selling Prices***

		Alternative Markup Percentage to Achieve the same Target Sales Price
Target sales price	₹250	
Variable costs		
(1) Manufacturing	₹150	(₹250 – ₹150) ÷ ₹150 = 67%
Selling and administrative	15.5	
(2) Unit variable costs	₹165	(₹250 – ₹165) ÷ ₹165 = 52%
Fixed costs		
Manufacturing	₹40	
Selling and administrative	₹30	
Unit fixed costs	₹70	
(3) Unit manufacturing costs	₹190	(₹250 – ₹190) ÷ ₹190 = 32%
(4) Unit full cost	₹235	(₹250 – ₹235) ÷ ₹235 = 6%
Target operating income	₹15	

SUMMARY

- While an organisation must recover all its costs in the long run to be viable, fixed costs may not be relevant for short-term decisions.
- The key steps in decision making are:
  - (i) Define the problem.
  - (ii) Develop alternative solutions.
  - (iii) Evaluate the alternatives.
  - (iv) Arrive at a decision

- The contribution margin (CM) of a product or service is the difference between its sales and variable costs. It represents the surplus available after covering variable costs to meet fixed costs and generate a profit.
- Cost–volume–profit analysis is an important tool of profit planning. It helps in answering questions like the following: At what volume of sales would the firm break-even? How much should the firm produce and sell in order to reach the target level of profit?
- One of the purposes of management accounting is to provide information relevant to decision making. Very broadly, costs and revenues that are expected to differ between the alternatives in future represent relevant information for decision making. In other words, we have to apply the differential analysis model.
- For purposes of planning, it is helpful to analyse the behaviour of costs in relation to volume. In this context, three types of cost patterns may be distinguished: fixed costs, variable costs, and semi-variable costs.
- Fixed costs arise essentially as a result of capacity creation and are invariant with respect to changes of activity. Variable costs, on the other hand, vary proportionately with output. Semi-variable costs have a fixed element and a variable element.
- Very broadly, costs and revenues that are expected to differ between the alternatives in future represent relevant information.
- In a perfect competition, a firm can sell any quantity at the given market price. In an imperfect competition, a firm's price has a bearing on the quantity it sells.
- Target prices are often fixed on a cost plus basis. There are different ways to arrive at the same target price. They represent different markups on different definitions of cost.

Budgeting

7

A budget is a quantitative expression of plans. It is the principal device to compel and discipline management planning. Without it, planning may not get the central focus that it deserves. It is commonly used by business firms, governmental agencies, non-profit institutions, and even households. While there is considerable variation in the scope, degree of formality, and level of sophistication applied to budgeting, most of the well-managed business firms use a budget which is a comprehensive and coordinated plan for the operations and resources of the firm. Such a budget is developed by a formal and intricate process.

How are budgets useful? Budgets provide several benefits in that they:

- Induce management to think systematically about the future.
- Serve as a device for coordinating the complex operations of the business.
- Provide a medium for communicating the plans of the firm.
- Motivate managers at all levels to perform well.
- Serve as a standard against which the actual performance may be judged.

This chapter is concerned with various aspects of budgeting. It is divided into nine sections which are as follows:

- Strategy and strategic planning
- Framework for budgeting
- Master budget
- Flexible budgeting
- Variance analysis
- Human aspects of budgeting
- Budgeting in India
- Dos and don'ts of budgeting
- Becoming budget savvy

7.1 STRATEGY AND STRATEGIC PLANNING

The exercise of annual budgeting is founded on the strategy followed by the firm. Strategy refers to the general direction in which a firm plans to move. Strategy involves finding the optimal fit between a firm's internal competencies and the opportunities in the external environment. Exhibit 7.1 shows schematically how strategies are formulated based on a concept advanced by Kenneth R. Andrews. In a multi-business firm (most companies are multi-business firms), strategy is formulated at two levels, viz., the corporate level and the business unit level.

EXHIBIT 7.1 ***Formulation of Strategies***

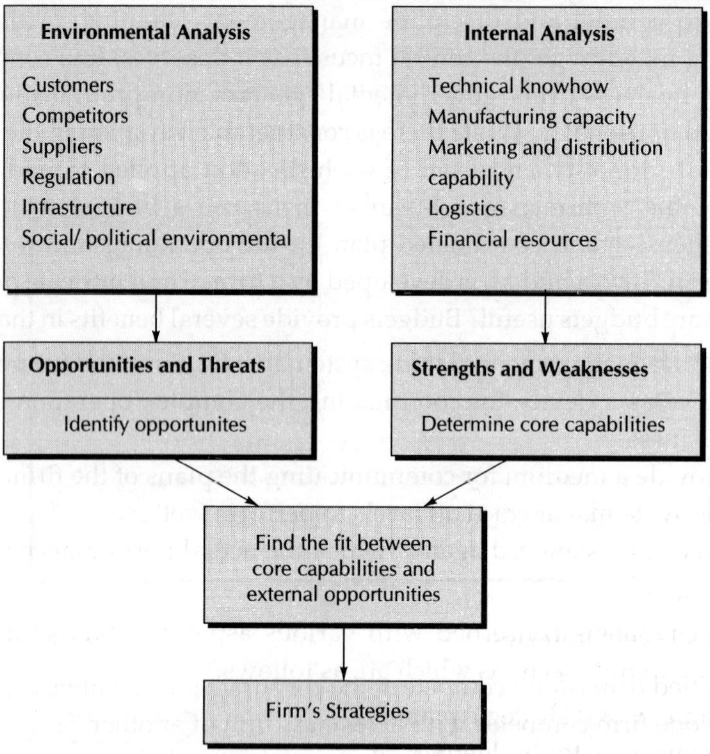

Corporate Level Strategy

At the corporate level, the key strategic issues are: What businesses should we be in? How much resources should we allocate to various businesses? Portfolio planning tools have been developed to guide such decisions. One such tool is the General Electric's Stoplight Matrix.

General Electric's Stoplight Matrix The General Electric Company is highly admired for the sophistication, maturity, and quality of its planning system. It uses a 3x3 matrix called the General Electric's Stoplight Matrix to guide the allocation of resources. This matrix calls for evaluating the businesses of a firm in terms of two key issues:

Business strength How strong is the firm vis-à-vis its competitors?

Industry attractiveness What is the attractiveness or potential of the industry?

The commitment of resources to various businesses is guided by how they are rated in terms of the above two dimensions. As shown in Exhibit 7.2, businesses which are favourably placed justify substantial commitment of funds; businesses which are unfavourably placed call for divestment; and businesses which are placed in between qualify for modest investment.

EXHIBIT 7.2 ***General Electric's Stoplight Matrix***

Industry Attractiveness \ Business Strength	Strong	Average	Weak
High	Invest	Invest	Hold
Medium	Invest	Hold	Divest
Low	Hold	Divest	Divest

Business Level Strategies

Diversified firms don't compete at the corporate level. Rather, a business unit of one firm competes with a business unit of another.

Among the various models that can be used as frameworks for developing a business level strategy, the Porter's generic model is perhaps the most popular. According to Michael Porter, there are three generic strategies that can be adopted at the business unit level: cost leadership, differentiation, and focus.

Cost Leadership A business unit may seek to achieve a position of cost leadership as its principal weapon of competition. Cost leadership may be gained by exploiting economies of scale, improving capacity utilisation, exercising tight control across the entire value chain, enhancing the productivity of R & D and marketing outlays, deriving advantage from cumulative learning, and simplifying the product/service design.

Does cost leadership mean sacrifice of quality? Usually, not. The typical motto of a cost leader is to "offer a product of acceptable quality at a low cost".

Firms that have successfully followed this strategy include Hero Honda in motorcycles, Reliance Industries in petrochemicals, Walmart in discount retailing, Mittal Steel in steel, and Dell Computers in computers.

Differentiation A differentiation strategy involves offering a product or service that is perceived by customers as distinctive or unique so that they are expected to pay a higher price. To succeed in this strategy the firm must identify some attributes of a product or service that customers really value, position itself to serve the customer need in a unique manner, and offer the differentiated product or service profitably.

Differentiation may be achieved through product quality, product range, bundled services, brand image, delivery convenience, and reputation. Differentiation strategies call for investments in R & D engineering capabilities, and marketing skills. Firms that pursue differentiation strategies build organisational structures and control systems that nurture creativity and innovation.

While a differentiated offering may be very pricey in some cases, it is not always so. Many firms that pursue this strategy seek to "offer a superior product or service at an affordable price."

Firms that have pursued the differentiation strategy include Mercedes in automobiles, Intel in microchips, Maytag in electrical appliances, Coca-Cola in beverages, Rolex in wrist-watches, and Raymond in textiles.

Focus A strategy of focus involves concentrating on a narrow line of products or a limited market segment. In the selected target market the company seeks to gain a competitive edge through cost leadership (cost focus) or product differentiation (differentiation focus).

Cost Focus A firm which pursues this strategy, concentrates on a narrow line of products or limited market segment. Within this domain, it achieves cost leadership through sustained efforts. McDonalds, for example, pursues a strategy of cost focus by offering limited menus to achieve economies of scale.

Differentiation Focus A strategy of differentiation focus involves concentrating on a limited market segment wherein the firm can offer a differentiated product based on its innovative capabilities. Porsche, for example, specialises in sports car, a market segment in which it competes with the likes of General Motors and Nissan. As a focused differentiator, it relies on its ability to innovate faster than a large differentiator.

Exhibit 7.3 shows the various generic competitive strategies suggested by Michael Porter in his classic work *Competitive Strategy.*[1]

EXHIBIT 7.3 ***Porter's Generic Competitive Strategies***

Sources of Competitive Advantage:

Strategic Scope	Unique Value as Perceived by Customer	Lowest Cost
Broad (industry-wide)	Overall Differentiation	Overall Cost Leadership
Narrow (segment only)	Focused Differentiation	Focused Cost Leadership

Strategic Innovation

Deregulation, globalisation, and digitalisation are reshaping the industrial landscape and creating discontinuities. In this environment, incremental improvements arising from business process re-engineering, total quality management, cost reduction, and the like cannot go beyond a point. To exploit discontinuities, strategic innovation is required and the pre-conditions for strategic innovation, according to Hamel and Scholes[2], are diversity of views and perspectives, new passions, and experimentation.

Diversity of Views and Perspectives There must be a diversity of views, insights, and perspectives. Without that, a company can become genetically blind. As Gary Hamel and Jim Scholes say: "A lack of genetic diversity makes it difficult for companies to, first, encompass and then, exploit the various trends that could be leveraged to create new wealth... Strategy innovation requires new

---

[1] Porter, Michael, *Competitive Strategy,* New York; Free Press, 1980.

[2] Gary Hamel and Jim Scholes "Mastering Strategy Innovation," *Business Today,* August 7, 1999.

ways of seeing. Reconceiving an organisation in terms of core competencies constitutes a new ways of seeing."

New Passions Often the emotional side of strategy is ignored. Since strategy reflects collective purpose and a shared destiny, an organisation should kindle the passions of its people. As Gary Hamel and Jim Scholes argue: " Inside, almost every individual has a deep passion for discovery and novelty. It is amazing to see the passions that are unleashed when an organisation goes to its members and invites them to participate in charting their collective destiny."

Experimentation Perfect foresight is an oxymoron in this age of discontinuities. While an organisation may be clear about its goals and broad direction in which it wants to move, its specific strategies can be discovered only through experimentation. As Gary Hamel and Jim Scholes argue: "The goal is not to develop perfect strategies, but to develop strategies that are directionally correct and then to progressively refine them through rapid experimentation and adjustment. This is the real work of the leader."

Strategic Planning

A distinction may be drawn between strategy formulation and strategic planning. Strategy formulation is concerned with determining strategies whereas strategic planning is concerned with implementing strategies. The strategic plan describes how strategies would be implemented.

While strategic formulation is a creative, innovative, and unstructured activity, strategic planning is a systematic and structured activity, which often follows a well-defined procedure and time table.

A formal strategic planning process offers several potential benefits: (a) It provides the framework to develop the annual budget. (b) It forces managers to think long-term. (c) It serves as a management development tool. (d) It helps in thinking about the actions required in the short-term to implement the long-term strategies.

Typically, the strategic planning process is completed just before the preparation of the annual budget. It involves the following steps:

1. Review and update the strategic plan from the previous year.
2. Decide on assumptions and guidelines and communicate the same to the operating units.
3. Get the strategic plan from the operating units.

4. Analyse and aggregate the business unit plans into an overall corporate strategic plan.
5. Get the plan approved by the board of directors and the CEO.

7.2 BUDGET PREPARATION

The strategic plan reflects the nature and size of several programmes that are proposed to be undertaken to implement the strategies of the firm. It has a multi-year horizon, which is normally three to five years. By contrast, the budget focuses on a single year. In a way, it is a slice of the strategic plan with a shorter focus.

There is one more important difference between a strategic plan and the annual budget. While the former is typically structured by product lines or other programmes, the latter is structured in terms of responsibility centres. A **responsibility centre** refers to an organisational unit headed by a manager who is responsible for its performance. Within a firm, there can be numerous responsibility centres that form a hierarchy. At the apex is the chief executive who is responsible for the overall performance of the firm. Under him are several presidents responsible for their functional activities and/or divisions, depending on the organisational structure. Under them arc operating managers and staff managers responsible for their plants or departments or zones or whatever. As one moves downwards, responsibility centres may consist of sections and sub-sections.

Responsibility centres are often classified on the basis of financial responsibility in four broad types: cost centres, revenue centres, profit centres, and investment centres.

- A **cost centre** is a responsibility centre headed by a person who is responsible for the costs incurred in that centre. Examples of cost centres are a production department in a factory, or a staff department like the personnel department.
- A **revenue centre** is a responsibility centre headed by a person who is responsible for generating revenues. The marketing department may be a revenue centre.
- A **profit centre** represents a wider area of responsibility headed by an individual who is accountable for the profit contribution it makes to the enterprise. Some examples of profit centres are: a production division, a service division, a bank branch.

- An **investment centre**, representing the broadest definition of managerial responsibility, is headed by an individual who is responsible for both the profit and the investment required to produce the profit.

The structuring of the budget in terms of responsibility centres is necessary because the budget is a tool for influencing, as well as appraising, managerial performance.

Controllability

Responsibility accounting seeks to ascribe responsibility to the originator of revenue, cost, and investment. Hence, it is necessary to separate controllable and non-controllable elements of cost, revenue, and investment for different responsibility centres. Broadly, we may say that an element of cost, revenue, or investment is controllable by the head of a responsibility centre, if it is significantly influenced by him. The application of this broad rule, however, poses problems. The difficulties are proportional to the complexity and inter-relationships found in the organisational structure. Often inter-twined organisational arrangements cause difficulties in separating controllable and non-controllable elements of revenues and costs. When this is so, the performance report of a responsibility centre must highlight items which are only partially controllable by it. Similarly, common allocated overhead items should be shown separately.

Once the gathering of data on revenues and costs is aligned along the lines of responsibilities, and controllable and non-controllable elements are reasonably separated, performance standards have to be established for the responsibility centres. Reflecting the goals of responsibility centres in terms of revenues, costs, volume, quality, etc., these standards guide the action of heads of responsibility centres. They are the benchmarks against which actual performance is compared. Hence, they must be made an integral part of the accounting and reporting system.

7.3 FRAMEWORK FOR BUDGETING

The Budget Period

In order to be operationally meaningful, the budget must be drawn up for a specific time period. Usually, the budget is drawn up for a year. The yearly budget may be divided into quarterly budgets or even monthly budgets. Generally, the budget period is divided into two parts with differing levels of detail applying to them. For example, the budget for the first quarter or six months may be drawn up on a monthly basis and for the remaining period on a quarterly basis. As the period for which the budget is drawn up on a quarterly basis approaches, the quarterly budgets may then be cast in terms of monthly budgets.

Some firms employ a rolling budget. Under this system, at the end of each quarter or each half year, the budget is extended by adding another quarter or another half year. Hence, the firm always has the budget for a year ahead of it. To illustrate, the budget system for a hypothetical company may be described: Exotica Limited finalises by December 15, 20X0, the budget for the year 20X1, drawn up on a quarterly basis. Come March 15, 20X1, it drops the first quarter of 20X1 (the quarter about to be completed) and includes the first quarter of 20X2 in its budget. At that time, of course, the budget estimates of the remaining three quarter of 20X1 are revised and updated.

Organisation for Budgeting

Though there seems to be no standardised organisation for budget preparation, in most of the large firms which develop formal budgets, a basic pattern exists. There is a budget committee and a budget director which guides and monitors the process of budgeting. In this, understandably, the line executives have a significant involvement.

Consisting of several top management executives, the budget committee: (i) sets broad guidelines for budgeting, (ii) coordinates the separate budgets prepared by different departments, (iii) reconciles inconsistencies among various departmental budgets, (iv) compiles the budget in its final form, and (v) sends the budget for the approval of the chief executive and the board of directors.

The budget director, working in liaison with the budget committee, heads a staff unit which helps the line organisation in preparing the budgets. Usually, he issues instructions on how the budgets have to be prepared, provides past data useful for estimation purposes, offers aid in computing various budgets figures, persuades people to submit their budgets on time, and assembles the budgets prepared by the line organisation. It should be emphasised that the budget director is responsible mainly for the mechanics of budget preparation, not the substance of budgets themselves. The line organisation provides, by its decisions and judgements, this content. Commenting on this, Robert Anthony says: "The budget organisation is like a telephone company, operating an important communication systems; it is responsible for the speed, accuracy, and clarity with which messages flow through the system, but not the content of the messages themselves."[3]

The Budget Base

What is the base or starting point for preparation of the budget? A commonly used base is the level of operations in the current year. Using this, the expected and planned changes in the forthcoming year are identified for purpose of developing the budget for that year. Under this approach, referred to as the incremental approach to budgeting, the focus of budgeting is on the increments in operations during the budget period. This approach can be quite appropriate in some cases. The sales budget for a product sold exclusively to the government or the salary budget of the corporate head office can be developed in this manner. The incremental approach to budgeting, however, suffers from one major limitation: it tends to perpetuate past follies and inefficiencies. A sales budget developed according to the incremental approach might overlook opportunities to penetrate different market areas; an expenses budget prepared in this way may gloss over wasteful elements.

To overcome the shortcomings of the incremental approach, an alternative has been proposed known as the zero-base approach to budgeting. It was pioneered by the Texas Instruments Company in the USA.

The basic feature of zero-base budgeting is that while preparing their budgets, the departments should not take anything for granted and start, as it were, on a clean slate. The budget-making for the ensuing year should be started from ground zero instead of treating the current budget as the base or the starting point. The concept of zero-base budgeting implies that all activities of the organisation should be viewed afresh. Priorities among competing claims for allocation of funds are to be settled on the basis of some evaluation technique such as cost-benefit analysis. The zero-base sales budget, for example, would be developed by examining all possible markets for the product rather than considering incremental changes over current sales operations. Similarly, a zero-base budget for manufacturing costs would be based on a careful assessment of operational requirements and not determined by using a 'present cost plus something' formula.

---

[3] Anthony R.A. *Management Accounting : Text and Cases*, Richard D Irwin Inc. Homewood: Illionois, 1964.

The zero-base approach obviously requires more effort and time. Further, it is likely to be opposed by heads of responsibility centres. They may not favour the searching scrutiny of every item in the budget every year. In view of these problems associated with this approach, a compromise solution may be worked out. The zero-base review can be done once every four (or five) years and the incremental approach applied in the intervening years.

Limiting Factor

In every firm, there is a critical factor which sets a limit to its level of activity. Often, the expected demand is the limiting factor which defines the scope and level of operations. When the demand is fairly strong, the limiting factor may be the production capacity of the firm which cannot be augmented in the short run. Or it may be the limited availability of power if the firm is located in a power-deficit region. Raw material availability may also sometimes be a limiting factor. Finally, for firms which do not have easy access to capital, finances may be a limiting factor.

Since it determines the scope and level of operations, the limiting factor is the most appropriate starting point for the budgeting exercise. It makes no sense, for example, to begin planning with the production capacity when the limiting factor is the expected demand. Sometimes it might so happen that in the planning process, the firm discovers some other factor which is more critical than the initial limiting factor. For example, the firm may begin its planning exercise from the level of sales forecast, the *prima facie* limiting factor, but discover later that its financial resources are more critical.

Participation

The budget guidelines prepared by the budget committee are transmitted down the organisational hierarchy. At each level, the management may provide more detailed information for guiding its subordinates till the guidelines reach the level of supervisors (foremen) who head the lowest level of responsibility centres. Each supervisor prepares budget estimates of items of expense controllable at his level. Expense items not controllable at his level are usually added later by the budget staff. The budget estimates prepared by the supervisor serve as the starting point for the negotiation between the supervisor (budgetee) and his superior. The superior may suggest modifications and changes which might be only partially acceptable to the supervisor (budgetee). Together, by a process of negotiation, they arrive at a budget that is reasonably acceptable to both of them. This kind of negotiation is repeated at successively higher levels of responsibility centres in the organisation. Of course, budgets established at higher levels may call for revision of budgets developed at lower levels in order to resolve inconsistencies. Put differently, the budgetary process may be somewhat iterative in nature. The process of budget determination ends when budgets at different levels are established in such a manner that they are mutually consistent.

7.4 MASTER BUDGET

Comprehensive in nature, the master budget covers all facets of the operations and finances of the firm. The master budget of a manufacturing firm usually has the following components:

A. Operating budget

1. Sales budget
2. Production budget
3. Materials and purchase budget
4. Labour cost budget
5. Manufacturing overhead budget
6. Non-manufacturing cost budget
7. Budgeted profit and loss statement

B. Financial budget

1. Capital expenditure budget
2. Cash budget
3. Budgeted balance sheet

Exhibit 7.4 shows in a condensed fashion the relationship among various parts of a master budget for a manufacturing firm.

Operating Budget

The operating budget, reflecting the projected profit and loss statement, is the centerpiece of the budgeting system. It is built up in terms of:

- Sales budget
- Production budget
- Materials and purchases budget
- Labour cost budget
- Manufacturing overhead budget
- Non-manufacturing cost budget

EXHIBIT 7.4 ***Components of Master Budget***

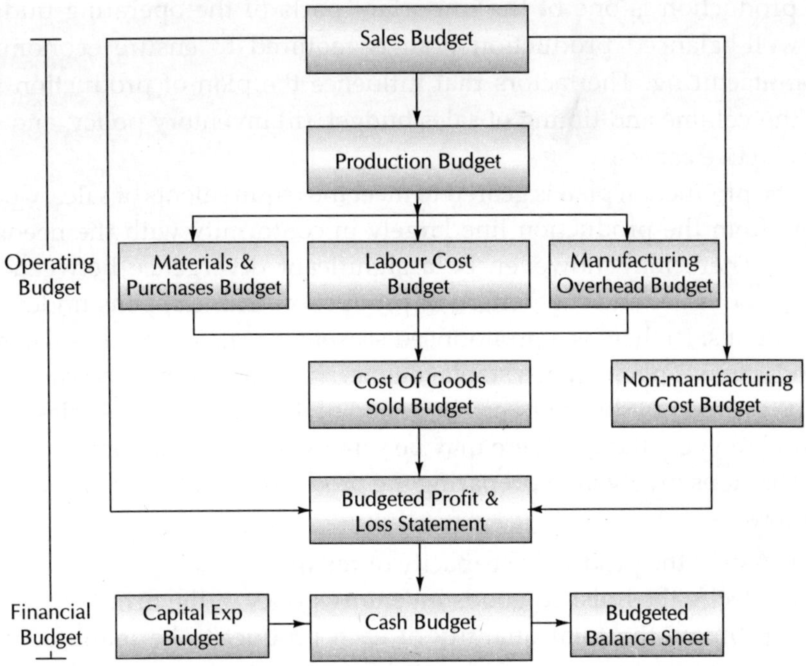

Sales Budget The sales forecast or budget for the forthcoming (budget) year is usually the starting point of the budgetary exercise. Production, inventory, and expenses are factors related to the level of sales. The short-term sales forecast, usually covering a period of one year, is part of a long-term sales forecast which may cover a period of three to five years. It focuses on the current slice of the long run sales forecast in much sharper relief. The sales forecast or sales budget underlies almost all other budgets. So a rational and intelligent effort should be made to develop a sales budget which the top management believes can be reasonably accomplished.

In developing the sales forecast, the following factors should be considered:

- The outlook of the industry and economy
- Past behaviour and emerging trends in sales
- Governmental regulations and controls affecting the industry
- Consumer attitudes, dispositions, tastes and preferences
- The nature and the extent of competition
- Sales promotion efforts of the firm

Production Budget In a manufacturing organisation, the budget of production is one of the important parts of the operating budget. A well-balanced production plan is required to ensure economical manufacturing. The factors that influence the plan of production are: (i) the volume and timing of sales budget, (ii) inventory policy, and (iii) productive capacity.

The production plan is geared to meet the requirements of sales. Goods flow from the production line largely in conformity with the needs of sales. There may, however, be a significant divergence between the pattern of sales and the pattern of production. This happens under two conditions: (i) there is a pronounced seasonal variation in sales whereas production is planned in a stable manner; (ii) production necessarily has to be carried out during a certain period of the year, whereas sales occur round the year though there may be some seasonal variations.

The steps involved in preparing the production budget are broadly as follows:

- Assess the productive capacity of the firm.
- Specify the finished goods inventory policy of the firm.
- Estimate the total quantity of each product to be manufactured during the budget period on the basis of sales forecast and finished goods inventory policy.
- Schedule the production during the budget period, taking into account the pattern of sales, the finished goods inventory policy, and the productive capacity.

Materials and Purchase Budgets Once the production budget defines the quantities to be produced, the next logical step is to estimate the material requirements and determine the purchase programme. In this context, the following principal budgets are developed:

- *Materials Budget* Materials used in a manufacturing unit are traditionally classified as direct and indirect. Direct materials are materials which can be easily traced to the product and indirect materials are materials which cannot be easily traced to the product. The materials budget generally is concerned only with direct materials. Indirect materials and supplies are covered by the manufacturing overhead budget. The materials budget shows the quantities, and often the prices, of materials planned to be purchased.
- *Purchase Budget* This budget shows : (i) the quantities of each type of raw material to be purchased, (ii) the schedule of purchases, and (iii) the estimated cost of purchases.

In developing the purchase budget, one has to take into account the following: (i) the quantities specified in the materials budget, (ii) the planned changes in material inventories, (iii) re-order levels of various inventory items, and (iv) economic order quantities of various inventory items.

- *Material Inventory Budget* This budget shows the planned raw material levels at certain points in the budgeting period.
- *Cost of Raw Materials Used Budget* This budget shows the estimated cost of raw materials to be used from inventory for production.

Labour Cost Budget Labour is generally classified as direct and indirect. Direct labour cost represents the wages paid to workers employed directly in the manufacturing activity. Indirect labour cost represents all other labour cost, such as supervisory salaries, wages paid to storekeepers, maintenance personnel, janitors, and so forth.

The budget for labour cost normally includes the cost of direct labour only. The cost of indirect labour is included in the manufacturing overhead budget.

The following approaches may be used for developing the labour cost budget:

- Estimate the labour cost per unit of production by multiplying the standard direct labour hours required for each unit of production by the average wage rate per hour. Multiply the number of units of finished goods planned to be produced by the labour cost per unit in order to get the labour cost budget.
- Estimate the labour cost on the basis of its relationship to some measure such as material cost.

When the above approaches cannot be used, the labour cost budget may be developed on the basis of information about: (i) permanent manpower employed in direct manufacturing activity and their remuneration rates, (ii) payments likely to arise on account of overtime work, and (iii) temporary manpower that may be needed and their remuneration rates.

Manufacturing Overhead Budget Manufacturing overhead is that part of factory cost which is not included in direct material and direct labour cost. Not directly identifiable with specific products or jobs, manufacturing overhead consists of: (i) indirect material, (ii) indirect labour, and (iii) miscellaneous factory expense items such as depreciation, utilities, supplies, repairs and maintenance, insurance, taxes etc.

To construct the manufacturing overhead budget, expense budgets for all the departments in the factory-production as well as service departments-have to be drawn up and aggregated. For this purpose, the expected volume of work to be done in each department has to be determined in terms of an indicator appropriate to its activity. Some measures of activity are given below:

- For producing departments:
  (a) Units of output
  (b) Direct labour hours
  (c) Direct machine hours
- For service departments:
  (a) Repairs and maintenance-direct repair hours or the number of machines to be maintained.
  (b) Purchase department-total purchase in rupees or the number of purchase orders to be placed.
  (c) General factory administration-number of employees in the plant or total direct labour hours.

Given the activity level of each department in terms of a suitable measure, departmental budgets are drawn up in terms of two basic components viz., the variable cost and the fixed cost. The former is related to the proposed level of activity; the latter is planned independently.

Budget for Non-Manufacturing Costs Non-manufacturing costs consist of expenses for selling and distribution, general administration, research and development, and financing. The budget for non-manufacturing costs are normally prepared along departmental lines. For each non-manufacturing department, the budget may be divided into fixed costs and variable costs. The variable costs of a non-manufacturing department, of course, would have to be related to some index of activity which is meaningful in its context.

Financial Budget

The financial budget comprises of the capital expenditure budget, the cash budget, and the budgeted balance sheet.

Capital Expenditure Budget The capital expenditure budget shows the list of capital projects selected for investment along with their estimated cost. Generally, this budget is prepared separately from the operating budget and often it too has its own budget cycle. Capital expenditure proposals emanating from different sources in the organisation are screened at various levels before they reach the capital budget committee, which is often a sub-committee of the budget committee. With the help of the controller, this committee prepares the capital budget document showing projects deemed worthwhile. This has to be approved by the board of directors which usually is the final decision making body on capital expenditures.

The proposals in the capital expenditure budget have to be suitably justified. Usually, the justification is in terms of quantitative criteria, such as net present value, accounting rate of return, internal rate of return, cost reduction per unit, and productivity gains. Hard-to-quantify considerations like growth opportunities, market image, technological competence, morale, labour unrest, and employee safety, could also be important.

Cash Budget The cash budget shows the cash inflows and outflows expected in the budget period. The major sources of cash inflows are: cash sales, collection of accounts receivable, dividend and interest income, disposal of fixed assets, long-term and short-term borrowing, and issue of equity capital. The major items of cash outflow are: cash purchases, payment of accounts payable, payment toward wages, salaries, rent, utilities and other operating expenses, tax payment, dividend payment, purchase of capital assets, and repayment of borrowings.

The projected surplus or deficit in the cash budget provide the basis for investment (if there is a surplus over the target cash balance that the firm wishes to maintain) and financing (when the projected cash balance falls below the target).

Budgeted Balance Sheet The projected balance sheet shows projected assets, liabilities, and owners' equity at the end of the budget period. The inputs required for its preparation are the initial balance sheet, the profit plan, the capital expenditure budget, the cash budget, and the investment and financing budget.

7.5 FLEXIBLE BUDGETING

The master budget that we have discussed in the previous section is a static or inflexible budget. Even though it can be easily revised, it is prepared on the assumption that the future level of activity is fixed.

Actual results can be compared with the original plan, irrespective of how the future unfolds. To illustrate, consider the case of Omega Company which manufactures a single product. The operating budget for the month of January 20X0 at a target level of sales of 5,000 units is shown in column 2 of Exhibit 7.5. The actual performance for the month of January 20X0 is shows in column 1 of Exhibit 7.5. Note that though the static budget envisaged a production and sales of 5,000, units, only 4,000 units were actually produced and sold. There were no opening or closing inventories.

The comparison between the master budget figures and actual performance figures is expressed in the form of variances as shown in column 3 of Exhibit 7.5. Looking at the variances column, we find that while there was an unfavourable variance (U) in sales, the variances relating to variable costs are favourable (F). These favourable variances, however, are deceptive because the actual level of activity was below the projected level. It makes little sense in such a case to compare actual results with a static budget.

Improved Basis

In order to improve the basis of comparison, a flexible budget can be used. Also referred to as a variable budget, the flexible budget is geared to a range of activity rather than a single level. It is prepared after analysing the behaviour of each element of cost with respect to volume. Since it is based on an understanding of cost behaviour patterns, it can be tailored easily to any level of activity.

EXHIBIT 7.5 ***Omega Company's Performance Report January 20X0***

	Actual	*Operating Budget*	*Variance*
Units	4,000	5,000	10,000 U
Sales	₹460,000	₹550,000	90,000 U
Variable Costs			
Direct Material	₹128,000	150,000	₹22,000 F
Direct Labour	₹105,000	125,000	₹20,000 F
Other variable costs	₹64,000	75,000	₹11,000 F
Total variable costs	₹297,000	350,000	53,000 F
Contribution margin	₹163,000	200,000	37,000 U
Fixed Costs			
Factory supervision	32,000	30,000	2,000 U
Depreciation of factory machines	20,000	20,000	

(Contd.)

EXHIBIT 7.5 (Contd.)

	Actual	Operating	Variance Budget
Other fixed factory costs	10,000	10,000	–
Fixed manufacturing costs	62,000	60,000	2,000 U
Fixed general and administration costs	45,000	46,000	1,000 F
Fixed selling costs	30,000	30,000	–
Total fixed costs	137,000	136,000	1,000 U
Operating Income (Loss)	26,000	64,000	38,000 U

Exhibit 7.6 shows the flexible budget for Omega Company. Here we find that the total variable cost per unit is ₹70 and the total fixed cost of the firm is ₹136,000. Hence, the graph of flexible budget is as shown in Exhibit 7.7. It is based on the following relationship.

Total costs = Fixed costs + Number of units x Unit variable cost

EXHIBIT 7.6 ***Omega Company's Flexible Budget for January 20X0***

	Budget Formula Per unit	Various Levels of Activity		
Units	–	4,000	5,000	6,000
Sales	₹110	440,000	550,000	660,000
Variable Costs				
Direct material	₹30	120,000	150,000	180,000
Direct labour	25	100,000	125,000	150,000
Other variable costs	15	60,000	75,000	90,000
Total variable costs	₹70	280,000	350,000	420,000
Contribution Margin	₹40	160,000	200,000	240,000
Fixed Costs				
Factory supervision		30,000	30,000	30,000
Depreciation of factory machines		20,000	20,000	20,000
Other fixed factory costs		10,000	10,000	10,000
Fixed manufacturing cost		60,000	60,000	60,000
Fixed general administration		46,000	46,000	46,000
Fixed selling costs		30,000	30,000	30,000
Total fixed costs		136,000	136,000	136,000
Operating Income (Loss)		24,000	64,000	104,000

From the preceding discussion, it is clear that as the flexible budget is prepared for a range of activity, it provides a meaningful basis of comparison. The essence of the flexible budget approach is that a budget can be tailored to any particular level of activity. Such a budget is helpful in planning when managers are trying to choose from among various activity ranges; they are equally helpful *ex post facto* for performance evaluation.

EXHIBIT 7.7 ***Omega Company's Graph of Costs***

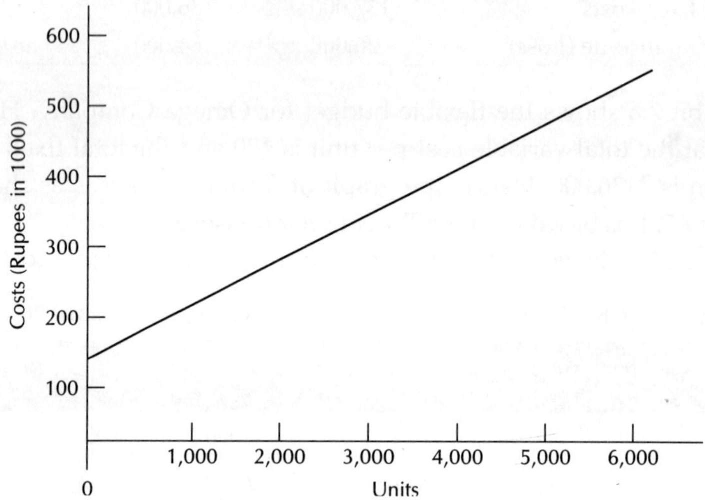

7.6 VARIANCE ANALYSIS

A flexible budget facilitates the analysis of variance. The variances may be divided into two broad categories:

- Variances arising from the difference between the planned and the actual volume of sales. Such variances may be called as *marketing variances* or *volume variances*.
- Variances caused by change in unit prices (or unit costs) are called *price variances* and variances caused by efficient or inefficient utilisation of inputs are called *efficiency variances*.

Exhibit 7.8 shows the following for Omega Company in the summary form: (i) marketing variances, and (ii) price and efficiency variances. It may be emphasised that a static budget fails to distinguish between these two types of variances which reflect two different facets of managerial performance. By isolating these variances, a flexible budget explains the difference between the master (or static) budget and the actual results in terms of different aspects of performance.

Column 4 of Exhibit 7.8 highlights the marketing variances. It shows clearly that due to an underachievement in the volume of sales by 1,000 units, sales revenues were less by ₹110,000 and therefore the contribution margin and operating income declined by ₹40,000. It may be noted that in this analysis, prices are held constant.

EXHIBIT 7.8 ***Omega Company's Summary of Performance for the Month Ended March 31, 20X0***

	(1) *Master (Static) Budget*	(2) *Actual Results at Actual Price*	(3) *Flexible Budget for Actual Output Achieved*	(4) 3–1 *Marketing Variances*	(5) 2–3 *Price and Efficiency Variances*
Units	5,000	4,000	4,000	1,000 U	
Sales	₹550,000	460,000	440,000	110,000 U	20,000 F
Variable Costs	350,000	297,000	280,000	70,000 F	17,000 U
Contribution Margin	200,000	163,000	160,000	40,000 U	3,000 F
Fixed Costs	136,000	137,000	136,000	—	1,000 U
Operating Income	64,000	26,000	24,000	40,000 U	2,000 F

Column 5 of Exhibit 7.8 shows the variance due to price changes and efficient/inefficient use of inputs. It presents the difference between actual costs and costs as per the flexible budget for an output of 4,000 units (the actual output). For more detailed analysis, a cost performance report of the kind shown in Exhibit 7.9 may be prepared.

EXHIBIT 7.9 ***Omega Company's Cost Performance Report for the Month ended March 31, 20X0***

	Actual Costs Incurred	*Flexible Budget*	*Price and Efficiency Variance*
Units	4,000	4,000	—
Variable Costs			
Direct material	128,000	120,000	8,000 U
Direct labour	105,000	100,000	5,000 U
Other variable costs	64,000	60,000	4,000 U
Total variable costs	297,000	280,000	17,000 U
Fixed Costs			
Factory supervision	32,000	30,000	2,000 U

(Contd.)

EXHIBIT 7.9 *(Contd.)*

	Actual Costs Incurred	*Flexible Budget*	*Price and Efficiency Variance*
Depreciation of factory machines	20,000	20,000	—
Other fixed factory costs	10,000	10,000	—
Fixed manufacturing costs	62,000	60,000	2,000 U
Fixed general and administration costs	45,000	46,000	1,000 F
Fixed selling costs	30,000	30,000	—
Total fixed costs	137,000	136,000	1,000 U

7.7 HUMAN ASPECTS OF BUDGETING

Many firms adopt a somewhat mechanistic approach to budgeting without an adequate consideration of its human aspects. Goals and objectives, however, are ultimately achieved through human beings. Hence the effect of budgets on people as well as the effect of people on budgets have to be properly understood. This section, discusses certain behavioural aspects relevant to budgeting.

Pressure

The traditional approach to budgeting was based on the assumption that human beings regard work as unpleasant, shirk responsibility, and ordinarily employ inefficient and wasteful methods. Such a conception of human behaviour led to a budgetary approach which emphasised that responsibility had to be established and a great deal of pressure applied in order to achieve the desired results.

Behavioural approach, however, has shown that while some pressure is beneficial, an excess of it leads to frustration. A budget is an effective motivational tool if it represents a challenging, yet attainable goal. If it is too demanding, it results in frustration and conflict; if too lax, it induces complacency.

Credibility

It is possible that the norms of performance reflected in the budget may be regarded as arbitrary and viewed with suspicion. To impart greater credibility to them, the following conditions must be satisfied:

- The norms of performance must be arrived at *scientifically* by the use of work study, time and motion study, and other industrial engineering studies.
- The norms of performance should be evolved by a *joint and participative* process involving the operating personnel, the administrative authorities, and the finance officers.

Inter-departmental Conflicts and Sub-Optimisation

Budgets may promote a narrow, department-centered outlook. In a system of responsibility budgeting, the primary objective of the head of a responsibility centre will be to show better performance for his centre. An over concern for better departmental or sectional performance might lead to inter-departmental conflicts and hurt the larger interests of the organisation. For example, the production manager, desirous of achieving a certain level of production, may produce a mix of products which does not conform to the one required by the marketing manager. Another example: In a bid to improve the average collection period, the credit manager may not extend credit to certain types of customers, though such an action might improve the profitability of the company. Such instances are many in industry and behaviour of this kind is referred to as sub-optimisation.

To mitigate sub-optimisation, departmental budgets and goals must be integrated with those of the over-all organisation. The criteria for evaluating the performance of various responsibility centres must reflect the over-all goals of the organisation to as great an extent as possible. This calls for the use of a combination of quantitative and qualitative criteria for performance evaluation.

Slack

No manager likes his actual performance to fall below the budgeted goal. Put differently, a manager seeks to avoid an unfavourable variance-a sign of failure. So when a manager is involved in setting the budget standards, he tends to include an element of slack or cushion to minimise the chances of failure. The production manager tends to over-estimate costs; the sales manager may under-estimate sales; and the finance manager seeks to maintain additional cash balance. The slack in the budget also permits a manager to pursue his personal goals in addition to organisational ones.

Some slack is necessary for the smooth working of the organisation. It provides managers elbow room to perform and reduces the conflict between individual and organisational goals. Hence, slack may be viewed as a lubricant necessary for the functioning of the budgetary system.

Though indispensable, slack is costly and has a tendency to increase particularly during prosperous periods. Too much slack can jeopardise the very existence of the firm. So, an organisation should seek to reduce slack whenever it tends to grow beyond permissible limits. Conscious and deliberate efforts should be made to attain the optimal level of slacks-a level at which efficiency is high and conflict tolerable.

Reward and Punishment

Budgetary systems can be used for rewarding good performance and punishing bad performance. A good performance, seen in a favourable variance, can be rewarded by higher monetary compensation, rapid advancement in the organisational hierarchy, and official recognition of good work. The punishment for bad performance, often judged by unfavourable variance, might be in the form of loss of additional compensation, non-promotion, or transfer to positions of lesser importance-in case of extreme bad performance, the employee may be asked to resign from the organisation.

While administering rewards and punishments, it should be borne in mind that the budget standards are based on certain anticipations which may not be realised. Hence, in determining rewards and punishments, actual conditions prevailing during the budget period should be taken into account. Sole reliance should not be placed on pre-determined budget standards. Slavish adherence to such standards may: (i) induce undue caution amongst managers at the time of budget preparation, and (ii) motivate them to act in ways not in the larger interest of the firm, in light of actual conditions. The reward and punishment system must motivate managers to act in the best interest of the firm. It should neither create undue fear in them nor blunt their initiative to act in ways appropriate to actual circumstances.

Gaming

Michael Jensen, an eminent financial economist and organisation theorist, argues that the traditional budgeting system which links bonuses to budgets is severely dysfunctional. He says: "It encourages managers to lie and cheat, lowballing targets and inflating results, and it penalizes them for telling the truth. It turns business decisions into elaborate exercises in gaming." Over a distinguished career in academia and consulting he has gathered a trove of horror stories.

What is the way out? The only way out, according to Jensen, is to sever the link between budgets and bonuses and to reward people purely for their accomplishments and not on their ability to achieve targets. This will take away the incentive to cheat. As he put it: "The only way to solve the problem is to remove all the kinks from the pay-for-performance line—to adopt a purely linear bonus schedule. Managers are still rewarded for good performance, but the rewards are independent of budget targets."

Arguing in a similar vein, he emphasises the desirability of having performance-related budgets. For example, the manager of a division may be told that he is allowed to spend 65 percent of his division's revenues on production and sales activities. The variable performance-related budget is similar to the compensation plan described earlier.

Playing the Budget Game

1. Always ask to negotiate the lowest target
2. Always manage to meet the numbers
3. Never exceed the target
4. Always focus on the sales target, not the customer
5. Always ask for more resources than you need
6. Always spend fully the allotted budget
7. Do not take risks
8. Learn the art of explaining variances

7.8 BUDGETING IN INDIA

During the last few decades or so, the character of budgeting in business firms in India has undergone a gradual but a very significant transformation. The following important changes are quite discernible to an observer of budgeting in Indian business firms.

Greater Technical Sophistication Typically, the budgetary exercise has become more sophisticated in technical terms, perhaps due to the growing influence of professionally qualified cost and management accountants. Some of the important indicators of increased technical sophistication are:

- Establishment of numerous cost-centres and profit-centres
- Development and updating of standards
- Segregation of revenues, product-wise and region-wise

- Analysis of costs in terms of their variability
- Introduction of the concept of product or regional contribution
- Application of the tools of variance analysis

Higher Degree of Participation Traditionally, business budgeting in India was more or less the exclusive concern of the accountant and the top management. Over the years, however, the process of budgeting has become much more participative. Marketing, production, engineering, purchase, and personnel departments now have a far greater involvement in determining their performance standards. To be sure, in many firms in India, the accounts department has a significant influence over the substance of the budget even now. However, its role in shaping the budget seems to be diminishing.

Stronger Linkage between Long-Range Planning and Budgeting In recent years, concerted attempts have been made in a large number of firms to bring about a closer integration between long-range planning and annual budgeting. Typically, these efforts have involved: (i) shortening of the horizon of long-range planning so that meaningful projections can be made, (ii) examining, sharpening, and stating of the premises of long-range planning in fairly explicit terms, and (iii) developing the long-range plan in more operational terms. While these efforts have strengthened the ties between long-range planning and annual budgeting, a lot more needs to be done on a continuing basis to forge these linkages.

7.9 DOS AND DON'TS OF BUDGETING

The budget is the principal instrument of planning and control. In order to improve its effectiveness, the following dos and don'ts must be borne in mind:

- The budget must receive the whole-hearted support of the top management. Their enthusiastic involvement is essential to the success of budgeting.
- The budget must set clear and realistic goals in all areas of operation. Vague and unrealistic goals cannot provide motivation.
- The budget must assign proper authority and responsibility to managers.
- All managers must be actively involved in the process of budget formulation.
- The budget must offer rewards for superior performance and impose penalties for inferior performance.

- The budget should not become too complex and detailed. Overly complex budget tend to be ignored.
- The budget should not be inflexible. Changing circumstances often invalidate budgetary assumptions. Hence, the budget must have inherent flexibility.
- The budget should not mask past inefficiencies. The tendency to do incremental budgeting that accepts historical performance uncritically must be checked.

7.10 BECOMING BUDGET SAVVY

Generally, budgeting is a top-down as well as a bottom-up exercise. The top management sets strategic goals and communicates the same to unit heads. The unit heads, in consultation with their teams, develop operating budgets for their units, which reflect organisation's strategic goals and as also their own goals. The budget proposals sent by the unit heads are reviewed by the top management. The top management may ask for adjustment and the negotiation process continues back and forth till the final budget is finalised. Put differently, the budgeting process is typically an iterative process.

As most managers participate in the budgeting exercise, they should develop a certain organisational savvy. Bear in mind the following tips for dealing with organisational issues that surround the budgeting process:

Know your firm's budgeting process As a manager you should know the time cycle of budgeting in your firm, the strategic goals set by the top management, the guidelines to be followed in preparing the budget, and the manner in which the budget is used in the organisation.

Seek clarification from the budget coordinator Talk to the budget coordinator in the controller's office or the finance person in your department on points where you need clarification. Make sure that you understand each line item in the budget you're developing.

Communicate with decision makers Know the concerns of decision makers and try to address them. Also educate them about your area of the business so that they appreciate the modifications that you may propose.

Remember that the key to success in any budgeting process is a credible two-way communication. As Richard Luecke notes: "Senior management has to communicate strategic goals in a way that makes sense. In turn, the unit heads communicate their resource needs and concerns when presenting budget proposals to management. All participants in the budget process have an obligation to listen to the various and sometimes conflicting positions".

Involve your team fully Since the final budget represents the commitment of your unit's team, involve every member of the team meaningfully throughout the budget period.

Monitor regularly As the performance numbers become available, compare the actual figures with the budgeted figures. If there is a significant variance, find out the cause for it and initiate prompt corrective action. Keep the finance people informed. Avoid throwing unpleasant surprises.

SUMMARY

- A budget is a quantitative expression of plans. It is commonly used by business firms, government agencies, non-profit institutions, and even households.
- Strategy refers to the general direction in which an organisation plans to move. It involves finding the optimal fit between a firm's internal competencies and the opportunities in the external environment. In a multi-business firm, strategy is formulated at two distinct levels viz. the corporate level and the business unit level.
- At the corporate level, the key strategic issues are: What businesses should we be in? How much resources should we allocate to various businesses? Portfolio planning tools have been developed to guide such decisions. One such tool is the General Electric's Stoplight Matrix.
- Among the various models that can be used as frameworks for developing a business level strategy, the Porter's generic model is perhaps the most popular. According to Michael Porter, there are three generic strategies that can be adopted at the business unit level: cost leadership, differentiation, and focus.
- A distinction may be drawn between strategy formulation and strategic planning. Strategy formulation is concerned with determining strategies whereas strategic planning is concerned with implementing strategies. The strategic plan describes how strategies would be implemented.

- Budgets, *inter alia,* induce managements to think systematically about the future, serve as a coordinating device, and serve as a standard for performance evaluation.
- The exercise of periodic budgeting is based on the framework of corporate strategy and long-range plans which reflect the basic objectives pursued by the firm and the key policies adopted to achieve these objectives.
- The operating budget of the firm may be constructed in terms of programmes or responsibility areas. The programme budget is developed in terms of products that are regarded as the principal programmes of the business. The responsibility budget shows the business plans in terms of the persons responsible for achieving them.
- Responsibility areas or centres may be divided into three broad types : cost centres, profit centres, and investment centres.
- There are two approaches to budgeting : the incremental approach and the zero-base approach.
- Comprehensive in nature, the master budget covers all facets of operations and finances of the firm. It has four major components : operating budget, capital expenditure budget, cash budget, and the projected financial position.
- The operating budget, reflected in the projected income statement, is the centre piece of the budgeting system. It is built up in terms of: (a) the sales budget, (b) the production budget, (c) the materials and purchases budget, (d) the labour cost budget, (e) the manufacturing overhead budget, and (f) the non-manufacturing cost budget.
- The capital expenditure budget shows the list of capital projects selected for investment along with their estimated cost. Generally, this budget is prepared separately from the operating budget and it often has its own budget cycle.
- The cash budget shows the cash inflows and outflows expected in the budget period.
- The projected balance sheet shows projected assets, liabilities, and owners' equity at the end of the budget period.
- The master budget is a static or inflexible budget. Hence, it is not very useful for comparison purposes. To improve the basis of comparison, a flexible budget may be used. Also referred to as variable budget, the flexible budget is geared to a range of activity rather than a single level. It is prepared after analysing the behaviour

of each element of cost with respect to volume. Since it is based on an understanding of cost behaviour patterns, it can be tailored easily to any level of activity.

- A flexible budget facilitates the analysis of variance. The variances may be divided into two broad categories : (a) Variances arising from the difference between the planned and the actual volume of sales. Such variances may be called marketing variances or volume variances. (b) Variances caused by change in unit prices (or cost) are called price variances and variances caused by efficient or inefficient utilisation of inputs are called efficiency variances.
- Behavioural research has shown that while some pressure is beneficial, an excess of it leads to frustration. A budget is an effective motivational tool if it represents a challenging, yet attainable goal.
- During the last two decades or so, the following changes in the realm of budgeting have taken place in India : greater technical sophistication, higher degree of participation, stronger linkage between budgeting and long-range planning, and better awareness of the concept of zero-base review.
- The budget is the principal instrument of planning and control. In order to improve its effectiveness, certain dos and donts must be borne in mind.
- As most managers participate in the budgetary process, they should develop a certain organizational savvy.

Cost Management

8

The need to manage costs across the entire organisation in a holistic manner was perhaps first realised by Japanese corporations keen on storming the US and European markets with unbelievably low priced products. Indeed, Japan's economic resurgence in the 1970s was driven by its ability to manufacture high quality products at low costs—costs that were far lower than those of their Western counterparts. To achieve cost leadership, Japanese firms employed techniques like Kaizen, Kanban, and Just-in-Time.

For many years, cost management was not an important concern for corporate India. A sheltered economy, a cost-plus pricing environment, limited competition, and absence of consumer power led to a neglect of cost management. The situation, however, has changed dramatically from the mid 1990s and the need to manage total cost has been driven home powerfully for corporate India, thanks to heightened competition, both domestic and global, sluggish industrial growth, substantial addition to manufacturing capacities, and acute price sensitivity of Indian consumers. In this environment, cost management has become critical to corporate success. Realising this many Indian companies have initiated concerted efforts to manage their costs.

This chapter discusses the key concepts and guidelines useful in cost management. It is divided into three sections:

- Strategic cost management
- Guidelines for total cost management
- Cost management in practice

8.1 STRATEGIC COST MANAGEMENT

Strategic cost management (SCM) is concerned with developing a sophisticated understanding of a firm's cost structure that helps in the search for sustainable competitive advantage. SCM blends three important themes drawn from the strategic management literature: value chain analysis, strategic positioning analysis, and cost driver analysis.

Value Chain Analysis

How should a firm organise its thinking about managing its costs? In the SCM framework, effective cost management requires a broad focus, which Michael Porter calls the value chain. The value chain of a firm is the linked set of value creating activities beginning with the basic raw material sources for component suppliers and ending with the end-use product delivered into the hands of the final customers. As Michael Porter puts it: "The value chain disaggregates a firm into its strategically relevant activities in order to understand the behavior of costs and the existing and potential sources of differentiation. A firm gains competitive advantage by performing these strategically important activities more cheaply and better than its competitors". Exhibit 8.1 depicts the generic value chain.

Exhibit 8.1 *The Generic Value Chain*

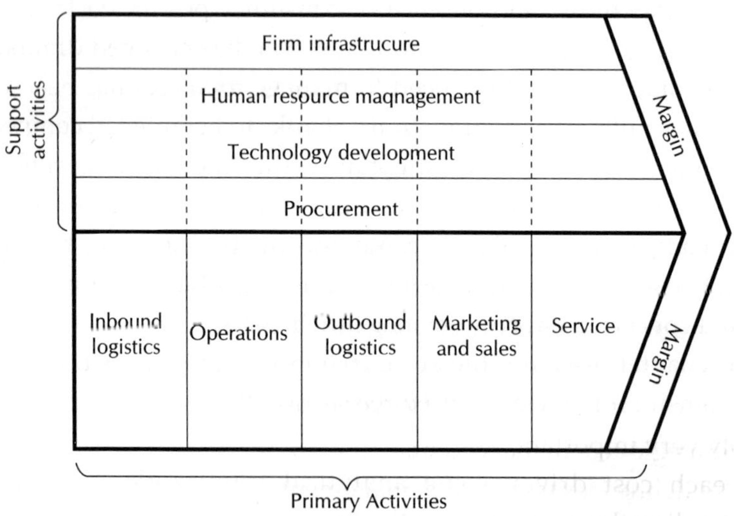

Source: Michael Porter, *Competitive Advantage*, The Free Press, New York, 1985

Value chain analysis highlights how profit can be enhanced by improving linkages with suppliers, linkages with customers, linkages within the value chain, and linkages across business unit value chains within the firm.

Strategic Positioning Analysis

In SCM, the role of cost analysis depends on how the firm chooses to compete. Michael Porter has defined two basic strategies for achieving competitive advantage viz., cost leadership and product differentiation.

A **cost leadership strategy** strives to provide the same or better value to customers at a lower cost than what is offered by competitors. A **differentiation strategy** seeks to increase customer value by providing to customers something that is not offered by others.

Since cost leadership and product differentiation involve different mindsets, they also involve different perspectives on cost analysis. If the primary strategic emphasis is on cost leadership, the following factors are important: role of engineered costs, flexible budgets for manufacturing cost control, budget targets, and competitor analysis. On the other hand, if the primary strategic emphasis is on product differentiation the foregoing factors are not so important but marketing cost analysis is critical to success.

Cost Driver Analysis

Management accounting draws on simple models of microeconomics and assumes that cost is primarily a function of only one cost driver, namely, output volume. SCM, on the other hand, builds upon richer models of the economics of industrial organisation and acknowledges that cost is driven by multiple factors that are interrelated in a complex fashion. Daniel Riley, cost management guru, divides cost drivers into two categories viz., structural and executional as shown in Exhibit 8.2.

There are other ways of developing the list of fundamental cost drivers. Whatever cost drivers are used, bear in mind that not all cost drivers are equally important all the time. In every case, there are some which are probably very important.

For each cost driver, some analytical framework is helpful in understanding the positioning of the firm.

EXHIBIT 8.2 *Cost Drivers*

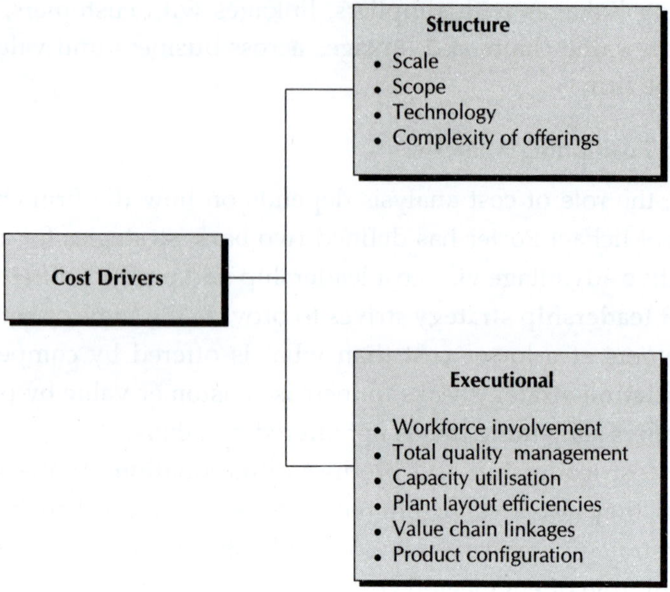

Other Themes

There are other themes emanating mainly from costing literature that are relevant for strategic cost management. They are briefly described below.

Life Cycle Costing Life cycle costs are all the costs associated with a product during its entire life cycle. Life cycle costing is defined by CAM-I as "the accumulation of costs for activities that occur over the entire life-cycle of product, from inception to abandonment by the manufacturer and the customer." Exhibit 8.3 shows the typical life cycle cost. From this exhibit it is clear that the bulk of the costs are locked in at the research, planning, and design stage. So, a great deal of care and circumspection needs to the exercised at these stages.

Target Costing A target cost is a market-based cost. It is derived from a sales price necessary to capture a predetermined market share.

Target cost = Sales price to get a target market share – Desired profit

The concept of target cost has been central to Japanese cost management. It has been expressed most vividly by Akio Morita, Chairman, Sony Corporation, in his book *Made in Japan*: "I dictated the selling price (of the Walkman) to suit a young person's pocketbook, even before we made the first machine... I said I wanted the first models ... to retail for no

Exhibit 8.3 ***Life Cycle Cost***

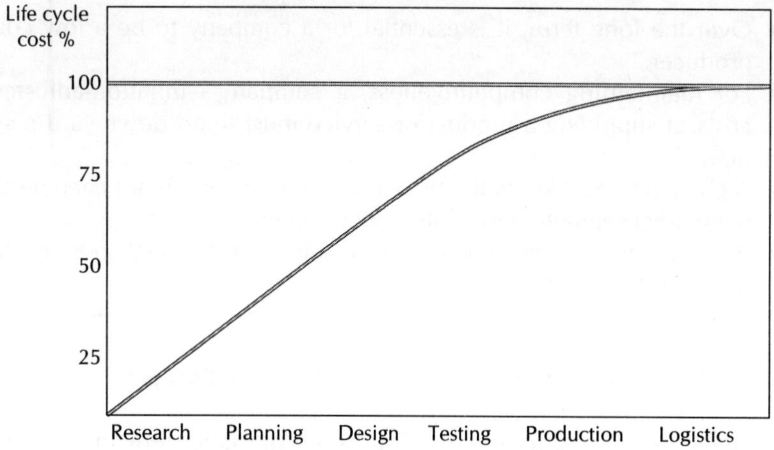

more than Yen 30,000. The accountants protested but I persisted. I told them I was confident we would be making out new product in very large numbers and our cost would come down as volume climbed."

Cost of Quality Juran has proposed a framework for cost of quality (COQ) analysis. His framework calls for measuring and monitoring costs in terms of a four part classification:

1. *Prevention* Costs incurred for preventing bad quality (quality circles).
2. *Appraisal* Costs incurred for monitoring the level of bad quality (scrap reporting systems).
3. *Internal failure* Costs incurred for fixing bad quality which is discovered before goods are shipped (rework labour).
4. *External failure* Costs incurred on account of bad quality that is not discovered before goods are shipped (warranty claims).

Value Engineering Also called value analysis, value engineering is a systematic approach to a product's design to improve its value, defined as the ratio of functionality to cost. Value can be improved by holding functionality constant while reducing cost or holding cost constant while increasing functionality.

Value engineering examines all the product's elements viz.,raw materials, manufacturing process, types of labour and equipments used, the purchased and self-manufactured components, and so on.

Vital Truths about Managing Costs

- Over the long term, it is essential for a company to be a low cost producer.
- For maintaining competitiveness, a company's inflation-adjusted costs of supplying a product or service must trend downward over time.
- A company must know the true cost and profit picture for each product/market segment and all its key customers.
- A company must focus on cash flow and balance sheet strengths as much as on profits.

8.2 GUIDELINES FOR TOTAL COST MANAGEMENT

What is total cost management? Total cost management encompasses strategy as well as operations, covers all functions, spans different dimensions, and subsumes everything and everywhere. *Inter alia*, total cost management seeks to:

- Design a product that can be manufactured at a low cost.
- Eliminate wastes and delays in the manufacturing process.
- Direct resources at simplifying the customer offering to precisely what the customer wants.
- Ensure that the right person is employed for the right job.
- Derive the greatest mileage from marketing and advertising expenditure.
- Minimise organisational overhead expenses.

The four ingredients of a system of total cost management are: total cost consciousness, total cost measurement, total cost responsibility, and total cost improvement.

An organisation committed to total cost management should pay heed to the following guidelines of total cost management.

Understand Your Cost Drivers As discussed above,Daniel Riley, cost management guru, divides cost drivers into two categories : structural and executional. Structural drivers emanate from strategic choices relating to the scale of operation (the volumes the company produces and sells), the scope of operation (the degree of vertical integration), the technologies employed by the firm, and the complexity of its offerings (the variety in products and services). The executional drivers relate to how well a company does what it does. The key factors here are workforce involvement, total quality management, capacity utilisation, plant layout efficiency, product configuration, and value chain linkages.

Focus on the Entire Value Chain A cost leadership strategy must focus on the entire value chain, not just the segments in which the firm is involved. In collaboration with its suppliers and customers, the firm should work toward cost savings in upstream as well as downstream activities. As John K. Shank and Vijay Govindrajan argue persuasively in their book *Strategic Cost Management*, a firm's competitive edge critically depends on its ability to manage its entire value chain relative to that of its rivals.

Marry Total Cost Management to Business Process Reengineering (BPR) According to James Champy and Michael Hammer, "BPR is the fundamental rethinking and radical redesign of business to achieve dramatic improvements in contemporary measures of performance such as cost, quality, service and speed." BPR is a logical ally of total cost management. The basic change demanded by the latter is provided by the former.

Do it Right the First Time as Total Quality Management Demands As Nanda Mazumdar and Rakhi Mazumdar say : "The very essence of Total Quality Management is the process of getting it right the first time every time, by designing a quality chain that uses the customer's needs to produce exactly what she needs, at a price that she is willing to pay, and in a way that enables the company to do this without rejection, rework, and redundancy." If you do it right the first time, the cost of poor quality, reflected in the cost of inspection, scrap, rework, and customer dissatisfaction will almost disappear.

Exercise Rigorous Cost Control at the Design and Product Development Stage It is an empirical fact that nearly 80 per cent of the costs are committed at the design and development stage. Hence bells and whistles should be eliminated at this stage because the customer will not pay for it. At Daewoo Anchor Electronics there is a basic principle called Tankism which demands that all products be developed in conformity with customer needs, without any superfluities. Elaborates T.S. Shin, CEO, Daewoo Anchor Electronics: "The objective is to concentrate on the core product to meet the customer needs- and nothing else." To do this of course the company should carefully assess what the customer wants. For example, when TVS- Suzuki commenced work on its 150 cc 4 stroke scooter, the Spectra, it conducted direct interviews with hundreds of customers in key market areas besides analysing the feedback provided by its sales force.

Team Up with Your Vendors Says S.V. Subramanian " The heart of supply chain management is the supplier vendor relationship . The closer and more dependent they are on each other, the better is the outcome. Despite the apprehension, single vendor relationships have proved fruitful."

To create the lowest possible cost structure, the buyer and the supplier must work in a cooperative manner, share their capabilities, and build an enduring mutually beneficial arrangement. The adversarial arm's length transaction will have to be supplanted by a collaborative arm in arm relationship.

Benchmark Against the Best Compare your cost against the best performers in your industry. This will help you to measure the competitive gap, provide the spur for greater efficiency, explore areas for improvement, and steal the learning curve of others. Madura Coats, for example, benchmarks it process and manufacturing costs against those of its parent, Coats Viyella, in 80 countries.

Resort to Flexible Manufacturing Systems To compete in future, firms will have to move to flexible manufacturing systems. Effective cost management calls for developing machineries, workflows, and worker skills that enable the firm to switch between products quickly while retaining the conventional economies of scale. As Korgaonkar says: "Only flexible manufacturing can provide adequate responses to changes in the marketing environment." For example, Bharat Forge's Machine Components Division uses a flexible manufacturing system to respond quickly to demand fluctuations. As Shirish Joshi of Bharat Forge explains: "The required change is made in the operating sequence of the machine. Since most machines are based on Programme Logic Controls, all this involves is transferring a new programme to them from the PC".

Switch to Just in Time (JIT) System The JIT inventory control system, originally developed by the Toyota Motor Company of Japan, simply implies that the firm should maintain a minimal level of inventory and rely on suppliers to provide parts and components "just-in-time" to meet its assembly requirements. In practice, companies classify their supplies into different categories and apply different strategies to each of them. For example, Bajaj Auto, a company that has one of the most efficient procurement systems, divides the thousands of components that go into its motorcycles into three categories viz., 'A' (the high value items), 'B' (the medium value items), and 'C' (the low value items). It allows managers to build inventories in inverse proportion to the average cost of each category. Thus, inventories for 'A' items are never more than for one shift. A similar classification and strategy has enabled Ashok Leyland to effect substantial savings.

Rely on Activity Based Costing The traditional system of costing accumulates indirect costs in too few pools and allocates them to cost objects using some gross cost drivers. Case studies suggest that the use of broad averages can unfairly burden high-volume products while treating very lightly low-volume products. The resulting cost information may lead to wrong product mix and pricing decisions. In today's environment, marked by high indirect costs, greater complexity in product offerings and heightened competition, there is a strong case for switching to activity based costing, which is more refined and accurate than the traditional system of costing.

Stretch Your Brands One way to enhance sales may be through a new brand aimed at a new market or a new set of customers. Launching a brand, however, is a very expensive proposition and hence, smart marketers try to extend existing brands. As Deepak Basu of Godfrey Phillip India (GPI) argues: "A line or brand extension has the advantage of the parent's pedigree which helps the extension and subsidises a major cost element." For example GPI launched Red and White Premium an extension of its existing Red and White Label. Likewise Smithline Beecham Healthcare extended its popular beverage brands Horlicks and Boost into biscuits.

Watch Your Adspend Adspend, now a major marketing cost, has to be managed cost effectively. Seasoned marketers say that there may be three ways to enhance the productivity of adspend. First focus on few brands because promoting one or two key brands in the right price segment seems to be a more sensible strategy. Second, use cheaper media alternatives. Third, consolidate media buying operations with a single agency (the agency of record) to bargain for discount.

Rationalise Your Distribution and Servicing Structure Costs tend to cascade the moment your product leaves the factory. For consumer products, for example, the distribution costs can be as high as 40 percent of the selling price. Hence, they have to be continually reviewed and pared. Inter alia, firms that manage their distribution costs well choose the cheapest channel, minimise the delivery time, streamline sales, customise offerings, and outsource their services.

Use Infotech to Cut Costs The improvements in information technology and telecommunications are creating unprecedented opportunities for lowering costs. As Anshu Tandon says : "From infotech enabled process improvements to information enriched transactions, from swifter exchange of data to better interaction between individuals, departments, and functions, convergence has opened several fronts in the attack on costs." Anjan Mukherjee echoes a similar view: "Organisations can use infotech to apply Total Cost Management across the entire value chain."

Manage Human Resources (HR) Costs Effectively Many companies have learnt that having too many wrong people and too few right ones has impaired their competitiveness. Hence effective management of HR costs is critical to a firm's success. As A. Sudhakar says: "As a strategic partner, HR can help define and reduce redundancy as well as overlap of work, and improve productivity to generate employee cost savings." Using HR for cost management, inter alia, involves zeroing in on non-performers and reducing headcounts, identifying skill gaps, hiring the right people, imparting training to prevent expensive hires, grooming talent in house, taking timely

Common Cost/Profit Ranges

Sales	100%
Cost of goods	65% and down
Gross margin	35% and up
R&D	0%–15%
Sales	5%–15%
General and Admin	10%–15%
Total	15%–45%
Earnings Before Taxes Target	15%
Assets Employed	60%
ROA Target(after tax)	15% and up

The ranges would be quite different for a process industry because of the much higher plant and equipment investment with the consequent greater pressure for high-capacity utilisation. The opposite is true of most service businesses with lower investments and fixed cost.

The ranges show that there will probably be significant differences in the percentages for any cost element, depending on the nature of the industry and its business strategy. Two numbers, however, are crucial: gross margin and asset turnover

- No manufacturing business can continuously generate satisfactory profits if gross margins drop much below 40 percent.
- The 60 percent of sales allowed for total assets employed is also a key variable.

initiatives for succession planning, offering competitive remuneration packages, motivating people through empowerment, and linking compensation to performance.

Trim Non-manufacturing Overheads Non manufacturing overhead costs are often soft pedalled because those who incur these costs are the ones who must initiate cost- cutting measures. Further, while there are structured tools for managing manufacturing overheads, there are hardly any for managing non-manufacturing overheads. To trim non-manufacturing costs seriously consider the following measures : move the office away from the city centre, subcontract services to outside agencies, rely on video and audio conferencing, minimise the supporting staff, ask executives to fly economy class and stay in lower priced hotels, monitor the use of phones and airconditioning, use car pools, link people through high speed communication channels, replace paper communication with email , and encourage people to work out of home.

8.3 COST MANAGEMENT IN PRACTICE

Here are some examples of cost management in practice

- Benchmarking a company's performance with the best can be a sobering experience. Managers of Xerox Corporation were dismayed to discover how poor its U.S. performance was in relation to its Fuji-Xerox Japanese subsidiary. This revelation prompted a serious reexamination of its strategy and brought about dramatic improvement in its operations.
- Dell Computers is obsessed about its low cost model. As Tom Meredith, former CFO of Dell, put it: "At Dell we are very, very focused on maintaining our low-cost model and our low-cost position in the market place."
- At Oracle Corporation, CEO Larry Ellison led the way by announcing a $1 billion cost reduction goal. This electrified the organisation. As John Henley, CFO, Oracle put it: " While only a target, announcing over $1 billion cost reduction goal upfront was extremely motivating. It put tremendous pressure on the company. There was no turning back; we were publicly committed. The target, while risky and potentially embarrassing, galvanized the company, as did linking bonuses to reduced costs and improved margins."
- General Electric began its well-publicized Six Sigma initiative in 1996 to improve efficiency and reduce costs in all its internal

operations. According to the company, this program "has flourished to the point where it has produced more than $2 billion in benefits in 1999, with much more to come this decade."

- Reliance Industries Limited has set up its Jamnagar refinery at a capital cost which is about two-thirds of that of most of the refineries in the world.
- Hindustan Unilever Limited brought about an annual savings of ₹1000 crore in packaging.
- Within five years, ICICI moved its customers' interactions from branches to ATMs and Internet/mobiles and achieved one of the lowest cost-income ratios in the world. As CEO Kamat put it: "Banks like ICICI have built technological capability to handle large volumes of low-ticket transactions. Managing this difficult equation has given us a significant technology cost advantage compared to banks in developed countries."
- After its dismal performance in 2000 Tata Motors launched an aggressive cost management programme. Within a span of just few years it cut its annual costs by about ₹2000 crores. Thanks to this effort, its break-even point reduced from 60 percent to 35 percent of its capacity.

SUMMARY

- SCM blends three important themes drawn from the strategic management literature: value chain analysis, strategic positioning analysis, and cost driver analysis.
- The value chain of a firm is the linked set of value creating activities beginning with the basic raw material sources for component suppliers and ending with the end-use product delivered into the hands of the final customers.
- Michael Porter has defined two basic strategies for achieving competitive advantage, which is cost leadership and product differentiation.
- A cost leadership strategy strives to provide the same or better value to customers at a lower cost than what is offered by customers. A differentiation strategy seeks to provide customer something that is not offered by others.
- Daniel Riley divides cost drivers into two categories which is structural and executional.

- Life cycle costing is defined by CAM-I as "the accumulation of costs for activities that occur over the entire life-cycle of product, from inception to abandonment by the manufacturer and the customer.
- A target cost is a market-based cost. It is derived from a sales price necessary to capture a predetermined market share.
- Juran has proposed a framework for cost of quality (COQ) analysis that looks at four types of costs: prevention, appraisal, internal failure, and external failure.
- Value engineering is a systematic approach to a product design to improve its value, defined as the ratio of functionality to cost.
- Total cost management encompasses strategy as well as operations, covers all functions, spans different dimensions, and subsumes everything and everywhere.
- The four ingredients of a system of total cost management are : total cost consciousness, total cost measurement, total cost responsibility, and total cost improvement.
- An organisation committed to total cost management should pay heed to the following guidelines : (i) Understand your cost drivers. (ii) Focus on the entire value chain. (iii) Marry total cost management to business process reengineering. (iv) Do it right the first time as total quality management demands. (v) Exercise rigorous cost control at the design and product development stage. (vi) Team up with your vendors. (vii) Benchmark against the best. (viii) Resort to flexible manufacturing systems. (ix) Switch to just-in-time system. (x) Rely on activity based costing. (xi) Stretch your brands. (xii) Watch your adspend. (xiii) Rationalise your distribution and servicing structure. (xiv) Use infotech to cut costs. (xv) Manage HR costs effectively. (xvi) Trim non-manufacturing overheads.

APPENDIX 8A

FRUGAL INNOVATIONS IN EMERGING MARKETS

Clayton Christensen coined the term "disruptive innovation" for new products that slash prices and new processes that radically alter the ways goods are made and delivered. Today many of these disruptive innovations are occurring in emerging markets. They will have a bigger impact in the West than lean production, the last great disruptive management innovation from the East.

There are several reasons for this. First, the market for corporate control is more vibrant and liquid than what it was two decades ago. While Japanese and Korean giants grew organically, the champions from emerging markets are aggressively pursuing cross border mergers and acquisitions. Second, the export machines of emerging markets are powered by many sectors, whereas the Japanese export machine depended on a few sectors, notably cars and electronics. Third, emerging market companies are obsessed to develop new markets to make up for their slim profit margins. Fourth, Western companies, which for decades dismissed the capabilities of companies in the East, are now looking at emerging markets as a source of innovation and growth.

Indeed, the West is ripe for frugal innovation, as governments and consumers are battling with deficits and debt burdens. The age of profligacy is giving way to the age of frugality. Since emerging markets are repositories of "value-for-money strategies" they can lead "cost innovation" which involves redesigning both products and processes from scratch to take out costs as this is a much more productive strategy than traditional cost cutting. As an example, Dr. Devi Shetty, founder of Narayana Hrudalaya, is setting up a 2000-bed hospital in Cayman Islands, a short flight from Miami where surgery will be offered at half the price charged by American hospitals.

Innovation in India

According to C.K. Prahalad, any innovation in India must conform to four key principles:

- It should provide a new price-performance envelope so that the products and services are affordable to all.
- It should be scalable, given the size of the country and the market.
- It must be ecologically sustainable.
- It must represent world-class quality.

Outstanding examples of innovations in India are Jaipur Foot, Amul, ITC e-Chaupal, Aravind Eye Care, and Narayana Hrudalaya.

Part III

Financial System and Valuation Concepts

Part III

Financial System and Valuation Concepts

9. The Financial System
10. The Time Value of Money
11. Risk and Return

The Financial System

9

The purpose of this book is to help you make better financial decisions. These decisions are made in the context of a financial system that constrains and facilitates them.

The financial system comprises of a variety of intermediaries, markets, and instruments that are related in the manner shown in Exhibit 9.1. It provides the principal means by which savings are transformed into investments. Given its role in the allocation of resources, the efficient functioning of the financial system is critical to a modern economy.

While an understanding of the financial system is useful to all informed citizens, it is particularly relevant to business managers. They participate in decisions which can be taken better if they know what instruments are available for financing business projects, what services are offered by financial intermediaries, how do financial markets work, what signals are provided by financial prices and returns, where can surplus funds be parked, what regulatory infrastructure applies to the financial system, so on and so forth.

This chapter provides a conceptual framework for understanding how the financial system works, so that you can make better financial decisions. It is divided into six sections as follows:

- Functions of the financial system
- Financial assets
- Financial markets
- Financial market returns
- Financial intermediaries
- Regulatory infrastructure

EXHIBIT 9.1 ***The Financial System***

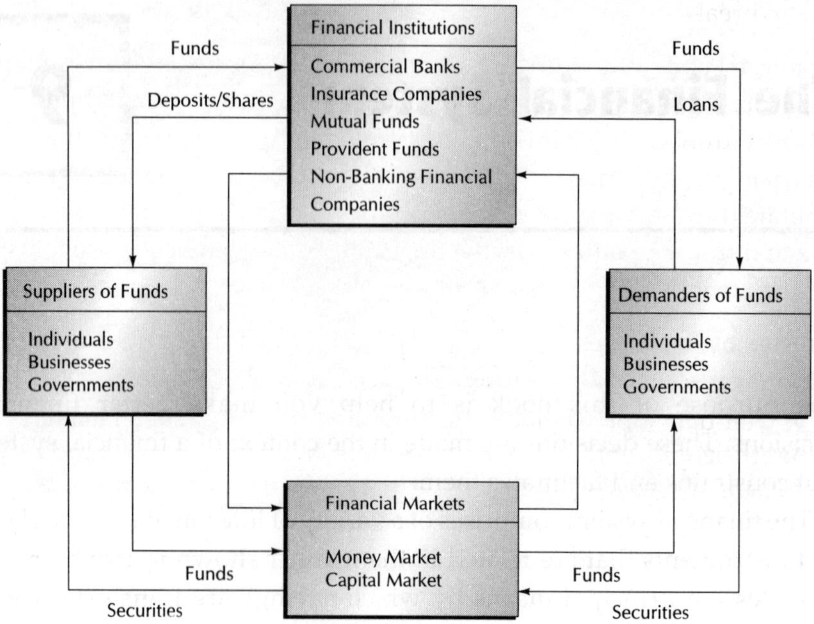

9.1 FUNCTIONS OF THE FINANCIAL SYSTEM[1]

The financial system performs the following interrelated functions that are essential to a modern economy:

- It provides a payment system for the exchange of goods and services.
- It enables the pooling of funds for undertaking large scale enterprises.
- It provides a mechanism for spatial and temporal transfer of resources.
- It provides a way for managing uncertainty and controlling risk.
- It generates information that helps in coordinating decentralised decision making.
- It helps in dealing with the incentive problem when one party has an informational advantage.

Payment System Depository financial intermediaries such as banks are the pivot of the payment system. Credit card companies play a supplementary role. To realise the importance of this function, simply

[1] Robert Merton *et al* (1994), *Cases in Financial Engineering* (Chapter 1), Harvard Business School Press.

look at the hardship and inconvenience caused when the payment system breaks down.

Pooling of Funds Modern business enterprises require large investments which are often beyond the means of an individual or even of hundreds of individuals. Mechanisms like financial markets and financial intermediaries, which are an integral part of the financial system, facilitate the pooling of household savings for financing business. If you look at it from the other side, the financial system enables households to participate in large indivisible enterprises.

Transfer of Resources The financial system facilitates the transfer of economic resources across time and space. As Robert Merton says:

> "A well-developed, smooth-functioning financial system facilitates the efficient life-cycle allocations of household consumption and the efficient allocation of physical capital to its most productive use in the business sector."
>
> "A well-developed, smooth-functioning capital market also makes possible the efficient separation of ownership from management of the firm. This in turn makes feasible efficient specialisation in production according to the principle of comparative advantage."

Risk Management A well-developed financial system offers a variety of instruments that enable economic agents to pool, price, and exchange risk. It provides opportunities for risk-pooling and risk-sharing for both household and business firms.

The three basic methods for managing risk are: hedging, diversification, and insurance. Hedging entails moving from a risky asset to a riskless asset. A forward contract, for example, is a hedging device. Diversification involves pooling and sub-dividing risks. While it does not eliminate the total risk, it redistributes it to diminish the risk faced by each individual. Insurance enables the insured to retain the economic benefits of ownership while laying off the possible losses. Of course, to do this a fee or insurance premium has to be paid.

Price Information for Decentralised Decision Making Apart from the manifest function of facilitating individuals and businesses to trade in financial assets, financial markets serve an important latent function as well. They provide information that helps in coordinating decentralised decision making. Robert Merton puts it thus:

> "Interest rates and security prices are used by households or their agents in making their consumption-saving decisions and in

choosing the portfolio allocations of their wealth. These same prices provide important signals to managers of firms in their selection of investment projects and financings."

Dealing with Incentive Problem When one party to a transaction has information that the other does not have, informational asymmetry exists. This leads to the problems of **moral hazard** and **adverse selection**, which are broadly referred to as agency problems. The nature of these problems may be illustrated with reference to insurance. A person who has taken a fire insurance policy is likely to become somewhat negligent. This is the moral hazard faced by the insurance company. A person who is more likely to experience fire losses will be inclined to take fire insurance. This is the adverse selection problem faced by the insurance company.

Financial intermediaries like banks and venture capital organisations can solve the problem of informational asymmetry by handling sensitive information discreetly and developing a reputation for profitable activity.

9.2 FINANCIAL ASSETS

Broadly speaking, an asset whether tangible or intangible is any possession that has value in exchange. A tangible asset is one whose value depends on its physical properties. Examples of tangible assets are land, buildings, machines, and vehicles. An intangible asset represents a claim to some future benefits. Financial assets, for example, are intangible assets as they represent claims to future cash flows. The terms financial asset, instrument, or security are used interchangeably.

The entity that offers future cash flows is called the **issuer** of the financial asset and the owner of the financial asset is called the **investor**. Here are some examples of financial assets:

- A 10-year bond issued by the Government of India carrying an interest rate of 7 percent.
- A 7-year non-convertible debenture issued by Reliance Industries Limited carrying an interest rate of 8 percent.
- A 3-year car loan provided by Citibank to an individual at an interest rate of 13 percent.
- Equity shares issued by NIIT to the general investing public through an initial public offering.
- A call option granted by Infosys Technologies Limited to an employee that gives him the right to buy 100 shares of Infosys at an exercise price of ₹1000.

Debt versus Equity Claims

A financial asset may entitle its owner to a fixed amount or a varying, residual amount. In the former case, the financial asset is called a debt security—the 10-year Government of India bond and the 7-year non-convertible debenture of Reliance Industries Limited are examples of debt security. In the latter case, the financial asset is referred to as an equity security—the equity shares issued by NIIT are an example of equity security.

Some securities straddle both the categories. Preference shares, for example, represent an equity claim that entitles the owner to get a fixed rupee amount. This payment, however, can be made only when the issuer earns a profit.

9.3 FINANCIAL MARKETS

A financial market is a market for creation and exchange of financial assets. If you buy or sell financial assets, you will participate in financial markets in some way or the other.

Functions of Financial Markets

Financial markets play a very pivotal role in allocating resources in an economy by performing three important functions:

1. Financial markets **facilitate price discovery**. The continual interaction among numerous buyers and sellers who participate in financial markets helps in establishing the prices of financial assets. Well-organised financial markets seem to be remarkably efficient in price discovery. That is why financial economists say: "If you want to know the value of a financial asset simply look at its price in the financial market.
2. Financial markets **provide liquidity** to financial assets. Investors can readily sell their financial assets through the mechanism of financial markets. In the absence of financial markets which provide such liquidity, the motivation of investors to hold financial assets will be considerably diminished. Thanks to negotiability and transferability of securities through the financial markets, it is possible for companies (and other entities) to raise long-term funds from investors with short-term and medium-term horizons. While

one investor is substituted by another when a security is transacted, the company is assured of long-term availability of funds.

3. Financial markets considerably **reduce the cost of transacting**. The two major costs associated with transacting are search costs and information costs. **Search costs** comprise explicit costs such as the expenses incurred on advertising when one wants to buy or sell an asset and implicit costs such as the effort and time one has to put in to locate a customer. **Information costs** refers to costs incurred in evaluating the investment merits of financial assets.

Classification of Financial Markets

There are different ways of classifying financial markets. One way is to classify financial markets by the type of financial claim. The **debt market** is the financial market for fixed claims (debt instruments) and the **equity market** is the financial market for residual claims (equity instruments).

A second way is to classify financial markets by the maturity of claims. The market for short-term financial claims is referred to as the **money market** and the market for long-term financial claims is called the **capital market**. Traditionally the cut off between short-term and long-term has been one year—though this dividing line is arbitrary, it is widely accepted. Since short-term financial claims are almost invariably debt claims, the money market is the market for short-term debt instruments. The capital market is the market for long-term debt instruments and equity instruments.

A third way to classify financial markets is based on whether the claims represent new issues or outstanding issues. The market where issuers sell new claims is referred to as the **primary market** and the market where investors trade outstanding securities is called the **secondary market**.

A fourth way to classify financial markets is by the timing of delivery. A **cash or spot** market is one where the delivery occurs immediately and a **forward or futures** market is one where the delivery occurs at a predetermined time in future.

A fifth way to classify financial markets is by the nature of its organisational structure. An **exchange-traded market** is characterised by a centralised organisation with standardised procedures. An **over-the counter market** is a decentralised market with customised procedures. Exhibit 9.2 presents a summary of the classification of financial markets.

EXHIBIT 9.2 ***Summary Classification of Financial Markets***

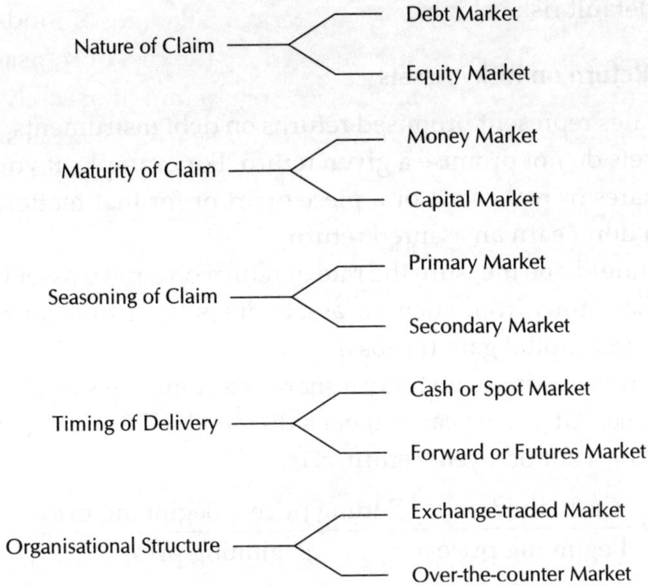

9.4 FINANCIAL MARKET RETURNS

Every day we are bombarded with news and reports on financial market returns like interest rates and equity returns over various media like newspapers, television, radio, and on-line computer service.

Interest Rates

An interest rate is a rate of return promised by the borrower to the lender. Different interest rates apply to different kinds of borrowing and lending. For example, the mortgage rate applies to a home loan whereas the term lending rate applies to a term loan for an industrial project.

The interest rate on any type of loan (or fixed income security) depends on several factors, the most important being the unit of account, the maturity, and the default risk. The **unit of account** is the medium such as rupees, dollars, pounds, yen, or gold in which payments are dominated. The **maturity** of a loan is the period over which it is paid back. **Default risk** is the possibility that the borrower may not honour his commitment to pay interest and principal as promised.

Generally, the interest rate is low when the unit of account depreciates very little due to of inflation, the maturity period is short, and the default risk is negligible. On the other hand, the interest rate is high when the unit of account depreciates due to inflation, the maturity period is long, and the default risk is high.

Rates of Return on Risky Assets

Interest rates represent promised returns on debt instruments. However, many assets do not promise a given return. For example, if you invest in equity shares or real estate or a piece of art or for that matter any risky asset you don't earn an assured return.

How should one measure the rate of return on a risky asset like equity stock? The return from such an asset comes from two sources : cash dividend and capital gain (or loss).

To illustrate, suppose you buy a share of a company's equity stock at a price of ₹100. After one year you get a dividend of ₹5 and the share price rises to ₹115. Your one-year return, *r*, is:

$$r = \frac{\text{Cash dividend}}{\text{Beginning price}} + \frac{\text{Ending price} - \text{Beginning price}}{\text{Beginning price}}$$

$$= \frac{5}{100} + \frac{115 - 100}{100}$$

$$= 5\% + 15\%$$

The first component is called the dividend income component (or dividend yield) and the second component is called the capital change component (or capital yield).

Inflation and Real Interest Rate

To make meaningful economic comparisons over time, the prices of goods and services must be corrected for the effects of inflation. A distinction has to be made between **nominal prices**, or prices in terms of some currency, and **real prices**, or prices in terms of purchasing power. This point may be illustrated with an example. Suppose the price of butter increases from ₹300 per kg in year 0 to ₹330 per kg in year 1. During this period the Consumer Price Index increases from 500 to 540, that is by 8 percent. So we say that even though the nominal price of butter increased by 10 percent, its real price rose by only 1.85 percent (1.10/1.08).

Just as a distinction is made between nominal and real prices, so too a distinction is made between nominal and real interest rates. The nominal interest rate on a bond is the rate of return in nominal terms whereas the real rate is the nominal rate corrected for the inflation factor. For example, if you earn a nominal rate of 15 percent in a year when the inflation rate is 10 percent, your real rate works out to ((1.15/1.10) – 1).

The general relationship between these rates is as follows:

$$1 + \text{Real rate} = \frac{1 + \text{Nominal rate}}{1 + \text{Inflation rate}}$$

Put differently,

$$\text{Real rate} = \frac{\text{Nominal rate} - \text{Inflation rate}}{1 + \text{Inflation rate}}$$

Determinants of Rates of Return

What factors determine the rates of return in a market economy? The principal factors are:

- Expected productivity of capital
- Degree of uncertainty characterising the productivity of capital
- Time preferences of people
- Degree of risk aversion

Expected Productivity of Capital Capital resources, comprising of tangible capital and intangible capital, help in producing goods and services. Tangible capital consists of physical assets like factories, mines, dams, railway networks, power stations, roads, and inventories. Intangible capital consists of non-physical assets like patents, copyrights, technical knowhow, and brand image.

The productivity of capital is expressed as a percentage per year, referred to as the return on capital. The expected return on capital varies across time and place. Inter alia, it depends on the state of technology, availability of other factors of production, and the strength of demand for goods and services produced by capital.

The returns earned by investors ultimately depend on how productive the capital is. Hence, the higher the expected productivity of capital, the higher the level of interest rates in the economy, and vice versa.

The Degree of Uncertainty about the Productivity of Capital The return on capital is subject to uncertainty stemming from a host of factors like technological changes, shifts in consumer preferences, erratic weather, policy changes, social unrest, and so on.

Equity securities have a claim to the profits earned on capital. Other things being equal, the higher the degree of uncertainty about the productivity of capital, the higher the risk premium required by equity investors, and vice versa.

Time Preferences of People People prefer current consumption to future consumption. Why? A principal reason is that they know that they are alive now and can enjoy current consumption whereas they are not sure whether they will be alive in future to enjoy deferred consumption. Other things being equal, the greater the preference of the society for current consumption, the higher the interest rate in the economy and vice versa.

Degree of Risk Aversion The return on capital in any economy, as we have learnt, is uncertain. The financial system provides a mechanism for partitioning the uncertain return on capital into different streams subject to different risks. Very broadly, it splits the uncertain return on capital into two components : a risk-free return earned on debt securities and a risky return earned on equity securities. The following relationship holds:

Risk-free return on debt securities < Expected return on capital
< Expected return on equity securities

Put differently, risk-averse people who want a risk-free return have to compensate risk-tolerant people for bearing risk in the form of risk premium. Other things being equal, the higher the degree of risk-aversion of the population, the higher will be the risk premium, and correspondingly the lower will be the risk-free rate.

9.5 FINANCIAL INTERMEDIARIES

Financial intermediaries are firms that provide services and products that customers may not be able to get on their own or get more efficiently on their own. A good example of a financial intermediary is a mutual fund that pools the financial resources of many people and invests in a basket of securities. The important products and services of financial intermediaries include checking accounts, savings accounts, loans, mortgages, mutual fund schemes, insurance contracts, credit rating, and so on.

Rationale for Financial Intermediaries

What is the rationale for financial intermediaries? Put differently, what are the benefits to individual investors when they invest indirectly through financial intermediaries rather than directly in operating companies? It seems that there are several advantages:

Diversification The pool of funds mobilised by financial intermediaries is invested in a broadly diversified portfolio of financial assets (stocks, money market instruments, bonds, and loans). Individual investors can scarcely achieve such diversification on their own. Remember that a diversified portfolio reduces risk.

Lower Transaction Cost The average size of a transaction of a financial institution is much higher than that of an individual investor. The transaction cost in percentage terms tends to decrease as the transaction size increases. Hence, financial intermediaries, compared to individual investors, incur lower transaction costs.

Economies of Scale Buying and holding securities (or for that matter granting loans and supervising them) calls for information gathering and processing and regular monitoring. These functions entail cost. Financial intermediaries, thanks to their bigger size and professional resources, enjoy economies of scale in performing these functions and hence they have a comparative advantage over individual investors.

Confidentiality Companies seeking funds or the continuing support of existing investors are required to disclose information that they like to keep confidential for competitive reasons. They would feel more comfortable in dealing with few financial intermediaries rather than numerous individual investors. Information shared with financial intermediaries may be kept confidential whereas information disclosed to numerous individual investors falls in the domain of public knowledge.

Signaling With greater professional expertise at their command, financial intermediaries can pick up and interpret signals and cues provided by companies which are likely to gravitate to them. In this manner, financial institutions perform a signaling function for the investing community.

Financial Intermediaries in India

The important financial intermediaries India, as elsewhere, are:

- Commercial banks
- Development financial institutions
- Insurance companies
- Small Savings, Provident Funds, and Pension Funds
- Mutual Funds
- Miscellaneous non-bank financial intermediaries

Commercial Banks

Commercial banks comprising of public sector banks, foreign banks, and private sector banks represent the most important financial intermediary in the Indian financial system.

The largest commercial Bank in India, the State Bank of India (SBI), was set up in 1955 when the Imperial Bank was nationalised and merged with some banks of the princely states. In 1969, in one fell swoop, the fourteen largest privately-owned commercial banks were nationalised. Subsequently, a few more privately-owned commercial banks were nationalised. As a result of these actions, public sector commercial banks, dominate the commercial banking scene in the country.

The changes in banking structure and control have resulted in (i) a wider geographical spread and deeper penetration of rural areas, (ii) a higher mobilisation of deposits, (iii) a reallocation of bank credit to priority activities, and (iv) a lower operational autonomy for bank management.

Foreign banks like Citibank have been in India for a long time and have been expanding their operations. The newest entrants on the commercial banking scene have been the private sector banks like HDFC Bank and ICICI Bank which were set up in mid-1990s in the wake of banking liberalisation. This segment has shown remarkable growth and vitality since the beginning.

Developmental Financial Institutions

Since independence a number of financial institutions have been set up to cater to the long term financing needs of various kinds. They are loosely referred to as developmental financial institutions. Inter alia, they include Industrial Financial Corporation of India (IFCI), Industrial Development Bank of India (IDBI), Industrial Credit and Investment Corporation of India (ICICI)—IDBI and ICICI have become commercial banks—Export Import Bank of India (EXIM Bank), Shipping Credit and Investment Corporation of India (SCICI), National Bank for Agriculture and Rural Development (NABARD), State Financial Corporations (SFCs), State Industrial Development Corporations (SIDCs), State Industrial Investment Corporations (SIICs), Small Industries Development Bank of India (SIDBI), Power Finance Corporation (PFC), Rural Electrification Corporation (REC), Indian Railway Finance Corporation (IRFC), National Housing Bank (NHB), and Infrastructure Leasing and Financial Services Limited (IL & FS).

Traditionally, these institutions focused on project finance; now they have broadened the scope of their activities. Earlier, they had a strong development orientation; now, they have a strong commercial orientation.

Insurance Companies

Till recently there were two insurance companies in India: the Life Insurance Corporation (LIC) of India and the General Insurance Corporation (GIC) of India (which is essentially a holding company that has four fully-owned subsidiary companies in its fold.). The Life Insurance Corporation of India, which provides life insurance, has massive resources at its command due to two reasons: (i) insurance policies usually incorporate a substantial element of savings, and (ii) insurance premiums are payable in advance. The subsidiaries of the General Insurance Corporation of India, which are engaged in the business of property insurance, too, have considerable resources with them because of the advance collection of insurance premiums.

With the liberalisation of the insurance sector many private sector players like ICICI—Prudential, Tata AIG, Birla Sunlife, and Metlife have set up insurance business in India.

Small Saving, Provident Funds, and Pension Funds

Post Office Savings Bank (POSB) Run by the Post and Telegraph Department on behalf of the Ministry of Finance, Government of India, the POSB is operated through the vast network of post offices. The POSB collects funds through various schemes like savings bank accounts, recurring and cumulative time deposit schemes, Public Provident Fund, and Kisan Vikas Patras.

Provident Funds A provident fund is a fund composed of the contributions made by an employee during his working life along with a matching contributions by the employer. The most important provident fund scheme in India is the Employees Provident Fund Scheme (EPF) which covers non-exempted establishments (industrial). For non-salaried earners a Public Provident Fund Scheme is available.

Pension Funds A pension fund is a pool of assets created with the contributions to a pension plan for financing pension plan benefits.

A pension fund is an intermediary that manages the assets and pays benefits to the retirees covered by the pension plan. Pension plans are sponsored by the government as an employer and private employers. The New Pension Scheme is open to even non-employers.

Mutual Funds

A mutual fund is a collective investment arrangement. In India three entities are central to a mutual fund: the **sponsor**, the **trust**, and the **asset**

management company. The sponsor promotes the mutual fund. The mutual fund is organised as a trust (with a board of trustees). It is, in a way, an umbrella organisation which floats various schemes in which the investing public can participate. The asset management company, organised as a separate joint stock company, manages the funds mobilised under various schemes.

Mutual funds have recorded a very impressive growth in India in the last several years. While there was only one mutual fund in India, viz. the Unit Trust of India, till 1986, presently there are a number of mutual funds in both the public sector as well as the private sector.

Miscellaneous Non-Bank Financial Intermediaries

In addition to the above mentioned financial intermediaries, the Indian financial system has a number of miscellaneous non-bank financial intermediaries, some of them engaged in fund—based activities and others provide a diverse range of financial services. The former may be called non-banking finance companies and the latter non-banking financial services companies.

Non-Banking Finance Companies (NBFCs) From the mid-1980s many non-banking financial companies have come into being in the public sector as well as the private sector—numerically, of course, most of them are in the private sector. Some of the well known non-banking finance companies are SBI Capital Markets, Kotak Mahindra Finance, Sundaram Finance, and Infrastructure Leasing and Finance Corporation.

Non-banking financial companies engage in a variety of fund-based as well as non-fund based activities. The principal fund-based activities are leasing, hire purchase, and bill discounting; the main non-fund based activities are issue management, corporate advisory services, loan syndication, and forex advisory services.

Non-Banking Financial Services Companies (NBFSCs) The important NBFSCs are merchant banks, venture capital funds, credit rating agencies, and depositories

Merchant Banks Merchant banks are firms which help businesses, governments, and other entities raise finances by issuing securities. They also facilitate mergers, acquisitions, and divestitures. The leading merchant banks in India are SBI Capital Markets, Enam Securities, JP Morgan, and ICICI Securities.

Venture Capital Firms Venture capital firms provide finance to high risk high return ventures. Young firms with limited managerial expertise often require advice in running the business in addition to finance. Venture capital firms provide managerial support as well as capital.

Credit Rating Agencies CRISIL, ICRA, and CARE are the important credit rating agencies. Apart from rating debt instruments, they provide opinions on Initial Public Offerings (IPOs) and corporate governance.

Depositories A depository is an institution which dematerialises physical certificates and facilitates the transfer of ownership through electronic book entries. The National Securities Depository Limited (NSDL), India's first depository, was set up in 1996. It was followed by the Central Securities Depositories Limited (CSDL).

9.6 REGULATORY FRAMEWORK

There are five entitities involved in regulating the financial sector : Ministry of Finance, Reserve Bank of India, Securities and Exchange Board of India, Insurance Regulatory and Developement Authority, and Pension Fund Regulatory and Developement Authority.

At present representatives of all these entities meet under the aegis of the High Level Coordination Committee (HLCC) which is currently a non-statutory body to debate and resolve the divergence in policy issues among different regulators. There is a proposal to give statutory powers to HLCC so that it can ensure compliance across markets.

From the point of view of corporates, the Reserve Bank of India and the Securities and Exchange Board of India are more important.

SUMMARY

- The financial system—consisting of a variety of institutions, markets, and instruments related in a systematic manner—provides the principal means by which savings are transformed into investments.
- The financial system provides a payment mechanism, enables the pooling of funds, facilitates the management of uncertainty, generates information for decentralised decision making, and helps in dealing with informational asymmetry.
- Financial assets represent claims against the future income and wealth of others. Financial liabilities, the counterparts of financial

assets, represent promises to pay some portion of prospective income and wealth to others.

- The important financial assets and liabilities in our economy are money, demand deposit, short-term debt, intermediate-term debt, long-term debt, and equity stock.
- A financial market is a market for creation and exchange of financial assets. Financial markets facilitate price discovery, provide liquidity, and reduce the cost of transacting.
- There are different ways of classifying financial markets. The important bases for classification are: type of financial claims, maturity of claims, new issues versus outstanding issues, timing of delivery, and nature of organisational structure.
- The interest rate on any type of loan (or fixed income security) depends on several factors, the most important being the unit of account, the maturity, and the default risk.
- Just as a distinction is made between nominal and real prices, so too a distinction is made between nominal and real interest rates. The nominal interest rate on a bond is the rate of return in nominal terms whereas the real rate is the nominal rate adjusted for the inflation factor.
- The principal determinants of rates of return in a market economy are : expected productivity of capital; degree of uncertainty characterising the productivity of capital; time preferences of people; and degree of risk-aversion.
- Financial intermediaries are firms that provide services and products that customers may not be able to get more efficiently by themselves in financial markets.
- Financial intermediaries seem to offer several advantages: diversification, lower transaction cost, economies of scale, confidentiality, and signaling benefit.
- The major financial intermediaries in India are commercial banks, developmental financial institutions, insurance companies, mutual funds, non-banking financial companies, and merchant banks.

The Time Value of Money 10

Money has time value. A rupee today is more valuable than a rupee a year hence. Why? There are several reasons:

- Individuals, in general, prefer current consumption to future consumption.
- Capital can be employed productively to generate positive returns. An investment of one rupee today would grow to $(1 + r)$ a year hence (r is the rate of return earned on the investment).
- In an inflationary period, a rupee today represents a greater real purchasing power than a rupee a year hence.

Many financial problems involve cash flows occurring at different points of time. For evaluating such cash flows, an explicit consideration of time value of money is required. This chapter discusses the method for dealing with time value of money and their applications to security valuation. It is divided into six sections which are as follows:

- Future value of a single amount
- Future value of an annuity
- Present value of a single amount
- Present value of an annuity
- Bond valuation
- Equity valuation

10.1 FUTURE VALUE OF A SINGLE AMOUNT

Suppose you have ₹1,000 today and you deposit it with a financial institution which pays 10 percent interest compounded annually, for a period of 3 years. The deposit would grow as follows:

		₹
First year:	Principal at the beginning	1,000
	Interest for the year	
	(₹1,000 × 0.10)	100
	Principal at the end	1,100
Second year:	Principal at the beginning	1,100
	Interest for the year	
	(₹1,100 × 0.10)	110
	Principal at the end	1,210
Third year:	Principal at the beginning	1,210
	Interest for the year	
	(₹1,210 × 0.10)	121
	Principal at the end	1,331

Formula

The general formula for the future value of a single amount is:

$$\text{Future Value} = \text{Present Value } (1 + r)^n$$

where r is the interest rate per year and n is the number of years over which compounding is done. The factor $(1 + r)^n$ is called the future value factor, $FV_{r,n}$. It is very tedious to calculate this factor unless you have a calculator. To reduce the tedium, tables are available. Exhibit 10.1 gives the value of this factor for several combinations of r and n. A comprehensive table is given in Appendix A at the end of this book.

Exhibit 10.1 *Value of $FV_{r,n}$ for Various Combinations of r and n*

n/r	*6 %*	*8 %*	*10 %*	*12 %*	*14 %*
2	1.124	1.166	1.210	1.254	1.300
4	1.162	1.366	1.464	1.574	1.689
6	1.419	1.587	1.772	1.974	2.195
8	1.594	1.851	2.144	2.476	2.853
10	1.791	2.159	2.594	3.106	3.707
12	2.012	2.518	3.138	3.896	4.817

Example If you deposit ₹1,000 today in a bank which pays 10 percent interest, compounded annually, how much will the deposit grow to after 8 years and 12 years?

The future value, 8 years hence, will be :

$$₹1{,}000\ (1.10)^8 = ₹1{,}000\ (2.144)$$
$$= ₹2{,}144$$

The future value, 12 years hence, will be :

$$₹1,000\ (1.10)^{12} = ₹1,000\ (3.138) = ₹3,138$$

Doubling Period

Investors commonly ask the question: How long would it take to double the amount at a given rate of interest? To answer this question, we may look at the future value factor table. Looking at Exhibit 10.1, we find that when the interest rate is 12 percent, it takes about 6 years to double the amount; when the interest rate is 6 percent it takes about 12 years to double the amount, so on and so forth. Is there a thumb rule which dispenses with the use of the future value factor table? Yes, there is one and it is called the Rule of 72. According to this thumb rule, the doubling period is obtained by dividing 72 by the interest rate. For example, if the interest rate is 8 percent, the doubling period is about 9 years (72/8). Likewise, if the interest rate is 4 percent, the doubling period is about 18 years (72/4). Though somewhat crude, it is a handy and useful thumb rule.

Shorter Compounding Periods

So far we have assumed that compounding is done annually. Now, consider the case where compounding is done more frequently. Suppose you deposit ₹1,000 with a finance company, which advertises that it pays 12 percent interest semi-annually—this means that the interest is paid every six months. Your deposit (if interest is not withdrawn) grows as follows:

First Six Months :	Principal at the beginning =	₹1,000.0
	Interest for 6 months = ₹1,000 × .12/2	₹60.0
	Principal at the end	₹1,060.0
Second Six Months :	Principal at the beginning	₹1,060.0
	Interest for 6 months ₹1,060 × .12/2	₹63.6
	Principal at the end	₹1,123.6

Note that if the compounding is done annually, the principal at the end of one year would be ₹1,000 (1.12) = ₹1,120.0. The difference of ₹3.6 (between ₹1,123.6 under semi-annual compounding and ₹1,120.0 under annual compounding) represents interest on interest for the second 6 months.

The general formula for the future value of a single cash amount when compounding is done more frequently than annually is:

$$\text{Future Value} = \text{Present Value } (1 + r/m)^{m \times n}$$

where r is the nominal annual interest rate expressed in decimals, m is the number of times compounding is done in a year, and n is the number of years over which compounding is done.

Example How much does a deposit of ₹5,000 grow to at the end of 6 years, if the nominal rate of interest is 12 percent and the frequency of compounding is 4 times a year? The amount after 6 years will be

$$₹5{,}000\ (1 + 0.12/4)^{4 \times 6} = ₹5{,}000\ (1.03)^{24}$$

$$= ₹5{,}000 \times 2.0328 = ₹10{,}164$$

Effective versus Nominal Rate

We have seen above that ₹1,000 grows to ₹1,123.6 at the end of the year if the nominal rate of interest is 12 percent and compounding is done semi-annually. This means that ₹1,000 grows at the rate 12.36 percent per annum. The figure of 12.36 per cent is called the **effective rate of interest**—the rate of interest under annual compounding, which produces the same results as that produced by an interest rate of 12 percent under semi-annual compounding.

The general relationship between the effective rate of interest and the nominal rate of interest is as follows:

$$r = (1 + k/m)^m - 1$$

where r is the effective rate of interest, k is the nominal rate of interest, and m is the frequency of compounding per year.

Example A bank offers 8 percent nominal rate of interest with quarterly compounding. What is the effective rate of interest?

The effective rate of interest is:

$$(1 + 0.08/4)^4 - 1 = 0.0824 = 8.24 \text{ percent}$$

Exhibit 10.2 gives the relationship between the nominal and effective rates of interest for different compounding periods. In general, the effect of increasing the frequency of compounding is not as dramatic as some would believe it to be—the additional gains dwindle as the frequency of compounding increases.

EXHIBIT 10.2 *Nominal and Effective Rates of Interest*

Nominal Rate %	Effective Rate %			
	Annual Compounding	Semi-annual Compounding	Quarterly Compounding	Monthly Compounding
8	8.00	8.16	8.24	8.30
12	12.00	12.36	12.55	12.68

10.2 FUTURE VALUE OF AN ANNUITY

An annuity is a series of periodic cash flows (payments and receipts) of equal amounts. The premium payments of a life insurance policy, for example, are an annuity. When the cash flows occur at the end of each period, the annuity is called a regular annuity or a deferred annuity. When the cash flows occur at the beginning of each period, the annuity is called an annuity due. Our discussion here will focus on a regular annuity—the formulae of course can be applied, with some modifications, to an annuity due.

Suppose you deposit ₹1,000 annually in a bank for 5 years and your deposits earn a compound interest rate of 10 percent. What will be the value of this series of deposits (an annuity) at the end of 5 years? Assuming that each deposit occurs at the end of the year, the future value of this annuity will be:

$$₹1,000\,(1.10)^4 + ₹1,000\,(1.10)^3 + ₹1,000\,(1.10)^2 + ₹1,000\,(1.10) + ₹1,000$$
$$= ₹1,000\,(1.464) + ₹1,000\,(1.331) + ₹1,000\,(1.21) + ₹1,000\,(1.10) + ₹1,000$$
$$= ₹6,105.$$

The time line of this annuity is shows in Exhibit 10.3.

Formula

In general terms, the future value of an annuity is given by the formula:

$$\text{Future value of an annuity} = \text{Constant Periodic flow}\left(\frac{(1+r)^n - 1}{r}\right)$$

where r is the interest rate per period and n is the duration of the annuity. The expression in the bracket is the future value annuity factor, $FVA_{r,n}$. Exhibit 10.4 shows the value of this factor for several combinations of r and n. A comprehensive table is given in Appendix A at the end of this book.

EXHIBIT 10.3 ***Time Line for an Annuity***

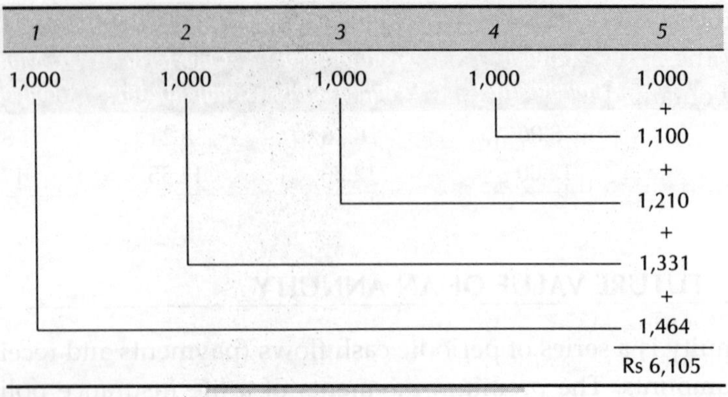

EXHIBIT 10.4 ***Value of $FVA_{r,n}$ for Various Combinations of r and n***

n/r	*6 %*	*8 %*	*10 %*	*12 %*	*14 %*
2	2.060	2.080	2.100	2.120	2.140
4	4.375	4.507	4.641	4.779	4.921
6	6.975	7.336	7.716	8.115	8.536
8	9.897	10.636	11.436	12.299	13.232
10	13.181	14.486	15.937	17.548	19.337
12	16.869	18.977	21.384	24.133	27.270

Example Four equal annual payments of ₹2,000 are made at the end of each year into a deposit account that pays 8 percent interest per year. What is the future value of this annuity at the end of 4 years?

$$₹2{,}000\ (FVA_{8\%,\ 4\ yrs}) = ₹2{,}000\ (4.507)$$

$$= ₹9{,}014$$

10.3 PRESENT VALUE OF A SINGLE AMOUNT

Suppose someone promises to give you ₹1,000 three year hence. What is the present value of this amount if the interest rate is 10 percent? The present value can be calculated by discounting ₹1,000 to the present point of time, as follows:

$$\text{Value three years hence} = ₹1{,}000$$

$$\text{Value two years hence} = ₹1{,}000\ (1/1.10)$$

$$\text{Value one year hence} = ₹1{,}000\ (1/1.10) \times (1/1.10)$$

$$\text{Value now (present value)} = ₹1{,}000\ (1/1.10) \times (1/1.10) \times (1/1.10)$$

Formula

The process of discounting, used for calculating the present value, is simply the inverse of compounding. The present value formula can be readily obtained by manipulating the compounding formula.

$$\text{Future Value} = \text{Present Value } (1 + r)^n$$

Dividing both the sides of the above equation by $(1 + r)^n$, we get,

$$\text{Present value} = \text{Future value} \times \left(\frac{1}{(1+r)^n}\right)$$

The factor $1/(1 + r)^n$ in the above equation is called the present value factor, $PV_{r,n.}$ Exhibit 10.5 gives the value of this factor for several combinations of r and n. A comprehensive table is given in Appendix A, at the end of the book.

Example Find the present value of ₹1,000 receivable 6 years hence, if the rate of discount is 10 percent.

The present value is:

$$₹1,000\ (PV_{10\%,\ 6}) = ₹1,000\ (0.564) = ₹564$$

EXHIBIT 10.5 *Value of $PV_{r,n}$ for Various Combinations of r and n*

n/r	*6 %*	*8 %*	*10 %*	*12 %*	*14 %*
2	0.890	0.857	0.826	0.797	0.770
4	0.792	0.735	0.683	0.636	0.592
6	0.705	0.630	0.564	0.507	0.456
8	0.626	0.540	0.467	0.404	0.351
10	0.558	0.463	0.386	0.322	0.270
12	0.497	0.397	0.319	0.257	0.208

10.4 PRESENT VALUE OF AN ANNUITY

Suppose you expect to receive ₹1,000 annually for 3 years, each receipt occurring at the end of the year. What is the present value of this stream of benefits if the discount rate is 10 percent? The present value of this annuity is simply the sum of the present values of all the inflows of this annuity:

$$₹1,000\ [1/1.10] + ₹1,000\ [1/1.10]^2 + ₹1,000\ [1/1.10]^3$$
$$= ₹1,000 \times 0.909 + ₹1,000 \times 0.826 + ₹1,000 \times 0.751$$
$$= ₹2486$$

The time line for this problem is shown in Exhibit 10.6.

EXHIBIT 10.6 ***Time Line of an Annuity***

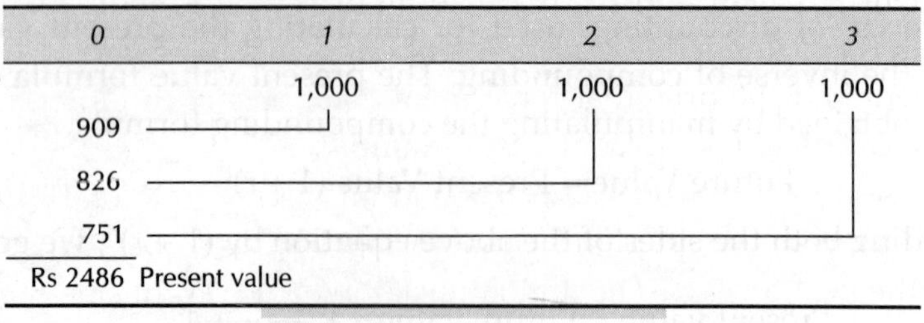

Formula

In general term, the present value of an annuity is given by the formula:

$$\text{Present value of an annuity} = \text{Constant Periodic flow} \times \left(\frac{1 - \dfrac{1}{(1+r)^n}}{r} \right)$$

where r is the interest rate per period and n, the duration of the annuity. The expression in the bracket is the present value annuity factor, $PVA_{r,n}$.

Exhibit 10.7 shows the value of this factor for several combinations of r and n. A more comprehensive table is given in Appendix A, at the end of this book.

EXHIBIT 10.7 ***Value of $PVA_{r,n}$ for Various Combinations of r and n***

n/r	6 %	8 %	10 %	12 %	14 %
2	1.833	1.783	1.737	1.690	1.647
4	3.465	3.312	3.170	3.037	2.914
6	4.917	4.623	4.355	4.111	3.889
8	6.210	5.747	5.335	4.968	4.639
10	7.360	6.710	6.145	5.650	5.216
12	8.384	7.536	6.814	6.194	5.660

Example What is the present value of a 4-year annuity of ₹10,000 discounted at 10 percent?

The $PVA_{10\%,4}$ is ₹3,170.

Hence, the present value of the annuity is

₹10,000 (3.170) = ₹31,700

Loan Amortisation Schedule

Most loans are repaid in equal periodic installments (monthly, quarterly, or annually), which cover interest as well as principal repayment. Such loans are referred to as **amortised loans**.

For an amortised loan we would like to know (a) the periodic installment payment and (b) the loan amortisation schedule showing the break up of the periodic installment payments between the interest component and the principal repayment component. To illustrate how these are calculated, let us look at an example.

Suppose a firm borrows ₹1,000,000 at an interest rate of 15 percent and the loan is to be repaid in 5 equal installments payable at the end of each of the next 5 years. The annual installment payment A is obtained by solving the following equation.

$$\text{Loan amount} = A \times \text{PVA}_{n=5,\, r=15\%}$$
$$1{,}000{,}000 = A \times 3.3522$$
$$\text{Hence } A = 298{,}312$$

The amortisation schedule is shown in Exhibit 10.8. The interest component is the largest for year 1 and progressively declines as the outstanding loan amount decreases.

EXHIBIT 10.8 ***Loan Amortisation Schedule***

Year	*Beginning Amount* (1)	*Annual Installment* (2)	*Interest* (3)	*Principal Repayment* (2)–(3) = (4)	*Remaining Balance* (1)–(4) = (5)
1	1,000,000	298,312	150,000	148,312	851,688
2	851,688	298,312	127,753	170,559	681,129
3	681,129	298,312	102,169	196,143	484,986
4	484,986	298,312	72,748	225,564	259,422
5	259,422	298,312	38,913	259,399	23*

a. Interest is calculated by multiplying the beginning loan balance by the interest rate.

b. Principal repayment is equal to annual installment minus interest.

* Due to rounding off error a small balance is shown.

Equated Monthly Installment

In the previous illustration we considered equated annual installments. In many cases, such as housing loans or car loans, however, the borrower has to repay the loan with interest in equated monthly installments (EMIs). The calculation of the EMI is similar to the calculation of the equated annual installment, except that the unit period is one month not one year.

The calculation of EMI may be illustrated with an example. Shyam takes a housing loan of ₹1,000,000 carrying an interest of 1 percent per month. The loan is to be repaid over 180 months.

What is the EMI?

The EMI is obtained by solving the following equation:

$$1{,}000{,}000 = A \times \text{PVA}_{n = 180,\, r = 1.00\%}$$

$$1{,}000{,}000 = A \times \frac{1 - \dfrac{1}{(1+r)^n}}{r}$$

$$1{,}000{,}000 = A \times \frac{1 - \dfrac{1}{(1.01)^{180}}}{.01}$$

$$1{,}000{,}000 = A \times 83.3217$$

$$A = \frac{1{,}000{,}000}{83.3217} = ₹12{,}002$$

Present value of a Perpetuity

A perpetuity is an annuity of infinite duration. In general terms:

$$\text{Present value of a perpetuity} = \text{Constant periodic flow} \left(\frac{1}{r}\right)$$

where r is the discount rate. The expression in the bracket is the present value perpetuity factor.

Put in words, it means that the present value perpetuity factor is simply 1 divided by the interest rate expressed in decimal form. Hence, the present value of a perpetuity is simply equal to the constant annual payment divided by the interest rate. For example, the present value of a perpetuity of ₹10,000 if the interest rate is 10 percent is equal to: ₹10,000/0.10 = ₹100,000. Intuitively, this is quite convincing because an initial sum of ₹100,000 would, if invested at the interest rate of 10 percent, provide a constant annual income of ₹10,000 forever, without any impairment of the capital value.

10.5 BOND VALUATION

Terminology

A bond or debenture (hereafter, referred to as only bond), akin to a promissory note, is an instrument of debt issued by a business or governmental unit. In order to understand the valuation of bonds, we need to be familiar with certain bond-related terms.

Par Value This is the value stated on the face of the bond. It represents the amount the firm borrows and promises to repay at the time of maturity. Usually, the par or face value of bonds issued by the business firms is ₹100 or ₹1,000.

Coupon Rate and Interest A bond carries a specific interest rate which is called the coupon rate. The interest payable to the bond holder is simply: par value of the bond × coupon rate. For example, the annual interest payable on a bond which has a par value of ₹100 and a coupon rate of 10 percent is ₹10 (₹100 × 10 percent).

Maturity Period Typically, corporate bonds have a maturity period of 3 to 10 years, whereas government bonds have maturity periods extending up to 20 years. At the time of maturity, the par (face) value plus perhaps a nominal premium is payable to the bondholder.

Basic Bond Valuation Model

As noted above, the holder of the bond receives a fixed annual interest payment for a certain number of years and a fixed principal repayment (equal to par value) at the time of maturity. Hence, the value of a bond is:

$$\text{Value} = I\,(\text{PVA}_{r,n}) + F\,(\text{PV}_{r,n})$$

where I is the annual interest payable on the bond, F is the principal amount (par value) of the bond, r is the required return on the bond, and n is the maturity period.

Example A ₹100 par value bond, bearing a coupon rate of 12 percent will mature after 8 years. The required rate of return on this bond is 14 percent. What is the value of this bond?

Since the annual interest payment will be ₹12 for 8 years, and the principal repayment will be ₹100 at the end of 8 years, the value of the bond will be:

$$\begin{aligned} V &= ₹12\,(\text{PVA}_{14\%,\,8\text{ yrs}}) + ₹100\,(\text{PV}_{14\%,\,8\text{ yrs}}) \\ &= ₹12\,(4.639) + ₹100\,(0.351) \\ &= ₹90.77 \end{aligned}$$

Example A ₹1,000 par value bond, bearing a coupon rate of 14 percent, will mature after 5 years. The required rate of return on this bond is 13 percent. What is the value of this bond? Since the annual interest payment will be ₹140 for 5 years and the principal repayment will be ₹1,000 at the end of 5 years, the value of the bond will be:

$$\begin{aligned} V &= ₹140\,(\text{PVA}_{13\%,\,5\text{ yrs}}) + ₹1{,}000\,(\text{PV}_{13\%,\,5\text{ yrs}}) \\ &= ₹140\,(3.517) + ₹1{,}000\,(0.543) \\ &= ₹1{,}035.4 \end{aligned}$$

Bond Valuation with Semi-annual Interest

Most of the bonds pay interest semi-annually. To value such bonds, we have to work with a unit period of six months and not one year. This means that the bond valuation equation has to be modified along the following lines:

- The annual interest payment I must be divided by two to obtain the semi-annual interest payment.
- The number of years to maturity must be multiplied by two to get the number of half-yearly periods.
- The discount rate has to be divided by two to get the discount rate applicable to half-yearly periods.

$$\text{Value} = I/2\,(\text{PVA}_{r/2,\,2n}) + F(\text{PV}_{r/2,\,2n})$$

Example A ₹100 par value bond carries a coupon rate of 12 percent and a maturity period of 8 years. Interest is payable semi-annually. Compute the value of the bond if the required rate of return is 14 percent.

The value of the bond is:

$$= 6\,(\text{PVA}_{7\,\%,\,16\text{ yrs}}) + 100\,(\text{PV}_{7\,\%,\,16\text{ yrs}})$$
$$= ₹6\,(9.447) + ₹100\,(.399)$$
$$= ₹90.6$$

Yield to Maturity

The yield to maturity (YTM) of a bond is the interest rate that makes the present value of the cash flows receivable from owning the bond equal to the price of the bond. Mathematically, it is the interest rate (r) which satisfies the equation:

$$P = \frac{C}{(1+r)} + \frac{C}{(1+r)^2} + \ldots + \frac{C}{(1+r)^n} + \frac{M}{(1+r)^n}$$

where P is the price of the bond, C is the annual interest, M is the maturity value, and n is the number of years left to maturity.

The computation of YTM requires a trial and error procedure. To illustrate this, consider a ₹1,000 par value bond, carrying a coupon rate of 9 percent, maturing after 8 years. The bond is currently selling for ₹800. What is the YTM on this bond? The YTM is the value of r in the following equation:

$$800 = \sum_{t=1}^{8} \frac{90}{(1+r)^t} + \frac{1000}{(1+r)^8}$$
$$= 90\,(\text{PVA}_{r,\,8\text{yrs}}) + 1{,}000\,(\text{PV}_{r,\,8\text{yrs}})$$

Let us begin with a discount rate of 12 percent. Putting a value of 12 percent for r we find that the right-hand side of the above expression is

$$₹90\ (PVA_{12\%,\ 8yrs}) + ₹1{,}000\ (PV_{12\%,\ 8yrs})$$
$$= ₹90(4.968) + ₹1{,}000(0.404)$$
$$= ₹851.1$$

Since this value is greater than ₹800, we may have to try a higher value for r. Let us try $r = 14$ percent. This makes the right-hand side equal to:

$$₹90\ (PVA_{14\%,\ 8yrs}) + ₹1{,}000\ (PV_{14\%,\ 8yrs})$$
$$= ₹90\ (4.639) + ₹1{,}000\ (0.351)$$
$$= ₹768.5$$

Since this value is less than ₹800, we try a lower value for r. Let us try $r = 13$ percent. This makes the right-hand side equal to:

$$₹90\ (PVA_{13\%,\ 8yrs}) + ₹1{,}000\ (PV_{13\%,\ 8yrs})$$
$$= ₹90\ (4.800) + ₹1{,}000\ (0.376)$$
$$= ₹808$$

Thus r lies between 13 percent and 14 percent. Using a linear interpolation in the range 13 percent to 14 percent, we find that r is equal to 13.2 percent.

$$13\% + (14\% - 13\%)\ \frac{808 - 800}{808 - 768.5} = 13.2\%$$

An Approximation If you are not inclined to follow the trial-and-error approach described above, you can employ the following formula to find the approximate YTM on a bond:

$$\text{YTM} \simeq \frac{C + (M - P)/n}{0.4M + 0.6P}$$

where YTM is the yield to maturity, C is the annual interest payment, M is the maturity value, P is the present value of the bond, and n is the years to maturity.

To illustrate the use of this formula, let us consider the bond discussed above. The approximate YTM of the bond works out to:

$$\text{YTM} = \frac{90 + (1000 - 800)/8}{0.4 \times 1000 + 0.6 \times 800} = 13.1\%$$

Thus, we find that this formula gives a value which is very close to the true value. Hence it is very useful.

The YTM calculation considers the current coupon income as well as the capital gain or loss the investor will realise by holding the bond to maturity. In addition, it takes into account the timing of the cash flows.

10.6 EQUITY VALUATION

As an equity shareholder, you expect to receive a stream of dividends from it, which extends indefinitely into the future. So the intrinsic value of an equity share may be expressed as follows:

$$\text{Value} = \frac{D_1}{(1+r)} + \frac{D_2}{(1+r)^2} + \ldots\ldots + \frac{D_n}{(1+r)^n} + \ldots\ldots$$

where $D_1, D_2, \ldots\ldots$ are the dividends receivable at the end of the year 1, year 2, and so on, and r is the rate of return required from the equity share.

The above equation is general enough to permit any pattern of dividends—constant, rising, declining, or randomly fluctuating. Two patterns are commonly employed in practice: constant dividends and constant growth of dividends.

If we assume that the dividends per share remains constant year after year, at a value of D, the dividend stream is a perpetuity. Hence, the value of the equity share will be:

$$\text{Value} = \frac{D}{r}$$

Dividends, however, tend to grow over time. If we assume that the dividend per share grows at a constant rate, denoted by the symbol g (growth rate), the value of the equity share is:

$$\text{Value} = \frac{D_1}{(1+r)} + \frac{D_1(1+g)}{(1+r)^2} + \frac{D_1(1+g)^2}{(1+r)^3} + \ldots\ldots$$

Note that, the dividend per share for year 2 is simply the dividend per share for year 1 multiplied by the growth factor $(1 + g)$, and so on.

If the above expression looks menacing, you can derive consolation from the fact that it simplifies to:

$$\text{Value} = \frac{D_1}{r - g}$$

Example The dividend paid by Ramesh Engineering Company is expected to grow at a rate of 8 percent per annum. The dividend expected on Ramesh's equity share a year hence is ₹2.00. What is the value of the share, if investors require a return of 18 percent on this share?

$$\text{Value} = \frac{2.00}{0.18 - 0.08} = ₹20.00$$

SUMMARY

- Money has time value. A rupee today is more valuable than a rupee a year hence.
- The general formula for the future value of a single amount is:

$$\text{Future value} = \text{Present value } (1 + r)^n$$

- According to the Rule of 72, the doubling period is obtained by dividing 72 by the interest rate.
- The general formula for the future value of a single cash amount when compounding is done more frequently than annually is:

$$\text{Future value} = \text{Present value } [1 + r/m]^{mn}$$

- An annuity is a series of periodic cash flows (payments and receipts) of equal amounts. The future value of an annuity is:

$$\text{Future value of an annuity} = \text{Constant periodic flow} \times [(1 + r)^n - 1)/r]$$

- The process of discounting, used for calculating the present value, is simply the inverse of compounding. The present value of a single amount is:

$$\text{Present value} = \text{Future value} \times 1/(1 + r)^n$$

- The present value of an annuity is:

$$\text{Present value of an annuity} = \text{Constant periodic flow} \times [1 - 1/(1 + r)^n]/r$$

- A perpetuity is an annuity of infinite duration. In general terms:

  Present value of a perpetuity = Constant periodic flow $[1/r]$
- The holder of a bond receives a fixed annual interest payment for a certain number of years and a certain principal repayment at the time of maturity. Hence, the value of the bond is:

$$\text{Value} = \text{Interest [Present value annuity factor]} + \text{Principal [Present value factor]}$$

- The yield to maturity (YTM) on a bond is the rate of return the investor earns when he buys the bond and holds it till maturity.
- The intrinsic value of an equity share is:

$$\text{Value} = \frac{D_1}{(1+r)} + \frac{D_2}{(1+r)^2} + \frac{D_3}{(1+r)^3} + \ldots\ldots$$

APPENDIX 10A

MICROSOFT EXCEL AS A FINANCIAL CALCULATOR

Excel is the greatest financial calculator ever made. All financial calculators have five financial keys, and Excel's basic time value functions are exactly analogous. The following table shows the equivalence between the calculator keys and Excel functions.

Purpose	*Calculator Key*	*Excel Function*
Solve for number of periods	N	**Nper (rate, pmt, pv**, *fv, type*)
Solve for periodic interest rate	I/Yr	**Rate (nper, pmt, pv**, *fv, type, guess*)
Solve for present value	PV	**PV (rate, nper, pmt**, *fv, type*)
Solve for annuity payment	PMT	**PMT (Rate, nper, pv**, *fv, type*)
Solve for future value	FV	**FV (Rate, nper, nper, pmt**, *pv, type*)

To solve a TVM problem in a financial calculator, you have to supply at least three of the variables. Likewise, you have to supply at least three of the arguments to each Excel function. Note that in the table, the bold function arguments are required whereas those in italics are optional.

Risk and Return

11

Risk is present in virtually every decision. When a production manager selects an equipment, or a marketing manager an advertising campaign, or a finance manager a portfolio of securities, all of them face uncertain cash flows. Assessing risks and incorporating the same in the final decision is an integral part of financial analysis.

The objective in decision making is not to eliminate or avoid risk—often it may be neither feasible nor necessary to do so—but to properly assess it and determine whether it is worth bearing. Once the risk characterising future cash flows is properly measured, an appropriate risk-adjusted discount rate should be applied to convert future cash flows into their present values.

To estimate the risk-adjusted discount rate—a task that we have glossed over so far—you should be able to measure and price financial risk. While the meaning of risk and return is grasped by almost every person, as a manager you need an explicit and quantitative understanding of these concepts and, more importantly, the nature of relationship between them. This chapter presents a framework that will help you in doing this. It is organised into five sections as follows:

- Risk as variability in return
- Risk reduction through diversification
- Measurement of market risk
- Relationship between risk and return
- Implications

11.1 RISK AS VARIABILITY IN RETURN

The rate of return on an asset for a given period (usually a period of one year) is defined as follows:

$$\text{Rate of return} = \frac{\text{Annual income} + \text{Ending price} - \text{Beginning price}}{\text{Beginning price}}$$

To illustrate, consider the following information about a certain equity stock:

* Price at the beginning of the year : ₹60.00
* Dividend paid at the end of the year : ₹2.40
* Price at the end of the year : ₹69.00

The rate of return on this stock is calculated as follows:

$$\frac{2.40 + (69.00 - 60.00)}{60.00} = 0.19 \text{ or } 19 \text{ per cent}$$

It is sometimes helpful to split the rate of return into two components, viz., current yield and capital gains/loss yield as follows:

$$\underbrace{\frac{\text{Annual income}}{\text{Beginning price}}}_{\textbf{Current yield}} + \underbrace{\frac{\text{Ending price} - \text{Beginning price}}{\text{Beginning price}}}_{\textbf{Capital gains/loss yield}}$$

The rate of return of 19 per cent in our example may be broken down as follows:

$$\frac{2.40}{60.0} + \frac{(69.00 - 60.00)}{60.00} = \underbrace{4 \text{ per cent}}_{\textbf{Current yield}} + \underbrace{15 \text{ percent}}_{\textbf{Capital gains yield}}$$

When you invest in a stock you know that its return can take various possible values. For example, it may be –5 percent, or 15 percent, or 35 percent. Further, the likelihood of these possible returns can vary.

Risk represents the variability of returns. It is commonly measured by variance or standard deviation of returns. To understand how it is calculated, let us consider the equity stock of Oriental Shipping. The return on the equity stock of Oriental Shipping depends on the state of the economy. The economy may be in three possible states, which is, boom, normal, and recession with probabilities of 0.30, 0.50, and 0.20. The probability distribution[1] of the rate of return on the equity stock of Oriental Shipping is given in Exhibit 11.1.

[1] The probability of an event represents the likelihood of its occurrence. When you define the probability of rate of return (or for that matter any other variable) remember that:

- The probability outcomes must be mutually exclusive and collectively exhaustive.
- The probability assigned to an outcome may vary between 0 and 1.
- The sum of the probabilities assigned to various possible outcomes is 1.

Based on the probability distribution of the rate of return, you can compute two key parameters, the expected rate of return and the standard deviation of rate of return.

EXHIBIT 11.1 ***Probability Distribution of the Rate of Return on Oriental Shipping Stock***

State of the Economy	*Probability of Occurrence*	*Rate of Return (%)*
Boom	0.30	50
Normal	0.50	20
Recession	0.20	–10

Given the probability distribution of the rate of return, we can calculate:

$$E(R) = \sum_{i=1}^{n} p_i R_i$$

$$\sigma = [\Sigma p_i \{R_i - E(R)\}^2]^{1/2}$$

where $E(R)$ is the expected rate of return, R_i is the return for the i th possible outcome, p_i is the probability associated with R_i, and σ is the standard deviation of return.

$E(R)$ and σ for the equity stock of Oriental Shipping are calculated in Exhibit 11.2.

EXHIBIT 11.2 ***Expected Return and Standard Deviation***

i. State of the Economy	*Oriental Shipping Stock* p_i	R_i	p_iR_i	$R_i - E(R)$	$(R_i - E(R))^2$	$p_i(R_i - E(R))^2$
1. Boom	0.30	50	15.0	27.0	729.0	218.7
2. Normal	0.50	20	10.0	–3.0	9	4.5
3. Recession	0.20	–10	–2.0	–33.0	1089.00	217.8
	$\Sigma p_iR_i = 23.0$				$\Sigma p_i(R_i - E(R))^2 = 441.0$	
	$\sigma = [\Sigma p_i(R_i - E(R))^2]^{1/2} = (441.0)^{1/2} = 21.0\%$					

11.2 RISK REDUCTION THROUGH DIVERSIFICATION

By combining risky securities in a portfolio, you can reduce risk. Consider the example given in Exhibit 11.3. Suppose there are two firms, Company A and Company B, operating in a Caribbean island , where tourism is the main industry. Company A makes and sells suntan lotion. It does well in sunny years but poorly in rainy years. The return on its stock will vary from 30% to –10%, depending on weather conditions, as shown in Exhibit 11.3.

Company B makes and sells disposable umbrellas. It does well during rainy years but poorly in sunny years. The return on its stock varies between 30 percent and –10 percent depending on weather conditions, as shown in Exhibit 11.3.

If you buy the stock of only Company A or Company B, you are exposed to a lot of risk. However, if you split your funds equally across the stocks of A and B, you can enjoy a stable return of 10 percent as shown in the last column of Exhibit 11.3.

Exhibit 11.3 ***Risk Reduction through Diversification***

Weather Conditions	*Return on Stock A, R_A*	*Return on Stock B, R_B*	*Return on Portfolio, R_P*
Sunny year	30%	–10%	0.5 (30) + 0.5 (–10) = 10%
Normal year	10%	10%	0.5 (10) + 0.5 (10) = 10%
Rainy year	–10%	30%	0.5 (–10) + 0.5 (30) = 10%

In this example, the returns on stocks A and B are perfectly negatively correlated. So, by appropriate diversification, it is possible to eliminate risk completely. In the real world, however, returns from most stocks tend to move together and hence it is not possible to eliminate risk completely. However, as long as returns on stocks do not move in a perfect lockstep, diversification reduces risk. In technical terms, diversification reduces risk if returns are not perfectly positively correlated.

The relationship between diversification and risk is shown graphically in Exhibit 11.4. When the portfolio has just one security, say stock 1, the risk of the portfolio, σ_p, is equal to the risk of single stock included in it, σ_1. As a second security-say stock 2- is added, the portfolio risk decreases. As more and more securities are added, the portfolio risk decreases, but at a decreasing rate, and reaches a limit. Empirical studies suggest that the bulk of the benefit of diversification, in the form of risk reduction, is achieved by forming a portfolio of about fifteen securities. Thereafter, the gain from diversification tends to be negligible.

Exhibit 11.4 ***Relationship Between Diversification and Risk***

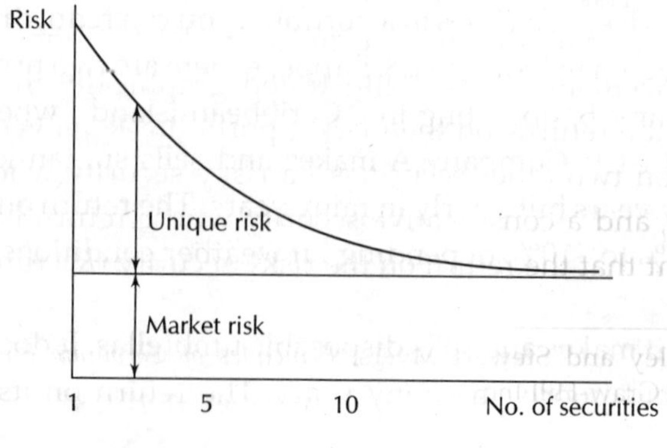

Market Risk versus Unique Risk

Notice that the portfolio risk does not fall below a certain level, irrespective of how wide the diversification is. Why? The answer lies in the following relationship which represents a basic insight of modern portfolio theory.

Total risk = Unique risk + Market risk

The **unique risk** of a security represents that portion of its total risk which stems from firm-specific factors like the development of a new product, a labour strike, or the emergence of a new competitor. Events of this nature primarily affect the specific firm and not all firms in general. Hence, the unique risk of a stock can be washed away by combining it with other stocks. In a diversified portfolio, unique risks of different stocks tend to cancel each other—a favourable development in one firm may offset an adverse happening in another and vice versa. Hence, unique risk is also referred to as diversifiable risk or unsystematic risk.

The **market risk** of a security represents that portion of its risk which is attributable to economy-wide factors like the growth rate of GNP, the level of government spending, money supply, interest rate structure, and inflation rate. Since these factors affect all firms to a greater or lesser degree, investors cannot avoid the risk arising from them, however diversified their portfolios may be. Hence, it is also referred to as systematic risk (as it affects all securities) or non-diversifiable risk.

11.3 MEASUREMENT OF MARKET RISK

The risk of a well-diversified portfolio, as we have seen, is represented by its market risk. As Brealey and Myers put it: " The risk of a well-diversified portfolio depends on the market risk of the securities included in the portfolio. Tattoo that statement in your forehead if you can't remember it any other way."[2]

The market risk of a security reflects its sensitivity to market movements. Different securities seem to display differing sensitivities to market movements. This is illustrated graphically in Exhibit 11.5 which shows the returns on the market portfolio (R_M) over time, along with returns on two other securities—a risky security whose return is denoted by R_r and a conservative security whose return is denoted by R_c. It is evident that the return on the risky security (R_r) is more volatile

---

[2] Richard Brealey and Stewart Myers, *Principles of Corporate Finance*, 4th ed., New York: McGraw-Hill Inc.

than the return on the market portfolio (R_M), whereas the return on the conservative security (R_c) is less volatile than the return on the market portfolio (R_M).

Exhibit 11.5 ***Behaviour of Returns over Time***

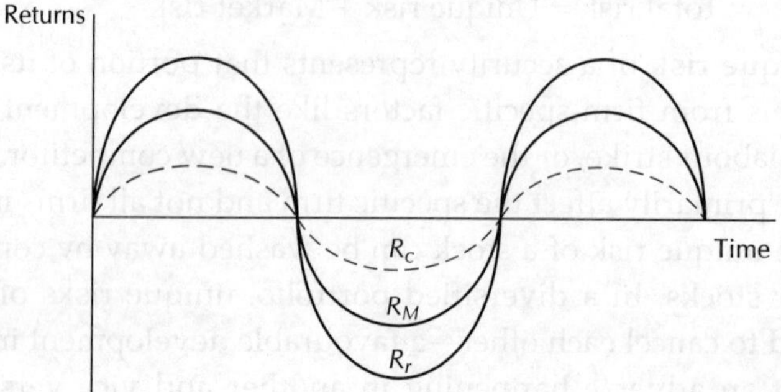

The sensitivity of a security to market movements is called beta (β). Beta reflects the slope of the linear regression relationship between the return on the security and the return on the market portfolio. It is the slope of the straight line in Exhibit 11.6.

Though not perfect, beta represents the most widely accepted measure of the extent to which the return on a security fluctuates with the return on the market portfolio. By definition, the beta for the market portfolio is 1. A security which has a beta of, say, 1.5 experiences greater fluctuation than the market portfolio. More precisely, if the market portfolio rises by 10 per cent, a security with a beta of 1.5 is expected to rise by 15 percent (1.5×10 percent). Conversely, if the market portfolio falls by 10 percent, the security is expected to fall by 15 percent. Individual security betas generally fall in the range 0.50 to 1.80 and rarely, if ever, assume a negative value.

Exhibit 11.6 ***Relationship between Security Return and Market Return***

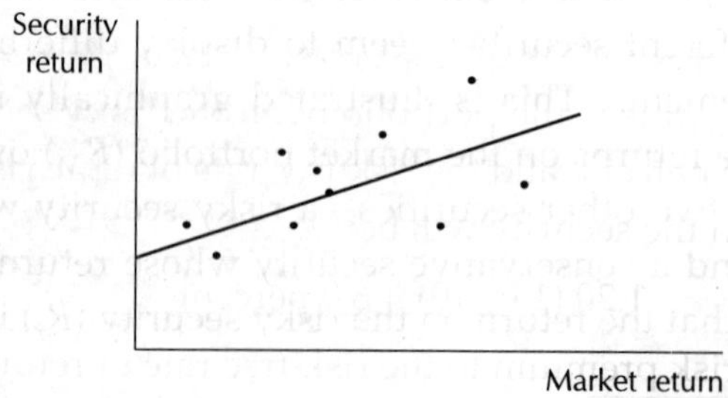

11.4 RELATIONSHIP BETWEEN RISK AND RETURN: THE CAPM

Before proceeding further, let us pause for a while and recapitulate the key elements of our story so far:

- Securities are risky because their returns are variable.
- The most commonly used measure of risk or variability in finance is standard deviation.
- The risk of a security can be split into two parts: unique risk and market risk.
- Unique risk stems from firm-specific factors, whereas market risk emanates from economy-wide factors.
- Portfolio diversification washes away unique risk, but not market risk. Hence, the risk of a fully diversified portfolio is represented by its market risk.
- The contribution of a security to the risk of a fully diversified portfolio is measured by its beta, which reflects its sensitivity to the general market movements.

Since beta is the relevant measure of a security's risk, the next logical question is: what is the relationship between the risk of a security, as measured by its beta, and its expected return?

According to the **capital asset pricing model (CAPM)**, which is an extension of the portfolio theory, risk and return are related as follows:

Expected rate of return = Risk-free rate of return + Risk premium

The above relation simply says that the expected rate or return on a security is equal to the risk-free rate of return (this is the rate of return earned on a risk-free investment like a bank deposit) plus the premium for bearing risk. What is this premium? It is equal to the following product:

$$\text{Beta of the security}\left(\text{Expected return on market portfolio} - \text{Risk-free rate of return}\right)$$

For example if the beta of a security is 1.20, the rate of return on market portfolio (this is the portfolio of all the risky securities listed in the market) is 15 percent, and the risk-free rate of return is 10 percent, the risk premium on the security will be:

$$1.20\,(15 - 10) = 6.0 \text{ percent}$$

Adding this risk premium to the risk-free rate of return of 10 percent, we find that the expected rate of return on the security works out to:

$$10 \text{ percent} + 6 \text{ percent} = 16 \text{ percent}$$

Exhibit 11.7 graphically shows the relationship between beta (systematic risk) and the expected rate of return. Called the security market line, this graphical portrayal clearly highlights the following points.

- As the beta of a security (or portfolio) increases, the expected rate of return from it increases.
- If the beta of a security (or portfolio) is zero, it will earn a rate of return equal to the risk-free rate of return.
- If the beta of a security (or portfolio) is unity, its expected rate of return will be equal to the general rate of return on equity stocks.
- A number of different expected rates of return are attainable by suitably adjusting the beta of the security (or portfolio).

EXHIBIT 11.7 ***Relationship between Beta (Market Risk) and Expected Rate of Return***

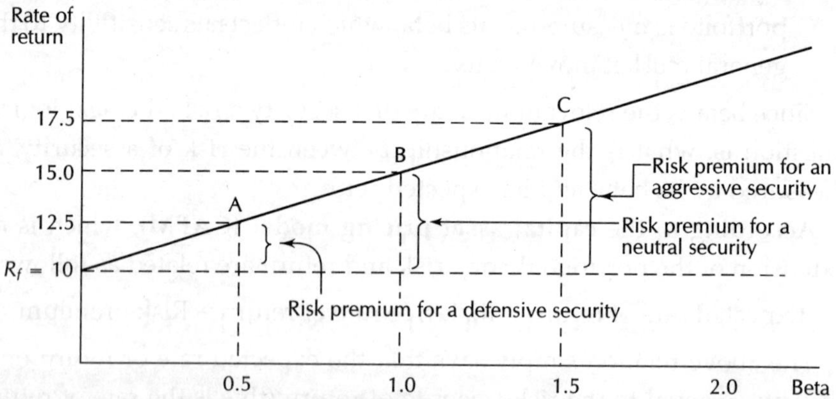

11.5 IMPLICATIONS

We have learnt about the components of risk, consequences of diversification, and the relationship between risk and return. The implications of our discussion are as follows.

1. Diversification in important. Owning a portfolio dominated by a small number of stocks is a risky proposition.
2. While diversification is desirable, an excess of it is not. There is hardly any gain in extending diversification beyond 10 to 15 stocks.
3. The performance of a well-diversified portfolio more or less mirrors the performance of the market as a whole.

4. In a well-ordered market, investors are compensated primarily for bearing market risk, but not unique risk. To earn a higher expected rate on return, one has to bear a higher degree of market risk.

SUMMARY

- Portfolio diversification washes away unique risk, but not market risk. Hence the risk of a fully diversified portfolio is its market risk.
- The contribution of a security to the risk of a fully diversified portfolio is measured by its beta, which reflects its sensitivity to the general market movements.
- According to the capital asset pricing model, risk and return are related as follows:

$$\text{Expected rate of return} = \text{Risk-free rate} + \text{Beta}\left(\text{Expected return on market portfolio} - \text{Risk-free rate}\right)$$

- In a well-ordered market, investors are compensated primarily for bearing market risk, but not unique risk. To earn a higher expected rate of return, one has to bear a higher degree of market risk.

APPENDIX 11A

BETA VALUES OF NIFTY JUNIOR STOCKS

Company	*Beta*	*Company*	*Beta*	*Company*	*Beta*
Asian Paints Ltd	0.65	ICICI Bank Ltd	1.29	Power Grid Corp of India Ltd	0.61
Axis Bank Ltd	1.19.	IndusInd Bank Ltd	1.34	Reliance Industries Ltd	1.09
Bajaj Finance Ltd	1.42	Infosys Ltd	0.78	State Bank of India	1.29
Bajaj Finserv Ltd	1.35	ITC Ltd	0.87	Sun Pharmaceutical Industries Ltd	0.73
Bharti Airtel Ltd	0.84	Kotak Mahindra Bank Ltd	1.16	Tata Consultancy Services Ltd	0.65
Dr Reddy's Laboratories Ltd	0.40	Larsen & Toubro Ltd	1.06	Tata Steel Ltd	1.44

(*Contd.*)

(*Contd.*)

Company	*Beta*	*Company*	*Beta*	*Company*	*Beta*
HCL Technologies Ltd	0.83	Mahindra & Mahindra Ltd	1.02	Tech Mahindra Ltd	1.02
HDFC Bank Ltd	1.08	Maruti Suzuki India Ltd	0.73	Titan Co Ltd	1.05
Hindustan Unilever Ltd	0.49	Nestle India Ltd	0.43	UltraTech Cement Ltd	0.88
Housing Development Finance Corp	1.27	NTPC Ltd	0.61	Wipro Ltd	0.97

* Beta are calculated for the period 01-Aug-2015 to 29-July-2016

Part IV

Financial Management

12. Financial Management: An Overview
13. Capital Budgeting
14. Financing Strategy
15. Sources of Finance
16. Working Capital Management

PART IV

Financial Management: An Overview

12

Suppose you are planning to start your own business. No matter what the nature of your proposed business is and how it is organised, you will have to address the following questions:

- What capital investments should you make? That is, what kinds of real estate, machineries, and R&D programmes should you invest in?
- How will you raise money to pay for the proposed capital investments? That is, what will be the mix of equity and debt in your financing plan?
- How will you handle the day-to-day financial activities like collecting your receivables and paying your suppliers?

While these are not the only concerns of financial management, they are certainly the central ones.

This chapter provides a broad overview of the field of financial management. It is organised into eight sections as follows:

- Financial decisions in a firm
- Goal of financial management
- The fundamental principle of finance
- Risk-return tradeoff
- Forms of business organisation
- Agency problem
- Organisation of the finance function
- Relationship of finance to economics and accounting

12.1 FINANCIAL DECISIONS IN A FIRM

As mentioned at the outset, there are three broad areas of financial decision making viz., capital budgeting, capital structure, and working capital management.

Capital Budgeting

The first and perhaps the most important decision that any firm has to make is to define the business or businesses that it wants to be. This decision has a significant bearing on how capital is allocated in the firm.

Once the managers of a firm choose the business or businesses they want to be in, they have to develop a plan to invest in buildings, machineries, equipments, research and development, godowns, showrooms, distribution network, information infrastructure, brands, and other long-lived assets. This is the capital budgeting process.

Considerable managerial time, attention, and energy is devoted to identify, evaluate, and implement investment projects. When you look at an investment project from the financial point of view, you should focus on the magnitude, timing, and riskiness of cash flows associated with it. In addition, consider the options embedded in the investment projects.

Capital Structure

Once a firm has decided on the investment projects it wants to undertake, it has to figure out ways and means of financing them.

The key issues in capital structure decision are: What is the optimal debt-equity ratio for the firm? Which specific instruments of equity and debt finance should the firm employ? Which capital markets should the firm access? When should the firm raise finances? At what price should the firm offer its securities?

An allied issue is the dividend decision of the firm. What is the optimal dividend payout ratio for the firm? Should the firm buyback its own shares?

Capital structure and dividend decisions should be guided by considerations of cost and flexibility, in the main. The objective should be to minimise the cost of financing without impairing the ability of the firm to raise finances required for value creating investment projects.

Working Capital Management

Working capital management, also referred to as short-term financial management, refers to the day-to-day financial activities that deal with current assets (inventories, debtors, short-term holdings of marketable securities, cash, etc.) and current liabilities (short-term debt, trade creditors, accruals, provisions, etc.).

The key issues in working capital management are : What is the optimal level of inventory for the operations of the firm? Should the firm grant credit to its customers and, if so, on what terms? How much cash should the firm carry on hand? Where should the firm invest its temporary cash surpluses? What sources of short-term finance are appropriate for the firm?

12.2 GOAL OF FINANCIAL MANAGEMENT

Finance theory rests on the premise that managers should manage their firm's resources with the objective of enhancing the firm's market value. This goal has been eloquently defended by distinguished finance scholars, economists, and practitioners. Here is a sampling of their views:

> "In a market-based economy which recognises the rights of private property, the only social responsibility of business is to create value and do so legally and with integrity. It is a profound error to view increases in a company's value as a concern just for its shareholders. Enlightened managers and public officials recognise that increases in stock prices reflect improvement in competitiveness—an issue which affects everyone who has a stake in the company or economy"[1].
>
> "The quest for value drives scarce resources to their most productive uses and their most efficient users. The more effectively resources are deployed, the more robust will be the economic growth and the rate of improvement in our standard of living. Adam Smith's 'invisible hand' is at work when investors' private gain is a public value"[2].

You may ask why are we overlooking the interests of customers, employees, and suppliers. No company can succeed unless it offers value for money to its customers, provides satisfactory employment conditions to its employees, and treats its suppliers fairly. Hence the question of neglecting the interests of these constituencies to promote the welfare of shareholders simply does not arise. More value for shareholders does

---

[1] Alfred Rappaport, *Let's Let Business Be Business* New York Times, February 4, 1990.

[2] Bennett Stewart, *The Quest for Value : A Guide to Senior Management*, New York: Harper & Row, 1991

not imply less value for customers, employees, or suppliers. On the contrary, only by focusing on creating value for its shareholders can a firm ensure that it has durable and mutually beneficial relationships with their customers, employees, and suppliers.

12.3 THE FUNDAMENTAL PRINCIPLE OF FINANCE

The key question that you have to ask before making a business decision is: Will the decision raise the market value of the firm? To answer this question, let us look at the fundamental principle of finance:

A business proposal – regardless of whether it is a new investment or acquisition of another company or a restructuring initiative – raises the value of the firm only if the present value of the future stream of net cash benefits expected from the proposal is greater than the initial cash outlay required to implement the proposal.

The difference between the present value of future cash benefits and the initial outlay represents the net present value or NPV of the proposal:

Net present value = Present value of future cash benefits – Initial cash outlay

Note that the costs and benefits of a business proposal have to be measured in cash. As shown in Exhibit 12.1, investors who finance a proposal invest cash and are hence interested only in cash returns.

Exhibit 12.1 ***Cash Alone Matters***

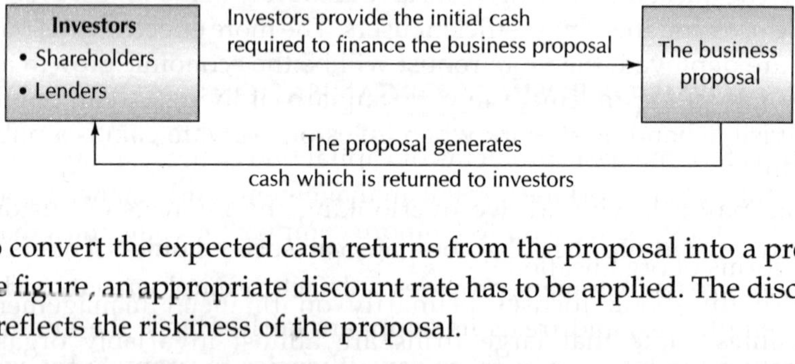

To convert the expected cash returns from the proposal into a present value figure, an appropriate discount rate has to be applied. The discount rate reflects the riskiness of the proposal.

12.4 RISK-RETURN TRADEOFF

A firm has to choose between alternative courses of action. Should the firm set up a plant which has a capacity of one million tons or two million tons? Should the debt-equity ratio of the firm be 2:1 or 1:1? Should the firm pursue a generous credit policy or niggardly credit policy? Should the firm carry a large inventory or a small inventory?

The alternative courses of action typically have different risk-return implications. A large plant may have a higher expected return and a higher risk exposure, whereas a small plant may have a lower expected return and a lower risk exposure. A higher debt-equity ratio, compared to a lower debt-equity ratio, may reduce the cost of capital but expose the firm to greater risk. A 'hot' stock, compared to a defensive stock, may offer a higher expected return but also a greater possibility of loss.

In general, when you make a financial decision, you have to answer the following questions: What is the expected return? What is the risk exposure? Given the risk-return characteristics of the decision, how would it influence value? Exhibit 12.2 shows schematically the relationship between the key financial decisions, return, risk, and market value.

EXHIBIT 12.2 ***Decisions, Return, Risk, and Market Value***

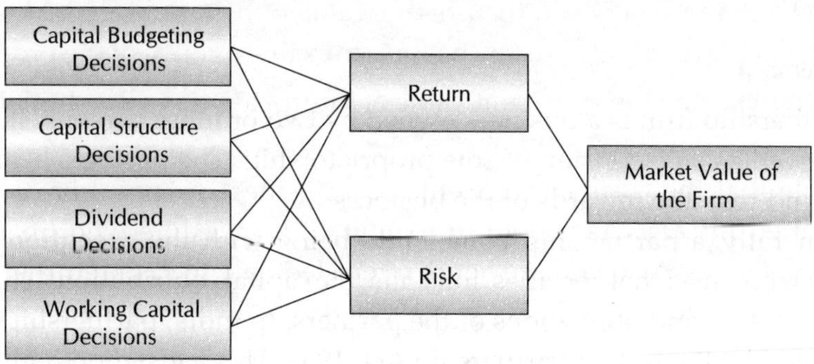

12.5 FORMS OF BUSINESS ORGANISATION

All firms face the basic problems of capital budgeting, capital structure, dividend policy, working capital management, and financial control. However, these issues tend to be more complex for companies than for other forms of organisation.

Since this book focuses primarily on financial management of companies—note that large firms are almost invariably organised as companies—you should know how a company differs from other forms of business organisation like sole proprietorship and partnership.

Sole Proprietorship

A sole proprietorship firm is a business owned by a single person. This is the simplest form of business, subject to minimal regulation. You can set up a sole proprietorship firm by obtaining a license—if the same is required for the business you want to engage in—and throwing open your doors. Thanks to its simplicity, most businesses begin as sole proprietorship firms. No wonder there are more sole proprietorships than any other form of organisation.

From a legal and tax point of view, a sole proprietorship firm has no separate status apart from its owner. The owner realises all the profits and bears all the losses. The owner indeed has unlimited personal liability for the debts of the business. By the same token, there is no distinction between business and personal income and all business income is taxed as personal income.

The equity capital of a sole proprietorship is limited to the personal wealth of the owner. Hence such firms often cannot grow beyond a point for want of capital. It may be somewhat difficult to transfer the ownership of a sole proprietorship firm as it involves sale of the entire business to the buyer.

Partnership

A partnership firm is a business owned by two or more persons. It may be viewed as an extension of sole proprietorship. The partners bear the risks and reap the rewards of the business.

Generally, a partnership comes into being with the execution of a partnership deed that specifies, inter alia, the capital contributions, shares, rights, duties, and obligations of the partners. In India, partnerships are governed by the Indian Partnership Act, 1932. This legislation regulates the relationship between the partners inter se as well as between the partners and the parties dealing with the partnership firm.

While a partnership firm can benefit from the varied experience and expertise of the partners and draw on their combined capital resources, its advantages and disadvantages are more or less similar to that of a sole proprietorship firm.

Company

A company is collectively owned by the shareholders who entrust the task of management to their elected representatives called the directors. The salient features of a company are as follows:

- The company is a distinct legal "person", separate from its owners, the shareholders. It can own assets, incur liabilities, enter into contracts, sue, and be sued in its name.

- The liability of the shareholders of a company is limited to the share capital subscribed to by them. Once this amount is fully paid up, they have no further obligation.
- A company must pay taxes on its profits. In addition, it has to pay taxes on dividend distribution. The dividend received by shareholders is tax-free in their hands.
- Setting up and managing a company is more complicated than setting up and managing other forms of organisation because companies are governed by the Indian Companies Act, a very elaborate and comprehensive piece of legislation.

A company may be a private limited company or a public limited company. The key differences between them are as follows:

- A private limited company must have at least two shareholders (members) whereas a public limited company must have at least seven shareholders. While there is no limit on the number of shareholders of a public limited company, the number of shareholders of a private company cannot exceed fifty.
- A public limited company invites members of the public to subscribe to its shares, whereas a private limited company cannot do so.
- A public limited company permits free transfer of shares whereas a private limited company usually imposes restrictions on such transfers.

On the whole, the public limited company is the most appropriate form of business organisation, except, of course when the business is small. The reasons are: (a) The risk to investors is limited. (b) The potential for growth is immense because of access to substantial funds. (c) Investors enjoy liquidity because of free transferability of securities. (d) The scope for employing talented managers is considerable.

12.6 AGENCY PROBLEM

In proprietorships and partnerships, owners are actively involved in management. But in companies, particularly large public limited companies, owners typically are not active managers. Instead, they entrust this responsibility to professional managers who may have little or no equity stake in the firm. There are several reasons for the separation of ownership and management in such companies:

- Most enterprises require large sums of capital to achieve economies of scale. Hence it becomes necessary to pool capital from thousands or even hundreds of thousands of owners. It is impractical for many owners to participate actively in management.

- Professional managers may be more qualified to run the business because of their technical expertise, experience, and personality traits.
- Separation of ownership and management permits unrestricted change in owners through share transfers without affecting the operations of the firm. It ensures that the 'know-how' of the firm is not impaired, despite changes in ownership.
- Given economic uncertainties, investors would like to hold a diversified portfolio of securities. Such diversification is achievable only when ownership and management are separated.

While there are compelling reasons for separation of ownership and management, a separated structure leads to a possible conflict of interest between managers and shareholders. Though managers are the agents of shareholders they are likely to act in ways that may not maximise the welfare of shareholders.

In practice, managers enjoy substantial autonomy and hence have a natural inclination to pursue their own goals. To prevent from being dislodged from their position, managers may try to achieve a certain acceptable level of performance as far as shareholder welfare is concerned. However, beyond that their personal goals like presiding over a big empire, pursuing their pet projects, diminishing their personal risks, and enjoying generous compensation and lavish perquisites tend to acquire priority over shareholder welfare.

The lack of perfect alignment between the interests of managers and shareholders results in agency costs which may be defined as the difference between the value of an actual firm and value of a hypothetical firm in which management and shareholder interests are perfectly aligned.

To mitigate the agency problem, effective monitoring has to be done and appropriate incentives have to be offered. Monitoring may be done by bonding managers, by auditing financial statements, by limiting managerial discretion in certain areas, by reviewing the actions and performance of managers periodically, and so on.

Incentives may be offered in the form of cash bonuses and perquisites that are linked to certain performance targets, stock options that grant managers the right to purchase equity shares at a certain price thereby giving them a stake in ownership, performance shares given when certain goals are achieved, and so on.

12.7 ORGANISATION OF THE FINANCE FUNCTION

Financial management is in many ways an integral part of the jobs of managers who are involved in planning, allocation of resources, and control. The responsibilities for financial management are dispersed throughout the organisation. For example:

- The engineer, who proposes a new plant, shapes the investment policy of the firm.
- The marketing analyst provides inputs in the process of forecasting and planning.
- The purchase manager influences the level of investment in inventories.
- The sales manager has a say in the determination of the receivables policy.
- Departmental managers, in general, are important links in the financial control system of the firm.

There are, however, many tasks of financial management and allied areas (like accounting) which are specialised in nature and which are attended to by specialists. These tasks and their typical distribution between the two key financial officers of the firm, the treasurer and the controller[3], are shown in Exhibit 12.3. Note that the treasurer is responsible mainly for financing and investment activities and the controller is concerned primarily with accounting and control.

EXHIBIT 12.3 ***Functions of the Treasurer and the Controller***

Treasurer	*Controller*
Obtaining finance	Financial accounting
Banking relationship	Internal auditing
Cash management	Taxation
Credit administration	Management accounting
Capital budgeting	and control

Typically, the head of finance who may be designated as Chief Finance Officer or as Director (Finance) supervises the work of the treasurer and the controller. In turn, these officers are assisted by several specialist managers working under them.

[3] Even though a firm may not have two separate financial officers designated as treasurer and controller, it is helpful to distinguish the functions of treasurership and controllership.

The finance officers, in addition to their specialised responsibility, have significant involvement in injecting financial discipline in corporate management processes. They are responsible for emphasising the need for rationality in the use of funds and for monitoring the operations of the firm to achieve desired financial results. In this respect the tasks of financial officers have assumed new dimensions. Instead of just looking after routine financing and accounting activities, they guide and participate in the tasks of planning, funds allocation, and control so that the financial point of view is sufficiently emphasised in the process of corporate management.

SUMMARY

- There are three broad areas of financial decision making, viz., capital budgeting, capital structure, and working capital management.
- Finance theory, in general, rests on the premise that the goal of financial management should be to maximise the wealth of shareholders.
- A business proposal raises the value of the firm only if the present value of the future stream of net cash benefits expected from the proposal is greater than the initial cash outlay required to implement the proposal.
- A confluence of forces appears now to be prodding Indian companies to accord greater importance to the goal of shareholder wealth maximisation.
- In general, when you take a financial decision, you have to answer the following questions: What is the expected return? What is the risk exposure? Given the risk-return characteristics of the decision, how would it influence value?
- The important forms of business organisation are: sole proprietorship, partnership, private limited company, and public limited company. While each form of organisation has certain advantages and limitations, the public limited company form of organisation generally appears to be the most appropriate form from the point of view of shareholder wealth maximisation.
- While there are compelling reasons for separation of ownership and management, a separated structure leads to a possible conflict of interest between managers and shareholders.

- The lack of perfect alignment between the interests of managers and shareholders results in the agency problem. To mitigate the agency problem, effective monitoring has to be done and appropriate incentives have to be offered.
- Financial management is in many ways an integral part of the jobs of managers who are involved in planning, allocation of resources, and control. The responsibilities for financial management are dispersed throughout the organisation. There are, however, many tasks of financial management and allied areas (like accounting) which are specialised in nature and attended to by two key financial officers of the firm viz., the treasurer and the controller.

Capital Budgeting 13

A steel company is considering building a new arc furnace; an insurance company is planning to install a computer system for information processing; the Government of India is thinking of an ambitious plan to link Ganges and Cauvery rivers; Gautam, a graduate student, is planning to buy a motorcycle; a pharmaceutical company is evaluating a major research and development programme. Essentially, each of these represents a capital expenditure proposal. The basic characteristic of a capital expenditure (also referred to as a capital investment or capital project or just project) is that it involves a current outlay (or current and future outlays) of funds in the hope of receiving a stream of benefits in future.

Capital expenditures, representing the growing edge of a business, are deemed to be very important for three inter-related reasons:

- They have long term consequences. Capital investment decisions have a bearing on the firm's operations for a long time to come.
- It may be difficult or expensive to reverse capital investment decisions because the market for used capital investments is often not well organised.
- Capital investment decisions often involve substantial outlays.

This chapter discusses the framework for capital budgeting. It is divided into nine sections:

- Capital budgeting process
- Key steps in project appraisal
- Costs and benefits
- Investment criteria
- Analysis of risk
- Cost of capital

- Value of options
- Overall corporate considerations
- Project appraisal by financial institutions

13.1 CAPITAL BUDGETING PROCESS

Capital budgeting is a complex process which may be divided into the following phases:

- Identification of potential investment opportunities
- Assembling of investment proposals
- Decision making
- Preparation of capital budget and appropriations
- Implementation
- Performance review

Identification of Potential Investment Opportunities

The capital budgeting process begins with the identification of potential investment opportunities. Usually, the planning body (it can be an individual or a committee, formal or informal) develops estimates of future sales which serve as the basis for setting production targets. This information, in turn, helps one to identify required investments in plant and equipment.

For imaginative identification of investment ideas, it is helpful to: (a) monitor external environment regularly to scout for investment opportunities; (b) formulate a well defined corporate strategy based on a thorough analysis of strengths, weaknesses, opportunities, and threats; (c) share corporate strategy and perspectives with persons who are involved in the process of capital budgeting; and (d) motivate employees to make suggestions.

Assembling of Investment Proposals

Investment proposals identified by the production department and other departments are usually submitted on a standarised capital investment proposal form. Generally, most of the proposals are routed through several persons before they reach the capital budgeting committee or some other body which assembles them. The purpose of this is primarily to ensure that the proposal is viewed from different angles. It also helps in creating a climate for the coordination of interrelated activities.

Investment proposals are usually classified into various categories for facilitating decision-making, budgeting, and control. An illustrative classification is given below:

- Replacement investments
- Expansion investments
- New product investments
- Obligatory and welfare investments

Decision Making

A system of rupee gateways usually characterises the capital investment decision making in practice. Under this system, executives are vested with the power to okay investment proposals up to certain limits. For example, in one company the plant superintendent can okay an investment outlay up to ₹100,000, the works manager up to ₹500,000, and the managing director up to ₹2,000,000. Investments requiring higher outlays need the approval of the board of directors.

Preparation of Capital Budget and Appropriations

Projects involving smaller outlays and those that can be decided by executives at lower levels are often covered by a blanket appropriation for expeditious action. Projects which need larger outlays are included in the capital budget after necessary approvals. Before undertaking such projects, an appropriation order is usually required. The purpose of this check is mainly to ensure that the position of funds of a firm is satisfactory at the time of implementation of the project. Further, it provides an opportunity to review the project during implementation.

Implementation

Translating an investment proposal into a concrete project is a complex, risky, and time consuming task. Delays in implementation, which are common, may lead to substantial cost overruns. For expeditious implementation at reasonable cost, the following are helpful:

- **Adequate formulation of projects** A major reason for delay in implementation is inadequate formulation of projects. If necessary homework in terms of preliminary studies and comprehensive, detailed formulation of the project has not been done, many surprises and shocks are likely to spring on the way. Hence, the need for adequate formulation of the project cannot be over-emphasised.

- **Use of the principle of responsibility accounting** Assigning specific responsibilities to project managers for completing the project within the defined time frame and cost limits is helpful for expeditious execution and cost control.
- **Use of network techniques** For project planning and control, several network techniques such as PERT (Programme Evaluation Review Technique) and CPM (Critical Path Method) are available. With the help of these techniques, monitoring of a project becomes easier.

Performance Review

Performance review, or post completion audit, is a feedback device. It is a means of comparing actual performance with projected performance. It is conducted most appropriately when the operations of a project have stabilised and is useful in several ways: (i) It throws light on how realistic were the assumptions underlying the project. (ii) It provides a documented log of experience that is highly valuable for decision making. (iii) It helps in uncovering judgemental biases. (iv) It induces a much needed caution amongst project sponsors.

13.2 KEY STEPS IN PROJECT APPRAISAL

Project appraisal involves six broad steps as shown in Exhibit 13.1. A brief description of these steps are as follows:

1. **Forecast the costs and benefits** A capital project involves costs and benefits extending over a period of time. Typically, costs are incurred in the form of initial cash outlays on fixed assets and net current assets. Benefits are derived in the form of cash inflows from the operations of the project over its economic life, plus terminal cash inflow from the liquidation of the project at the end of its economic life.
2. **Assess the riskiness of the project** Costs and benefits associated with a capital project are almost invariably subject to risk. There may be a lot of variability characterising factors like project cost, sales quantity, selling price, material cost, energy cost, project life,

and salvage value. The actual values of these variables often turn out to be different from their forecast values. Hence, you should try to get a handle over how the variability in these factors can affect the attractiveness of the project.

3. **Estimate the cost of capital** The cost of capital is the discount rate used for evaluating a capital project. Under appropriate conditions, it is measured as the weighted average cost of different sources of capital employed for financing the project. The cost of a specific source of finance is defined as the rate of discount that equates the present value of the expected post-tax payments to that source of finance, with the net funds received from that source.
4. **Apply suitable investment criteria** The stream of costs and benefits of the project has to be converted into a measure indicating how worthwhile is the project. For this purpose, several investment criteria are used. They fall into two broad categories: discounted cash flow criteria and non-discounted cash flow criteria. While the former calls for discounting the future benefits using an appropriate discount rate, the latter does not involve any discounting.
5. **Value the options** The traditional approach to project appraisal calls for judging a project on the basis of its net present value, obtained by discounting the project cash flow stream using an appropriate cost of capital. This approach, however, is incomplete, as it fails to capture the value of real options embedded in the project. Hence, the traditional NPV analysis needs to be expanded to include the value of real options inherent in the project.
6. **Consider the overall corporate perspective** Capital investments in plant, machinery, buildings, research facilities, product development, marketing programmes, and so on are tangible expressions of a company's strategy. Hence, capital investment decisions must be evaluated from the overall perspective of the firm. In such an evaluation, due consideration should be given to general economic outlook, prospects of industries in which the firm operates, and the competitive position and core competencies of the firm.

The following sections discuss at length the various steps involved in project appraisal. For pedagogic convenience, investment criteria are discussed before risk and cost of capital.

EXHIBIT 13.1 ***Key Steps in Project Appraisal***

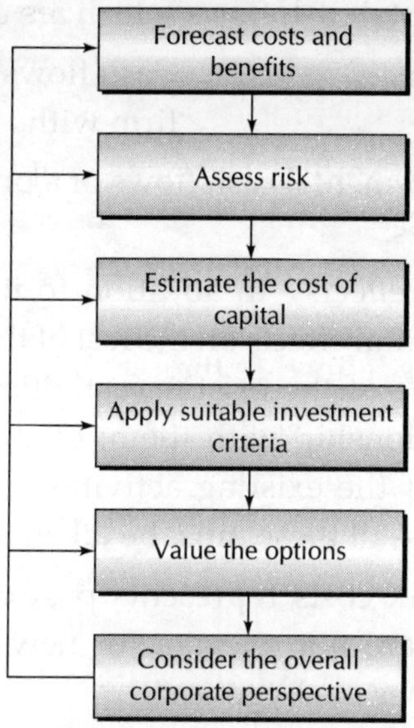

13.3 COSTS AND BENEFITS

Capital expenditures typically involve current and near future costs that are expected to generate benefits in the future.

Basic Principles

While measuring the costs and benefits of a capital expenditure proposal, you must bear in mind the following guidelines:

Focus on Cash Flows Costs and benefits must be measured in terms of cash flows—costs are cash outflows and benefits are cash inflows. Cash flows matter because they represent the purchasing power.

Since accounting figures are based on the accrual principle, they have to be adjusted to derive the cash flows. For example, depreciation and other non-cash charges, which are deducted in computing profits from the accounting point of view, have to be added back as they do not entail cash outflows.

Estimate cash flows on a post-tax basis. Some firms look at pre-tax cash flows and, to compensate that, apply a discount rate greater than the cost of capital. However there is no reliable basis for making such adjustments. Hence, as a rule, work with post tax cash flows.

Measure Cash Flows on an Incremental Basis The value of a project depends on its incremental cash flows which are defined as:

Cash flows of the firm with the project	–	Cash flows of the firm without the project

In estimating the incremental cash flows of a project, bear in mind the following sub-guidelines:

Consider all incidental effects In addition to its direct cash flows, a project may have incidental effects on the rest of the firm. It may enhance the profitability of some of the existing activities of the firm as it has a complementary relationship with them; or it may detract from the profitability of some of the existing activities as it has a competitive relationship with them—all these must be taken into account.

Ignore sunk costs Sunk costs represents past outlays that cannot be recovered and, hence, are not relevant for new investment decisions. Remember that, "bygones are bygones".

Include opportunity costs If a project requires the use of some resources already available with the firm, the opportunity cost of these resources should be charged to the project. The opportunity cost of a resource is the value of net cash flows that can be derived from it if it were put to its best alternative use. Suppose a project requires a vacant piece of land within the factory premises of the firm. The cost of this land represents a sunk cost and hence is not relevant for the new project. But the project should be charged with the opportunity cost of this land which represents the benefit that can be derived by putting it to its best alternative use, which in this case may simply be leasing the land to another firm.

Question the allocation of overhead costs Accountants normally allocate organisational overhead costs to various divisions or projects on some basis. Hence, when a project is proposed, a portion of the organisational overhead costs is allocated to it. This may, however, have no relationship with the incremental organisational overhead cost associated with the project. Remember that, what matters is the incremental overhead costs (along with other incremental costs), attributable to the project and not the allocated overhead costs.

Do not forget net working capital Apart from investment in fixed assets like land, building, machinery, and technical know how, a project also requires investment in current assets like cash, receivables (debtors), and inventories. A portion of current assets is supported by non-interest bearing current liabilities like accounts payable (creditors) and provisions.

The difference between current assets and non-interest bearing current liabilities is the net working capital. It is financed by equity, preference, and debt. While estimating the investment outlay of a project, do not forget the investment in net working capital.

Exclude Financing Costs When you define project cash flows, exclude financing costs like interest on debt and dividend on preference and equity. Why? The weighted average cost of capital used for discounting the project cash flows reflects the cost of debt, preference, and equity capital. Hence, if interest on debt and dividend on preference and equity are deducted in estimating project cash flows, the cost of capital will be counted twice. Guard against this error.

Treat Inflation Consistently Interest rates are usually expressed in nominal terms, not real terms. For example, if Tata Steel issues a debenture carrying an interest rate of say, 10 percent, the 10 percent rate is a nominal rate. This means that, if you buy a ₹100 debenture you will get a nominal return of 10 percent. If the inflation rate happens to be, say, 5 percent, your real return will be correspondingly less. To figure out your real return, use the following formula:

$$(1 + \text{Real return}) = \frac{(1 + \text{Nominal return})}{(1 + \text{Inflation rate})}$$

Applying this to the Tata Steel debenture, you get

$$(1 + \text{Real return}) = \frac{(1 + 0.10)}{(1 + 0.05)} = 1.048$$

Hence, the real return is 4.8 percent.

Since discount rates are usually quoted in nominal terms, you should, for reasons of consistency, estimate the project cash flows too in nominal terms. This means that you must consider the trends in prices and costs in nominal terms.

You can, of course, work with real cash flows (cash flows that abstract away the impact of inflation). If you do so, make sure that the discount rate too is stated in real terms.

Components of the Cash Flow Stream

The cash flow stream of a project may be divided into three parts as follows:

- **Initial flows** These represent the cash outflows associated with investment in various project components. Initial flows are defined as:

Outlays on plant, machinery, and other fixed assets

–

Tax shields relating to investment in plant, machinery, and other fixed asset

+

Outlays on net working capital

- **Operational flows** These are cash inflows expected during the operational phase of the project. The operational cash inflow for a given year is equal to:

  Profit after tax

  +

  Depreciation and other non cash charges

- **Terminal flows** Cash flows expected from the disposal of assets when the project is terminated are referred to as terminal flows. Terminal flows are defined as:

  Post tax salvage value of fixed assets

  +

  Post tax salvage value of net working capital

Illustration

Naveen Enterprises is considering a capital project about which the following information is available:

- The investment outlay on the project will be ₹100 million. This consists of ₹80 million on plant and machinery and ₹20 million on net working capital. The entire outlay will be incurred at the beginning of the project.
- The project will be financed with ₹45 million of equity capital, ₹5 million of preference capital, and ₹50 million of debt capital. Preference capital will carry a dividend rate of 15 percent and debt capital will carry an interest rate of 15 percent.
- The life of the project is expected to be 5 years. At the end of 5 years, fixed assets will fetch a net salvage value of ₹30 million whereas net working capital will be liquidated at its book value.
- The project is expected to increase the revenues of the firm by ₹120 million per year. The increase in costs on account of the project is expected to be ₹80 million per year (This includes all items of cost other than depreciation, interest, and tax). The effective tax rate will be 30 percent.

- Plant and machinery will be depreciated at the rate of 25 percent per year as per the written down value method. Hence, the depreciation charges will be:

First year	:	₹20.00 million
Second year	:	₹15.00 million
Third year	:	₹11.25 million
Fourth year	:	₹8.44 million
Fifth year	:	₹6.33 million

Given the above details, the project cash flows are shown in Exhibit 13.2.

EXHIBIT 13.2 ***Project Cash Flows***

(₹ *in million*)

	0	1	2	3	4	5
A. Fixed assets	(80)					
B. Net working capital	(20)					
C. Revenues		120	120	120	120	120
D. Costs (other than depreciation and interest)		80	80	80	80	80
E. Depreciation		20	15	11.25	8.44	6.33
F. Profit before tax		20	25	28.75	31.56	33.67
G. Tax		6	7.5	8.63	9.47	10.10
H. Profit after tax		14	17.5	20.12	22.09	23.57
I. Net salvage value of fixed assets						30
J. Recovery of net working capital						20
K. Initial outlay	(100)					
L. Operating cash flow (H + E)		34.0	32.5	31.37	30.53	29.9
M. Terminal cash flow (I + J)						50.0
N. Net cash flow (K + L + M)	(100)	34.0	32.5	31.37	30.53	79.9
Book value of investment	100	80	65	53.75	45.31	38.98

13.4 INVESTMENT CRITERIA

Once the stream of costs and benefits has been defined, it must be evaluated to determine whether the project is worthwhile or not. Several criteria have been proposed for such evaluation, of which, the important ones are:

- Payback period
- Average rate of return

- Net present value
- Internal rate of return

Payback Period

The payback period is the length of the time required to recover the initial cash outlay on the project. For example, a project involves a cash outlay of ₹6,00,000 and generates cash inflows of ₹1,00,000, ₹2,50,000, ₹2,50,000 and ₹2,00,000 in the first, second, third, and fourth years, respectively. In this case, the payback period is 3 years because the sum of cash inflows during 3 years is equal to the initial outlay. When the annual cash inflow is a constant sum, the payback period is simply the initial outlay divided by the annual cash inflow. For example, a project which has an initial cash outlay of ₹1,000,000 and a constant annual cash inflow of ₹3,00,000 has a payback period of ₹10,00,000/₹3,00,000 = $3\frac{1}{3}$ years.

To figure out the payback period of Naveen Enterprise's capital project, let us look at the cumulative cash flow, till it turns positive.

(*₹ in million*)

Year	*Cash flow*	*Cumulative cash flow*
0	– 100.00	– 100.00
1	34.00	– 66.00
2	32.50	– 33.50
3	31.37	– 2.13
4	30.53	+ 28.40

Since the cumulative cash inflow is negative at the end of year 3 but positive at the end of year 4, the payback period is between 3 and 4 years.

According to the payback period criterion, the shorter the payback period, the more desirable the project. Firms using this criterion generally specify the maximum acceptable payback period. If this is n years, only projects with a payback period of n years or less are deemed worthwhile.

Evaluation A widely used investment criterion, the payback period seems to offer the following advantages:

- It is simple, both in concept and application. It does not use complicated concepts or tedious calculations and has few hidden assumptions.
- It is a rough and ready method for dealing with risk. It favours projects which generate substantial cash inflows in earlier years while discriminating against those which bring substantial cash

inflows in later years. Now, if risk tends to increase with futurity—and in general this may be true—the payback criterion can be helpful in weeding out risky projects.

- Since it emphasises earlier cash inflows, it is a sensible criterion when the firm is pressed with problems of liquidity.

The limitations of payback criterion, however, are very serious:

- It fails to consider the time value of money. In the payback calculation, cash inflows are simply added without suitable discounting. This violates the most basic principle of financial analysis, which stipulates that cash flows occurring at different points of time can be added or subtracted only after suitable compounding or discounting.
- It ignores cash flows beyond the payback period. This leads to discrimination against projects which generate substantial cash inflows in later years.
- It is a measure of a project's capital recovery, not its profitability.
- Though it measures a project's liquidity, it does not indicate the liquidity position of the firm as a whole, which is more important.

Average Rate of Return

The average rate of return, also called the accounting rate of return, is defined as:

$$\frac{\text{Profit after tax}}{\text{Book value of the investment}}$$

The numerator of this ratio is the average annual post-tax profit over the life of the investment; the denominator is the average book value of assets committed to the project.[1] To illustrate the calculation of average rate of return, consider the data for the project of Naveen Enterprises.

(₹ in million)

Year	*Book value of investment*	*Profit after tax*
1	100.00	14.00
2	80.00	17.5
3	65.00	20.12
4	53.75	22.09
5	45.31	23.57

[1] There are ways and ways of defining the average rate of return. We have used a definition that is commonly recommended.

The average rate of return is:

$$\frac{1/5(14.0 + 17.5 + 20.12 + 22.09 + 23.57)}{1/5(100 + 80 + 65 + 53.75 + 45.31)} = 28.07 \text{ percent}$$

Evaluation Traditionally a popular investment appraisal criterion, the average rate of return has the following virtues:

- It is simple to calculate.
- It is based on accounting information which is readily available and familiar to businessmen.
- It considers benefits over the entire life of the project.

Its short-comings, however, seem to be considerable:

- It is based on accounting profit, not cash flow.
- It does not take into account the time value of money.

Net Present Value

The net present value of a project is the sum of the present value of all the cash flows associated with it. The cash flows are discounted at an appropriate discount rate (cost of capital).

The net present value of Naveen Enterprise's project is calculated below, using a discount rate of 15 percent which is the cost of capital applicable to this project. For details of how the cost of capital is computed, refer to Section 13.6.

(₹ in million)

Year	*Cash flow*	*Discount factor*	*Present value*
0	– 100.00	1.00	– 100.00
1	34.00	0.870	29.58
2	32.50	0.756	24.57
3	31.37	0.658	20.64
4	30.53	0.572	17.46
5	79.90	0.497	39.71
			Sum = 31.96

The decision rule associated with the net present value is: accept the project, if the net present value is positive and reject the project, if the net present value is negative. A net present value of zero suggests indifference.

Discount Rate and Net Present Value For projects that have cash outflows followed by cash inflows - most projects are like this - the net present value declines as the discount rate increases. Typically, the relationship between the discount rate and net present value is depicted in Exhibit 13.3.

EXHIBIT 13.3 ***Discount Rate and Net Present Value***

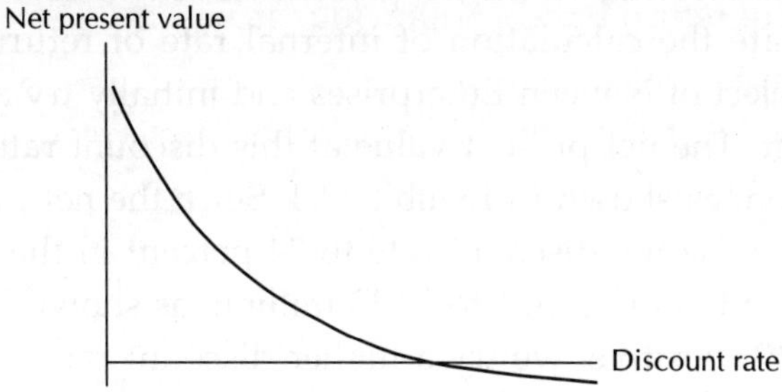

Evaluation Conceptually sound, the net present value criterion has considerable merits:

- It takes into account the time value of money.
- It considers the cash flow stream in its entirety.
- It squares neatly with the financial objective of maximisation of the wealth of shareholders. The net present value represents the contribution to the wealth of shareholders.

While this criterion has hardly any shortcoming, a problem regarding its use may be mentioned. The net present value is an absolute measure and not a relative measure. Decision makers, however, are generally more comfortable with a relative measure (like the accounting rate of return or the internal rate of return).

Internal Rate of Return

The internal rate of return of a project is the discount rate that makes its net present value equal to zero. It is represented by the point of intersection in Exhibit 13.3. Note the key differences between net present value and internal rate of return.

Net Present Value	*Internal Rate of Return*
• Assumes that the discount rate (cost of capital) is known. • Calculates the net present value, given the discount rate.	• Assumes that the net present value is zero. • Figures out the discount rate that makes net present value zero.

To calculate the internal rate of return of a project, you have to try a few discount rates till you find one that makes its net present value zero.

In this iterative procedure, bear in mind the following guidelines: If the net present value is positive, raise the discount rate to decrease the net present value; on the other hand, if the net present value is negative, lower the discount rate to increase the net present value. Remember the objective is to drive down the net present value to zero.

To illustrate the calculation of internal rate of return, let us work with the project of Naveen Enterprises and initially try a discount rate of 20 percent. The net present value at this discount rate works out to ₹15.88 million, as shown in Exhibit 13.4. Since the net present value is positive, we raise the discount rate to 24 percent in the next iteration. The net present value drops to ₹5.13 million, as shown in Exhibit 13.4. Since it is still positive, we try a higher discount rate, viz. 28 percent. At this discount rate, the net present value becomes—₹4.02 million as shown in the last column of Exhibit 13.4. Thus, we know that the internal rate of return lies between 24 percent and 28 percent. If resort to linear interpolation in this range the internal rate of return is calculated as follows:

Exhibit 13.4 ***How the Discount Rate Impacts on the Net Present Value***

Year	*Cash flow*	*Discounting rate: 20%*		*Discounting rate: 24%*		*Discounting rate: 28%*	
		Discount factor	*Present Value*	*Discount factor*	*Present Value*	*Discount factor*	*Present Value*
0	–100	1.000	–100.00	1.000	–100.00	1.000	–100.00
1	34.00	0.833	28.32	0.806	27.40	0.781	26.55
2	32.50	0.694	22.56	0.650	21.13	0.610	19.83
3	31.37	0.579	18.16	0.524	16.44	0.477	14.96
4	30.53	0.482	14.72	0.423	12.91	0.373	11.39
5	79.90	0.402	32.12	0.341	27.25	0.291	23.25
		NPV = 15.88		NPV = 5.13		NPV = – 4.02	

$$\text{Smaller discount rate} + \frac{\text{NPV at the smaller rate}}{\text{Sum of the absolute values of the NPV at the smaller and the bigger discount rates}} \times [\text{Bigger discount rate} - \text{Smaller discount rate}]$$

$$24\% + \frac{5.13}{5.13 + 4.02}\,[28\% - 24\%] = 26.24 \text{ percent}$$

Evaluation A popular discounted cash flow method, the internal rate of return criterion has several virtues:

- It takes into account the time value of money.
- It considers the cash flow stream in its entirety.
- It makes sense to businessmen who are wonted to think in terms of rate of return and find an absolute quantity such as net present value, somewhat difficult to work with.

The internal rate of return criterion, however, has its own limitations:

- There may be multiple rates of return. If the cash flow stream of a project has more than one change in sign, there is a possibility of multiple rates of return.
- The internal rate of return criterion can be misleading when the choice is between mutually exclusive projects that have substantially different outlays. Consider projects *P* and *Q*.

	Cash flows 0	Cash flows 1	Internal rate of return	Net present value (at 12%)
P	– 10,000	+ 20,000	100%	7,857
Q	– 50,000	+ 75,000	50%	16,964

Both the projects are good, but *Q* with its higher net present value contributes more to the wealth of the shareholders. Yet, from an internal rate of return point of view, *P* looks better than *Q*. Hence, the internal rate of return criterion seems unsuitable for ranking projects of different scales.

13.5 ANALYSIS OF RISK

Capital investments are almost invariably subject to risk arising from a variety of factors like technological developments, emergence of new competition, shifts in consumer preferences, natural disasters, changes in macroeconomic environment, volatility of financial prices, and so on. Due to the presence of risk, actual outcomes tend to deviate from expected outcomes.

The risks characterising capital investments are likely to vary widely across projects. An unrelated diversification project tends to be more risky than an expansion project which, in turn, may be more risky than a replacement project.

Analysing project risks is one of the most difficult and controversial issues in finance. Several approaches have been suggested and no single approach can be regarded as ideal for all the situations. You can look at a project in isolation and assess the variability of its returns per se; at a broader level, you can look at a project in the context of the firm and evaluate its contribution to the total risk of the firm; at a still broader level, you can look at a project from the point of a diversified investor in the capital market and measure its market (or systematic) risk.

In theory, there is a strong case for looking at a project from the point of view of the total firm risk or, even better, from the point of view of the market risk. In practice, however, for reasons of simplicity and pragmatism, managers often look at the stand-alone risk of the project. How is the project risk measured? What adjustment is made for risk? The following discussion addresses these issues.

Measurement of Risk

For measuring the risk of a project, the commonly employed techniques are sensitivity analysis and break even analysis. For large complex projects, simulation analysis and decision tree analysis may also be attempted.

Sensitivity Analysis Since the future is uncertain, you may like to know what happens to the viability of the project when some variable like sales or investment deviates from its expected value. In other words, you may want to do "what if" analysis or sensitivity analysis.

To understand the nature of sensitivity analysis, let us consider an example. Suppose you are the general manager of Apex Flour Mills, that is considering setting up a new flour mill near Bangalore. Based on previous experience, the project staff of Apex has developed the figures shown in Exhibit 13.5.

EXHIBIT 13.5 *Cash Flow Forecast for Apex Flour Mill Project*

₹ in '000s

		Year 0	*Year 1-10*
1.	Investment	(20,000)	
2.	Sales		18,000
3.	Variable costs (66 2/3 % of sales)		12,000
4.	Fixed costs		1,000
5.	Depreciation		2,000
6.	Pre tax profit		3,000
7.	Taxes		1,000

(Contd.)

EXHIBIT 13.5 ***(Contd.)***

		Year 0	*Year 1-10*
8.	Profit after taxes		2,000
9.	Cash flow from operation		4,000
10.	Net cash flow	(20,000)	4,000

Since the cash flow from the operations is an annuity, the NPV of the flour mill project is:

$$- 200{,}00{,}000 + 40{,}00{,}000 \times \text{PVA}(r = 12\%, n = 10)$$
$$- 200{,}00{,}000 + 40{,}00{,}000\ (5.650)$$
$$= 26{,}00{,}000$$

The NPV based on the expected values of the underlying variables, looks positive. You are, however, aware that the underlying variables can vary widely and hence you would like to explore the effect of such variations on the NPV. So you define the optimistic and pessimistic estimates for the underlying variables. These are shown in the left hand columns of Exhibit 13.6. With this information, you can calculate the NPV for the optimistic and pessimistic values of each of the underlying variables. To do this, vary one variable at a time. For example, to study the effect of an adverse variation in sales (from the expected ₹18 million to the pessimistic ₹15 million), you maintain the values of the other underlying variables at expected levels. (This means that the investment is held at ₹20 million, variable costs as a proportion of sales are held at $66\frac{2}{3}$ per cent, fixed costs are held at ₹1 million, so on and so forth.)

EXHIBIT 13.6 ***Sensitivity of NPV to Changes in the Value of Key Variables***

(₹ in million)

	Range			*NPV*		
Key Variable	*Pessimistic*	*Expected*	*Optimistic*	*Pessimistic*	*Expected*	*Optimistic*
Investment (₹ in million)	24.00	20.00	18.00	– 0.65	2.60	4.22
Sales (₹ in million)	15.00	18.00	21.00	– 1.17	2.60	6.40
Variable costs as a percent of sales	70.00	66.70	65.00	0.34	2.60	3.73
Fixed costs	1.3	1.0	0.8	1.47	2.60	3.33

The NPV, when the sales are at their pessimistic level and other variables at their expected level, is shown on the right side of Exhibit 13.6. Likewise, you can calculate the effect of the variations in the values of the other underlying variables. The NPVs for the pessimistic, expected, and optimistic forecasts are shown on the right side of Exhibit 13.6.

A very popular method of assessing risk, sensitivity analysis has certain merits:

- It shows how robust or vulnerable a project is to changes in values of the underlying variables.
- It indicates where further work may be done. If the net present value is highly sensitive to changes in some factor, it may be worthwhile to explore how the variability of that critical factor may be contained.
- It is intuitively very appealing as it articulates the concerns that project evaluators normally have.

Notwithstanding its appeal and popularity, sensitivity analysis suffers from several shortcomings:

- It merely shows what happens to NPV when there is a change in some variable, without providing any idea of how likely that change will be.
- Typically, in sensitivity analysis, only one variable is changed at a time. In the real world, however, variables tend to move together.
- It is inherently a very subjective analysis. The same sensitivity analysis may lead one decision maker to accept the project while another may reject it.

Break even Analysis In sensitivity analysis, we ask what will happen to the project if sales decline or costs increase or something else happens. As a project analyst, you will also be interested to know how much should be produced and sold at a minimum to ensure that the project does not lose money. Such an exercise is called break even analysis and the minimum quantity at which loss is avoided is called the break even point. To figure out how the break even quantity is calculated, let us look at the flour mill project for which the following estimates were obtained:

Sales	₹18 million
Variable costs	12 million
Fixed costs	1 million
Depreciation	2 million

Note that the ratio of variable costs to sales is 0.667 (12/18). This means that every rupee of sales makes a contribution of ₹0.333. Put differently, the contribution margin ratio is 0.333. Hence, the break even level of sales will be:

$$\frac{\text{Fixed costs} + \text{Depreciation}}{\text{Contribution margin ratio}} = \frac{1+2}{0.333} = ₹9 \text{ million}$$

By way of confirmation, you can verify that the break even level of sales is indeed ₹9 million.

	₹ in million
Sales	9
Variable costs	6
Fixed costs	1
Depreciation	2
Profit before tax	0
Tax	0
Profit after tax	0

Adjustment of Risk

Given the information on the risk characteristics of the project, measured in whatever way, you have to adjust for risk. You may do it by adjusting the discount rate, or the cash flows, or the payback period.

Adjusting the Discount Rate A popular method to account for risk is to use a risk adjusted discount rate. If the risk of the project is similar to that of the existing investments of the firm, use the average cost of capital of the firm as the discount rate; if the risk of the project is greater than the risk of the existing investments of the firm, use a discount rate greater than the average cost of capital of the firm; finally, if the risk of the project is less than the risk of the existing investments of the firm, use a discount rate lower than the average cost of capital of the firm.

While this method is appealing, it is often applied in an *ad hoc* manner. The adjustment of the discount rate is done in a subjective manner.

Adjusting the Cash Flows Instead of adjusting the discount rate, one may adjust the cash flow. For example, if the expected cash flow for year 1 is say ₹120,000, it may be adjusted downward to ₹110,000. Doing so implies that an expected ₹120,000 is deemed equivalent to a certain ₹110,000. Put differently ₹110,000 is the certainty equivalent of an expected ₹120,000. Once the expected cash flows are converted into their certainty equivalents, the risk free discount rate is applied to compute the net present value. Remember that when the adjustment is made to the cash flows, the discount rate must be the risk free rate. If the discount rate too is adjusted, it will tantamount to double counting of risk which is not correct. Conceptually, this method is superior to the other methods of risk adjustment. However, it is very inconvenient to apply in practice because a certainty equivalent factor has to be specified for every cash flow—a somewhat difficult proposition.

Adjusting the Payback Period When the payback period is used as an investment criterion, it is common to use a flexible payback yardstick. If the project is perceived to be highly risky, a shorter payback norm, say 3 years, may be applied. On the other hand, if the project is regarded as very safe, a longer payback norm, say 6 years, may be used.

While this approach is intuitively appealing, it is characterised by a high degree of subjectivity. It is very difficult to objectively establish the payback period that accurately reflects risk.

13.6 COST OF CAPITAL

The cost of capital of any investment (project, business, or company) is the rate of return the suppliers of capital would expect to receive if the capital were invested elsewhere in an investment (project, business, or company) of comparable risk. Before discussing the technical details of how the cost of capital is computed, let us reiterate two points.

- The cost of capital reflects **expected** returns, not historical returns.
- The cost of capital represents an **opportunity cost**. It reflects the returns investors expect from investments of similar risk.

To illustrate the calculation of cost of capital, let us look at the financing plan for the project of Naveen Enterprises.

- Equity capital : ₹45 million
  (2 million equity shares are proposed to be issued to fetch a net price of ₹22.5 each. While the issue price will be ₹25 per share, the issue expenses will be 10 percent. The expected dividend per share for the following year is ₹1.8).
- Preference capital : ₹5 million
  (50,000 preference shares of ₹100 each are proposed to be issued to an institutional investor at par. The

preference shares will carry a dividend of 15 percent)

- Debt capital : ₹50 million
  (0.5 million non convertible debentures of ₹100 each will be privately placed with a mutual fund. The debentures will carry an interest rate of 15 percent)

For our present discussion we assume that the risk of the project of Naveen Enterprises is comparable to the risk of the firm as a whole; further, the financing pattern of the project is comparable to the financing pattern of the firm as a whole.

Cost of Debt

The cost of debt is the return required by the creditors of the firm on new borrowings. You can observe the cost of debt, directly or indirectly. Since it is the interest rate the firm must pay on its new borrowings, you can estimate it by looking at the interest rates prevailing in the financial markets. For example, if the firm has outstanding bonds, you can use the yield to maturity on these bonds as a proxy for the cost of new borrowings. Alternatively, if you know that the new bonds of the firm would have a rating of say, AAA, you can look at the interest rate on recently issued AAA bonds.

While figuring out the cost of debt, remember that the coupon rate on the firm's outstanding debt is irrelevant. It merely represents a historical cost, not the current cost of debt. What matters is the cost of debt today and this is reflected in the yield prevailing in today's market.

The return required by the suppliers of debt capital to Naveen Enterprises is 15 percent. Hence, this represents the pre-tax cost of debt. Since the interest paid on debt capital is a tax deductible expense, the post-tax cost of debt is equal to:

$$\text{Pre-tax cost of debt } (1 - \text{tax rate})$$
$$= 15\% \, (1 - 0.3) = 10.5\%$$

Cost of Preference

Since preference capital carries a fixed rate of dividend, the cost of preference capital can be determined fairly easily. It is the dividend rate the firm must pay on a new issue of preference capital. Alternatively, it can be estimated by looking at the yields on outstanding preference shares that are similarly rated.

The cost of preference capital for Naveen Enterprises is 15 percent. Note that the preference dividend, unlike the interest on debt, is not a tax deductible payment. Hence, there is no tax adjustment here.

Cost of Equity

Theoretically, the cost of equity is the return expected by capital providers from investments of similar risk. So, you can argue that the cost of equity can be found out by asking equity investors how much return they expect. This is not feasible because the number of equity shareholders for most companies is fairly large, sometimes running into hundreds of thousands. Further, even if you could ask them, they may not be able to define their expectation the way seasoned bankers or investors do. Many of them may simply say "I want a high return". This is not helpful in arriving at a concrete estimate of the cost of equity.

Given the practical difficulties in directly ascertaining the return expected by equity shareholders, financial analysts try to deduce investor expectation by indirect ways. Three methods are commonly employed in practice:

- CAPM approach
- Bond yield plus risk premium approach
- Dividend discount model approach

CAPM Approach According to the capital asset pricing model (which was introduced in Chapter 11), risk and return are related as follows:

$$E(R) = R_f + \beta\,[E(R_M) - R_f]$$

In words,

$$\text{Expected return on a risky asset} = \text{Risk-free rate return} + \text{Beta of the asset}\left(\text{Expected return on market portfolio} - \text{Risk-free rate of return}\right)$$

To illustrate the CAPM approach, let us assume that $R_f = 10$ percent and $E\,(R_M) = 18$ percent. The expected return on equity stocks of companies with different betas is given below:

Beta	*Expected return* $= R_f + \beta\,[E(R_M) - R_f]$
0.5	10 + 0.5 (18 – 10) = 14%
1.0	10 + 1.0 (18 – 10) = 18%
1.5	10 + 1.5 (18 – 10) = 22%

To apply, the CAPM approach, the following inputs are required: R_f, the risk-free rate, $[E(R_M) - R_f]$, the market risk premium, and β, the beta of the stock.

While there is a disagreement among finance practitioners as to how these inputs have to be estimated, for our purposes the following will suffice:

- The risk-free rate may be estimated as the yield on a long-term government bond that has a maturity of 10 years or more.
- The market risk premium may be estimated as the difference between the average return on the market portfolio and the average risk free rate over the past 10 to 30 years - the longer the period, the better it is.
- The beta of the stock may be calculated by regressing the monthly returns on the stock over the monthly returns on the market index over the past 60 months or more.

The CAPM is regarded by many as a fairly rigorous and objective approach to determining the required return on equity. This approach, however, is based on the assumption that investors eliminate unsystematic risk by efficient diversification and hence require compensation only for systematic risk which is reflected in beta. Market imperfections may impede efficient diversification by investors, exposing them to unsystematic risk. When this occurs, investors will require compensation for unsystematic risk, a factor which is not found in the CAPM relationship. Another shortcoming of the CAPM relates to the instability of the betas of individual securities. Studies have shown that individual securities have unstable betas. This makes the use of a historical beta as a proxy for the future beta somewhat questionable. Notwithstanding these shortcomings, the CAPM approach is a useful approach for estimating the required rate of return of equity stocks.

Bond Yield Plus Risk Premium Approach Analysts who do not have faith in the CAPM approach often resort to a subjective procedure to estimate the cost of equity. They add a judgmental risk premium to the observed yield on the long-term bonds of the firm to get the cost of equity :

Cost of equity = Yield on long-term bonds + Risk premium

The logic of this approach is fairly simple. Firms that have risky and consequently high cost debt will also have risky and consequently high cost equity. So it makes sense to base the cost of equity on a readily observable cost of debt.

The problem with this approach is how to determine the risk premium. Should it be 2 percent, 4 percent, or *n* percent? There seems to be no objective way of determining it. Most analysts look at the operating and financial risks of the business and arrive at a subjectively determined risk premium that normally ranges between 2 percent and 6 percent. While this approach may not produce a precise cost of equity, it will give a reasonable ballpark estimate.

Dividend Discount Model Approach In Chapter 10 we learnt that the price of an equity is equal to the present value of the dividends expected from it.

If we assume that the dividend per share grows at a constant rate, the price of the equity share is:

$$P_0 = \frac{D_1}{r - g}$$

where P_0 is price, D_1 is the dividend expected a year from now, r is the return expected by shareholders, and g is the growth rate in dividends.

Solving the above equation for r, we get :

$$r = \frac{D_1}{P_0} + g$$

Thus, the expected return of shareholders, which in equilibrium is also the required return, is equal to the dividend yield plus the expected growth rate.

For a publicly traded company, it is fairly easy to determine the dividend yield. However, estimating the expected growth rate, g, is difficult. You can estimate g by using the following methods:

1. You can get a handle over g by relying on analysts' forecasts for the future growth rates. Analysts' forecasts may be available from a variety of sources. Since different sources are likely to give different estimates, a simple approach may be to obtain multiple estimates and then average them.
2. You can look at dividends for the preceding 5-10 years, calculate the annual growth rates, and average them. Suppose you observe the following dividends for some stock.

Year	*Dividend*	*Rupee change*	*Growth*
1	₹3.00	—	—
2	₹3.50	₹0.50	16.7
3	₹4.00	₹0.50	14.3

4	₹4.25	₹0.25	6.3
5	₹4.75	₹0.50	11.8

If you average the four growth rates, the result is 12.3 percent ; so you can use this as an estimate of the expected growth rate, g.

3. You can use the retention growth rate method. Here, you first forecast the firm's average retention rate (this is simply 1 minus the dividend payout rate) and then multiply it by the firm's expected future return on equity (ROE).

   $$g = (\text{Retention rate})\ (\text{Return on equity})$$

   For example, if the forecasted retention rate and return on equity are 0.60 and 15 percent, the expected growth rate is:

   $$g = (0.6)\ (15\%) = 9 \text{ percent.}$$

The dividend growth model is simple. It is easy to understand and easy to apply. However, there are some problems associated with it.

- First, it cannot be applied to companies that do not pay dividends or to companies that are not listed on the stock market. Even for companies that pay dividends, the assumption that dividends will grow at a constant rate may not be valid.
- Second, it does not explicitly consider risk. There is no direct adjustment for the risk associated with the estimated growth. Of course, there is an implicit adjustment for risk as the current stock price is used.

Average Cost of Capital

Once the specific costs of debt, preference, and equity capital are determined, the average cost of capital is calculated as the weighted arithmetic average of these specific costs.

For Naveen Enterprises, the weights applicable to the various sources of finance are as follows:

- Equity capital 45/100
- Preference capital 5/100
- Debt capital 50/100

The average cost of capital is calculated as follows:

Source of finance	*Component cost (percent)*	*Weight*	*Product of component cost and weight*
Equity capital	20.00	0.45	9.00
Preference capital	15.00	0.05	0.75
Debt capital	10.50	0.50	5.25
			15.00

13.7 VALUE OF OPTIONS

The DCF valuation assumes that a firm adopts a passive approach toward its real assets. It ignores the options embedded in real assets. Remember that the DCF method was initially developed for valuing bonds and stocks. Investors in these assets are generally passive. Barring exceptional circumstances, they can hardly do anything to enhance the interest or dividend they get from financial assets.

Now look at the real assets in which firms invest. Smart managers know that they can add value to those assets by exploiting options embedded in them. These options enable them to magnify gains and curtail losses.

Taxonomy of Real options

There are several important options found in capital projects. They may be classified as follows:

Investment Timing Option The firm may invest in a project now or defer the investment by a year or so. Delaying the investment may help in resolving some uncertainty about the value of the project. The "wait and watch" option is a common real option.

Expansion Option If the initial project does well, the firm has the option to make follow on investments aimed at expanding capacity. In many cases, capacity expansion can be achieved at a modest cost by making debottlenecking investments.

Growth Option A firm may undertake an R&D programme, or build a small plant to serve a new market, or make a modest strategic investment decision in a new line of business. Per se, each of them may be a negative NPV investment. However, such an investment provides the platform for future growth which may be very valuable. Michael Porter calls it as a 'beachhead' as it opens up new opportunities in future. For example, Proctor and Gamble acquired the Charmin Paper Company which served as a beachhead to launch a cluster of products like disposable diapers, paper towels, and bathroom tissues.

Shutdown Option A project may be temporarily shut down if it is economical to do so. For example, an iron ore mining project may be closed for a while if the output price of the iron ore is depressed. In general, shutdown options are more valuable when the variable costs are high. A shutdown option reduces the downside risk of the project.

Abandonment Option If the project does not perform well and there is very little promise for improvement, the firm can consider the exit option. The firm need not continue with an uneconomic activity indefinitely. An abandonment or exit option, like a shutdown option, reduces the downside risk of the project.

Flexibility Option Apart from the options that naturally exist in most projects, managers can incorporate flexibility in designing the project. The designed-in options may take the form of input flexibility options, and output flexibility options.

An **input flexibility** option allows a firm to switch between alternative inputs. For example, an electric power plant may go for a flexible dual-fuel boiler which can switch between gas or oil as fuel, depending on which resource of energy is cheaper at a given point of time.

An **output flexibility** options allows a firm to alter the product mix. Oil refineries, for example, are typically designed with this flexibility. This permits them to switch from one product mix to another, depending on which product mix is the most profitable at a given point of time.

Relative Values of Cash Flows and Options

A variety of analytical and numerical methods have been proposed for valuing real options. While these methods are too advanced for this book, the key insights provided by them can be combined with well-informed judgment to get a broad sense of the value of real options.

In general, real options are more valuable when:

- The environmental uncertainty is high.
- The degree of managerial flexibility is high.

Exhibit 13.7 presents a matrix showing the combined effect of environmental uncertainty and managerial flexibility on the relative

EXHIBIT 13.7 *Relative Values of Cash Flows and Options*

Environmental Uncertainties	Managerial flexibility: Low	Managerial flexibility: High
High	Cash flows : 75 Options : 25	Cash flows : 50 Options : 50
Low	Cash flows : 95 Options : 5	Cash flows : 75 Options : 25

values of cash flows and options. The percentages shown, however, are merely suggestive. They have to be specified by the project evaluator to reflect his informed judgment.

13.8 OVERALL CORPORATE CONSIDERATIONS

The capital budget of a firm, in order to be meaningful and viable, must satisfy several conditions, arising from overall corporate considerations.

Consistency with Strategy The capital budget is the principal instrument for implementing the strategy of the firm. To ensure the consistency of capital budget with the strategy of the firm, the following should be done:

- Strategy formulation and long range planning should precede capital budgeting.
- During the capital budgeting exercise, investment proposals should be viewed in the context of the critical premises of strategy and long range plans.

Compatibility with Resources The capital budget of a firm must be compatible with its resources, viz., financial capacity and managerial capability.

The financial capacity of a firm may be estimated as: Operating cash flow-fixed funding requirements + potential funding sources.

Assessing the managerial capability is more difficult than estimating financing capacity. The methods of evaluation in this area being weak, there may be a tendency to gloss over it or side-step it. However, inability to identify critical managerial limitations and organisational imbalances can seriously vitiate funds allocation. Indeed, this is one of the most vulnerable facets of capital budgeting.

Controllability As the business environment is continually changing and evolving, even the best conceived business plans may turn out to be ill advised and poorly timed. Hence, sound controls should be instituted in the process of capital budgeting. This involves the following:

- The base level spending and expansion investment should be segregated.
- Sound profitability criteria should be applied to expansion investments.
- Projects included in the capital budget should be thoroughly reviewed prior to actual implementation.

- Major projects should be divided into sub- phases for purposes of controlling expenditures.
- Actual costs must be periodically compared against planned costs.

13.9 PROJECT APPRAISAL BY FINANCIAL INSTITUTIONS

Financial institutions appraise a project from the marketing, technical, financial, economic, and managerial angles. The principal issues considered and the criteria employed in such appraisal are discussed below.

Market Appraisal The importance of the potential market and the need to develop a suitable marketing strategy cannot be over-emphasised. Hence efforts are made to:

- Examine the reasonableness of the demand projections by utilising the findings of available surveys, industry association projections, Planning Commission projections since scrapped, and independent market surveys (which may sometimes be commissioned).
- Assess the adequacy of the marketing infrastructure in terms of promotional effort, distribution network, transport facilities, stock levels, etc.
- Judge the knowledge, experience, and competence of the key marketing personnel.

Technical Appraisal The technical review done by financial institutions focuses mainly on the following aspects:

- Product mix
- Capacity
- Process of manufacture
- Engineering know-how and technical collaboration
- Raw materials and consumables
- Location and site
- Building
- Plant and equipments
- Manpower requirements
- Break-even point

Technical Appraisal The technical review is done by qualified and experienced personnel available in the institutions and/or outside experts (particularly where large and technologically sophisticated projects are involved).

Financial Appraisal The financial appraisal seeks to assess the following:

Reasonableness of the Estimate of Capital Cost While assessing the capital cost estimates, efforts are made to ensure that (a) padding or under-estimation of costs is avoided, (b) specification of machinery is proper, (c) proper quotations are obtained from potential suppliers, (d) contingencies are provided for, and (e) inflation factors are considered.

Reasonableness of the Estimate of Working Results The estimate of working results is sought to be based on (a) a realistic market demand forecast, (b) price computations for inputs and outputs that are based on current quotations and inflationary factors, (c) an approximate time schedule for capacity utilisation, and (d) cost projections that distinguish between fixed and variable costs.

Adequacy of Rate of Return The general norms for financial desirability are as follows:

- Internal rate of return : 15 percent
- Return on investment : 20–25 percent after tax
- Debt-service coverage ratio : 1.5 to 2.0

In applying these norms, however, a certain degree of flexibility is shown on the basis of the nature of the project, the risks inherent in the project, and the status of the promoter.

Appropriateness of the Financing Pattern The institutions consider the following in assessing the financial pattern:

- A general debt-equity ratio norm of 1 : 1.
- A requirement that promoters should contribute a certain percentage of the project cost.
- Stock exchange listing requirements.
- The means of the promoter and his capacity to contribute a reasonable share of the project finance.

Economic Appraisal The economic appraisal looks at the project from the larger social point of view. The methodology adopted by financial institutions for the purpose of economic evaluation (also referred to as social cost benefit analysis) is labeled as 'Partial Little Mirrlees' approach. In addition to the calculation of the economic rate of return as per this approach, they also look at two other economic indicators: (i) effective rate of protection, and (ii) domestic resource cost. Admittedly, the economic review done by financial institutions is not very rigorous and sophisticated. Also, the emphasis placed on this review has diminished. Now it is hardly done.

Managerial Appraisal In order to judge the managerial capability of the promoters, the following questions are raised:

- How resourceful are the promoters?
- How sound is the understanding of the project by the promoters?
- How committed are the promoters?

Resourcefulness This is judged in terms of the prior experience of the promoters, the progress achieved in organising various aspects of the project, the skill with which the project is presented, and the ability to raise committed capital and unforeseen shortfall in financing.

Understanding This is assessed in terms of the credibility of the project plan (including, inter alia, the organisation structure, the staffing plan, the estimated costs, the financing pattern, the assessment of various inputs, and the marketing programme) and the details furnished to the financial institutions.

Commitment This is gauged by the resources (financial, managerial, material, and other) applied to the project and the zeal with which the objectives of the project, short-term as well as long-term, are pursued. Managerial review also involves an assessment of the calibre of the key technical and managerial personnel working on the projects, the schedule for training them, and the remuneration structure for rewarding and motivating them.

SUMMARY

- Capital expenditures are very important for three inter-related reasons: (i) they have long-term consequences, (ii) they are difficult to reverse, and (iii) they involve substantial outlays.
- Capital budgeting, a complex process, may be divided into the following phases: (i) identification of potential investment opportunities, (ii) assembling of investment proposals, (iii) decision-making, (iv) preparation of capital budget and appropriations, (v) implementation, and (vi) performance review.
- Project appraisal involves six broad steps: (a) Forecast the costs and benefits. (b) Apply suitable investment criteria. (c) Assess the riskiness of the project. (d) Estimate the cost of capital. (e) Value the options. (f) Consider the overall corporate perspective.
- While measuring the costs and benefits of a capital expenditure proposal, bear in mind the following guidelines: (a) Focus on post-

tax cash flows. (b) Measure cash flows on an incremental basis. (c) Exclude financing costs. (d) Treat inflation consistently.

- The cash flow stream of a project may be divided into three parts: (a) initial investment, (b) operating cash inflows, and (c) salvage value.
- Several criteria have been proposed for project evaluation. The popular ones are: payback period, average rate of return, net present value, and internal rate of return.
- The payback period is the length of time required to recover the initial cash outlay on the project. According to this criterion, a project is acceptable if its payback period is less than a certain specified period.
- The average rate of return, also called the accounting rate of return, may be defined as:

$$\frac{\text{Profit after tax}}{\text{Book value of the investment}}$$

  A project is acceptable if its average rate of return exceeds a certain cut-off rate of return.
- The net present value of a project is equal to the sum of the present values of all the cash flows (outflows and inflows) associated with the project. A project is acceptable if its net present value exceeds zero.
- The internal rate of return of a project is the discount rate which makes its net present value equal to zero. A project is acceptable if its internal rate of return exceeds the cost of capital.
- Capital investments are almost invariably subject to risk arising from a variety of factors like competition, technological changes, shifts in consumer preferences, and so on.
- For measuring the risk of a project the commonly employed techniques are sensitivity analysis and break-even analysis.
- Sensitivity analysis is essentially "what if" analysis. It seeks to answer questions like: What will happen to the viability of a project when some variable like sales or investment or project life deviates from its expected value.
- Break-even analysis focuses on the minimum quantity that must be sold to ensure that the project does not lose money.
- The commonly used methods for risk adjustment are: adjusting the discount rate, adjusting the cash flows, and adjusting the payback period.

- All capital has a cost though it is not uniform. It tends to vary from one source of capital to another, from one firm to another, and from one point in time to another.
- The marginal cost of capital is the post-tax return the firm must earn on its proposed capital investments to satisfy the expectations of investors who provide funds to support such capital investments. It is calculated as the weighted arithmetic average of the specific cost of debt, preference, and equity capital proposed to be employed by the firm.
- More often than not, a project has a payoff in the form of new investment opportunities that may possibly open up if the project is undertaken.
- Valuing the options embedded in real life projects is difficult. Yet, if you can identify the options and specify the circumstances under which they would be exercised, you can make an informed estimate of their values.
- The capital budget of a firm, in order to be meaningful and viable must satisfy several overall corporate considerations: (i) It must be consistent with the long range strategic plans for the business. (ii) It must be compatible with the resources of the firm. (iii) It must be controllable.
- Financial institutions appraise a project from the marketing, technical, financial, and managerial angles.

14 Financing Strategy

The key issues to be addressed while formulating the financing strategy of a firm are:

- What should be the capital structure of the firm?
- Which financing instruments should the firm employ?
- What method of offering should the firm use?
- Which markets should the firm tap?
- When and at what price should the issue be made?
- What should be the distribution policy?
- How should a firm communicate with its investors?
- What should a firm do to improve the standard of corporate governance?

These issues are inter- related as shown in the financing octagon depicted in Exhibit 14.1. However for pedagogic convenience we will discuss them sequentially.

EXHIBIT 14.1 *The Financing Octagon*

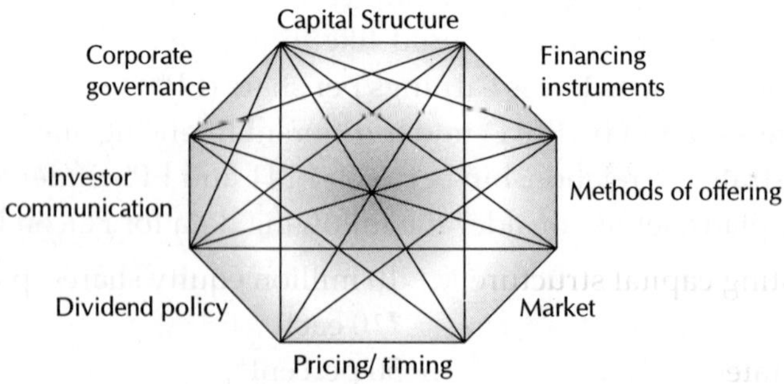

14.1 CAPITAL STRUCTURE

The two broad sources of finance available to a firm are: shareholders' funds and loan funds. Shareholders' funds come mainly in the form of equity capital and retained earnings and secondarily in the form of preference capital. Loan funds come in a variety of ways like debenture capital, term loans, deferred credit, fixed deposit, and working capital advance. Ignoring preference capital (which is of minor significance) the basic differences between shareholders' funds (referred to as equity) and loan funds (referred to as debt) are as follows:

Equity

- Equity shareholders have a residual claim on the income and wealth of the firm.
- Dividend paid to equity shareholders is not a tax deductible payment.

Debt

- Lenders have a fixed claim in the form of interest and principal payment.
- Interest paid to lenders is a tax deductible payment.

What are the key considerations in determining the debt equity ratio (the capital structure) of the firm? The important considerations in planning the capital structure are:

- Earnings per share
- Risk
- Control
- Flexibility
- Nature of assets

Earnings Per Share

Earnings per share, which is simply equity earnings divided by the number of outstanding equity shares, is regarded as an important financial number that firms would like to improve. Hence we need to understand how sensitive is earnings per share (EPS) to changes in profit before interest and tax (PBIT) under different financing alternatives.

To illustrate the relationship between PBIT and EPS under alternative financing plans, let us consider the following data for Falcon Limited

- Existing capital structure : 10 million equity shares, par value ₹10 each
- Tax rate : 50 percent

Falcon Limited plans to raise additional capital of ₹100 million for financing an expansion project. In this context, it is evaluating two alternative financing plans: (i) issue of equity shares (10 million equity shares of ₹10 per share), and (ii) issue of debentures carrying 14 percent interest.

What will be the EPS under the two alternative financing plans for two levels for PBIT say ₹20 million and ₹40 million? Exhibit 14.2 shows the value of EPS at these two levels of PBIT under the alternative financing plans.

EXHIBIT 14.2 ***Earnings Per Share Under Alternative Financing Plans***

	Equity Financing		*Debt Financing*	
	PBIT 20,000,000	*PBIT 40,000,000*	*PBIT 20,000,000*	*PBIT 40,000,000*
Interest	–	–	14,000,000	14,000,000
Profit before tax	20,000,000	40,000,000	6,000,000	26,000,000
Tax	10,000,000	20,000,000	3,000,000	13,000,000
Profit after tax	10,000,000	20,000,000	3,000,000	13,000,000
No of equity shares	20,000,000	20,000,000	10,000,000	10,000,000
EPS	0.50	1.00	0.30	1.30

In general, the relationship between profit before interest and taxes and earnings per share is as follows:

$$\text{Earnings per share} = \frac{[\text{PBIT} - \text{Interest}](1 - \text{Tax rate}) - \text{Preference dividend}}{\text{Number of equity shares}}$$

The break even PBIT for the two alternative financing plans is the level of PBIT at which EPS is the same under both the financing plans. It can be graphically obtained by plotting the relationship between PBIT and EPS under the two alternatives and noting the point of intersection. This is shown in Exhibit 14.3 for the example of Falcon limited. From this figure we find that the break even level of PBIT is ₹28 million. If PBIT is below

EXHIBIT 14.3 ***Break-even PBIT Level***

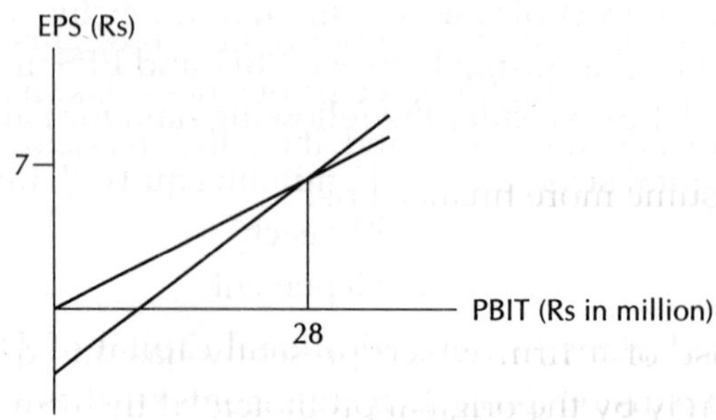

₹28 million equity financing is preferable to debenture financing; if PBIT is higher than ₹28 million, the opposite holds.

Risk

The two principal sources of risk in a firm are business risk and financial risk.

Business risk refers to the variability of profit before interest and taxes. It is influenced, inter alia, by the following factors.

- *Demand Variability* Other things being equal, the higher the variability of demand for the products manufactured by the firm, the higher is its business risk.
- *Price Variability* A firm which is exposed to a higher degree of volatility for the prices of its products is, in general, characterised by a higher degree of business risk in comparison with similar firms which are exposed to a lesser volatility for the prices of their products.
- *Variability of Input Prices* When input prices are highly variable, business risk tends to be high.
- *Proportion of Fixed Costs* If fixed costs represent a substantial proportion of total costs, other things being equal, business risk is likely to be high. This is because when fixed costs are high, PBIT is more sensitive to variations in demand

Financial risk represents the risk emanating from financial leverage. When a firm employs a high proportion of debt in its capital structure, i.e, when it has a high degree of financial leverage, it carries a high burden of fixed financial commitment. Equity shareholders, who have a residual interest in the income and wealth of the firm, are naturally exposed to the risk arising from such fixed commitments. Equity shareholders face this risk, also referred to as financial risk, in addition to business risk.

Generally, the affairs of the firm are, or should be, managed is such a way that the total risk borne by equity shareholders, which consists of business risk plus financial risk, is not unduly high. This implies that if the firm is exposed to a high degree of business risk, its financial risk should be kept low. On the other hand, if the firm has a low business risk profile, it can assume more financial risk.

Control

Consider the case of a firm which presently has an equity capital of 1000 owned entirely by the original promoters. If the firm wants to raise additional capital, say another 1000, it may go for debt finance, or a rights issue of equity capital, or a public issue of equity capital , or a combination of two or more of these. The pros and cons of the three basic ways of raising additional finance are shown below:

	Pros	*Cons*
• Rights issue of equity capital	No dilution of control	Severe limits on the financing
	No financial risk	Higher cost
• Debt capital	No dilution of control	Financial risk
	Lower cost	
• Public issue of equity capital	No financial risk	Dilution of control
		Higher cost

Since the rights issue option severely limits the financing ability of the firm—the present owners may lack the resources or inclination or both—the options which may merit serious considerations are debt capital and public issue of equity capital. In evaluating these options, among other things, the issue of control is important.

Flexibility

Flexibility refers to the ability of a firm to raise capital from any source it wishes to tap. It provides manoeuvrabilty to the finance manager. Generally, if the return earned on equity is satisfactory, the firm can raise further equity capital as there is no restriction on the amount of equity capital a firm can raise. However, as the debt equity ratio is normally not permitted to exceed a certain level (which may be specified by some regulatory authority, or determined by financial institutions, or indicated by the capital market), the firm cannot presume that it can always raise further capital by issuing debt securities. Hence, flexibility for practical purposes may mean that the firm does not exhaust fully its debt capacity. Put differently, it implies that the firm maintains reserve borrowing power to enable it to raise debt capital to fund unforeseen needs.

Nature of Assets

The nature of a firm's assets has an important bearing on its capital structure. If the assets are primarily tangible (plant and machinery and buildings), debt finance is used more. For example, electric utility companies use more debt because their assets are mainly tangible, physical in nature. On the other hand, if the assets are primarily intangible (brands and technical know how) debt finance is used less. For example, software companies use very little debt as there assets are mainly intangible.

What explains the link between the nature of assets and the use of debt finance? The major explanation is that lenders are more willing to lend against tangible assets and less inclined to lend against intangible assets.

A Checklist

When should the firm use more equity and when should the firm use more debt. Here is a checklist:

Use more equity when	*Use more debt when*
• The corporate tax rate applicable to the firm is negligible.	• The corporate tax rate applicable to the firm is high.
• Business risk exposure is high.	• Business risk exposure is low.
• Dilution of control is not an important issue.	• Dilution of control is an important issue.
• The assets of the firm are mostly intangible.	• The assets of the firm are mostly tangible.
• The firm has many valuable growth options.	• The firm has few growth options.

14.2 FINANCING INSTRUMENTS

Equity and debt come in a variety of forms and are raised in different ways. The important forms are shown in Exhibit 14.4 which shows the menu of financing available to a firm. The various forms of financing have been discussed in greater detail in the following chapter.

Public and Private Sources of Capital

A firm can raise equity and debt capital from both public and private sources. Capital raised from public sources is in the form of securities offered to public through an offer document filed with the Securities and Exchange Board of India[1]. These securities can be traded on public secondary markets like the National Stock Exchange or the Bombay Stock Exchange, which are recognised stock exchanges that facilitate the trading of public securities.

Private capital comes either in the form of loans given by banks and financial institutions or in the form of securities like equity shares, preference shares, and debentures which are privately placed with

[1] This, however does not apply when a firm raises fixed deposits or issues commercial paper.

EXHIBIT 14.4 *Menu of Financing*

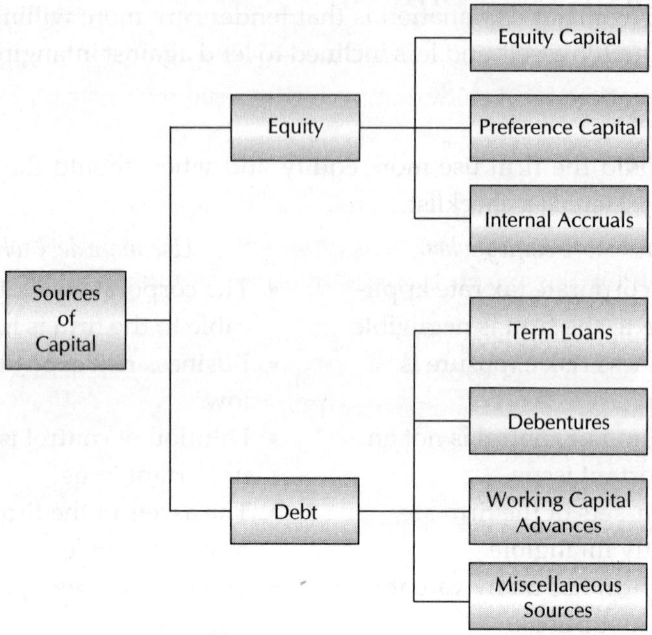

a small group of sophisticated investors like venture capital firms, financial institutions, insurance companies, mutual funds, and wealthy individuals.

The Typical Pattern of Financing

When a company is formed, it first issues equity shares to the promoters (founders) and also, in most cases, raises loans from banks, financial institutions, and other sources. As the need for financing increases, the company may issue shares and debentures privately to promoters' relatives, friends, business partners, employees, financial institutions, banks, mutual funds, venture capital funds, and others—venture capital funds are likely to be an important source of finance for a nascent venture. Such investors are specific and small in number.

As the company grows further, it may have to raise capital from the public. The first issue of equity shares to the public by an unlisted company is called the initial public offering (IPO). Subsequent offerings are called seasoned offerings.

Apart from equity shares, a firm may issue preference shares[2] and debentures to the general investing public through a public issue.

[2] Over the years preference shares have declined in importance

14.3 METHODS OF OFFERING

There are different ways in which a company may raise finances in the primary market: public offering, rights issue, and private placement.

Public Offering

A public offering or public issue involves sale of securities to the members of the public. The three types of public offering are: the initial public offering (IPO), the seasoned equity offering, and the bond offering.

Initial Public Offering The first public offering of equity shares of a company, which is followed by a listing of its shares on the stock market, is called the initial public offering (IPO).

Decision to Go Public The decision to go public (or more precisely the decision to make an IPO so that the securities of the company are listed on the stock market and are publicly traded) is a very important issue. It is a complex decision, which calls for carefully weighing the benefits against costs.

Benefits	*Costs*
• Access to a larger pool of capital	• Dilution
• Respectability	• Loss of flexibility
• Lower cost of capital compared to private placement	• Disclosures and accountability
• Liquidity	• Periodic costs

Eligibility for IPOs An Indian company, excluding certain banks and infrastructure companies, can make an IPO if it satisfies the following conditions.[3]

- The company has a certain track record of profitability and a certain minimum networth.
- The securities are compulsorily listed on a recognised stock exchange, which means that a certain minimum percent of each class of securities is offered to the public.
- The promoter group (promoters, friends, relatives, associates, etc.) is required to make a certain minimum contribution to the post-issue capital.
- The promoters' contribution to the equity is subject to a certain lock-in period.

[3] The guidelines for making an IPO tend to change. Readers are advised to refer to the latest guidelines at www.sebi.gov.in

The IPO Process From the perspective of merchant banking, the IPO process consists of four major phases: (a) hiring the merchant bankers, (b) due diligence and prospectus preparation, (c) marketing, and (d) subscription and allotment.

The company wishing to go public has to hire the merchant bankers to manage its offering. The selection of a merchant banker is usually referred to as a 'beauty contest'. Typically, it involves meeting different merchant bankers, discussing the plans for going public, and getting a valuation estimate. Understandably, the choice of the merchant banker is guided mainly by the valuation estimate offered. Often, a company going for an IPO selects two or more merchant bankers to manage the issue. The primary manager is called the "lead manager" and the other managers are called "co-managers".

Once the managers are selected, *due diligence and prospectus preparation* begin. The merchant bankers understand the company's business and plans, examine various documents and records, prepare the draft prospectus, file the same with the regulatory authorities, and arrange for its printing. Merchant bankers, lawyers, accountants, and company managers have to toil for countless hours to complete the legal formalities that finally culminate in the printing of the prospectus. Since book building is commonly used, the issue price is not fixed in advance, but a price band is given.

The next phase of an IPO is the *marketing phase.* After all the regulatory approvals are in place, the company embarks on a *road show* to promote the issue. A road show involves presentation by the management of the company to potential investors (mostly institutional) in different locations. Concurrently, the issue is advertised in various media primarily targeted at retail investors.

The final phase of the IPO involves receiving *subscription and allotment* of shares. The subscription is normally kept open for five to ten days. During this period, investors can submit their bid-cum-application forms. After the subscription is closed, the merchant bankers fix the final issue price, determine the pattern of allotment, complete the allotment of shares, and secure the listing on one or more recognised stock exchanges.

Seasoned Equity Offering For most companies their IPO is seldom their last public issue. As companies need more finances, they are likely to make further trips to the capital market with seasoned equity offerings, also called secondary or follow on offerings.

While the process of a seasoned equity offering is similar to that of an IPO, it is much less complicated. The company may employ the merchant bankers who handled the IPO. Further, with the availability of secondary market prices, there is no need for elaborate valuation. Finally, prospectus preparation and road shows can be completed with less effort and time than that required for the IPO.

Bond Offering The bond offering process is similar to the IPO process. There are, however, some differences:

- The prospectus for a bond offering typically emphasises a company's stable cash flows, whereas the prospectus for an equity offering highlights the company's growth prospects.
- Pure debt securities are typically offered through the 100 percent retail route because the book building route is not appropriate for them.
- Debt securities are generally secured against the assets of the issuing company and that security should be created within six months of the close of the issue of debentures.
- A debt issue cannot be made unless credit rating from a credit rating agency is obtained and disclosed in the offer document.
- It is mandatory to create a debenture redemption reserve for every issue of debentures.
- It is necessary for a company to appoint one or more debenture trustees before a debenture issue.

Rights Issue

A rights issue involves selling securities in the primary market by issuing rights to the existing shareholders. When a company issues additional equity capital, it has to be offered in the first instance to the existing shareholders on a pro rata basis. This is required under the Companies Act, 2013. The shareholders, however, may by a special resolution forfeit this right, partially or fully, to enable a company to issue additional capital only to the public.

Procedure for Rights Issue A company making a rights issue sends a letter of offer along with a composite application form consisting of four forms (A, B, C and D) to the shareholders. Form A is meant for the acceptance of the rights and application for additional shares. This form also shows the number of rights shares the shareholder is entitled to. It also has a column through which a request for additional shares may be made. Form B is to be used if the shareholder wants to renounce the rights in favour of someone else. Form C is meant for application by the renouncee in whose favour the rights have been renounced, by the original allottee, through Form B. Form D is to be used to make a request for split forms. The composite application form must be mailed to the company within a specific period, which is usually 30 days.

Rights Issue versus Public Issue A rights issue offers several advantages over a public issue. The floatation costs of a rights issue are significantly lower than those of a public issue. Theoretically, the subscription price of a rights issue is irrelevant because the wealth of a shareholder who subscribes to the rights issue or sells the rights remains unchanged, irrespective of what the subscription price is. Hence, the problem of transfer of wealth from existing shareholders to new shareholders does not arise in a rights issue.

Private Placement

A private placement is an issue of securities to a select group of persons not exceeding 49. Private placement of shares and convertible debentures by a listed company can be of two types.

Preferential Allotment When a listed company issues shares or debentures to a select group of persons in terms of the provisions of Chapter VII of SEBI (ICDR) Regulations, it is referred to as a private placement. The issuer has to comply with various provisions, relating to pricing, disclosures, lock-in period and so on, apart from the requirements of the Companies Act.

Qualified Institutional Placement (QIP) A QIP is an issue of equity shares or convertible securities to Qualified Institutional Buyers in terms of the provisions of Chapter VIII of SEBI (ICDR) Regulations.

Private Placement of Debentures In India, corporates, financial institutions, infrastructure companies, and others depend considerably on privately placed debentures which are subscribed to mainly by mutual funds, banks, insurance organisations, provident funds, and pension funds.

For quite some time the regulatory framework for private placement of debentures was very lax. Information and disclosures to be included in the Private Placement Memorandum were not defined, credit rating was not mandatory, listing was not compulsory, and banks and financial institutions could subscribe to these issues without too many constraints.

The regulatory framework changed significantly in late 2003 when SEBI and RBI tightened their regulations over the issuance of privately placed debentures and the subscription of the same by banks and financial institutions. The key features of the new regulatory dispensation are:

- The disclosure requirements for privately placed debentures are similar to those of publicly offered debentures.
- Debt securites shall carry a credit rating of not less than investment grade from a credit rating agency registered with SEBI.
- Debt securities shall be issued and traded in demat form.
- Debt securities shall be compulsorily listed.
- The trading in privately placed debt shall take place between QIBs and HNIs (High Networth Individuals) in standard denomination of ₹10 lakh.
- Banks should not invest in non-SLR securities of original maturity of less than one year other than commercial paper and certificates of deposits which are covered under RBI guidelines.
- Banks should not invest in unrated non-SLR securities.

How Do the Various Methods of Offering Compare

How do the three methods compare broadly in terms of the amount that can be raised, the cost of issue, dilution of control, degree of underpricing, and market perception? Exhibit 14.5 presents a summary comparison for an equity issue. As far as a debt issue is concerned, dilution of control is a non-issue and the market perception is positive under all the methods.

EXHIBIT 14.5 *Summary Comparison of the Various Methods*

	Public Issue	*Rights Issue*	*Private Placement*
• Amount that can be raised	Large	Moderate	Moderate
• Cost of issue	High	Negligible	Negligible
• Dilution of control	Yes	No	Yes
• Degree of underpricing	Large	Irrelevant	Small
• Market perception	Negative	Neutral	Neutral

14.4 MARKETS

A firm planning to raise finances may tap one or more of the following capital markets:

Indian Capital Market A firm accessing the Indian Capital market has to conform to the regulations of the Securities and Exchange Board of India (SEBI).

Euro Capital Market The euro capital market is a global market beyond the purview of any national regulatory body. Many firms in India have accessed this market since the early 1990s using instruments like Global Depository Receipts (GDRs) and Euro Convertible Bonds (ECBs). Firms interested in accessing this market have to take the approvals of the Ministry of Finance, Foreign Investment Promotion Board, and Reserve Bank of India.

Foreign Domestic Capital Market Some Indian firms have accessed or are in the process of accessing the domestic capital market of US (through instruments like Yankee bonds and American Depository Receipts), U.K., and Japan. Obviously, an Indian firm interested in accessing foreign domestic capital market has to obtain clearances from Indian authorities as well as the regulatory bodies of the foreign country.

How do the three markets compare in terms of access, market size, cost of issue, disclosure and transparency requirements, and prices/rates? Exhibit 14.6 provides a summary comparison of the three markets.

EXHIBIT 14.6 ***A Summary Comparison of the Three Markets***

	Indian Capital Market	*Euro Capital Market*	*Foreign Domestic Market*
• Access	Easy	Restricted	Highly Restricted
• Market	Small	Large	Large
• Cost of Issue	High	Low	Low
• Disclosure & transparency	Less onerous	Onerous	Highly onerous
• Prices/Rates	Not so attractive	Attractive	More attractive

14.5 PRICING AND TIMING

Along with the choice of instrument, method of offering, and the market, the firm issuing securities has to determine when and at what price should its issue be made. Since pricing and timing are closely inter-related they may be discussed together.

If the capital market is efficient in the sense that the market price is always equal to the intrinsic value, the simple guideline with respect to pricing and timing would be: "Raise finances whenever they are required by issuing securities at prevailing market prices".

Since the market price and intrinsic value may diverge in real life situations, pricing and timing are important issues. Bear in mind the following guidelines while resolving these issues.

Decouple Financing and Investment Decisions Opportunities for smart moves on investment and financing side of the business often do not sychronise. Hence financing decisions should be decoupled from investment decisions, As Warren Buffett says: "Therefore, we simply borrow when conditions seem non-oppressive and hope that we will later find intelligent expansion or acquisition opportunities, which as we have said are more likely to pop up when conditions in the debt market are clearly oppressive. Our basic principle is that if you want to shoot rare, fast moving, elephants, you should always carry a loaded gun".

Never Be Greedy If present conditions are favourable for a certain type of financing, take advantage of it. Driven by greed, do not wait for an even better possible tomorrow. The advice of Bernard Baruch formulated for the stock market investor applies equally well to the participant in financial market: "Leave the first 10 percent and the last 10 percent for someone else".

Ensure Inter-generational Fairness Tapping the equity market when it is buoyant does not mean that the firm should price its equity issue far above its intrinsic value. If it does so, existing shareholders will benefit at the expense of new shareholders. While it may appear alluring in the short run, it may not be advisable in the long run. Firms which succumb to such a temptation for immediate gains may eventually alienate new investors and lose credibility in the capital market. To ensure inter-generational fairness among equity shareholders, the firm should price its issue at more or less the intrinsic value and to more or less guarantee an encouraging response to its issue, the firm should approach the market when it feels that the market price is higher than the intrinsic value by a margin of say 10 to 20 percent.

14.6 DISTRIBUTION POLICY

Very broadly, the distribution policy is concerned with issues like how much of its earnings should a firm pay by way of dividends, what are the implications of bonus issues and stock-splits, and when does it make sense to buy back shares.

Key Considerations Influencing Dividend Policy

The key considerations influencing a firm's dividend policy are as follows:

Earnings Prospects If the firm expects its earnings to grow in future it may be inclined to pay more by way of dividends. On the other hand, if it is uncertain about its earnings prospects it may pay less by way of dividends.

Funding Requirements An important factor influencing the payout ratio of a firm is its requirement for funds in the foreseeable future. This is usually assessed with the help of financial forecasts prepared in the context of long range planning. Generally, firms which have substantial investment opportunities and consequently considerable funding needs tend to keep the dividend payout ratio low to conserve resources for growth.

Dividend Record The past dividend record of a firm has a bearing on its current dividend payment. Firms generally pursue a policy of gradually varying (this mostly implies increasing but occasionally means decreasing) the rupee level of dividend over time.

Liquidity Position Dividends entail cash payment. Hence, the liquidity position of the firm has a bearing on its dividend decision. A firm may be unable to distribute more than a small fraction of its earnings, despite its desire to do so, if it is hard pressed for liquidity.

Shareholder Preference The preference of shareholders may influence the dividend payout ratio of the firm. When equity shareholders have greater interest in current dividend vis-à-vis capital gains, the firm may be inclined to follow a liberal dividend payout policy. On the other hand, if equity shareholders have a strong preference for capital gains, the firm may plough back a larger proportion of its earnings.

Control External financing , unless it is through a rights issue, involves dilution of control. If external finances are raised through a public issue of equity capital, the existing shareholders will have to share control with the new shareholders. Internal financing by way of retained earnings, on the other hand, leads to no dilution of control. Hence, if the shareholders and management of the firm are averse to dilution of control, the firm should rely more on retained earnings.

Bonus Shares

Share issued to existing shareholders as a result of the capitalisation of reserves are bonus shares. Exhibit 14.7 illustrates the nature of this capitalisation

EXHIBIT 14.7 ***Effect of a Bonus Issue on the Equity Portion of the Balance Sheet***

Part A : Equity Portion Before the Bonus Issue	
Paid up Share Capital	₹10,000,000
(1,000,000 shares of ₹10 each fully paid)	
Reserves and Surplus	₹30,000,000
Part B : Equity Portion After the Bonus Issue in the Ratio 1:1	
Paid up Share Capital	₹20,000,000
(2,000,000 shares of ₹10 each fully paid)	
Reserves and Surplus	₹20,000,000

In the wake of the bonus issue:

- The shareholders' proportional ownership remains unchanged.
- The book value per share, the earnings per share, and the market price share decrease, but the number of shares increases.

From the above it appears that the issue of bonus shares is more or less a financial gimmick without any real impact on the welfare of equity shareholders. Yet, firms do issue bonus shares and shareholders eagerly look forward to such issues. Why? The primary reason is that shareholders regard a bonus issue as a firm indication that the prospects of the company have brightened. Further, they feel reassured that the management is investor friendly. A secondary reason is that the bonus issue brings the price of the share in a more popular trading range.

Stock Splits

In a stock split, the par value per share is reduced and the number of shares is increased proportionately. Exhibit 14.8 illustrates the nature of this change.

EXHIBIT 14.8 ***Effects of a Stock Split on the Equity Portion of the Balance Sheet***

Part A: Equity Portion of the Balance Sheet	
Paid up share capital	₹5,000,000
(500,000 shares of ₹10 each)	
Reserves and surplus	₹10,000,000

(Contd.)

EXHIBIT **14.8** *(Contd.)*

Part B: Equity Portion After Stock Split in Ratio 10:1	
Paid up share capital	₹5,000,000
(5000,000 shares of ₹1 each)	
Reserves and surplus	₹10,000,000

Comparison Between Bonus Issue and Stock Split

A comparison between a bonus issue and a stock split is given below:

Bonus Issue	*Stock Split*
• The par value of the stock remains constant.	• The par value of the stock is reduced.
• A part of reserves is capitalised.	• There is no capitalistion of reserves
• The shareholders' proportional ownership remains unchanged.	• The shareholders' proportional ownership remains unchanged.
• The book value per share, the earnings per share, and the market price per share decline.	• The book value per share, the earnings per share, and market price per share decline.
• The market price per share is brought within a more popular trading range.	• The market price per share is brought within a more popular trading range.

Share Buybacks

A share buyback means that a company repurchases its own shares from the market. A common practice in countries like US and UK, buyback of shares have now been permitted in India and many companies have share buyback programmes.

Motives for Share Buyback Why do companies resort to share buyback? Some of the common explanations for share buyback are:

- The management believes that the stock of the company is undervalued.
- The company has excess cash but lacks profitable investment opportunities.
- It represents a defensive strategy against a potential takeover.
- The management wants to signal to investors its confidence in the future earnings of the firm.
- It may be used to increase the leverage of the firm.

Regulation of Buyback The key provisions of the Companies Act with respect to buyback are as follows:

- The buyback programme should be authorised by a special resolution passed in the general meeting of the company. Further, it should be completed within a period of 12 months from the date of approval by the shareholders.
- The post buyback debt-equity ratio of the company should not exceed 2 : 1.
- The buyback should not exceed 25 % of the total paid-up capital and free reserves of the company.
- After completing a buyback programme, a company should not make a further issue of equity securities within a period of 24 months except by way of a bonus issue or in discharge of a subsisting obligation (like conversion of warrants, debentures or preference shares into equity shares, stock option scheme, and sweat equity scheme).
- The buyback may be funded by the following means: (a) free reserves and share premium, (b) cash generated from the disposal of capital assets, (c) a public equity issue made exclusively for the purpose of buyback, and (d) a debenture issue.

Procedural Guidelines for buybacks have been issued by the Securities and Exchange Board of India (SEBI) The important guidelines are:

- The buyback can be done through a tender offer, Dutch auction route, reverse book-building, reverse rights, or through stock market purchases. Promoters, however, are barred from offering their shares if stock market purchases are made.
- The buyback cannot be done through negotiated deals (where a block of shares is picked up from a single/few investor, spot deals and private placement).
- The buyback process has to be handled by a merchant banker/s duly appointed by the company. The merchant banker/s will be held responsible for due diligence, pro-rata acceptance of shares, and so on.

14.7 INVESTOR COMMUNICATION

To ensure that the intrinsic value of a company is fully reflected in its stock price, the company should communicate intelligently with the investors. What a company should do and should not do in this respect can be appreciated by understanding how the stock market really works. Share prices are not determined by a polling process in which all investors have an equal say. Rather, they are influenced by the actions of influential investors or lead steers. As Bennett Stewart and David M. Glassman put it: " Stock prices, like all prices, are set not by average investors; they are set 'at the margin' by the smartest money in the game. The herd is led by influential investors—lead steers as we call them. They care about cash flow and risk; they are not fooled by accounting illusion".

Given the dominant role of 'lead steers', the company should bear in mind the following guidelines while communicating with an efficient market.

Deemphasise Financial Disclosure The advocates of the 'disclosure' view of financial communication believe that the stock market is influenced by investors who assess companies by their reported financial results. Hence they argue that a company must paint a picture of steady earnings growth and cover any deficiencies by resorting to creative accounting. As a Wall Street Journal editorial put it: " A lot of executives apparently believe that if they figure out a way to boost reported earnings their stock price will go up even if the higher earnings do not represent an underlying economic change."

Empirical evidence on market efficiency, however, strongly supports the view that the market is very intelligent in penetrating through the veil of accounting reports and seeing a company's underlying economic performance. Hence efforts to artificially inflate reported earnings or creatively manage the bottom line are futile.

Avoid Financial Hype Many managers believe that the securities of a company should be marketed like any other product. This implies that the company should hire a public relations firm, sell its story through imaginative advertisements, and hype itself in the best tradition of Madison Avenue. This approach is guided by the " demand and supply view" which assumes that securities can be sold at higher prices by stimulating their demand through high pressure selling tactics.

The "demand and supply view" is not a valid view in a market dominated by rational lead steers. The "intrinsic value view" prevails in such a market. If prices rise because unsophisticated investors are momentarily swayed by financial hype, lead steers will sell and align price with intrinsic value. They may even short sell. As Bennett Stewart and David M. Glassman put it: " This means that in a market dominated by forward—looking investors, shares can change hands without changing price".

Cut 'Lead Steers' into the Planning Process Meaningful communication with 'lead steers' calls for cutting them into the planning process of the company. This means that, inter alia, they should be provided information about the following: (a) average operating profit over a business cycle from capital already committed to the business, (b) new investments projected in the foreseeable future, (c) expected rate of return over the lives of investment, (d) target capital structure and financing policy, (e) acquistion/divestiture strategy, (f) international performance , and (g) management compensation plan.

14.8 CORPORATE GOVERNANCE

Corporate governance is concerned basically with the agency problem that arises from the separation of finance and management (or, in more popular terms, ownership and control.) It refers to the constraints that managers put on themselves or that investors impose on managers to induce investors to provide funds *ex ante* and check misallocation of resources *ex post* facto by managers. More specifically, corporate governance covers issues like the legal rights of investors, the role of large investors, the system of electing the board of directors, the composition of the board, the composition of the various sub-committees of the board, the compensation of the board members, the resposibilities of the board and its sub-committees, the ability of the board to maintain surveillance, the system of checks and balances, the incentives offered to managers to protect investors from dissipation of resources, the standards of financial reporting and corporate disclosures, and so on.

A great deal of concern has been expressed in recent years about the poor quality of corporate governance, in general, in India.This was also echoed in the 1999 Budget speech of Union finance minister Yashwant Sinha when he said ".... if investors have to be drawn back to the capital market, companies have to put their houses in order by following internationally accepted practice of corporate governance. This is necessary to enhance investor confidence".

Legal Provisions Under the Companies Act

The key provisions of the Companies Act with respect to corporate boards are:

- **Strength** A public limited company must have at least three directors.

- **Meetings** The board of directors must meet at least once in a quarter.
- **Composition** There is no fixed number of non-executive directors. No person can be a director of more than twenty companies.
- **Powers** The board of directors has the powers to (a) borrow, lend, and invest funds, (b) recommend dividends, and (c) appoint the managing director.
- **Remuneration** The total remuneration of the directors is subject to a ceiling of 11 percent of net profits.
- **Duties** The board has the duty to present the financial statements and directors' report to members.
- **Liabilities** The board is punishable for breach of trust, dishonesty, and fraud.
- **Audit committee** There shall be an audit committee in all companies having a paid up capital of not less than ₹50 million.

The SEBI Code

The key elements of the SEBI code, which is based on the recommendations of the Kumaramangalam Birla Committee report, are as follows:

- At least one-half of the board shall comprise non-executive directors and at least one-third of the board shall comprise of independent directors.
- An audit committee of at least three non-executive directors shall be set up, the majority of them being independent. It shall meet at least thrice a year.
- The remuneration paid to all directors shall be disclosed in the annual report.
- A Management Discussion and Analysis Report should form part of the annual report.
- Details of new appointees as directors shall be provided to the shareholders.
- The annual report shall have a section on corporate governance.
- The auditors of the company should give a certificate regarding compliance on corporate governance.

Reforming Corporate Governance

True, there are a number of provisions in the regulatory framework (the Companies Act, the Securities and Exchange Board of India Act, and so on) to guard the interest of investors. However, enlightened companies will have to go beyond them and ensure that they are not run primarily for the benefit of dominant shareholders[4].

To build a healthy, mutually beneficial, relationship with all its investors, it behoves on every company to improve the standards of its corporate governance. Some of the ways of strengthening corporate governance are:

- Regard institutional investors as strategic partners, not adversaries
- Separate the office of the chairman from that of the chief executive officer
- Expand the role of non-executive directors
- Ensure that the board of directors is informationally well equipped
- Link managerial compensation to performance
- Give employees stock options
- Improve corporate accounting and reporting practices

Reform of corporate governance thus calls for a multi pronged approach. It is indeed a tall order. Is it feasible to achieve such reforms? A cynic might say that vested interests tend to perpetuate inefficient corporate governance and the political and economic market place is not likely to deliver efficient governance. I do not share this view. Although our understanding of the politics of corporate governance is rather limited, I am convinced that the heightened competition that we are witnessing in all spheres of economic activity will lead to improvement in the quality of corporate governance. Access to external capital on economical terms is now a major competitive weapon and there seems to be no better way to ensure this than to improve the quality of corporate governance. Enlightened self- interest should prod a company to raise its standards of corporate governance. After all, as Gordon Donaldson put it, the price of independence is active self discipline.

SUMMARY

- The important considerations in planning the capital structure of a firm are: earnings per share, risk, control, flexibility, and nature of assets.
- A firm should use more equity when (a) the corporate tax rate applicable to the firm is negligible, (b) business risk exposure is high,

[4] The dominant shareholder is the controlling family in the case of a private sector firm or the foreign parent in the case of a subsidiary of a foreign company, or the government in the case of a public sector undertaking.

(c) dilution of control is not an important issue, (d) the assets of the firm are mostly intangible, and (e) valuable growth options exist.

- A firm should use more debt when: (a) the corporate tax rate applicable to the firm is high, (b) business risk exposure is low, (c) dilution of control is an important issue, (d) the assets of the firm are mostly tangible, and (e) the firm has few growth options.
- The market for financial securities may be divided into two segments: the primary market and the secondary market. New issues are made in the primary market whereas outstanding issues are traded in the secondary market.
- There are three ways in which a company may raise finances in the primary market: (i) public issue, (ii) rights issue, and (iii) private placement.
- A firm planning to raise finances may tap one or more of the following capital markets: Indian capital market, euro capital market, and foreign domestic capital market.
- Since the market price and intrinsic value may diverge in real life situations, pricing and timing are important issues. Remember the following guidelines while resolving these issues: (i) Decouple financing and investment decisions. (ii) Never be greedy. (iii) Ensure inter-generational fairness.
- The key considerations influencing a firm's dividend policy are: earnings prospects, funding requirements, dividend record, liquidity position, shareholder preference, and control.
- Bonus shares are issued to existing shareholders as a result of the capitalisation of reserves.
- In a stock split, the par value per share is reduced and the number of shares is increased proportionately.
- Given the dominant role of 'lead steers', a company should bear in mind the following guidelines while communicating with the market: (i) Deemphasise creative accounting. (ii) Avoid financial hype. (iii) Cut 'lead steers' into the planning process
- Corporate governance is concerned basically with the agency problem that arises from the separation of finance and management. To build a healthy, mutually beneficial, long-term relationship with its investors, it behoves on every company to improve the standard of its corporate governance.

Sources of Finance 15

To support its investments, a firm must find the means to finance them. Equity and debt represent two broad sources of finance for a business firm. Equity (referred to as shareholders' funds on balance sheets in India) consists of equity capital, retained earnings, and preference capital. Debt (referred to as loan funds on balance sheets in India) consists of term loans, debentures, and short-term borrowings.

We have already looked at various sources of finance in some context or the other. Our task here is to present a reasonably systematic picture of financing by assembling various pieces in a coherent manner. The concepts of financing are fairly simple and logical though the language may be somewhat unfamiliar.

This chapter describes the sources of finance required to support investments in fixed assets and working capital. It is divided into seven sections as follows:

- Equity capital
- Preference capital
- Internal accruals
- Term loans
- Debentures
- Working capital advances
- Miscellaneous sources

15.1 EQUITY CAPITAL

Equity capital represents ownership capital as equity shareholders collectively own the company. They enjoy the rewards and bear the risks of ownership. However, their liability, unlike the liability of the owner in a proprietary firm and the partners in a partnership concern, is limited to their capital contributions.

Some Terms

Authorised, Issued, Subscribed, and Paid-up Capital The amount of capital that a company can potentially issue, as per its memorandum, represents the **authorised capital**. The amount of capital offered by the company to the investors is called the **issued capital**. The amount of issued capital which is subscribed to by the investors is called the **subscribed capital**. The actual amount paid up by the investors is called the **paid-up capital**—typically the issued, subscribed, and paid-up capital are the same.

Par Value, Issue Price, Book Value, and Market Value The **par value** of an equity share is the value stated in the memorandum and written on the share scrip. The par value of equity shares is generally Re. 1 and ₹10 (the most popular denominations). One also comes across par values like ₹2, ₹5, ₹50, and ₹1,000.

The **issue price** is the price at which the equity share is issued. Typically when a company issues shares to the public, it sets the issue price higher than the par value. Sonata Software (India) Limited, for example, set its issue price at ₹80 per share as against the par value of ₹10 per share. When the issue price exceeds the par value, the difference is referred to as the share premium. It may be noted that the issue price cannot be, ordinarily, lower than the par value.[1]

The **book value** of an equity share is equal to:

$$\frac{\text{Paid-up equity capital} + \text{Reserves and surplus}}{\text{Number of outstanding equity shares}}$$

Quite naturally, the book value of an equity share tends to increase as the ratio of reserves and surplus to paid-up equity capital increases.

The **market value** of an equity share is the price at which it is traded in the market. This price can be easily established for a company which is listed on the stock market and actively traded. For a company which is listed on the stock market but traded very infrequently, it is difficult to obtain a reliable market quotation. For such a company, the market quotation may reflect the sale of a few shares in a past period and hence may not reflect the current market value of the firm. For a company which

[1] Technically, shares may be issued at a discount although procedural complexity makes it infrequent.

is not listed on the stock market, one can merely conjecture as to what its market price would be if it were traded. The market price is determined by a variety of factors like current earnings, growth prospects, risk, and company size.

Rights of Equity Shareholders

Right to Income Equity shareholders have a residual claim to the income of the firm. The income left after satisfying the claims of all other investors belongs to the equity shareholders. This income is simply equal to profit after tax minus preferred dividend.

The income of equity shareholders may be retained by the firm or paid out as dividends. It may be noted here that equity shareholders are entitled to dividend that is declared by the board of directors. The dividend decision is the prerogative of the board of directors.

Right to Control Equity shareholders as owners of the firm elect the board of directors and have the right to vote on every resolution placed before the company. The board of directors, in turn, selects the management which controls the operations of the firm.

Hence, equity shareholders, in theory, exercise an indirect control over the operations of the firm. How effective is such indirect control? Often it is weak and ineffective because of the apathy and indifference of most of the shareholders who rarely bother to cast their votes, by post or through a proxy, let alone attend the annual general meetings. Scattered and ill-organised, equity shareholders fail to exercise their collective power effectively. Usually, the management of the firm, with the support of a well organised but not a very substantial group of shareholders, is able to hold the reins of control.

Pre-emptive Right The pre-emptive right enables existing equity shareholders to maintain their proportional ownership by purchasing the additional equity shares issued by the firm. The law requires companies to give existing equity shareholders the first opportunity to purchase, on pro rata basis, additional issues of equity capital. For example, if the company has 1,000,000 outstanding shares of equity stock and proposes to issue 200,000 additional equity shares, an equity shareholder owning 1000 shares has the right to purchase 200 of the 200,000 new shares before those are offered to anyone else. The equity shareholders may, however, forfeit this right, partially or totally.

Right in Liquidation As in the case of income, equity shareholders have a residual claim over the assets of the firm in the event of liquidation. Claims of all others—statutory authorities, debenture holders, secured lenders, unsecured lenders, other creditors, and preferred shareholders—are prior to the claim of equity shareholders. More often than not equity shareholders do not get anything in the event of liquidation because the liquidation value of assets is not adequate to meet fully the claims of others.

Advantages and Disadvantages of Equity Capital

An important source of long-term financing, equity capital offers the following advantages:

- There is no compulsion to pay dividends. If the firm has insufficiency of cash it can skip equity dividends without suffering any legal consequences.
- Equity capital has no maturity date and hence the firm has no obligation to redeem.
- Because equity capital provides a cushion to lenders, it enhances the creditworthiness of the company. In general, other things being equal, the larger the equity base, the greater the ability of the firm to raise debt finance on favourable terms.

The disadvantages of raising finances by issuing equity shares are as follows:

- Sale of equity shares to outsiders dilutes the control of existing owners.
- The cost of equity capital is high, usually the highest. The rate of return required by equity shareholders is generally higher than the rate of return required by other investors.
- Equity dividends are paid out of profit after tax, whereas interest payments are tax-deductible expenses. Further, the company paying equity dividends has to pay the dividend distribution tax. All this makes the relative cost of equity more.
- The cost of issuing equity shares is generally higher than the cost of issuing other types of securities. Underwriting commission, brokerage costs, and other issue expenses are high for equity issues.

15.2 PREFERENCE CAPITAL

Preference capital represents a hybrid form of financing – it partakes some characteristics of equity and some attributes of debentures. It resembles equity in the following ways: (i) preference dividend is payable only out of distributable profits; (ii) preference dividend is not an obligatory payment (the payment of preference dividend is entirely within the discretion of directors); and (iii) preference dividend is not a tax-deductible payment and dividend distribution tax is payable on preference dividend.

Preference capital is similar to debentures in several ways: (i) the dividend rate of preference capital is usually fixed; (ii) the claim of preference shareholders is prior to the claim of equity shareholders; and (iii) preference shareholders do not normally enjoy the right to vote.

Features of Preference Capital

The important features of preference capital are as follows:

- Barring a few exceptions, preference shares in India carry a cumulative feature with respect to dividends. This means that unpaid dividends are carried forward and payable in future. Note that a company cannot declare equity dividends unless preference dividends are paid with arrears.
- Preference shares are typically redeemable after three to fifteen years.
- Preference shares do not carry voting rights. A preference shareholder, however, is entitled to vote under certain circumstances, if preference dividend is skipped.

Advantages and Disadvantages of Preference Capital

Preference capital offers the following advantages:

- There is no legal obligation to pay preference dividend. A company does not face bankruptcy or legal action if it skips preference dividend.
- Redemption of preference shares can be delayed without significant penalties.
- Preference capital is generally regarded as part of net worth. Hence, it enhances the creditworthiness of the firm.
- Preference shares do not, under normal circumstances, carry voting right. Hence, there is no dilution of control.

Preference capital, however, suffers from some serious shortcomings:

- Compared to debt capital, it is a more expensive source of financing because the dividend paid to preference shareholders is not, unlike debt interest, a tax-deductible expense.

- Though there is no legal obligation to pay preference dividends, skipping them can adversely affect the image of the firm in the capital market.
- Compared to equity shareholders, preference shareholders have a prior claim on the assets and earnings of the firm.
- If a firm skips preference dividends for three years, it has to grant voting right to preference shareholders on matters affecting them.

15.3 INTERNAL ACCRUALS

The internal accruals of a firm consist of depreciation charges and retained earnings. Depreciation represents the allocation of capital expenditure to various periods over which the capital expenditure is expected to benefit the firm. Suppose a machine costs ₹100,000 and has an economic life of 5 years at the end of which its expected salvage value is 0. If the machine is depreciated using the straight line method the annual depreciation charge will be ₹20,000. Each year a depreciation cost of ₹20,000 is shown in the profit and loss account. This cost merely represents a periodic writeoff of a capital cost incurred in the beginning. Put differently, it is a non-cash charge. Hence, it is considered an internal source of finance.

Retained earnings are that portion of equity earnings (profit after tax less preference dividends) which are ploughed back in the firm. Because retained earnings are the sacrifice made by equity shareholders, they are referred to as internal equity. Companies normally retain 20 percent to 80 percent of profit after tax for financing growth. If you look at a sample of corporate balance sheets you will find that reserves and surplus (other than share premium reserve and revaluation reserve), which essentially represent accumulated retained earnings, are an important source of long-term financing. Even this is an understatement of the contribution of retained earnings to long-term financing because a portion of reserves and surplus would have been capitalised by the firm if it had issued bonus shares.

Advantages and Disadvantages of Internal Accruals

Internal accruals are viewed very favourably by most corporate managements for the following reasons:

- Internal accruals are readily available. Management does not have to talk to outsiders (shareholders or lenders)

- Use of internal accruals, in contrast to external equity, eliminates issue costs and losses on account of underpricing.
- There is no dilution of control when a firm relies on internal accruals.
- The stock market generally views an equity issue with skepticism. Internal accruals, however, do not carry any negative connotation.

The disadvantages of internal accruals include the following

- The amount that may be available by way of internal accruals may be limited.
- The opportunity cost of retained earnings is quite high as it is equal to the cost of equity—remember that retained earnings, in essence, represent dividends denied to equity shareholders.
- The opportunity cost of depreciation generated funds is equal to the weighted average cost of capital of the firm.
- Many firms do not fully appreciate the opportunity costs of retained earnings and depreciation-generated funds. They tend to impute a low cost to internal accruals. Comforted by the easy availability of internal accruals and the notion that they have a low cost, managements may invest in sub-marginal projects that have a negative NPV.

15.4 TERM LOANS

So far we looked at the sources of finance which fall under the broad category of equity finance (or shareholders' funds). Now we turn our attention to long-term debt. Firms obtain long term debt mainly by raising term loans or issuing debentures.

Historically term loans given by financial institutions and banks have been the primary source of long-term debt for private firms and most public firms. Term loans, also referred to as term finance, represent a source of debt finance which is generally repayable in less than 10 years. They are employed to finance acquisition of fixed assets and working capital margin. Term loans differ from short-term bank loans which are employed to finance short-term working capital need and tend to be self-liquidating over a period of time, usually less than one year[2].

[2] In practice, of course, due to the phenomenon of "roll over", their effective maturity may be longer.

Features of Term Loans

The following features of term loans may be discussed.

- Currency
- Security
- Interest payment and principal repayment
- Restrictive covenants

Currency Financial institutions give rupee term loans as well as foreign currency term loans. The most significant form of assistance provided by financial institutions, rupee term loans are given directly to industrial concerns for setting up new projects as well as for expansion, modernisation, and renovation projects. These funds are provided for incurring expenditure on land, building, plant and machinery, technical know-how, miscellaneous fixed assets, preliminary expenses, preoperative expenses, and margin money for working capital.

Financial institutions provide foreign currency term loans for meeting the foreign currency expenditure towards import of plant, machinery and equipment, and payment of foreign technical know-how fees. The periodic liability for interest and principal remains in the currency/currencies of the loan and is translated into rupees at the prevailing rate of exchange for making payments to the financial institutions.

Security Term loans typically represent secured borrowing. Usually assets, which are financed with the term loan, provide the **prime** security. Other assets of the firm may serve as **collateral** security.

All loans provided by financial institutions, along with interest, liquidated damages, commitment charges, expenses, etc., are secured by way of:

- First equitable mortgage of all immovable properties of the borrower, both present and future; and
- Hypothecation of all movable properties of the borrower, both present and future, subject to prior charges in favour of commercial banks for obtaining working capital advance in the normal course of business.

Interest Payment and Principal Repayment The interest and principal repayment on term loans are definite obligations that are payable irrespective of the financial situation of the firm. To the general category of borrowers, financial institutions charge an interest rate that is related to the credit risk of the proposal, subject usually to a certain floor rate. Financial institutions impose a penalty for defaults. In case of default of payment of instalments of principal and/or interest, the borrower is liable to pay by way of liquidated damages additional interest calculated at the rate of 2 percent per annum for the period of default on the amount of principal and/or interest in default. In addition to interest, lending institutions levy a commitment fee on the unutilised loan amount.

The principal amount of a term loan is generally repayable over a period of 4 to 10 years after an initial grace period of 1 to 2 years. Typically, term loans provided by financial institutions are repayable in equal semi-annual instalments or equal quarterly instalments.

Note that the interest burden declines over time, whereas the principal repayment remains constant. This means that the total debt servicing burden (consisting of interest payment and principal repayment) declines over time. This pattern of debt servicing burden, typical in India, differs from the pattern obtaining in western economies where debt is typically amortised in equal periodic instalments.

Restrictive Covenants In order to protect their interest, financial institutions impose restrictive conditions on the borrowers. While the specific set of restrictive covenants depends on the nature of the project and the financial situation of the borrower, loan contracts often require that the borrowing firm:

- Broad-base its board of directors and finalise its management set-up in consultation with and to the satisfaction of the financial institutions;
- Make arrangements to bring additional funds in the form of unsecured loans/deposits for meeting overruns/shortfalls;
- Refrain from undertaking any new project and/or expansion or make any investment without the prior approval of the financial institutions;
- Obtain clearances and licenses from various government agencies;
- Repay existing loans with the concurrence of financial institutions;
- Refrain from additional borrowings or seek the consent of financial institutions for additional borrowings.

Further, loan agreements impose restrictions on the transfer of shareholding by promoters/associates.

Term Loan Procedure

The procedure associated with a term loan involves the following steps:

Submission of Loan Application The borrower submits an application form which seeks comprehensive information about the project. The application form covers, inter alia, the following aspects:

- Promoters' background
- Particulars of the industrial concern
- Particulars of the project (capacity, process, technical arrangements, management, location, land and buildings, plant and machinery, raw materials, effluents, labour, housing, and schedule of implementation)
- Cost of project
- Means of financing
- Marketing and selling arrangements
- Profitability and cash flow
- Economic considerations
- Government consents

Initial Processing of Loan Application When the application is received, an officer of the financial institution reviews it to ascertain whether it is complete for processing. If it is incomplete the borrower is asked to provide the required additional information. When the application is considered complete, the financial institution prepares a 'Flash Report' which is essentially a summarisation of the loan application. On the basis of the 'Flash Report', it is decided whether the project justifies a detailed appraisal or not.

Appraisal of the Proposed Project The detailed appraisal of the project covers the marketing, technical, financial, managerial, and economic aspects. The Appraisal Memorandum is normally prepared within two months after site inspection. Based on that a decision is taken whether the project will be accepted or not.

Issue of the Letter of Sanction If the project is accepted, a financial letter of sanction is issued to the borrower. This communicates to the borrower the assistance sanctioned and the terms and conditions relating thereto.

Acceptance of the Terms and Conditions by the Borrowing Unit On receiving the letter of sanction from the financial institution, the borrowing unit convenes its board meeting at which the terms and conditions associated with the letter of sanction are accepted and an appropriate resolution is passed to that effect. The acceptance of the terms and conditions has to be conveyed to the financial institution within a stipulated period.

Execution of Loan Agreement The financial institution, after receiving the letter of acceptance from the borrower, sends the draft of the agreement to the borrower to be executed by authorised persons and properly stamped as per the Indian Stamp Act, 1899. The agreement, properly executed and stamped, along with other documents as required by the financial institution must be returned to it. Once the financial institution also signs the agreement, it becomes effective.

Creation of Security The term loans (both rupee and foreign currency) and the deferred payment guarantee assistance provided by the financial institutions are secured through a mortgage, by way of deposit of title deeds, of immovable properties and hypothecation of movable properties. As the creation of mortgage, particularly in the case of land, tends to be a time consuming process, the institutions permit interim disbursements[3]. The mortgage, however, has to be created within a year from the date of the first disbursement. Otherwise the borrower has to pay an additional charge.

Disbursement of Loans Periodically, the borrower is required to submit information on the physical progress of the projects, financial status of the project, arrangements made for financing the project, contribution made by the promoters, projected funds flow statement, compliance with various statutory requirements, and fulfillment of the pre-disbursement conditions. Based on the information provided by the borrower, the financial institution will determine the amount of term loan to be disbursed from time to time. Before the entire term loan is disbursed, the borrower must fully comply with all terms and conditions of the loan agreement.

Monitoring Monitoring of the project is done at the implementation stage as well as at the operational stage. During the implementation stage, the project is monitored through (i) regular reports, furnished by the promoters, which provide information about placement of orders, construction of buildings, procurement of plant, installation of plant and machinery, trial production, etc., (ii) periodic site visits, (iii) discussion with promoters, bankers, suppliers, creditors, and others connected with the project, (iv) progress reports submitted by the nominee directors, and (v) audited accounts of the company.

---

[3] The interim security, prior to the creation of the final security, usually comprises all the stipulated security but the mortgage.

During the operational stage, the project is monitored with the help of (i) quarterly progress report on the project, (ii) site inspection, (iii) reports of nominee directors, and (iv) comparison of performance with projections.

The most important aspect of monitoring, of course, is the recovery of dues represented by interest and principal repayment.

15.5 DEBENTURES

Traditionally not very popular, debentures have emerged as an important instrument from the mid-1990s. Akin to promissory notes, debentures are instruments for raising debt finance. Debenture holders are the creditors of the company. The obligation of a company toward its debenture holders is similar to that of a borrower who promises to pay interest and principal at specified times. Debentures often provide more flexibility than term loans as they offer greater choice with respect to maturity, interest rate, security, repayment, and special features.

Features

The important features of debentures are as follows:

- When a debenture issue is sold to the investing public a trustee is appointed through a trust deed. The trustee, usually a bank or financial institution or insurance company, is supposed to ensure that the borrowing firm fulfills its contractual obligations.
- Debenture issues in India are typically secured by mortgages/ charges on the immovable properties of the company and a floating charge on its other assets (subject to prior charges created in favour of the company's bankers over the current assets). However, the order of priority of mortgages/charges may vary across different debenture issues. Occasionally, companies issue unsecured debentures. These are debentures that are not backed by specific assets of the firm, but by its general credit.
- Corporate debt may be short-term, medium-term or long term. Short-term corporate debt of less than one year is called commercial paper. Medium term debentures may have a maturity of 1 year to 5 years. Long-term debentures typically have a maturity period of 5 to 12 years.
- Publicly issued debentures that have a maturity period of 18 months or more have to be compulsorily credit rated.

- Debentures are typically redeemable in nature. For all debenture issues with a maturity period of more than 18 months, a Debenture Redemption Reserve (DRR) has to be created. The company should create a DRR equivalent to at least 50 per cent of the amount of issue before redemption commences.
- Debentures may carry a fixed rate of interest or floating rate of interest or zero rate of interest.
- Debentures may carry a 'call' feature which provides the issuing company the option to redeem the debentures at a certain price before the maturity period. Sometimes debentures may have a 'put' feature which gives the holder the right to seek redemption at specified times at predetermined prices.

Debt Rating

Ratings of debt securities issued by companies, quasi-government organisations, and the government, first originated in the U.S. where several firms offer such services. In India, too, there are credit rating agencies such as CRISIL, ICRA, CARE, Brick works and Fitch.

A debt rating essentially reflects the probability of timely payment of interest and principal by the borrower. The higher the debt rating, the greater the likelihood that the borrower will fulfill its obligation to pay interest and principal.

Debt ratings (or debt rating agencies) are supposed to offer low-cost information, serve as a basis for a proper risk-return trade-off, and impose healthy discipline on borrowers.

Rating Methodology Despite variations across individual rating agencies, the following features appear to be common in the rating methodology employed by different agencies:

1. Two broad types of analyses are done: (i) industry and business analysis, and (ii) financial analysis.
2. The key factors considered in industry and business analysis are: (i) growth rate and relationship with the economy, (ii) industry risk characteristics, (iii) structure of industry and nature of competition, and (iv) managerial capability of the issuer.
3. The important factors considered in financial analysis are: (i) earning power, (ii) business and financial risks, (iii) asset protection, (iv) cash flow adequacy, (v) financial flexibility, and (vi) quality of accounting.

4. Subjective judgment seems to play an important role in the assessment of the issue/issuer on various factors.
5. While each factor is normally scored separately, no mechanical formula is used for combining the scores on different factors to arrive at the rating conclusion. In the ultimate analysis, all variables are viewed as interdependent.
6. The rating is expressed in alphabetic symbols. A typical example is the following set of rating symbols employed by CRISIL for corporate debt securities.

AAA	:	Highest safety
AA	:	High safety
A	:	Adequate safety
BBB	:	Low safety
BB	:	Inadequate safety
B	:	High risk
C	:	Substantial risk
D	:	In default

7. Industry risk characteristics are likely to set the upper limit on rating.

Advantages and Disadvantages of Debt Financing

Term loans and debentures are two important ways of raising long-term debt. The advantages of debt financing are as follows:

- Interest on debt is a tax-deductible expense, whereas equity and preference dividend are paid out of profit after tax.
- Debt financing does not result in dilution of control because debt holders (term lending institutions and debenture holders) are not entitled to vote.
- Debt holders do not partake in the value created by the company as payments to them are limited to interest and principal.
- Issue costs of debt are significantly lower than those on equity and preference capital.
- The burden of servicing debt is generally fixed in nominal terms. Hence debt provides protection against high unanticipated inflation.

Debt financing is not an unmixed blessing. It has serious disadvantages associated with it:

- Debt financing entails fixed interest and principal repayment obligation. Failure to meet these commitments can cause a great deal of financial embarrassment and even lead to bankruptcy.

- Debt contracts impose restrictions that limit the borrowing firm's financial and operating flexibility. These restrictions may impair the borrowing firm's ability to pursue value-maximising strategies.
- If the rate of inflation turns out to be unexpectedly low, the real cost of debt will be greater than expected.

15.6 WORKING CAPITAL ADVANCES

Working capital advances by commercial banks represent the most important source for financing current assets.

Forms of Bank Finance

Working capital advance is provided by commercial banks in three primary ways : (i) cash credits/overdrafts, (ii) loans, and (iii) purchase/ discount of bills. In addition to these direct forms, commercial banks help their customers in obtaining credit from other sources through the letter of credit arrangement.

Cash Credits/Overdrafts Under a cash credit or overdraft arrangement, a pre-determined limit for borrowing is specified by the bank. The borrower can draw as often as required provided the outstandings do not exceed the cash credit/overdraft limit. The borrower also enjoys the facility for repaying the amount, partially or fully, as and when he desires. Interest is charged only on the running balance, not on the limit sanctioned. A minimum charge may be payable irrespective of the level of borrowing, for availing of this facility. This form of advance is highly attractive from the borrower's point of view because while the borrower has the freedom of drawing the amount in instalments as and when required, the interest is payable only on the amount actually outstanding.

Loans These are advances of fixed amounts to the borrower . The borrower is charged with interest on the entire loan amount, irrespective of how much he draws. In this respect, this system differs markedly from the overdraft or cash credit arrangement wherein interest is payable only on the amount actually utilised. Loans are payable either on demand or in periodical instalments. When payable on demand, loans are supported by a demand promissory note executed by the borrower. There is often a possibility of renewing the loan.Working capital loans now represent the dominant form of bank finance in India.

Purchase / Discount of Bills A bill arises out of a trade transaction. The seller of goods draws the bill on the purchaser. The bill may be either clean or documentary (a documentary bill is supported by a document of title to goods like a railway receipt or a bill of lading) and may be payable on demand or after a usance period which does not exceed 90 days. On acceptance of the bill by the purchaser, the seller offers it to the bank for discount/purchase. When the bank discounts/purchases the bill, it releases the funds to the seller. The bank presents the bill to the purchaser (the acceptor of the bill) on the due date and gets its payment.

Letter of Credit A letter of credit is an arrangement whereby a bank helps its customer to obtain credit from its (customer's) suppliers. When a bank opens a letter of credit in favour of its customer for some specific purchases, the bank undertakes the responsibility to honour the obligation of its customer, should the customer fail to do so.

Application and Processing

A customer seeking a working capital advance is required to submit an appropriate application form—there are different types of application forms for different categories of advances. The information furnished in the application covers, inter alia, the following: the name and address of the borrower and his establishment; the details of the borrower's business; the nature and amount of security offered. The application form has to be supported by various ancillary statements like the financial statements and financial projections of the firm.

The application is processed by the branch manager or his field staff. This primarily involves an examination of the following factors: (i) ability, integrity, and experience of the borrower in the particular business, (ii) general prospects of the borrower's business, (iii) purpose of advance, (iv) requirement of the borrower and its reasonableness, (v) adequacy of the margin, (vi) provision of security, and (vii) period of repayment.

Sanction and Terms and Conditions

Once the application is duly processed, it is put up for sanction to the appropriate authority. The sanctioning powers of various officials—like Branch Manager, Regional Manager, General Manager, etc—are defined by virtue of the position they occupy.

If the sanction is given by the appropriate authority, along with the sanction of advance the bank specifies the terms and conditions applicable to the advance. These usually cover the following: (i) the amount of loan or the maximum limit of the advance, (ii) the nature of the advance, (iii) the period for which the advance will be valid, (iv) the rate of interest applicable to the advance, (v) the primary security to be charged, (vi) the insurance of the security, (vii) the details of the collateral security, if any, to be provided, (viii) the margin to be maintained, and (ix) other restrictions or obligations on the part of the borrower. It is a common banking practice to incorporate important terms and conditions on a stamped security document to be executed by the borrower. This helps the bank to create the required charge on the security offered and also obligates the borrower to observe the stipulated terms and conditions.

Security

For working capital advances, commercial banks seek security either in the form of hypothecation or in the form of pledge.

Hypothecation Under this arrangement, the owner of the goods (hypothecator) borrows money against the security of movable property, usually inventories. The owner does not part with the possession of property. The rights of the lender (hypothecatee) depend upon the arrangement between the lender and the borrower. Should the borrower default in paying his dues, the lender can file a suit to realise his dues by selling the goods hypothecated.

Pledge In a pledge arrangement, the owner of the goods (pledgor) deposits the goods with the lender (pledgee) as security for the borrowing. Transfer of possession of goods is a precondition for pledge. The lender is expected to take reasonable care of goods pledged with him. The pledge contract gives the lender the right to sell goods and recover dues, should the borrower default in paying debt.

Margin Amount

Banks do not provide hundred per cent finance. They insist that the customer should bring a portion of the required finance from other sources. This portion is known as the margin amount. The margin amount tends to vary from asset to asset.

15.7 MISCELLANEOUS SOURCES

Apart from the above mentioned sources of finance, there are several other ways in which finance may be obtained. These include:

- Deferred credit
- Lease finance
- Hire purchase
- Unsecured loans and deposits
- Subsidies and sales tax deferments
- Short term loans from financial institutions
- Commercial paper
- Factoring

Deferred Credit

Many a time the suppliers of machinery provide deferred credit facility under which payment for the purchase of machinery is made over a period of time. The interest rate on deferred credit and the period of payment vary rather widely. Normally, the supplier of machinery, when he offers deferred credit facility, insists that a bank guarantee should be furnished by the buyer.

Lease Finance

A lease represents a contractual arrangement whereby the lessor grants the lessee the right to use an asset in return for periodic lease rental payments. While leasing of land, buildings, and animals has been known from times immemorial, the leasing of industrial equipments is a relatively recent phenomenon, particularly on the Indian scene.

There are two broad types of lease: finance lease and operating lease. A **finance lease** or capital lease, is essentially a form of borrowing. Its salient features are:

- It is an intermediate term to long-term non-cancellable arrangement. During the initial lease period, referred to as the 'primary lease period', which is usually 3 years or 5 years or 8 years, the lease cannot be cancelled.
- The lease is more or less fully amortised during the primary lease period. This means that during this period, the lessor recovers, through the lease rentals, his investment in the equipment along with an acceptable rate of return. Thus, a finance lease transfers substantially all the risks and rewards incidental to ownership to the lessee.
- The lessee is responsible for maintenance, insurance, and taxes.
- The lessee usually enjoys the option for renewing the lease for further periods at substantially reduced lease rentals.

An **operating lease** can be defined as any lease other than a finance lease. The salient features of an operating lease are:

- The lease term is significantly less than the economic life of the equipment.
- The lessee enjoys the right to terminate the lease at short notice without any significant penalty.
- The lessor usually provides the operating know-how and the related services and undertakes the responsibility of insuring and maintaining the equipment. Such an operating lease is called a 'wet lease'. An operating lease where the lessee bears the costs of insuring and maintaining the leased equipment is called a 'dry lease'.

From the above features of an operating lease it is evident that this form of lease does not result in a substantial transfer of the risks and rewards of ownership from the lessor to the lessee. The lessor structuring an operating lease transaction has to depend on multiple leases or on the realisation of a substantial resale value (on expiry of the first lease) to recover the investment cost plus a reasonable rate of return thereon. Therefore, specialising in operating lease calls for an in-depth knowledge of the equipments and the secondary (resale) market for such equipments. Of course, the prerequisite is the existence of a resale market. Given the fact that the resale market for most of the used capital equipments in our country lacks breadth, operating leases are not in popular use. In the recent years there have been attempts to structure car lease and computer lease transactions in the operating lease format.

At present, the following are the key characteristics of lease finance in India

- Most leases in India are finance leases, not operating leases.
- Lease finance is available for identifiable performing assets.
- Lease finance is available in small volumes.
- There is a great deal of flexibility in structuring lease finance.
- Lease of immovable assets is not possible by banks
- Lease tenors up to eight years are available.

Hire Purchase

Finance companies usually offer the facility of leasing as well as hire-purchase to its clients. What are the features of a hire-purchase arrangement? What is the difference between leasing and hire purchase, from the point of view of lessee (hirer)?

The main features of a hire-purchase arrangement are as follows:

- The hiree (the counterpart of lessor) purchases the asset and gives it on hire to the hirer (the counterpart of lessee).
- The hirer pays regular hire purchase instalments over a specified period of time. These instalments cover interest as well as principal repayment. When the hirer pays the last instalment, the title of the asset is transferred from the hiree to the hirer.
- The hiree charges interest on a flat basis. This means that a certain rate of interest, say 8 percent, is charged on the initial investment (made by the hiree) and not on the diminishing balance.
- The total interest collected by the hiree is allocated over various years. For this purpose the 'sum of the years digits' method is commonly employed.

The following differences between leasing and hire purchase, from the point of view of the lessee (hirer), may be noted.

Leasing	*Hire-Purchase*
• The lessee cannot claim depreciation.	• The hirer is entitled to claim depreciation.
• The entire lease rental is a tax-deductible expense for the lessee.	• Only the interest component of the hire purchase instalment is a tax-deductible expense for the hirer.
• The lessee, not being the owner of the asset, does not enjoy the salvage value of the asset.	• The hirer, being the owner of the asset, enjoys the salvage value of the asset.

Unsecured Loans and Deposits

Unsecured loans are typically provided by the promoters to fill the gap between the promoters' contribution required by financial institutions and the equity capital subscribed to by the promoters. These loans are subordinate to the institutional loans. The rate of interest chargeable on these loans is less than the rate of interest on the institutional loans. Finally these loans cannot be taken back without the prior approval of financial institutions.

Deposits from public, referred to as public deposits, usually represent unsecured borrowing of one to three years (five years in the case of non-banking finance companies) duration. Many existing companies prefer to raise public deposits instead of term loans from financial institutions because restrictive covenants do not accompany public deposits. However, it may not be possible for a new company to raise public deposits. Further, it may be difficult for it to repay public deposits within three years.

Subsidies and Sales Tax Deferments

Governments and development agencies may provide subsidies for certain kinds of projects. Of late, however, these have decreased in importance. Previously the central government as well as the state governments provided subsidies to industrial units located in backward areas. The central subsidy has been discontinued but the state subsidies continue. The state subsidies vary between 5 percent to 25 percent of the fixed capital investment in the project, subject to certain ceilings.

To attract industries, the states provide incentives in the form of sales tax deferments and sales tax exemptions.

Under the sales tax deferment scheme, the payment of sales tax on the sale of finished goods may be deferred for a period ranging between five to twelve years. Essentially it implies that the project gets an interest-free loan, represented by the quantum of sales tax deferred, during the deferment period.

Under the sales tax exemption scheme, some states exempt the payment of sales tax applicable on purchases of raw materials, consumables, packing, and processing materials from within the state which are used for manufacturing purposes. The period of exemption ranges from three to nine years depending upon the state and the specific location of the project within the state.

Short-term Loans from Financial Institutions

Financial institutions provide short-term loans to companies with good track record. To be eligible for such a loan, a company must satisfy certain conditions relating to dividend track record, debt-equity ratio, current ratio, and interest coverage ratio.

Short-term loans provided by financial institutions have the following features:

- They are totally unsecured and are given on the strength of a demand promissory note.
- The loan is given for a period of one year and can be renewed for two consecutive years, provided the original eligibility criteria are satisfied.

Commercial Paper

Commercial paper represents short-term unsecured promissory notes issued by firms which enjoy a fairly high credit rating. Generally, large firms with considerable financial strength are able to issue commercial paper. The important features of commercial paper are as follows:

- The maturity period of commercial paper ranges from 90 to 180 days.
- Commercial paper is sold at a discount from its face value and redeemed at its face value. Hence the implicit interest rate is a function of the size of the discount and the period of maturity.
- Commercial paper is either directly placed with investors or sold through dealers.
- Commercial paper is usually bought by investors who intend holding it till its maturity. Hence there is no well developed secondary market for commercial paper.

Factoring

A factor is a financial institution which offers services relating to management and financing of debts arising from credit sales. While factoring is well-established in western countries, only two factors, the SBI Factoring and Commercial Services Limited and Canbank Factoring Limited, which have been mandated by the Reserve Bank of India to operate in the western region and the southern region respectively, have made some tangible progress. The Punjab National Bank and the Bank of Allahabad are expected to set up factoring agencies to serve northern region and the eastern region, respectively.

Features of a Factoring Arrangement The key features of a factoring arrangement are as follows:

- The factor selects the accounts of the client that would be handled by it and establishes, along with the client, the credit limits applicable to the selected accounts.
- The factor assumes responsibility for collecting the debt of accounts handled by it. For each account, the factor pays to the client at the end of the credit period or when the account is collected, whichever comes earlier.
- The factor advances money to the client against not-yet-collected and not-yet-due debts. Typically, the amount advanced is 70 to 80 percent of the face value of the debt and carries an interest rate

which may be equal to or marginally higher than the lending rate of commercial banks.

- Factoring may be on a recourse basis (this means that the credit risk is borne by the client) or on a non-recourse basis (this means that the credit risk is borne by the factor). Presently, factoring in India is done on a recourse basis.
- Besides the interest on advances against debt, the factor charges a commission which may be 1 to 2 percent of the face value of the debt factored.

SUMMARY

- The two broad sources of finance available to a firm are: shareholders' funds (equity funds) and loan funds (debt funds).
- Equity capital represents ownership capital as equity shareholders collectively own the firm. Equity shareholders enjoy the rewards as well as bear the risk of ownership.
- The rights of equity shareholders consist of: (i) the right to residual income, (ii) the right to control, (iii) the pre-emptive right to purchase additional equity shares issued by the firm, and (iv) the residual claim over assets in the event of liquidation.
- Preference capital represents a hybrid form of financing–it partakes some characteristics of equity and some attributes of debentures.
- The internal accruals of a firm consist of depreciation charges and retained earnings.
- Term loans represent a source of debt finance which is generally repayable in less than 12 years. They are employed to finance acquisition of fixed assets and working capital margin.

Working Capital Management

16

Up to now, we discussed topics like capital budgeting, capital structure, and dividend policy which fall in the domain of long-term financial management. This chapter introduces working capital management or short-term financial management which is concerned with decisions relating to current assets and current liabilities.

The key difference between long-term financial management and short-term financial management (also referred to as working capital management) is in terms of the timing of cash. While long-term financial decisions like buying capital equipment or issuing debentures involve cash flows over an extended period of time (5 to 15 years or even more), short-term financial decisions typically involve cash flows within a year or within the operating cycle of the firm.

There are two concepts of working capital: gross working capital and net working capital. Gross working capital is the total of all current assets. The constituents of current assets are shown in Part A of Exhibit 16.1. Net working capital is the difference between current assets and current liabilities. The constituents of current liabilities are shown in Part B of Exhibit 16.1. Management of working capital refers to the management of current assets as well as current liabilities. The major thrust, of course, is on the management of current assets. This is understandable because current liabilities arise in the context of current assets.

Working capital management is a significant facet of financial management. Its importance stems from two reasons:

- Investment in current assets represents a substantial portion of total investment.
- Investment in current assets and the level of current liabilities have to be geared quickly to changes in sales. To be sure, fixed asset investment and long-term financing are also responsive to variation

EXHIBIT 16.1 ***Constituents of Current Assets and Current Liabilities***

Part A: Current Assets
Inventories
Raw materials and components
Work-in-process
Finished goods
Others
Sundry debtors
Loans and advances
Cash and bank balances
Part B: Current Liabilities
Sundry creditors
Trade advances
Borrowings (short-term)
Commercial banks
Others
Provisions

in sales. However, this relationship is not as immediate as it is in the case of working capital components.

This chapter discusses various facets of working capital management. It is divided into ten sections as follows:

- Characteristics of current assets
- Factors influencing working capital requirements
- Working capital policy
- Operating cycle and cash cycle
- Cash requirement for working capital
- Cash management
- Credit management
- Inventory management
- Management of payables and accruals
- Ten commandments of working capital management

16.1 CHARACTERISTICS OF CURRENT ASSETS

In the management of working capital, two characteristics of current assets must be borne in mind: (i) short life span and (ii) swift transformation into other asset forms.

Current assets have a short life span. Cash balances may be held idle for a week or two, accounts receivable may have a life span of 30 to 120 days, and inventories may be held for 30 to 100 days. The life span of current assets depends upon the time required in the activities of procurement, production, sales, and collection and the degree of synchronisation among them.

Each current asset is swiftly transformed into other asset forms: cash is used for acquiring raw materials; raw materials are transformed into finished goods (this transformation may involve several stages of work-in-process); finished goods, generally sold on credit, are converted into sundry debtors (accounts receivable); and finally sundry debtors, on realisation, generate cash. Exhibit 16.2 shows the cycle of transformation.

The short life span of working capital components and their swift transformation from one form into another has certain implications:

Exhibit 16.2 *Current Assets Cycle*

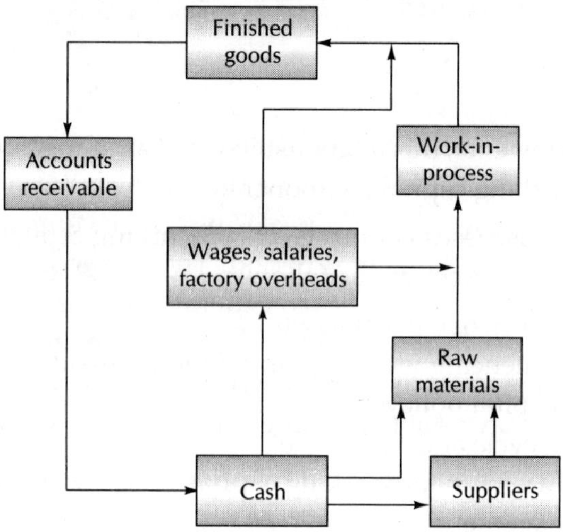

- Decisions relating to working capital management are repetitive and frequent.
- The difference between profit and present value is insignificant.
- The close interaction among working capital components implies that efficient management of one component cannot be undertaken without simultaneous consideration of other components. For example, if the firm has a large accumulation of finished foods inventory, it may have to provide more liberal credit terms or show laxity in credit collection. Another example: If the firm has a cash crunch, it may have to offer generous discounts.

16.2 FACTORS INFLUENCING WORKING CAPITAL REQUIREMENTS

The working capital needs of a firm are influenced by numerous factors. The important ones are:

- Nature of business
- Seasonality of operations
- Production policy
- Market conditions
- Conditions of supply

Nature of Business The working capital requirement of a firm is closely related to the nature of its business. A service firm, like an electricity undertaking or a transport corporation, which has a short operating cycle and which sells predominantly on cash basis, has a modest working capital requirement. On the other hand, a manufacturing concern like a machine tools unit, which has a long operating cycle and which sells largely on credit, has a very substantial working capital requirement.

Seasonality of Operations Firms which have marked seasonality in their operations usually have highly fluctuating working capital requircments. To illustrate, consider a firm manufacturing ceiling fans. The sale of ceiling fans reaches a peak during the summer months and drops sharply during the winter period. The working capital needs of such a firm are likely to increase considerably in summer months and decrease significantly during the winter period. On the other hand, a firm manufacturing a product like lamps, which have fairly even sales round the year, tends to have stable working capital needs.

Production Policy A firm marked by pronounced seasonal fluctuation in its sales may pursue a production policy which may reduce the sharp variations in working capital requirements. For example, a manufacturer of ceiling fans may maintain a steady production throughout the year rather than intensify the production activity during the peak business season. Such a production policy may dampen the fluctuations in working capital requirements.

Market Conditions The degree of competition prevailing in the market place has an important bearing on working capital needs. When competition is intense, a larger inventory of finished goods is required to promptly serve customers who may not be inclined to wait because other manufacturers are ready to meet their needs. Further, generous credit terms may have to be offered to attract customers in a highly competitive market. Thus, working capital needs tend to be high because of greater investment in finished goods inventory and accounts receivable.

If the market is strong and competition weak, a firm can manage with a smaller inventory of finished goods because customers can be served with some delay. Further, in such a situation the firm can insist on cash payment and avoid lock-up of funds in accounts receivable – it can even ask for advance payment, partial or total.

Conditions of Supply The inventory of raw materials, spares, and stores depends on the conditions of supply. If the supply is prompt and adequate, the firm can manage with small inventory. However, if the supply is unpredictable and scant then the firm, to ensure continuity of production, would have to acquire stocks as and when they are available and carry larger inventory on an average. A similar policy may have to be followed when the raw material is available only seasonally and production operations are carried out round the year.

16.3 WORKING CAPITAL POLICY

Two important issues in working capital policy are:

- What should be the level of investment in current assets?
- What mix of long-term financing and short-term financing should the firm employ to support current assets?

Level of Current Assets

Under a flexible policy (also referred to as a 'conservative policy'), the investment in current assets is high. This means that the firm maintains a huge balance of cash and marketable securities, carries large amounts of inventories, and grants generous terms of credit to customers which leads to a high level of debtors. Under a restrictive policy (also referred to as an 'aggressive policy'), the investment in current assets is low. This means that the firm keeps a small balance of cash and marketable securities, manages with small amounts of inventories, and offers stiff terms of credit which leads to a low level of debtors.

What are the consequences of flexible and restrictive policies? Very broadly, a flexible policy results in fewer production stoppages (on account of inventory shortages), ensures quick deliveries to customers, and stimulates sales because liberal credit is granted to customers. Of course, these benefits come at the cost of higher investment in current assets. A restrictive current assets policy, on the other hand, may lead to frequent production stoppages, delayed deliveries to customers, and loss of sales. These are the costs that the firm may have to bear to keep its investment in current assets low.

Determining the optimal level of current assets involves a trade-off between costs that rise with current assets and costs that fall with current assets. The former are referred to as **carrying costs** and the latter as **shortage costs**. Carrying costs are mainly in the nature of the cost of financing a higher level current assets. Shortage costs are mainly in the form of disruption in production schedule, loss of sales, and loss of customer goodwill. Exhibit 16.3 shows graphically how these costs behave in relation to the level of current assets. The optimal level of current assets is denoted by CA*, as the costs (the sum of carrying costs and shortage costs) are minimised at that level. Often the total cost curve is fairly flat around the optimal level. Hence, it may be difficult to precisely identify the optimal level. You must be satisfied if the level of current assets is in a range close to the optimal point.

EXHIBIT 16.3 *Carrying Costs and Shortage Costs*

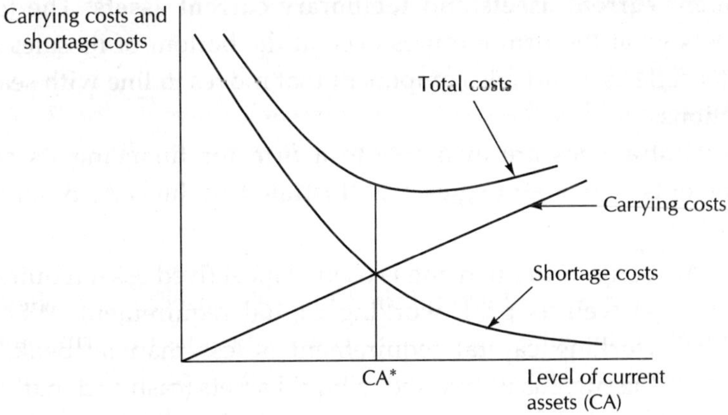

Current Assets Financing Policy

After establishing the level of current assets, the firm must determine how these should be financed. What mix of long-term capital and short-term debt should the firm employ to support its current assets?

Exhibit 16.4 depicts how total assets—and hence the capital requirements—change over time for a growing firm. For the sake of simplicity, assets are divided into two classes, viz., **fixed assets** and **current assets**. Fixed assets are assumed to grow at a constant rate

EXHIBIT 16.4 ***Capital Requirements and Their Financing***

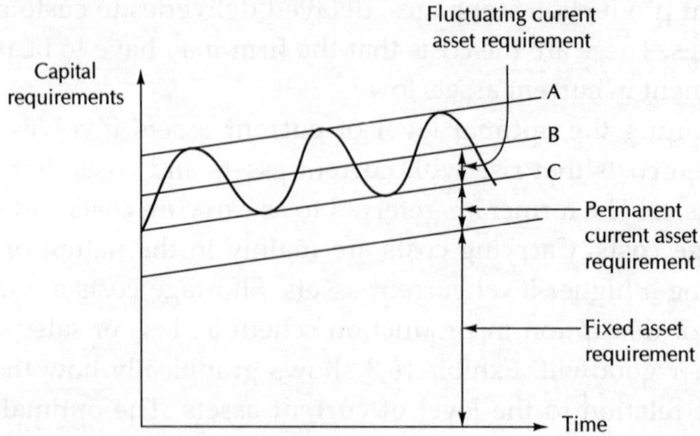

which reflects the secular rate of growth in sales. Current assets, too, are expected to display the same long-term rate of growth; however, they exhibit substantial variation around the trend line, thanks to seasonal (or even cyclical) patterns in sales and/or purchases.

The investment in current assets may be broken into two parts: **permanent current assets** and **temporary current assets**. The former represents what the firm requires even at the bottom of its sales cycle; the latter reflects a variable component that moves in line with seasonal fluctuations.

Several strategies are available to a firm for financing its capital requirements. Three strategies are illustrated by lines A, B, and C in Exhibit 16.4

Strategy A: Long-term financing is used to meet fixed asset requirement as well as peak working capital requirement. When the working capital requirement is less than its peak level, the surplus is invested in liquid assets (cash and marketable securities).

Strategy B: Long-term financing is used to meet fixed assets requirement, permanent working capital requirement, and a portion of fluctuating working capital requirement. During seasonal upswings, short-term financing is used; during seasonal downswings, surplus is invested in liquid assets.

Strategy C: Long-term financing is used to meet fixed asset requirement and permanent working capital requirement. Short-term financing is used to meet fluctuating working capital requirement.

The Matching Principle

According to this principle, the maturity of the sources of financing should match the maturity of the assets being financed. This means that fixed assets and permanent current assets should be supported by long-term sources of finance whereas fluctuating current assets must be supported by short-term sources of finance. Strategy C in Exhibit 16.4 reflects the matching principle.

The rationale for the matching principle is fairly straightforward. If a firm finances a long-term asset (say, machinery) with a short-term debt (say, commercial paper), it will have to periodically re-finance the asset. This is risky as well as inconvenient. Hence, it makes sense to ensure that the maturity of the assets and the sources of financing are properly matched.

16.4 OPERATING CYCLE AND CASH CYCLE

The investment in working capital is influenced by four key events in the production and sales cycle of the firm:

- Purchase of raw materials
- Payment for raw materials
- Sale of finished goods
- Collection of cash for sales

Exhibit 16.5 depicts these events on the cash flow line. The firm begins with the purchase of raw materials which are paid for after a delay which represents the accounts payable period. The firm converts the

EXHIBIT 16.5 *Operating and Cash Cycle*

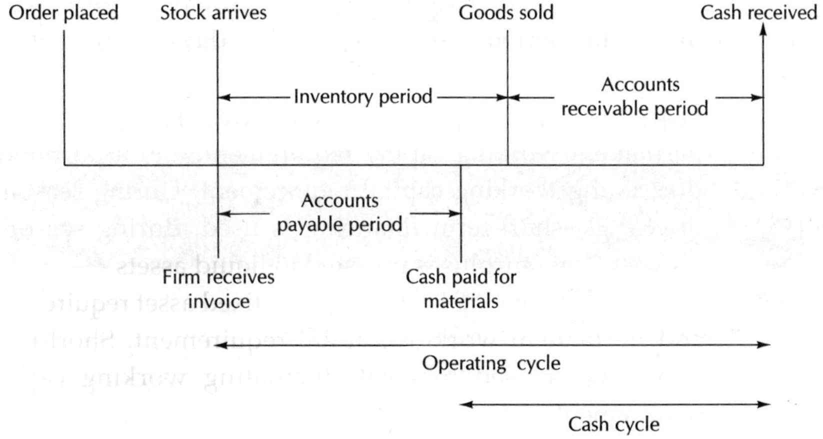

raw materials into finished goods and then sells the same. The time lag between the purchase of raw materials and the sale of finished goods is the inventory period. Customers pay their bills some time after the sales. The period that elapses between the date of sales and the date of collection of receivables is the accounts receivable period (debtors period).

The time that elapses between the purchase of raw materials and the collection of cash for sales is referred to as the operating cycle, whereas the time between the payment for raw material purchases and the collection of cash for sales is referred to as the cash cycle. The operating cycle is the sum of the inventory period and the accounts receivable period, whereas the cash cycle is equal to the operating cycle less the accounts payable period.

From the financial statements of the firm, we can estimate the inventory period, the accounts receivable period, and the accounts payable period.

$$\text{Inventory period} = \frac{\text{Average inventory}}{\text{Annual cost of good sold}/365}$$

$$\text{Accounts receivable period} = \frac{\text{Average accounts receivable}}{\text{Annual sales}/365}$$

$$\text{Accounts payable period} = \frac{\text{Average accounts payable}}{\text{Annual cost of goods sold}/365}$$

Exhibit 16.6 provides the relevant information for Horizon Limited. Based on this, we can calculate several things.

$$\text{Inventory period} = \frac{(96+102)/2}{720/365} = 50.1 \text{ days}$$

$$\text{Accounts receivable period} = \frac{(86+90)/2}{800/365} = 40.2 \text{ days}$$

EXHIBIT 16.6 ***Financial Information for Horizon Limited***

Profit and Loss Account Data			*Balance Sheet Data*	
			Beginning of 20 X 0	*End of 20 X 0*
Sales	800	Inventory	96	102
Cost of goods sold	720	Accounts receivable	86	90
		Accounts payable	56	60

$$\text{Account payable period} = \frac{(56+60)/2}{720/365} = 29.4 \text{ days}$$

$$\text{Operating cycle} = \underset{\substack{\text{Inventory}\\\text{period}}}{50.1} + \underset{\substack{\text{Accounts}\\\text{receivable}\\\text{period}}}{40.2} = 90.3 \text{ days}$$

$$\text{Cash cycle} = \underset{\substack{\text{Operating}\\\text{cycle}}}{90.3} - \underset{\substack{\text{Accounts}\\\text{payable}\\\text{period}}}{29.4} = 60.9 \text{ days}$$

Thus, Horizon Limited takes about two months to collect payment from its customers from the time it pays for its inventory purchases.

It is helpful to monitor the behaviour of overall operating cycle and its individual components. For this purpose, time-series analysis and cross-section analysis may be done. In time-series analysis, the duration of the operating cycle and its individual components is compared over a period of time for the same firm. In cross-section analysis, the duration of the operating cycle and its individual components is compared with that of other firms of a comparable nature.

16.5 CASH REQUIREMENT FOR WORKING CAPITAL

As a manager, you will be interested in figuring out how much cash you should arrange to meet the working capital needs of your firm. To do this, you may follow a two step procedure:

Step 1 Estimate the cash cost of various current assets required by the firm. The cash cost of a current asset is:

Value of the current asset
- Profit element, if any, included in the value.
- Non-cash charges like depreciation, if any, included in the value.

To illustrate, suppose the value of sundry debtors (receivables) is shown to be ₹10 million on the balance sheet. If the profit margin is 25 percent and the depreciation element in the cost of goods sold is ₹0.5 million, the cash cost of sundry debtors is obtained as follows:

Value in the balance sheet	₹10.0 million
Profit margin	₹2.5 million
Cost of goods sold	₹7.5 million
Depreciation element	₹0.5 million
Cash cost of sundry debtors	₹7.0 million

Step 2 Deduct the spontaneous current liabilities from the cash cost of current assets. A portion of the cash cost of current assets is supported by trade credit and accruals of wages on expenses, which may be referred to as spontaneous current liabilities. The balance left after such deduction has to be arranged from other sources.

Example The above procedure may be illustrated with the help of an example. Max Limited sells goods at a profit margin of 25 percent counting depreciation as part of the cost of manufacture. Its annual figures are as follows:

• Sales (Two months credit is given)	₹240 million
• Material cost (Suppliers give three months credit)	72
• Wages (Wages are paid one month in arrears)	48
• Manufacturing expenses outstanding at the end of the year (Cash expenses are paid one month in arrears)	4
• Administrative and sales expenses (These are paid as incurred)	30

Max Limited keeps two months' stock of raw materials and one month's stock of finished goods. It wants to maintain a cash balance of ₹5 million. Estimate the requirement of working capital on cash cost basis, assuming a 10 percent safety margin. Ignore work in process.

The requirement of working capital on cash cost basis is worked out below:

A: Current Assets

(₹ in million)

Item	*Calculation*	*Amount*
Debtors	$\frac{\text{Total cash cost}}{12} \times 2 = \frac{198 \times 2}{12}$	33.0
Raw material stock	$\frac{\text{Material cost}}{12} \times 2 = \frac{72 \times 2}{12}$	12
Finished goods stock	$\frac{\text{Cash manufacturing cost}}{12} \times 1 = \frac{168}{12}$	14
Cash balance	A predetermined amount	5
	A: Current assets	64

(Contd.)

(Contd.)

B: Current Liabilities

(₹ *in million)*

Item	Calculation	Amount
Sundry creditors	$\frac{\text{Material cost}}{12} \times 3 = \frac{72 \times 3}{12}$	18
Manufacturing expenses outstanding	One month's cash manufacturing expenses	4
Wages outstanding	One month's wages	4
	B: Current liabilities	26
Working capital (A-B)		38
Add 10% safety margin		3.8
Working capital required		₹41.8

Working Notes

(₹ *in million)*

1. Sales		240
Less: Gross profit (25%)		60
Total manufacturing cost		180
Less: Materials	72	
Wages	48	120
Manufacturing expenses		60
2. Cash manufacturing expenses (₹4 million × 12)		48
3. Depreciation: (1) – (2)		12
4. Total cash cost		
Total manufacturing cost		180
Less: Depreciation		12
Cash manufacturing cost		168
Add: Administration and selling expenses		30
Total cash cost		198

16.6 CASH MANAGEMENT

Cash, the most liquid asset, is of vital importance to the daily operations of business firms. While the proportion of corporate assets held in the form of cash is very small, often between 1 and 3 percent, its efficient management is crucial to the solvency of the business. In a very important sense, cash is the focal point of fund flows in a business and is generally referred to as the "lifeblood of a business enterprise."

Why does a firm need cash? There are three primary motives for a firm to hold cash: (a) to meet the needs of day-to-day transactions (**transactions motive**); (b) to protect the firm against uncertainties characterising some of the its cash flows (**precautionary motive**); and (c) to take advantage of unexpected investment opportunities (**speculative motive**).

While cash serves these functions, it is an idle resource with an opportunity cost. The liquidity provided by holding cash is at the expense of profits that could accrue from alternative investment opportunities. Hence, the firm should plan and control cash carefully.

Cash Budgeting

Cash forecasts or budgets are the principal tools of cash management. They are routinely prepared by business firms. They are helpful in: (a) estimating cash requirement, (b) planning short-term financing, (c) scheduling payments in connection with capital expenditure projects, (d) planning purchases of materials, (e) developing credit policies, and (f) checking the accuracy of long-term forecasts.

A firm can use multiple short-term forecasts of varying length and detail, suited to meet different needs. The commonly used designs for short-term cash forecasts are: (i) one year divided into quarters or months, (ii) one quarter divided into months, (iii) one month divided into weeks, and (iv) a week divided into days.[1] The point to be emphasised here is that the multiple formats serve different purposes and should not be regarded as mutually exclusive.

Receipts and Disbursement Method The principal method of cash forecasting is the receipts and disbursements method. Under this method, the cash forecast shows the timing and magnitude of expected cash receipts and disbursements over the forecast period. It includes all expected receipts and disbursements, irrespective of how they are classified in accounting. The items of cash receipts and cash payment along with the bases for estimating these are shown in Exhibit 16.7.

From the exhibit, it is clear that the receipts and payments method of cash forecasting calls for information about estimated sales, plans for production, purchasing and financing, and the capital expenditure budget. The most crucial input in the entire process, of course, is the

[1] Of course, I would not like to press the point further for an already hard-pressed firm.

EXHIBIT 16.7 ***Items of Cash Receipts and Payments and the Basis of their Estimation***

	Item	*Basis of Estimation*
Receipts	Cash sales.	Estimated sales and its division between cash and credit sales.
	Collection of accounts receivables.	Estimated sales and its division between cash and credit sales and the collection pattern.
	Interest and dividend receipts.	Firm's portfolio of securities and return expected from the portfolio.
	Increase in loans/ deposits and issue of securities.	Financing plan.
	Sale of assets.	Proposed disposal of assets.
Payments	Cash purchases.	Estimated purchases and its division between cash purchases and credit purchases.
	Payment of credit purchases.	Estimated purchases and its division between cash and credit purchases and the terms of credit purchases.
	Wages and salaries.	Manpower employed and wages and salaries structure.
	Manufacturing expenses.	Production Plan.
	General, administrative and selling expenses.	Administrative and sales personnel and proposed sales promotion and distribution expenditure.
	Capital equipment purchases.	Capital expenditure budget and the payment pattern associated with capital equipment purchases.
	Repayment of loans and retirement of securities.	Financing plan.

figure of estimated sales. This is because various business plans are closely related to the estimated sales.

Illustration The preparation of cash forecasts may be illustrated by an example. Beta Company manufactures razor blades. Its estimated sales for the period January 20 × 1 through June 20 × 1 are as follows: ₹100,000 a month from January through March and ₹120,000 per month from April through June. The sales of November and December of the previous year have been ₹100,000 each. Cash and credit sales are expected to be 20 percent and 80 percent respectively. The receivables from credit sales are expected to be collected as follows: 50 percent of receivables, on an average, one month from the date of sale; and the remaining 50 percent, on an average, two months from the date of sale. No bad debt losses are expected to occur. Other anticipated receipts are: (i) ₹5,000 from the sale of a machine in March, and (ii) ₹2,000 interest on securities in June. Given this information, the forecasted cash receipts have been tabulated in Exhibit 16.8.

EXHIBIT 16.8 ***Forecast of Cash Receipts in rupees***

	January	*February*	*March*	*April*	*May*	*June*
1. Sales	100,000	100,000	100,000	120,000	120,000	120,000
2. Credit sales	80,000	80,000	80,000	96,000	96,000	96,000
3. Collection of accounts receivables	80,000	80,000	80,000	80,000	88,000	96,000
4. Cash sales	20,000	20,000	20,000	24,000	24,000	24,000
5. Receipt from machine sale			5,000			
6. Interest						2,000
Total cash receipts (3 + 4 + 5 + 6)	100,000	100,000	105,000	104,000	112,000	122,000

We now consider the forecast of cash payment. Beta Company plans to purchase materials worth ₹40,000 in January and February, and materials worth ₹48,000 each month from March through June. The payments are made approximately a month after the purchase. The purchases for the previous year's December month have been ₹40,000 for which payment will be made in January. Miscellaneous cash purchases of ₹2,000 per month are planned from January through June. Wage payments are expected to be ₹15,000 per month, January through June. Manufacturing expenses are anticipated at ₹20,000 per month and general administrative and selling expenses at ₹10,000 per month. Dividend payment of ₹20,000 and tax payment of ₹20,000 are scheduled for June 20X1. A proposed cash purchase of a machine worth ₹50,000 is to be made in March 20X1. Based on this information the expected payments are shown in Exhibit 16.9.

EXHIBIT 16.9 ***Forecast of Cash Payments in Rupees***

	January	*February*	*March*	*April*	*May*	*June*
1. Material purchases	40,000	40,000	48,000	48,000	48,000	48,000
2. Credit material purchases	40,000	40,000	48,000	48,000	48,000	48,000
3. Payment of accounts payable	40,000	40,000	40,000	48,000	48,000	48,000
4. Miscellaneous cash purchases	2,000	2,000	2,000	2,000	2,000	2,000
5. Wages	15,000	15,000	15,000	15,000	15,000	15,000
6. Manufacturing exp.	20,000	20,000	20,000	20,000	20,000	20,000
7. General admn. expense	10,000	10,000	10,000	10,000	10,000	10,000
8. Dividend	-	-	-	-	-	20,000
9. Tax	-	-	-	-	-	20,000
10. Capital expenditure	-	-	50,000	-	-	-
Total payments (3 + 4 + 5 + 6 + 7 + 8 + 9 + 10)	87,000	87,000	137,000	95,000	95,000	135,000

Assuming that the cash balance as on 1st January is ₹22,000 and that the minimum cash balance required by the firm is ₹20,000, we can prepare a summary statement. Shown in Exhibit 16.10, this statement calculates the surplus/deficit in relation to the minimum required.

From Exhibit 16.10, it can be seen that cash shortage is expected to occur only during March and is likely to disappear in April as the business operations result in cash inflows. The shortage expected in March is due to the proposed capital expenditure of ₹50,000. The management can avoid this shortage by a adopting one or more of the following means: (i) postponing the asset acquisition to April, (ii) deferring a portion of the payment for the capital asset to April, and (iii) resorting to short-term borrowing for the month of March.

Evaluation The receipts and disbursements method of cash forecasting is used commonly because of two advantages: it provides a complete picture of the expected cash flows, and it is a sound vehicle for exercising control over day-to-day transactions. However, this method has some

EXHIBIT 16.10 *Summary Cash Forecast in Rupees*

	January	*February*	*March*	*April*	*May*	*June*
1. Opening cash balance	22,000					
2. Receipts	100,000	100,000	105,000	104,000	112,000	122,000
3. Payments	87,000	87,000	137,000	95,000	95,000	135,000
4. Net cash flow (2 – 3)	13,000	13,000	(32,000)	9,000	17,000	(13,000)
5. Cumulative net cash flow	13,000	26,000	(6,000)	3,000	20,000	7,000
6. Opening cash balance + Cumulative net flow (1 + 5)	35,000	48,000	16,000	25,000	42,000	29,000
7. Minimum cash balance required	20,000	20,000	20,000	20,000	20,000	20,000
8. Surplus or deficit in relation to the minimum cash balance required (6 – 7)	15,000	28,000	(4,000)	5,000	22,000	9,000

drawbacks too. Its reliability is impaired by delays in collection or sudden demands for large payments and other similar factors. It fails to provide a clear picture of important changes in the company's working capital movement, especially those relating to inventories and receivables.

Monitoring Collections and Disbursements

To enhance the efficiency of cash management, collection and disbursements must be carefully monitored. In this respect, the following are helpful.

Prompt Billing Often, there is a time lag between the despatch of goods or provision of service and the sending of bills. In one company this time lag, on an average, was about five days. By preparing and sending the bills promptly, a firm can ensure quicker remittance. It should be realised that it is in the area of billing that the company's control is great and there is a sizeable opportunity to free cash. To tap this opportunity, the treasurer should work with the controller and others and try to: (a) accelerate invoice data, (b) mail bills promptly, and (c) identify payment location.

Expeditious Collection of Cheques An important aspect of efficient cash management is to process the cheques received very promptly. Yet many firms deposit cheques received with some delay.

In addition to quick handling of cheques, a firm receiving remittances by cheques from different parts of the country can decentralise its collections and cut down the delay in the conversion of cheques to the head office into cash. Instead of asking customers to remit their cheques to the head office, a regional/local office of the company can be advised to process them locally. The regional/local office of the bank can be instructed to remit the collections (beyond a certain minimum balance) to the head office account by telegraphic or telex transfer or net banking. With the vast network of branches set up by the major banks, regional/local collection centers can be easily established. To ensure that the system of collection works according to plan, it is helpful to periodically audit the actual transfers by the collecting banks and ensure that they are in conformity with the instructions given.

Control of Payables By controlling its payables properly, a firm can conserve its cash resources. This involves several things:

- Payments should be made only as and when they fall due.
- Payables and their disbursement can be centralised. This helps in consolidating working funds at the head office, scheduling payments more effectively, reducing unproductive bank balances at the regional/local offices, and investing surplus funds more effectively.
- Arrangements can be made with suppliers to set the due dates of their bills so that they match the company's period of peak receipts. Synchronisation of cash outflows and inflows helps a company to get greater mileage from its cash resources.

Playing the Float When a firm issues a cheque, the balance in its book is reduced. In the bank's books, however, the balance is not reduced till the payment has been made by the bank. The amount of cheques issued by the firm but not paid for by the bank is knows as the 'payment float'.

Now consider what happens when a firm receives a cheque and deposits it with its bank. The firm increases the balance in its books, but in the bank's books it is not increased until the cheque has been cleared. The amount of cheques deposited by the firm in the bank but not cleared is referred to as the 'collection float'. The difference between the 'payment float' and the 'collection float' is called the net float. When the net float is positive, the balance in the books of the bank is higher than the balance in the books of the firm. So long as the bank shows a positive balance, a negative cash balance in the books of the firm may not be viewed with alarm. If a firm enjoys a positive 'net float', it can issue cheques even if it means having an overdrawn bank account in its books. Such an action is referred to as 'playing the float' and its is considered risky. Within limits, however, a firm can play this game with reasonable safety and get a higher mileage from its cash resources. Net banking, however, has reduced the scope of this game.

Investment of Surplus Funds

Companies often have surplus funds for short periods of time before they are required for capital expenditures, loan repayment, or some other purpose. These funds may be deployed in a variety of ways. At one end of the spectrum is the term deposit (to be made for a minimum period of 30 days) in a bank, virtually a risk free investment, that offers a relatively modest rate of interest; at the other end of the spectrum is the investment in equity shares which can produce highly volatile returns. In between lie several avenues like units/shares of mutual funds schemes, public sector bonds, treasury bills, inter-corporate deposits, and bill discounting. This section looks at the options availatble for deploying surplus funds.

Fixed Deposits with Banks Banks accept term deposits for periods ranging from 15 days to 5 years.Generally the rate of interest increases with the period of deposits.

Units/Shares of Mutual Fund Schemes A wide range of mutual fund schemes are available in India. A firm with short-term surplus funds may participate in open-ended schemes as they ensure ready liquidity. These schemes accept funds as well as permit withdrawals on a continuing basis. The most appropriate open-ended schemes for short-term investment purposes seem to be the money-market mutual fund schemes. These schemes invest in money-market instruments like treasury bills, commercial paper, and certificates of deposit.

Certificates of Deposits A certificate of deposit (CD) represents a negotiable receipt of funds deposited in a bank for a fixed period. It may be in a registered form or a bearer form. The latter is more popular as it can be transacted more readily in the secondary market. Like treasury bills, CDs are issued at a discount and redeemed at par. CDs are issued in physical form and are freely transferable after an initial lock-in period which may be 90 days or so.

CDs are a popular form of short-term investment for companies for the following reasons: (i) Banks are normally willing to tailor the denominations and maturities to suit the needs of the investors. (ii) CDs are transferable. (iii) CDs are generally risk free. (iv) CDs generally offer a higher rate of interest than treasury bills or term deposits.

Commercial Paper Commercial paper represents short-term unsecured promissory notes issued by firms that are generally considered to be financially strong. Commercial paper usually has a maturity period of 90 days to 180 days. It is sold at a discount and redeemed at par. Hence, the implicit rate is a function of the size of discount and period of maturity. Commercial paper is either directly placed with investors or sold through dealers. Commercial paper does not presently have a well developed secondary market in India.

The main attraction of commercial paper is that it offers an interest rate that is typically higher than that offered by treasury bills or certificates of deposit. However, its disadvantage is that it does not have an active secondary market. Hence, it makes sense for firms that plan to hold it till maturity.

16.7 CREDIT MANAGEMENT

While business firms would like to sell on cash, the pressure of competition and the force of custom persuades them to sell on credit. Firms grant credit to facilitate sales. It is valuable to customers as it augments their resources–it is particularly appealing to those customers who cannot borrow from other sources or find it very expensive or inconvenient to do so.

The credit period extended by business firms usually ranges from 15 days to 60 days. When goods are sold on credit, finished goods get converted into accounts receivable (or sundry debtors as they are referred to in India) in the books of the seller. In the books of the buyer, the obligation arising from credit purchase is represented as accounts payable (trade creditors).

A firm's investment in accounts receivable depends on how much it sells on credit and how long it takes to collect receivables. For example, if a firm sells ₹1 million worth of goods on credit a day and its average collection period is 40 days, its accounts receivable will be ₹40 million. Accounts receivable constitute the third most important asset category for business firms, after plant and equipment and inventories. Hence, it behoves on a firm to manage its credit well.

Terms of Payment

Terms of payment vary widely in practice. At one end, if the seller has financial sinews, it may extend liberal credit to the buyer till it converts goods bought into cash. At the other end, the buyer may pay cash in advance to the seller and finance the entire trade cycle. Most commonly, however, some in-between arrangement is chosen wherein the trade is financed partly by the seller, partly by the buyer, and partly by some financial intermediary. The major terms of payment are discussed below:

Cash Terms When goods are sold on cash terms, the payment is received either before the goods are shipped (cash in advance) or when the goods are delivered (cash on delivery). Cash in advance is generally insisted upon when goods are made to order. In such a case, the seller would like to finance production and eliminate marketing risks. Cash on delivery is often demanded by the seller if it is in a strong bargaining position and/or the customer is perceived to be risky.

Open Account Credit sales are generally on open account. This means that the seller first ships the goods and then sends the invoice (bill). The credit terms (credit period, cash discount for prompt payment, the period of discount, and so on) are stated in the invoice which is acknowledged by the buyer. There is no formal acknowledgement of indebtedness by the buyer.

- *Credit Period* The credit period refers to the length of time the customer is allowed to pay for its purchases. It is usually mentioned in days from the date of invoice. If a firm allows 30 days, say, of credit with no discount for early payment, its credit terms are stated as 'net 30'.
- *Cash Discount* Firms generally offer cash discount to induce customers to make prompt payment. For example, credit terms of 2/10, net 30 mean that a discount of 2 percent is offered if the payment is made by the tenth day; otherwise, the full payment is due by the thirtieth day.

- *Billing* To streamline billings, it is a common practice to send a single bill every month. For example at the end of every month, the customer may be sent a consolidated bill for the purchases made from the 26th of the previous month to the 25th of the current month.

Consignment When goods are sent on consignment, they are merely shipped but not sold to the consignee . The consignee acts as the agent of the seller (consignor). The title of the goods is retained by the seller till they are sold by the consignee to a third party. Periodically, sales proceeds are remitted by the consignee to the seller.

Draft When goods are shipped on open account or consignment, the seller does not have strong evidence of the buyer's obligation. So, a more secure arrangement, usually in the form of a draft, is sought. A draft represents an unconditional order issued by the seller asking the buyer to pay on demand (demand draft), or at a certain future date (time draft), the amount specified on it. It is typically accompanied by shipping documents that are delivered to the drawee when he pays or accepts the draft. When the drawee accepts a time draft it becomes a trade acceptance. The seller may hold the acceptance till it matures or get it discounted.

The draft performs three useful functions: (i) It serves as a written evidence of a definite obligation. (ii) It helps in reducing the cost of financing to some extent. (iii) It represents a negotiable instrument.

Letter of Credit Commonly used in international trade, the letter of credit is now used in domestic trade as well. A letter of credit, or L/C is issued by a bank on behalf of its customer (buyer) to the seller. As per this document, the bank agrees to honour the draft drawn on it for the supplies made to the customer if the seller fulfills the conditions laid down in the L/C.

The L/C serves several useful functions: (i) It virtually eliminates credit risk, if the bank has a good standing. (ii) It reduces uncertainty as the seller knows the conditions that should be fulfilled to receive payment. (iii) It offers safety to the buyer who wants to ensure that payment is made only in conformity with the conditions of the L/C.

Credit Policy

The important dimensions of a firm's credit policy are:

- Credit standards
- Credit period

- Cash discount
- Collection programme

These variables are related and have a bearing on the level of sales, bad debt loss, discount taken by customers, and collection expenses. For purposes of expository convenience, however, we examine each of these variables independently.

Credit Standards A pivotal question in the credit policy of the firm is: What standard should be applied in accepting or rejecting an account for credit granting? A firm has a wide range of choices in this respect. At one end of the spectrum, it may decide not to grant credit to any customer, however strong his credit rating may be. At the other end, it may decide to grant credit to all customers, irrespective of their credit rating. Between these two extreme positions lie several possibilities which are often the more practical ones.

In general, liberal credit standards tend to push sales up by attracting more customers. This is, however, accompanied by a higher incidence of bad debt loss, a larger investment in receivables, and a higher cost of collection. Stiff credit standards have the opposite effects. They tend to depress sales, reduce the incidence of bad debt loss, decrease the investment in receivables, and lower the collection cost.

Credit Period The credit period refers to the length of time allowed to customers to pay for their purchases. It generally varies from 15 days to 60 days. When a firm does not extend any credit, the credit period would obviously be zero. If a firm allows, say, 30 days of credit with no discount to induce early payment, its credit terms are stated as "net 30".

Lengthening of the credit period pushes sales up by inducing existing customers to purchase more and attracting additional customers. This is, however, accompanied by a larger investment in receivables and a higher incidence of bad debt loss. A shortening of the credit period would have the opposite effects. It will tend to lower sales, decrease investment in receivables, and reduce the incidence of bad debt loss. Exhibit 16.11 illustrates how the effect of lengthening the credit period on profit may be figured out.

Cash Discount Firms generally offer cash discount to induce prompt payment. The percentage of discount and the period for which it is available are reflected in the credit terms. For example, credit terms of 2/10, net 30 mean that a discount of 2 percent is offered if the payment is made by the 10th day; otherwise the full payment is due by the 30th day.

EXHIBIT 16.11 ***Effect of Lengthening the Credit Period on Residual Income***

Excel Limited presently has an annual turnover of ₹100 million and an average collection period of 30 days. The marketing director of the company believes that a longer credit period will stimulate additional sales. Of course, it is likely to be accompanied by higher defaults. The expected impacts of longer credit periods on sales and defaults are given below:

Credit policy	*Increase in collection period*	*Increase in sales*	*Bad debts percentage*
1	15 days	₹5 million	2%
2	30 days	₹10 million	4%

The selling price of the product is ₹50 and the variable cost per unit is ₹30. The bad debts percentage currently is 1 percent. Excel requires a return of 20 percent on its investments. Assume that a year consists of 360 days.

The effect of extending the credit periods by 15 days and 30 days is shown below:

	Credit Period		
	Existing 30 days ₹(in million)	*Option 1 45 days ₹(in million)*	*Option 2 60 days ₹(in million)*
A. Expected sales	100.00	105.00	110.00
B. Contribution (40%)	40.00	42.00	44.00
C. Bad debts	1.00	2.1	4.4
D. Average receivables $\frac{\text{Sales}}{360} \times \text{Credit period}$	8.333	13.125	18.333
E. Investment in receivables (60% of D)	5.00	7.875	11.00
F. Required return on investment in receivables (20% of E)	1.00	1.575	2.20
G. Residual Income (B-C-F)	38.00	38.325	37.40

Since the residual income is maximised under option I, Excel is advised to increase the credit period from the present 30 days to 45 days.

Liberalising the cash discount policy can result in the discount percentage being increased and/or the discount period being lengthened. Such an action tends to enhance sales (because the discount is regarded as price reduction), reduce the average collection period (as customers pay promptly), and increase the cost of discount. Exhibit 16.12 illustrates the effect of changing the cash discount policy on the residual income (the income left after making a charge on investment) for Naveen Enterprises.

EXHIBIT 16.12 *Effect of Changing the Cash Discount Policy on Profit*

Naveen Enterprises has annual sales of ₹5 million. Naveen currently extends a credit of 60 days to its customers. However, it does not offer any discount for prompt payment. The chief executive officer of Naveen is considering a plan to offer discount of 2/10, net 60. It is expected that 50 per cent of the customers will avail of discount and the average collection period of the firm will reduce to 35 days from the current 60 days. The ratio of variable cost to sales for Naveen is 70 percent. Naveen imputes an interest cost of 25 percent on its investment. Should Naveen offer discount for prompt payment? Assume that there are 360 days to a year.

In this case, cash discount for prompt payment may be offered provided the savings in interest on account of reduced investment in receivables exceeds cash discount given to customers. Hence, the analysis may be done as follows:

A. Annual credit sales	₹5,000,000
B. Cash discount availed on one half of sales $0.5 \times 5{,}000{,}000 \times \frac{2}{100}$	₹50,000
C. Present investment in receivables $\frac{5{,}000{,}000}{360} \times 60 \times 0.7$	₹583,333
D. Expected investment in receivables $\frac{5{,}000{,}000}{360} \times 35 \times 0.7$	₹340,278
E. Reduction in investment in receivables	₹243,055
F. Savings in capital charge on reduced investment in receivables (25% of E)	₹60,764

Since the savings in capital charge on reduced investment in receivables (₹60,764) exceeds the cash discount given by the firm (₹50,000), it is advisable to offer cash discount for prompt payment.

Collection Programme Aimed at timely collection of receivables, the collection programme of the firm consists of the following:

- Monitoring the state of receivables.
- Despatch of letters to customers whose due date is approaching.
- Telegraphic, telephonic, or electronic advice to customers around the due date.
- Threat of legal action to overdue accounts.
- Legal action against overdue accounts.

A rigorous collection programme tends to decrease sales, shorten the average collection period, reduce bad debts percentage, and increase the collection expense. A lax collection programme, on the other hand, would push sales up, lengthen the average collection period, increase the bad debt percentage, and perhaps reduce the collection expense.

Credit Evaluation

Before granting credit, the firm must ask the question: How creditworthy is the customer? In judging the creditworthiness of an applicant, three basic factors – the three C's – are character, capacity, and collateral. **Character** refers to the willingness of the customer to honour his obligations. It reflects integrity, a moral attribute considered very important by credit managers. **Capacity** refers to the ability of the customer to pay on time. It depends on the financial situation (particularly the working capital position and profitability) and the general business conditions affecting the performance of the customer. **Collateral** represents the security offered by the firm in the form of mortgages.

There are several ways in which you can find out whether a customer is likely to pay his debt. These are discussed as follows:

Analysis of Financial Statements Financial statements contain a wealth of information about the customer's financial condition and performance. A searching analysis of these statements can provide useful insights into credit worthiness. The following financial ratios are helpful in this respect:

- Current ratio
- Acid-test ratio
- Debt-equity ratio
- PBIT to total assets ratio
- Return on equity

Obtaining Bank Reference The banker of the prospective client is another source of information about his financial condition. This information can be obtained indirectly through the bank of the credit granting firm to ensure a higher degree of candour.

Analysis of Firm's Experience Consulting one's own experience is very important, if the firm has had previous dealings with the customer. It is worth asking: How prompt has he been in making payments? How well has he honoured his word in the past? When the customer is being approached/considered for the first time, the impression of the company's salesman about the integrity of the customers is important.

Monitoring Receivables

An important aspect of credit management is to monitor the payment of receivables. Several measures can be employed by the credit manager for this purpose. We will discuss the following measures: (i) average collection period, (ii) ageing schedule, and (iii) collection matrix.

Average Collection Period The average collection period is a measure commonly used to monitor the payment behaviour of customers. It is defined as:

$$\frac{\text{Receivables}}{\text{Average credit sales per day}}$$

To illustrate the calculation of this measure, consider the monthly sales and month -end accounts receivables for a product line, given in Exhibit 16.13. If the average collection period is calculated at the end of each quarter, we get the following picture:

Quarter	*Average Collection Period*
First	$\frac{320}{(150+156+158)/90} = 62 \text{ days}$
Second	$\frac{320}{(150+170+180)/91} = 58 \text{ days}$
Third	$\frac{360}{(190+200+210)/92} = 55 \text{ days}$
Fourth	$\frac{420}{(220+230+240)/92} = 56 \text{ days}$

Looking at the average collection period, we see that it decreased slightly over the year, suggesting that collection improved a bit.

EXHIBIT 16.13 ***Sales and Receivables Data***

Month	*Sales*	*Receivables*	*Month*	*Sales*	*Receivables*
January	150	400	July	190	340
February	156	360	August	200	350
March	158	320	September	210	360
April	150	310	October	220	380
May	170	300	November	230	400
June	180	320	December	240	420

Ageing Schedule An ageing schedule shows the age-wise distribution of accounts receivable at a given time. For example, the ageing schedule at the end of various quarters may be as follows:

Outstanding Accounts Receivable

Age	*1st Quarter*	*2nd Quarter*	*3rd Quarter*	*4th Quarter*
0-30 days	40%	42%	44%	46%
31-60 days	30%	28%	26%	25%
61-90 days	20%	22%	23%	20%
91-120 days	9%	8%	5%	7%
> 120	1%	–	2%	2%

A comparison of ageing schedule at periodic intervals helps to identify changes in the payment behaviour of customers.

Collection Matrix The average collection period and the ageing schedule have traditionally been very popular measures for monitoring receivables. However, they suffer from a limitation in that they are influenced by the sales pattern as well as the payment behaviour of the customers. If sales are increasing, the average collection period and the ageing schedule will differ from what they would be if sales are constant. This holds even when the payment behaviour of customers remains unchanged. The reason is simple: a greater portion of sales is billed currently. Similarly, decreasing sales lead to the same results. The reason here is that a smaller portion of sales is billed currently.

In order to correctly study the changes in the payment behaviour of customers, it is helpful to look at the pattern of collections associated with credit sales. Exhibit 16.14 shows an illustrative collection matrix. For example, the credit sales during the month of January are collected as follows: 13 percent in January (the month of sales), 42 percent in February

EXHIBIT 16.14 *Collection Matrix*

Percentage of receivables collected during the	*January sales*	*February sales*	*March sales*	*April sales*	*May sales*	*June sales*
Month of sales	13	14	15	12	10	9
First following month	42	35	40	40	36	35
Second following month	33	40	21	24	26	26
Third following month	12	11	24	19	24	25
Fourth following month	–	–	–	5	4	5

(the first following month), 33 percent in March (the second following month), and 12 percent in April (the third following month).

From the collection pattern, one can judge whether the collection is improving, stable, or deteriorating. A secondary benefit of such an analysis is that it provides a historical record of collection percentages that can be useful in projecting monthly receipts for each budgeting period.

16.8 INVENTORY MANAGEMENT

Inventories consist of raw materials, work in process, finished goods, and stores and spares. They represent a significant proportion of total assets – generally varying between 15 and 45 percent with an average of around 30 percent. Given the substantial investment in inventories, the importance of inventory management cannot be over emphasised.

Need for Inventories

What purpose is served by inventories? Before we answer this question, a distinction must be drawn between 'process' or 'movement' inventories and 'organisation' inventories. Process or movement inventories are required because it takes time to complete a process/operation and to move a product from one stage to another. The average quantity of such inventories would be equal to:

Average output of the process (or average usage at the end of the movement) × Time required for the process (or time required in movement)

For example

- If the average output of a process is 500 units per day and the process time is 15 days the average process inventory will be 7,500 units.
- If the average sales at the warehouse is 100 units a week and the transit (movement) time required to ship the goods from the plant to the warehouse is 3 weeks, the average movement inventory will be 300 units.

Organisation inventories are maintained to widen the latitude in planning and scheduling successive operations. Raw material inventory enables the firm to decouple its purchasing and production activities to some extent. It provides flexibility in purchasing and production. The firm can wait for an opportune buying moment without letting its production schedule be affected. Similarly, the production schedule need not be influenced by immediate purchasing activity.

Process inventory[2] provides flexibility in production scheduling which allows an efficient schedule and high utilisation of capacity. Without in-process inventory, a bottleneck at any stage in the production process renders the machines and facilities at subsequent stages idle. This results in delay and unutilised facilities.

Finished goods inventory enables a firm to decouple its production programme and marketing activities so that desirable results can be achieved on both fronts. If adequate finished goods inventory is available, the marketing department can meet the needs of customers promptly, irrespective of the quantity and composition of goods flowing out of the production line at the time. By the same token, the volume and composition of current output from the production line can be determined independently of the volume and composition of the current offtake in the market.

Order Quantity–EOQ Model

There are two basic questions relating to inventory management:

- What should the size of the order be?
- At what level should the order be placed?

To answer the first question, the basic Economic Order Quantity (EOQ, hereafter) model may be helpful. Before discussing the EOQ model, let us distinguish between three types of costs in the context of inventory management: ordering costs, carrying costs, and shortage costs.

- **Ordering costs** relating to purchased items are expenses on the following: requisitioning, preparation of purchase order, expediting, transport, and receiving and placing in storage. Ordering costs pertaining to items manufactured in the company include the following expenses: requisitioning, set-up, and receiving and placing in storage.
- **Carrying costs** include expenses on the following: interest on capital locked up in inventory, storage, insurance, obsolescence, and taxes. Carrying costs are generally about 25 percent of the value of inventories held.
- **Shortage costs** arise when inventories are short of requirement for meeting the needs of production or the demand of customers.

[2] Process inventory here refers to work-in-progress inventory. It is distinguished from process or movement inventory mentioned earlier, though a part of work-in-progress inventory does represent process or movement inventory.

Inventory shortages may result in one or more of the following: high costs concomitant with crash procurement, inefficient and uneconomic production schedules, and customer dissatisfaction and loss of sales. When shortage results in failure to meet customer demand, measurement of shortage costs is relatively difficult because the effects are both long-term and short-term as well as somewhat intangible in nature.

When a firm orders large quantities in a bid to reduce the total ordering costs, other things being equal, the average inventory tends to be high, thereby increasing the carrying costs. Also, when a firm carries a large safety stock to reduce shortage costs, its carrying costs tend to be high. In view of such relationships, minimisation of overall costs of inventory management requires consideration of trade-offs among these costs.

Exhibit 16.15 shows a graph illustrating the behaviour of the total carrying costs, the total ordering costs, and the sum of these costs. The total carrying costs vary directly with the order size (as the average level of inventory is one-half of the order size). In contrast, the total ordering costs vary inversely with the order size.

EXHIBIT 16.15 ***Behaviour of Inventory Related Cost***

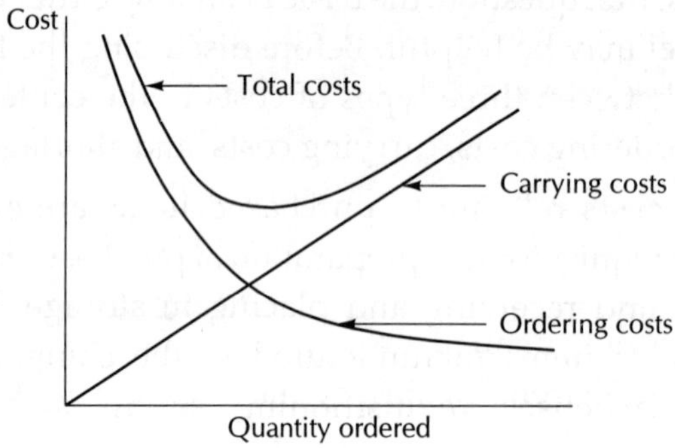

The total costs of ordering and carrying are minimised when:

$$Q = \sqrt{\frac{2FU}{PC}} \tag{16.1}$$

where Q is the economic order quantity, F is the cost per order, U is the annual usage/demand, P is the price per unit, and C is the carrying cost as percentage of inventory value

The EOQ model can be illustrated with the help of the following data relating to a hypothetical company:

U = annual sales = 20,000 units

F = fixed cost per order = ₹2,000

P = purchase price per unit = ₹12

C = carrying cost = 25 percent of inventory value

Plugging in these values in the above equation, we get,

$$Q = \sqrt{\frac{2 \times 2{,}000 \times 20{,}000}{12 \times 0.25}} = 5164$$

Order Point

The standard EOQ model assumes that materials can be produced instantaneously. This implies that the firm can place an order for replenishment when the inventory level drops to zero. In real life, however, procurement of materials requires time. Hence, the order (or re-order) level must be such that inventory at the time of ordering suffices to meet the needs of production during the procurement period.

If the usage rate of materials and the lead time for procurement are known with certainty, the ordering level will simply be:

Lead time in days of procurement × Average daily usage

When the usage rate and lead time are likely to vary, the re-order level should be higher than the normal consumption requirement during the procurement period. Such a step provides a measure of safety in face of variability of usage and lead time. In other words, the re-order level should be equal to:

Normal consumption + Safety stock

ABC Analysis

In most inventories, a small proportion of items accounts for a very substantial usage (in terms of the monetary value of annual consumption) and a large proportion of items accounts for a very small usage (in terms of the monetary value of annual consumption). Based on this empirical reality, ABC analysis advocates, in essence, a selective approach to inventory control which calls for a greater concentration of effort on inventory items that account for the bulk of usage value. This involves classifying inventories into three broad categories, A, B and C. Category A, representing the most important items, generally consists of 15 to 25 percent of inventory items and accounts for 60 to 70 percent of annual usage value. Category B, representing items of moderate importance, generally consists of 20 to 30 percent of inventory items and accounts for 15 to 25 percent of annual usage value. Category C, representing items of least importance, generally consists of 40 to 60 percent of inventory items and accounts for 10 to 15 percent of annual usage value.

Graphically the cumulative percentage of items and the cumulative percentage of usage is as shown in Exhibit 16.16.

EXHIBIT 16.16 ***Graph of Cumulative Percentage of Items and Cumulative Percentage of Usage***

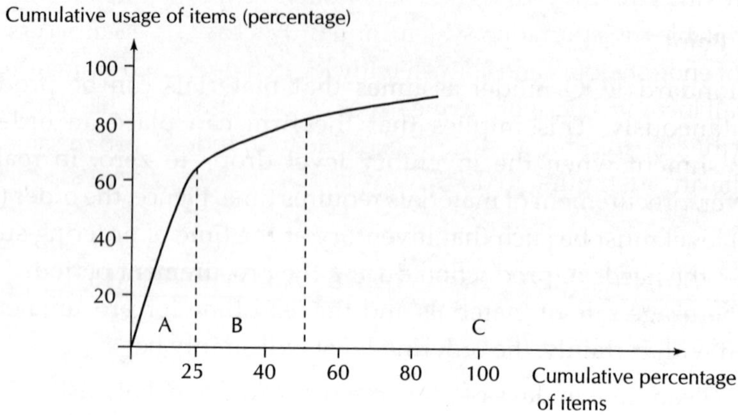

Monitoring and Control of Inventories

A firm may establish a programme of inventory monitoring and control consisting of the following elements.

- Exercise of vigilance against imbalances of raw materials and work-in-process which tend to limit the utility of stocks to the scarcest item.
- Vigorous efforts to expedite completion of unfinished production jobs in order to get them into a saleable condition.
- Active disposal of goods that are surplus, obsolete, or unusable.
- Shortening of the production cycle.
- Change in design to maximise the use of standard parts and components available off the shelf.
- Strict adherence to production schedules.
- Special pricing to dispose off unusually slow moving items.
- Making the seasonal sale fluctuations as even as possible.

Just-in-Time Inventory Control The just-in-time inventory control system, originally developed by Taiichi Okho of Japan, simply implies that the firm should maintain a minimal level of inventory and rely on suppliers to provide parts and components "just-in-time" to meet its assembly requirements. This may be contrasted with the traditional inventory management system which calls for maintaining a healthy level of safety stock to provide a reasonable protection against uncertainties of consumption and supply. The traditional system may be referred to as a "just-in-case" system. The just-in-time inventory system, while conceptually very appealing, is difficult to implement because it involves a significant change in the total production and management system. It requires inter alia: (i) a strong and dependable buyer/supplier relationship, (ii) a reliable transportation system, and (iii) an easy physical access in the form of enough doors and conveniently located docks and storage areas to dovetail incoming supplies to the needs of assembly lines. Nevertheless, it is worthwhile to come as close as possible to it. Indeed, progressive firms in India are attempting to do so.

16.9 MANAGEMENT OF PAYABLES AND ACCRUALS

So far we have discussed the management of current assets. We now turn our attention to the management of current liabilities which comprise mainly of trade creditors (also called accounts payables) and accruals.

Trade Credit

Trade credit represents the credit extended by the suppliers of goods and services. It is a spontaneous source of finance in the sense that it arises in the normal transactions of the firm without specific negotiations, provided the firm is considered creditworthy by its suppliers. It is an important source of finance representing 25 percent to 50 percent of short-term financing.

Obtaining Trade Credit The confidence of suppliers is the key to securing trade credit. What do suppliers look for in granting trade credit? Among other things, suppliers consider the following:

- *Earnings record over a period of time* If the firm has a fairly good earnings record with a portion of it ploughed back in the business, it is looked upon favourably.
- *Liquidity position of the firm* Suppliers naturally look at the ability of the firm to meet its obligations in the short run. Such ability is usually measured by the current ratio and the acid test ratio.
- *Record of payment* If the firm has been prompt and regular in paying the bulk of the suppliers in the past, it is deemed to be creditworthy.

Cultivating Good Supplier Relationships While a well-established, successful enterprise may have no difficulty in obtaining trade credit, a new company or one with financial problems will probably face difficulty in obtaining it. The confidence of suppliers, a pre-condition for obtaining trade credit, can be earned by discussing the financial situation, by showing realistic plans, and more important, by honouring commitments. The last point, namely, honouring commitments, is very important. Broken promises erode confidence more than poor operating results. It is better to make modest commitments which may not be fully satisfying to the supplier and honour them rather than make tall promises, that gratify the supplier, and fail to honour them.

Cost of Trade Credit The cost of trade credit depends on the terms of credit offered by the supplier. If the terms are, say, 30 days net, then trade credit is cost-free for 30 days because the amount payable is the same whether the payment is made on purchase or on the 30th day. However, if the supplier offers discount for prompt payment and the terms are, say, 2/10, net 30, there is a cost associated with trade credit availed beyond the discount period. Here, we may divide the 30-day period into two parts as follows:

10 days	20 days
Discount period	Non-discount period

The cost of trade credit during the discount period is nil, whereas the cost of trade credit during the non-discount period is:

$$\frac{\text{Discount\%}}{\text{1-Discount\%}} \times \frac{360}{\text{Credit period-Discount period}}$$

In our example, this works out to:

$$\frac{0.02}{1-0.02} \times \frac{360}{30-10} = 36.7 \text{ percent}$$

The cost of trade credit for several credit terms are:

Credit Terms	*Cost of Trade Credit*
1/10, net 20	36.4 percent
2/10, net 45	21.0
3/10, net 60	22.3
2/15, net 45	24.5

In general, the cost of additional trade credit is very high and unless the firm is hard pressed financially, it should not forego the discount for prompt payment.

Accruals

The major accrual items are wages and taxes. These are simply what the firm owes to its employees and to the government. Wages are usually paid on a weekly, fortnightly, or monthly basis—between payments, the amounts owed but not yet paid is shown as accrued wages on the balance sheet. Income tax is payable quarterly and other taxes may be payable half-yearly or annually. In the interim, taxes owed but not paid may be shown as accrued taxes on the balance sheet.

Accruals vary with the level of activity of the firm. When the activity level expands, accruals increase and when the activity level contracts, accruals decrease. As they respond more or less automatically to changes in the level of activity, accruals are treated as part of spontaneous financing.

Since no interest is paid by the firm on its accruals, they are often regarded as a 'free' source of financing. However, a closer examination would reveal that this may not be so. When the payment cycle is longer, wages may be higher. For example, an employee earning ₹1000 per week and receiving weekly payment may ask for a slightly higher compensation if the payment is made monthly. Likewise, when the payment period is longer, tax authorities may raise the tax rates to some extent. Even when such adjustments are made, the fact remains that between established payment dates, accruals do not carry any explicit interest burden.

While accruals are a welcome source of financing, they are typically not amenable to control by management. The payment period for employees is determined by the practice in industry and provisions of law. Similarly, tax payment dates are given by law and postponement of payment normally results in penalties.

16.10 TEN COMMANDMENTS OF WORKING CAPITAL MANAGEMENT

Here are the ten commandments of working capital management.

1. Find ways and means to shorten the operating cycle and cash cycle.
2. Match the maturity of the sources of financing to those of assets.
3. Centralise cash management and invest surplus funds judiciously.
4. Establish credit policy sensibly.
5. Monitor closely the collection of receivables and employ ingenious ways for collection.
6. Maintain a tight vigil over inventories.

7. Employ Materials Requirements Planning, Just-in–Time, and Electronic Data Interchange systems.
8. Take cash discounts if you have comfortable liquidity.
9. Stretch payables within reasonable bounds.
10. Build a long-term relationship of trust with banker.

SUMMARY

- There are two concepts of working capital: gross working capital and net working capital. Gross working capital is the total of all current assets net working capital is the difference between current assets and current liabilities.
- Working capital management is a significant facet of financial management. Financial managers spend a great deal of time on working capital management.
- In the management of working capital, two characteristics of current assets must of borne in mind:
  (i) short life span, and
  (ii) swift transformation into other asset forms.
- The working capital needs of a firm are influenced by numerous factors. The important ones are:
  (i) nature of business,
  (ii) seasonality of operations,
  (iii) production policy,
  (iv) market conditions, and
  (v) conditions of supply.
- An important working capital policy decision is concerned with the level of investment in current assets. Determining the optimal level of current assets involves a trade-off between costs that rise with current assets and costs that fall with current assets. The former are referred to as *carrying costs* and the latter as *shortage costs.*
- Several strategies are available to a firm for financing its needs. An important one is based on the matching principle. According to this principle, the maturity of the sources of finance should match the maturity of the assets being financed. This means that fixed assets and permanent current assets should be supported by long-term sources of finance whereas fluctuating current assets must be supported by short-term sources of finance.
- The operating cycle of a firm begins with the acquisition of raw materials and ends with the collection of receivables. If the accounts

payable period is subtracted from the operating cycle, one gets the cash cycle.

- Information about the operating cycle is helpful in (i) forecasting working capital, and (ii) control of working capital.
- The cash requirements for working capital may be estimated with the help of a two-step procedure: (i) Estimate the cash cost of various current assets required by the firm. (ii) Deduct the spontaneous current liabilities from the cash cost of current assets.
- Cash, the most liquid asset, is of vital importance to the daily operations of business firms. Crucial for the solvency of the business, it is referred to as the "life blood of a business firm".
- There are three primary reasons for a firm to hold cash: (i) to meet the needs of day-to- day transactions; (ii) to protect the firm against uncertainties characterising its cash flows; and (iii) to take advantage of unexpected investment opportunities. While cash serves these functions, it is an idle resource which has an opportunity cost. Hence, it should be carefully planned and controlled.
- The principal method of short-term cash forecasting is the receipts and disbursements method. The cash budget, prepared under this method, shows the timing and magnitude of expected cash receipts and payments over the forecast period, irrespective of how they are classified in accounting.
- To enhance the efficiency of cash management, collections and disbursements must be properly monitored. In this context, the following are helpful: prompt billing, expeditious collection of cheques, control of payables, and playing the float.
- Companies often have surplus funds for short periods of time before they are required for capital expenditures, loan repayment, or some other purpose. These funds can be deployed in a variety of ways.
- Business firms sell on credit. Credit is granted to facilitate sales.
- The important dimensions of a firm's credit policy are: credit standards, credit period, cash discount, and collection effort.
- In general, liberal credit standards tend to push sales up by attracting more customers. This is, however, accompanied by a higher incidence of bad debt loss, a larger investment in receivables, and a higher cost of collection. Stiff credit standards have opposite effects.
- Lengthening of the credit period pushes sales up. This is, however, accompanied by a larger investment in receivables and a higher incidence of bad debt loss. Shortening of the credit period has the opposite effects.

- Liberalising the cash discount policy tends to enhance sales, reduce the average collection period, and increase the cost of discount. Tightening the cash discount policy has the opposite effects.
- A rigorous collection programme tends to decrease sales, shorten the average collection period, reduce bad debt percentage, and increase the collection expense. A lax collection programme has the opposite effects.
- In judging the creditworthiness of an applicant the three basic factors—the three Cs—are character, capacity, and collateral.
- There are several ways in which you can find out whether a customer is likely to pay his debts: analysis of financial statements, obtaining bank reference, analysis of firm's experience, and numerical credit scoring.
- Traditionally, two methods have been commonly suggested for monitoring accounts receivable: days' sales outstanding and ageing schedule. While these methods are popularly used, they have a serious deficiency: they are based on an aggregation of sales and receivables. To overcome the weakness of the traditional methods, the payment pattern approach has been suggested.
- Inventories generally represent a very significant proportion of total assets. Hence the importance of inventory management cannot be overemphasised.
- A distinction may be drawn between 'process or movement' inventories and 'organisation' inventories. The former are required because it takes time to complete a process/operation and to move the product from one stage to another; the latter are maintained to widen the latitude in planning and scheduling successive operations.
- A basic question relating to inventory management is: What should be the size of the order? To determine the optimal order quantity, the Economic Order Quantity model may be employed.
- In most inventories, a small proportion of items accounts for a very substantial usage (in terms of the monetary value of annual consumption) and a large proportion of items accounts for a small usage. ABC analysis, based on this empirical reality, advocates in essence a selective approach to inventory control which calls for a greater concentration of effort on inventory items accounting for the bulk of usage value.
- The firm should establish a comprehensive programme to monitor investment in inventories. Ideally it should strive to adopt the 'Just-in-time' inventory control system.

- Trade credit represents the credit extended by the suppliers of goods and services. It is a spontaneous current liability. The cost of trade credit depends on the terms of credit offered by the supplier. When the supplier offers discount for prompt payment, trade credit availed beyond the discount period is quite costly.
- The major accrual items are wages and taxes. These are simply what the firm owes to its employees and to the government. Accruals vary spontaneously with the level of activity of the firm. While accruals are a welcome source of financing, they are typically not amenable to control by management.

APPENDIX 16A

SUPPLY CHAIN MANAGEMENT

The concept of supply chain management rests on two basic ideas. First, practically every product that reaches an end user is the result of the cumulative efforts of several organisations. Collectively, these organisations are referred to as the supply chain. Second, while supply chains have existed for a long time, most organisations traditionally have paid attention to only what was happening within their "four walls". Few businesses understood, let alone managed, the entire chain of activities involved in delivering products to the final customer. As a result, supply chains were often disjointed and ineffective.

Supply chain management (SCM) has been defined as the "design, planning, execution, control, and monitoring of supply chain activities with the objective of creating net value, building a competitive infrastructure, leveraging worldwide logistics, synchronizing supply with demand and measuring performance globally".

A cross-functional approach, supply chain management includes managing the movement of raw materials into an organisation, certain aspects of internal conversion of materials into finished goods, and the movement of finished goods towards the end consumer. It involves coordination and collaboration with channel partners such as suppliers, intermediaries, third-party service providers, and customers. In essence, supply chain management seeks to integrate supply and demand management within and across companies. Some have called the loosely coupled network of businesses that cooperate to provide product and services as the *Extended Enterprise.*

PART V

Special Topics

17. Mergers, Acquisitions, and Restructuring
18. International Finance
19. Value-based Management
20. Business Performance Measurement
21. Corporate Valuation
22. Risk Management: Basics of Financial Engineering
23. Macroeconomics: A Primer

Part V

Special Topics

17. Mergers, Acquisitions and Restructuring
18. International Finance
19. Value-Based Management
20. Business Performance Measurement
21. Corporate Valuation
22. Risk Management: Basics of Financial Engineering
23. Macroeconomics: A Primer

Mergers, Acquisitions, and Restructuring

17

Mergers, takeovers, divestitures, spinoffs, leveraged buyouts, and so on, collectively referred to as corporate restructuring, have become a major force on the financial and economic landscape all over the world. Essentially an American phenomenon till the mid 1970s, corporate restructuring seems to have become a dominant global theme since then.

On the Indian scene, too, corporates are looking seriously at mergers, acquisitions, and restructuring. Indeed, corporate restructuring has become the order of the day. Most of business groups and their companies seem to be engaged in some kind of restructuring or the other. From the house of Tatas to the house of AV Birla, from an engineering giant like Larsen & Toubro to a banking behemoth like State Bank of India, from the troubled Suzlon to the distressed Air India, everyone seems to be singing the anthem of corporate restructuring. The pace and intensity of corporate restructuring has increased since the beginning of the liberalisation era, thanks to greater competitive pressures and a more permissive environment.

Corporate restructuring can occur in myriad ways. The vast array of transactions that business firms resort to are summarised in Exhibit 17.1. Though the classification is somewhat arbitrary, it helps in clarifying the emphasis of various restructuring practices.

This chapter discusses the nature, mechanics, and rationale of different kinds of corporate restructuring transactions. In addition it looks at rehabilitation schemes and privatisation. It is divided into nine sections:

- Mergers
- Purchase of a division/plant
- Takeovers
- Managing an acquisition
- Business alliances

- Portfolio restructuring
- Financial restructuring
- Rehabilitation schemes
- Privatisation

Exhibit 17.1 *Major Types of Transactions*

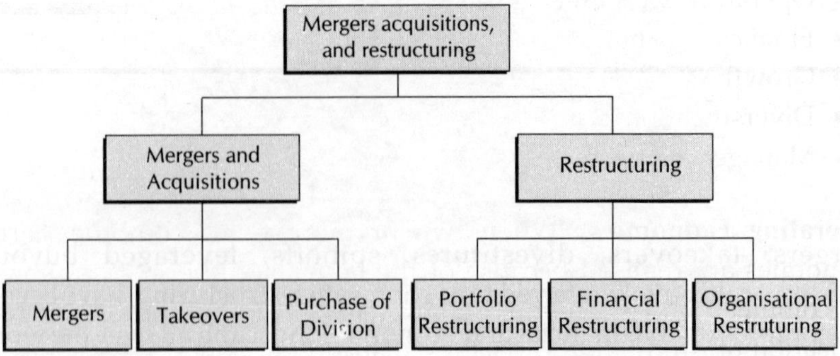

17.1 MERGERS

A merger refers to a combination of two or more companies into one company. It may involve absorption or consolidation. In an absorption, one company acquires another company. Example: Ashok Leyland Limited absorbed Ductron Casting Limited. In a consolidation, two or more companies combine to form a new company. Example: Hindustan Computers Limited, Hindustan Instruments Limited, Indian Software Company Limited, and Indian Reprographics Limited combined to form HCL Limited. Mergers in India, called amalgamations in legal parlance (hereafter we shall use the terms mergers and amalgamations interchangeably), are usually of the absorption variety. The acquiring company (also referred to as the amalgamated company or the merged company) acquires the assets and liabilities of the acquired company (also referred to as the amalgamating company or the merging company or the target company). Typically, the shareholders of the amalgamating company get shares of the amalgamated company in exchange for their shares in the amalgamating company.

Mergers may be classified into several types: (i) horizontal, (ii) vertical, and (iii) conglomerate. A **horizontal merger** represents a merger of firms engaged in the same line of business. A **vertical merger** represents a merger of firms engaged in different stages of production in an industry. A **conglomerate merger** represents a merger of firms engaged in unrelated lines of activities.

Reasons of Mergers

The principal economic rationale for a merger is that the value of the merged entity is expected to be greater than the sum of the independent values of the merging entities. What are the sources of additional value? The important ones are:

- Operating economies
- Financial economies
- Growth
- Diversification
- Managerial effectiveness

Operating Economies When two or more firms combine, certain economies are realised because of the larger volume of operations of the combined entity. These economies arise because of more intensive utilisation of production capacities, distribution networks, engineering services, research and development facilities, data processing systems, so on and so forth. Economies of scale are most prominent in the case of horizontal mergers where the scope for more intensive utilisation of resources is greater. In vertical mergers, the principal sources of benefits are improved coordination of activities, lower inventory levels, and higher market power of the combined entity. Finally, even in conglomerate mergers there is scope for reduction or elimination of certain overhead expenses.

Financial Economies A principal reason for mergers is to avail of financial economies in one or more of the following forms.

- When a firm with accumulated losses and/or unabsorbed tax shelters merges with a profit –making firm, tax shields are utilised better.
- The merged entity may enjoy a higher debt capacity because the earnings of the merged entity tend to be more stable than the independent earnings of the merging entities. Further, it may be able to borrow at a lower interest rate.

Growth If a firm has decided to enter or expand in a particular industry, merger with another firm in that industry, rather than internal expansion, may offer several strategic advantages: (i) As a pre-emptive move it can prevent a competitor from establishing a similar position in that industry. (ii) If offers a special 'timing' advantage because the merger alternative enables a firm to 'leap frog' several stages in the process of expansion. (iii) It may entail less risk and even less cost. (iv) In a 'saturated' market, simultaneous expansion and replacement (through a merger) makes more sense than creation of additional capacity through internal expansion.

Diversification A commonly stated motive for mergers is to achieve risk reduction through diversification. The extent to which risk is reduced, of course, depends on the correlation between the earnings of the merging entities. While negative correlation brings greater reduction in risk, positive correlation brings lesser reduction in risk.

Managerial Effectiveness One of the potential gains of merger is an increase in managerial effectiveness. This may occur if the existing management team, which is performing poorly, is replaced by a more effective management team. Often a firm, plagued with managerial inadequacies can gain immensely from the superior management that is likely to emerge as a sequel to the merger. Another allied benefit of a merger may be in the form of greater congruence between the interests of the managers and the shareholders.

A common argument for creating a favourable environment for mergers is that it imposes a certain discipline on management. If lacklustre performance renders a firm more vulnerable to potential acquisition, existing managers will strive hard continually to improve their performance.

Legal Procedure

The procedure for mergers (referred to as amalgamation in the legal parlance) generally involves the following steps:

- Intimate the stock exchanges, where the amalgamating and amalgamated companies are listed, about the amalgamation proposal.
- Get the draft amalgamation proposal approved by the respective boards of the amalgamating and amalgamated companies.
- Apply to the NCLTs for convening the meetings of shareholders and creditors and get their permission.
- Despatch the notice of meetings of shareholders and creditors.
- Hold the meetings of shareholders and creditors and obtain their approval.

- Petition the NCLT for confirming the scheme of amalgamation (as approved by shareholders and creditors) and passing the orders.
- File the order of the NCLT with the Registrar of Companies.
- Transfer the assets and liabilities of the amalgamating company to the amalgamated company.
- Issue securities of the amalgamated company in exchange for the securities of the amalgamating company.

Tax Aspects of Amalgamations

- For tax purposes, the depreciation chargeable by the amalgamated company has to be based on the written down value of the assets before amalgamation. For accounting (company law) purposes, however, the depreciation charge may be based on the consideration paid for the assets.
- The amalgamated company can carry forward the accumulated losses and unabsorbed depreciation of the amalgamating company when certain conditions are satisfied.
- The amalgamated company can amortise certain expenditures incurred by the amalgamating company.
- Capital gains tax is not applicable to the amalgamating company or its shareholders if they get shares in the amalgamated company.

Exchange Ratio

The shareholders of the amalgamating company are given the shares of the amalgamated company in exchange for the shares held by them in the amalgamating company. For example when TOMCO was merged with Hindustan Lever Limited, shareholders of TOMCO were given the shares of Hindustan Lever Limited in the ratio of 2:15; that means 2 shares of Hindustan Lever Limited were given in lieu of 15 shares of TOMCO. How is the exchange ratio determined? The commonly used bases for establishing the exchange ratio are: earnings per share, market price per share, and book value per share.

Earnings Per Share Suppose the earnings per share of the acquiring firm are ₹5.00 and the earnings per share of the target firm ₹2.00.An exchange ratio based on earnings per share will be 0.4(2/5).This means 2 shares of the acquiring firm will be exchanged for 5 shares of the target firm.

While earnings per share reflect *prime facie* the earning power, there are some problems in an exchange ratio based solely on current earnings per share of the merging companies because it fails to take into account the following:

- The difference in the growth rates of earnings of the two companies.
- The gains in earnings arising out of merger.
- The differential risks associated with the earnings of the two companies.

Moreover, there is the measurement problem of defining the normal level of current earnings. The current earnings per share may be influenced by certain transient factors like a windfall profit, or an abnormal labour problem, or a large tax relief. Finally, how can earnings per share, when they are negative, be used?

Market Price Per share The exchange ratio may be based on the relative market prices of the shares of the acquiring firm and the target firm. For example, if the acquiring firm's equity share sells for ₹50 and the target firm's equity share sells for ₹10, the exchange ratio based on the market price is 0.2(10/50). This means that 1 share of the acquiring firm will be exchanged for 5 shares of the target firm.

When the shares of the acquiring firm and the target firm are actively traded in a competitive market, market prices have considerable merit. They reflect current earnings, growth prospects, and risk characteristics. When the trading is meagre, market prices, however, may not be very reliable. In the extreme case market prices may not be available if the shares are not traded. Another problem with market prices is that they may be manipulated by those who have a vested interest.

Book Value Per Share The relative book values of the two firms may be used to determine the exchange rate. For example, if the book value per share of the acquiring company is ₹25 and the book value per share of the target company is ₹15, the book value based exchange ratio is 0.6 (15/25).

The proponents of book value contend that it provides a very objective basis. This, however, is not a convincing argument because book values are influenced by accounting policies which reflect subjective judgements. There are still more serious objections against the use of book value.

- Book values do not reflect changes in purchasing power of money.
- Book values often are highly different from true economic values.

17.2 PURCHASE OF DIVISION/PLANT

With the step-up in corporate restructuring activity, purchase and sale of divisions or plants are becoming commonplace. Here are some prominent examples:

- Oswal Agro Limited bought the petrochemical plant of Union Carbide Limited.
- India Cement Limited bought the cement division of Coromandal Fertilizers Limited.
- Heinz India Limited bought the foods division of Glaxo India Limited.
- SRF bought the nylon tyre cord division of CEAT Limited.
- Lafarge bought the cement plant of TISCO.

The counterpart for purchase is divestiture. If firm A purchases a plant or factory or business division of firm B, from the point of firm B it represents a divestiture. Purchases (and divestitures) are expected to grow in importance in the years to come as firms restructure themselves with greater freedom in the more liberalised industrial environment.

Typically, when a division is purchased, the acquiring company takes over the assets of that division along with its accompanying liabilities. For example, when India Cements Limited bought the cement division of Coromandal Fertilisers Limited it took over the liabilities associated with that division as well.

Valuing a Division

Three approaches are commonly used for valuing a business or a division thereof - after all a division is a mini-business:

- Adjusted book value approach
- Direct comparison approach
- Discounted cash flow approach

17.3 TAKEOVERS

A takeover generally involves the acquisition of a certain block of equity capital of a company which enables the acquirer to exercise control over the affairs of the company. In theory, the acquirer must buy more than 50 per cent of the paid up equity of the acquired company to enjoy complete control. In practice, however, effective control can be exercised with a smaller holding, usually between 20 and 40 per cent, because the remaining shareholders, scattered and ill-organised, are not likely to challenge the control of the acquirer.

Some examples of takeovers witnessed in recent years in India are: Goenkas took over Spencers and Harrison Malayalam; Hindujas took over Ashok Leyland; India Cement Limited took over Raasi Cement Limited; Holcim took over ACC; Daichi Sankyo took over Ranbaxy Laboratories. A takeover is friendly if the incumbent management approves it; on the other hand, a takeover is hostile if the incumbent management opposes it.

Pros and Cons of Takeovers

Proponents of takeover argue that takeovers improve the quality of management, facilitate forward and backward linkages with the other operations of the acquirer, and afford scope for realising synergistic benefits. T. Boone Pickens Jr., a very eloquent votary of takeovers, regards takeovers as a device for punishing weak managements and protecting the interest of the small shareholders. The leitmotif of a book[1] written by him is that companies should be run in the interest of shareholders and not management or, as some executives claim, "the society at large". He defends takeovers as a device to protect the interest of shareholders.

Pickens' view, of course, has been disputed vigorously by the opponents of takeovers. Warren Law[2], in a very incisive criticism, challenged the premise of Pickens that takeovers help in rescuing poorly managed companies from the inept managers. According to him, managers do much more for their companies and shareholders than the raiders (or predators) who are primarily motivated by a desire to make a 'fast buck' and see their pictures on magazine covers.

While the popular controversy on takeovers continues, scientific research supports takeovers. In the words of Michael Jensen and Richard Ruback: "In brief, the evidence seems to indicate that corporate takeovers generate positive gains, that target firm shareholders benefit, and that bidding firm shareholders do not lose."

Hence, takeovers may be regarded as a legitimate device in the market for corporate control provided they are properly regulated. Basically, this means that the framework for regulating takeovers should seek to: (a) impart transparency to the process, (b) protect the interest of small shareholders (c) facilitate the realisation of

---

[1] T. Boone Pickens. Jr. *Boone* New York, Houghton Miflin Co, 1986.

[2] Warren Law "A Corporation is More Than Its Stock" *Harvard Business Review*, 1986.

economic gains, (d) prevent concentration of economic power, and (e) provide financial support to desirable takeover proposals.

Guidelines for Takeovers

The Securities and Exchange Board of India has issued detailed guidelines for regulating substantial acquisition of shares and takeovers. The key guidelines are:

- The acquirer should intimate the target company and the concerned stock exchange as soon as its holding reaches 5 percent of the voting capital of the target company.
- No sooner the holding of the acquirer reaches 25 percent of the voting capital of the target company, it should intimate the concerned stock exchange and offer to other shareholders of the company to buy a minimum of 26 percent of the voting capital of the target company through an offer document at a price that is subject to a floor, as determined by certain guidelines.
- The offer document should give financial information of the offerer company (acquirer), disclose the intentions of the offerer company about the proposed changes in the business of the target company, and provide long-term commercial justification for the proposed offer.

The purpose of these guidelines is to (a) impart greater transparency to takeover deals, (b) ensure a greater amount of disclosure through public announcement and offer documents, and (c) protect the interest of small shareholders.

17.4 MANAGING AN ACQUISITION

Several studies on mergers and acquisitions in the last three decades or so have found that more often than not these transactions do not produce the anticipated gains. As Warren Hellman said: "So many mergers fail to deliver what they promise that there should be a presumption of failure. The burden of proof should be on showing that anything really good is likely to come out of one."

Five Sins of Acquisitions

It appears that acquisitions are plagued by five sins: straying too far afield, striving for bigness, leaping without looking, overpaying, and failing to integrate well.

Straying Too Far Afield Very few firms have the ability to successfully manage diverse businesses. As one study revealed, 42 percent of the acquisitions that turned sour were conglomerate acquisitions in which the acquirer and the acquired companies lacked familiarity with each other's business. The temptation to stray into unrelated areas that appear exotic and very promising is often strong. However, the reality is that such forays are often very risky.

Striving for Bigness Size is perhaps a very important yardstick by which most organisations, business or otherwise, judge themselves. Hence, there is a strong tendency on the part of managers, whose compensation is significantly influenced by size, to build big empires. The focus on size may lead to unwise acquisitions. Hence, when evaluating an acquisition proposal keep the attention focused on how it will create value for shareholders and not on how it will increase the size of the company.

Leaping before Looking Failure to investigate fully the business of the seller is rather common. The problems here are: (i) the seller may exaggerate the worth of intangible assets (brand image, technical know-how, patents and copyrights, and so on), (ii) the accounting reports may be deftly window-dressed, and (iii) the buyer may not be able to assess the hidden problems and contingent liabilities or may simply brush them aside because of its infatuation with the target company. Veterans in this game strongly argue that the negotiating parties must searchingly examine the other side's motivations.

Overpaying In a competitive bidding situation, the naïve ones tend to bid more. Often the highest bidder is one who overestimates value out of ignorance. Though he emerges as the winner he happens to be in a way the unfortunate winner. This is referred to as the "winner's curse" hypothesis.

Failing to Integrate Well Even the best strategy can be ruined by poor implementation. A precondition for the success of an acquisition is the proper post-acquisition integration of two different organisations. This is a complex task which may not be handled well. As Copeland et al. say: "Relationships with customers, employers, and suppliers can easily be disrupted during the process; and this disruption may cause damage to the value of the business. Aggressive acquirers often believe they can improve the target's performance by injecting better talent, but end up chasing much of the talent out."

A Disciplined Acquisition Programme

As the chances of failure in an acquisition can be high, it should be planned carefully. It pays to develop a disciplined acquisition programme consisting of the following steps:

1. Manage the pre-acquisition phase
2. Screen candidates
3. Evaluate the remaining candidates
4. Determine the mode of acquisition
5. Negotiate and consummate the deal
6. Manage the post-acquisition integration

Step 1: Manage the Pre-acquisition Phase A good starting point of a merger and acquisition programme for an acquiring company is to institute a thorough valuation of the company itself. This will enable the acquiring company to understand well its strengths and weaknesses and deepen the acquirer's insights into the structure of its industry. It will also help in identifying ways and means of enhancing the value of the acquiring firm so that the firm can minimise the chances of becoming a potential acquisition candidate itself.

Armed with this knowledge, managers of the acquiring firm can do brainstorming that will throw up worthwhile acquisition ideas. Opportunities that strengthen or leverage the core business, or provide functional economies of scale, or result in transfer of skill or technology need to be identified.

Of course, the entire exercise of identifying acquisition targets must be kept very confidential. Should the market come to know of a proposed takeover, the price of the target will rise and perhaps jeopardise the deal itself.

Step 2: Screen Candidates The ideas generated in the brainstorming sessions and the suggestions received from various quarters (merchant bankers, consultants, corporate planners, and so on) will have to be filtered. Screening criteria that make sense from the acquiring company's perspective need to be used. For example, an acquirer may eliminate companies that are:

- Too large (market capitalisation of equity in excess of ₹1000 crore), or
- Too small (revenues less than ₹100 crore), or
- Engaged in a totally unrelated activity, or

- Commanding a high price-earnings multiple (in excess of 25), or
- Not export-oriented (exports account for less than 20 per cent of the turnover), or
- Not amenable to acquisition (existing management is not inclined to relinquish control).

A company should be well prepared before the acquisition opportunity actually arises. It should do advance analysis of possible acquisition candidates so that it can rapidly initiate action, no sooner an opportunity surfaces, without succumbing to the temptation of making expensive mistakes.

Step 3: Evaluate the Remaining Candidates The screening criteria applied in step 2 will narrow down the list of candidates to a fairly small number. Each of them should be examined thoroughly. A comprehensive evaluation must cover in great detail the following aspects: operations, plant facilities, distribution network, sales, personnel, and finances (including hidden and contingent liabilities). Special attention should be paid to the quality of management. Experienced, competent, and dedicated management is a scarce resource. When a company is acquired, the quality of its management is as, if not more, important as the rest of its assets.

Each candidate ought to be valued as realistically as possible. Valuation should not be clouded by wishful thinking and it should not be vitiated by an obsession to acquire the target company.

Most important, valuation must not be exaggerated by considerations of 'synergistic benefits' which may be elusive rather than real.

Acquisitions are unique investment decisions because there are no dry runs, the entire money has to be paid upfront, exit costs after integration are prohibitively high, and managing a synergy in many ways is akin to managing a complex new venture. No wonder, acquirers have lost with impunity billions of dollars in their pursuit of poorly understood acquisitions.

As acquisition premiums typically range between 20 per cent and 60 per cent of the pre-acquisition market value, an acquiring firm must formulate a clear and coherent strategy that will enable the firm to earn the premium that it will most probably have to pay.

Step 4: Determine the Mode of Acquisition As discussed earlier, the three major modes of acquisition are merger, purchase of assets, and takeover. In addition, one may look at leasing a facility or entering into a management contract. Though these do not tantamount to acquisition, they give the right to use and manage a complex of assets at a much lesser cost and commitment. They may eventually lead to acquisition.

The choice of the mode of acquisition is guided by the regulations governing them, the time frame the acquirer has in mind, the resources the acquirer wishes to deploy, the degree of control the acquirer wants to exercise, and the extent to which the acquirer is willing to assume contingent and hidden liabilities. Exhibit 17.2 shows how the three methods compare.

Step 5: Negotiate and Consummate the Deal For successful negotiation, the acquiring firm should know how valuable is the acquisition candidate to the firm, to the present owner, and to other potential acquirers.

The process of negotiating acquisitions is notoriously susceptible to rising commitments. As Warren Buffett says the thrill of the chase may blind the acquirer to the outcome of it. Given this inherent pitfall, it makes sense to divide the task of acquisitions analysis and negotiation between two teams. The first team should evaluate the acquisition target from the strategic, operating, and organisational points of view and prepare a game plan of what needs to be done to improve the overall performance. Ideally, it should consist of operating managers who would be entrusted with the responsibility of actually running the business if the deal goes through. The second team should consist of financial and legal persons entrusted with the task of carrying out the actual negotiations. It must retain the emotional capacity to withdraw from the deal unless the financial and legal terms are attractive.

EXHIBIT 17.2 ***Modes of Acquisition : How Do They Compare***

	Takeover	*Purchase*	*Merger*
Object	Shares	Unit	Company
Process	Open offer/ Market	Clearances	Approvals
Taxation(Shareholders)	Attracted	NA	Nil
Taxation (Company)	NA	Attracted	NA
Stamp Duty	0 to ½%	Applicable (High)	Nil
Pricing	Market driven	Valuation	Valuation
Extent of Acquisition	26-51%	100% of the unit	100% of the company
Consideration	Cash/shares	Cash	Cash / shares
To whom	Members	Company	Members

Step 6: Manage the Post-acquisition Integration Generally, after the acquisition, the new controlling group tends to be much more ambitious and is inclined to assume a higher degree of risk. It seeks to (i) quicken the pace of action in an otherwise staid organisation, (ii) encourage a proactive, rather than a reactive, stance towards external developments, and (iii) emphasise achievement over adherence to organisational procedures.

The changes sought to be introduced by the new controlling group are likely to challenge deep-seated values, beliefs, styles, traditions, and practices. This may induce a sense of insecurity and discomfort—and even repugnance and hostility—in some quarters. Such reaction arises partly because they genuinely believe that the objectives, strategies, value, and style of the new controlling group may not subserve the interest of the organisation. Many competent professional managers believe that managing a complex, multi-product, multi-technology enterprise requires a culture and set of values that may be alien to the new group. Hence it depends upon the new group to make adjustments in their values and styles and introduce changes which are worked out cooperatively. Mutual trust and confidence should be the bedrock for introducing changes meant to galvanise the enterprise to reach greater heights of achievement.

17.5 BUSINESS ALLIANCES

Business alliances such as joint ventures, strategic alliances, equity partnerships, licensing, franchising alliances, and network alliances have grown significantly. In many situations, well-designed business alliances are viable alternatives to mergers and acquisitions. No wonder they have become commonplace in diverse fields like high-technology, media and entertainment, automobiles, pharmaceuticals, oil exploration, and financial services. Here are some conspicuous examples:

- General Motors and Toyota entered into an unprecedented joint venture agreement in the 1980s.
- Merck has over 100 R&D alliances with a variety of entities.
- In 1999, IBM announced business alliances worth $ 30 billion with companies like Cisco and Dell computers.
- Oracle has over 15,000 alliances with its business partners.

Business alliances come in a variety of forms. The most commonly used forms are: joint ventures, strategic alliances, equity partnerships, licensing, franchising alliances, and network alliances.

Rationale for Business Alliances

Business alliances are motivated by a desire to share risks and gain access to new markets, reduce costs, receive favourable regulatory treatement, or acquire (or exit) a business.

Sharing Risks and Resources Developing new technologies can be a very risky and expensive proposition. Further, such endeavours require pooling technical capabilities of different organisations. Hence, firms in high technology industries form business alliances so that diverse know-how can be pooled, adequate funding can be arranged, and acceptable risk sharing mechanisms can be worked out.

Access to New Markets The cost of accessing a new market may be prohibitive because huge outlays are required on advertising, promotion, warehousing, and distribution. To solve this problem, a company may enter into an alliance to market its products or services through the sales force, distribution outlets, or Internet site of another firm.

Cost Reduction Business alliances can help in reducing costs through sharing or combining of facilities in joint manufacturing operations and mutually beneficial purchaser-supplier relationships.

Favourable Regulatory Treatment Regulatory authorities like the Department of Justice in the U.S. generally look upon JVs more favourably than mergers or acquisitions.

Prelude to Acquisition or Exit A JV or strategic alliance may be a prelude to acquire another company. Alternatively it may be used as a means for exiting a business.

What Makes a Business Alliance Succeed

The following factors are critical to the success of a business alliance:

- The partners have complementary strengths.
- The cost of developing a new product is exorbitant for a single firm.
- The partners have the ability to cooperate with one another.
- There is clarity of purpose, roles, and responsibilities.
- The apportionment of risks and rewards are perceived as equitable by all parties.
- The partners have similar time horizons and financial expectations.

17.6 PORTFOLIO RESTRUCTURING

Portfolio restructuring essentially involves modifying the business portfolio through divestitures and demergers.

Divestitures

A divestiture involves the sale of a division or plant or unit of one firm to another. From the seller's perspective, it is a form of **contraction**, from the buyer's point of view, it represents **expansion**. For example, when Coromandal Fertilizers Limited sold its cement division of India Cements Limited, the size of Coromandal Fertilizers Limited contracted whereas the size of India Cements Limited expanded. Hence, a divestiture is the obverse of a purchase.

Motives of Divestiture Divestiture decisions are prompted by a variety of motives. The more important ones are discussed below:

Raising Capital A common motive for divestitures is to raise capital. Cash strapped firms seem to resort to divestiture to shore up their liquidity. CEAT, for example, sold its nylon tyre cord plant at Gwalior to SRF for ₹3250 million so that it could settle its outstandings and raise funds to concentrate on tyre manufacturing.

Curtailment of Losses A prominent reason for divestiture is to cut losses. More broadly it may imply that the unit that is proposed to be divested is earning a sub-normal rate of return.

Strategic Realignment The seller may divest a unit which no longer fits with its strategic plan. Often such a unit tends to be in an unrelated line and may demand a lot of managerial time and attention. After divestment, the seller can concentrate on its core business. ICI appears to be a good example. It sold its fibre division to Terene Fibres India and fertilisers division to Chand Chap Fertilisers and Chemicals and seeds division to Hysum India. These divestitures, ICI believes, will enable it to focus on paints and industrial chemicals, in line with its parent's global strategy.

Efficiency Gain A divestiture results in an efficiency gain when the unit divested is worth more as part of some other firm or as a stand-alone business. This happens when there is a reverse synergy, sometimes referred to as 'anergy'. This means that the value of the parts is greater than the whole. In simple arithmetic, it implies that 5 – 3 = 3 !. Remember that a merger is motivated by the possibility of synergistic benefit, where the whole is expected to be more valuable than the sum of the parts 2 + 3 = 6 !.

Demergers

A demerger results in the transfer by a company of one or more of its undertakings to another company. The company whose undertaking is transferred is called the **demerged** company and the company (or the companies) to which the undertaking is transferred is referred to as the **resulting** company.

A demerger may take the form of a spinoff or a split-up. In a spinoff an undertaking or division of a company is spun off into an independent company. After the spinoff, the parent company and the spun off company are separate corporate entities. For example, the the telecommuncations business of Reliance Industries Limited was spun off as a separate company which was rechristened Reliance Communications Limited. In a split-up, a company is split up into two or more independent companies. As a sequel, the parent company disappears as a corporate entity and in its place two or more separate companies emerge. For example, the Ahmedabad Advance Mills was split up into two separate companies, viz., the New Ahmedabad Advance Mills and the Tata Metal Strips. Though spinoffs and splitups are different in form, their economic substance is the same.

Rationale Spinoffs and splitups are regarded as devices for enhancing corporate values by raising efficiency and performance. The principal sources of efficiency gain and performance improvement are as follows:

Sharper Focus A spinoff[3] may facilitate a sharper business focus by removing a poor business "fit". For example, when Itek Corporation of the U.S. spun off its vision products division, Itek's management said: "With the separation of vision products, Itek is once again a high technology company. While the separation of vision products was costly, we are now in a position to totally dedicate our efforts and resources where Itek has expertise and leadership".

Improved Incentives and Accountability A spinoff strengthens managerial incentives and heightens its accountability. For example, the president's letter in the 1980 Annual Report of Peabody International describes the effects of Peabody's spinoff of GEO International : "Speaking from personal experience, one of the most exciting benefits has been a rekindling of the entrepreneurial spirit and initiative within

---

[3] Since spinoffs are similar to splitups from the economic point of view, what is said of a spinoff applies to a split-up as well

both Peabody and GEO. Managers in both companies now feel that their individual efforts can make a significant difference in bottom line results".

Tax Aspects of Demerger The Income Tax Act stipulates the following conditions for a transaction to be recognised as a demerger:

- All the assets and liabilities of the undertaking are transferred from the demerged company to the resulting company.
- The transfer is effected on a going concern basis and at book value.
- Shareholders holding not less than 75 percent in value of the shares in the demerged company become shareholders of the resulting company or companies by virtue of the demerger.
- In consideration of the demerger, the resulting company issues its shares to the shareholders of the demerged company on a proportionate basis.

When a transaction satisfies the above conditions, the following tax provisions are applicable:

- Tax benefits and concessions available to an undertaking should be available to the said undertaking on its transfer to the resulting company.
- Accumulated losses and unabsorbed depreciation can be carried forward from the demerged company to the resulting company.
- Neither the companies nor the shareholders are subject to capital gains tax.
- Expenses incurred wholly for the purpose of demerger are allowed as a deduction in five annual installments of 20 percent each.

The above benefits, however, will not apply should there be another demerger of the resulting company within a period of ten years from the date of demerger.

17.7 FINANCIAL RESTRUCTURING

Financial restructuring involves a significant change in the financial structure of the firm and/or the pattern of ownership and control. Financial restructuring is done in a variety of ways. The more common ones are:

- Going public
- Debt – equity swap
- Leveraged buyout

Going Public

Most of the partnership firms and private limited companies and to some extent even sole proprietorship concerns – that have attained some size and stature – seem to debate whether they should go public and if so when and on what terms.

Whether to Go Public For many firms the decision relating to going public is an agonising one. What are the *'pros'* and *'cons'* that are relevant to such a decision? The potential advantages that seem to induce many companies to go public are:

Access to Capital A private limited company may find it very difficult to grow beyond a certain point for want of capital. Hence, the principal motivation for going public is to have access to larger capital.

Respectability Heading a public limited company is deemed to be more respectable than leading a private limited company. Many entrepreneurs believe that they have "arrived" in some sense if their company goes public.

Ability to Attract Talent Competent and ambitious executives would like to work for organisations that offer greater prospects for growth. Other things being equal, public limited companies have greater growth potential compared to private limited companies. Hence, they can attract superior talent.

Foreign Alliances Foreign companies may be more comfortable in working with public limited companies. Hence a firm, interested in seeking an alliance with a foreign partner, would be better off if it is organised as a public limited company.

A public limited company, of course, is not an unmixed blessing. There may be several disadvantages in going public:

Dilution When a private limited company goes public, the existing shareholders will have to accept some dilution of their ownership stake. They no longer remain the absolute owners of the company.

Loss of Flexibility The affairs of a public limited company are subject to fairly comprehensive regulations. Hence, when a private limited company is transformed into a public limited company there is some loss of flexibility.

Disclosures Law requires a public limited company to disclose more information to investors and others. Hence, it cannot maintain a strict veil of secrecy over its expansion plans and product market strategies as its private counterpart can do.

Accountability Understandably, the degree of accountability of a public limited company is higher. It has to explain a lot to its shareholders.

When and on What Terms On the whole, many private limited companies may find that the pros of going public outweigh the cons of going public. Once they are convinced, in principle, that they should go public, the next question is when and on what terms?

Generally, a private limited company should wait till it has been profitable for at least three years. There is a SEBI guideline which says that a company should have been profitable for at least three years to enjoy freedom in pricing its issue. As far as the actual timing of the public issue is concerned, it is a matter of judgement. Companies would naturally like to go public when the stock market is buoyant. However, given the lead time required for a public issue and the unpredictability of the stock market, successful timing seems to depend as much on luck as on skill.

Debt–Equity Swap

When a firm finds it difficult to service its existing debt, it may explore the possibility of converting the debt into equity. Such a conversion is referred to as a debt–equity swap. For example, when Indian Drugs and Pharmaceuticals Limited was not in a position to meet the interest burden, let alone the principal repayment obligation, on its outstanding debt, it sought to swap its debt into equity.

Remember that financially troubled firms seek to avoid debt and embrace equity. Why? As Bennett Stewart and David Glassman put it "Equity is soft, debt hard. Equity is forgiving, debt insistent. Equity is a pillow, debt is a sword. Equity and debt are the yin and yang of corporate finance".

Leveraged Buyout

A leveraged buyout involves a transfer of ownership consummated mainly with debt. Generally, a leveraged buyout involves an acquisition of a division or unit of a company; occasionally it entails the purchase of an entire company.

To illustrate the essence of a leveraged buyout transaction, a simple example may be given. Trilok Limited has three divisions, namely the plastics division, the textiles division, and the garments division. Trilok is interested in divesting the plastics division. While the assets of this division have a replacement cost of ₹1400 million, they will fetch only

₹900 million if liquidated. Trilok is willing to sell the division if it gets ₹1000 million. Four key executives of the plastics division are keen on acquiring it through a leveraged buyout operation. They are willing to invest ₹80 million.

They approach Financial Engineering Limited (FEL), a merchant banking firm, for assistance. FEL prepares projections for the plastics division on the assumption that it will be run as an independent company by the four key executives. FEL figures out that the cash flows of this operation would support a debt of ₹1000 million. FEL finds a finance company which is willing to provide debt finance to the extent of ₹850 million for the project. FEL also locates a private investor who is prepared to invest ₹70 million in the equity of this project. The plastics division of Trilok is acquired by an independent company, run by the four key executives, which is financed through debt to the tune of ₹850 million and through equity participation to the extent of ₹150 million.

Risks and Rewards The sponsors of a leveraged buyout are lured by the prospect of wholly (or largely) owning a company or a division thereof with the help of substantial debt finance. They assume considerable risks in the hope of reaping handsome rewards. The success of the entire operation depends on their ability to improve the performance of the unit, contain its business risks, exercise cost controls, and liquidate disposable assets. If they fail to do so, the high fixed financial costs can jeopardise the venture.

17.8 REHABILITATION SCHEMES

There are hundreds of large sick units, thousands of medium scale sick units, and countless number of small scale sick units. Thousands of crores of bank funds have been locked in these sick units. In addition, the unpaid arrears of excise duty, sales tax, provident fund, wages, power bills, and so on are considerable.

The incidence of industrial sickness has been a cause of great concern to the government, financial institutions, banks, entrepreneurs, employees, and others.

Causes of Sickness

Industrial sickness is caused by a variety of factors like market recession, infrastructure bottlenecks, technical shortcomings, changes in government policies, and so on. Of course, managerial deficiency is often the most important factor. A study of RBI put it this way: "A broad generalisation regarding important causes of industrial sickness emerges. It is observed that the factor most often responsible for industrial sickness can be defined as 'management'. This may take the form of poor production management, poor labour management, poor resources management, lack of professionalism, dissension within the management, or even dishonest management".

Revival Programme

When an industrial unit is identified as sick, a viability study should be conducted to assess whether the unit can be revived/rehabilitated and a suitable plan for rehabilitation must be formulated[4]. This may involve one or more of the following elements.

Settlement with Creditors A sick unit is normally in straitened financial circumstances and is not able to honour its commitments to its creditors (financial institutions, debenture holders, commercial banks, suppliers, and government authorities). To alleviate its financial distress, a settlement scheme has to be worked out which may involve one or more of the following: rescheduling of principal and interest payment; waiver of interest; conversion of debt into equity; and payment of arrears in installments.

Provision of Additional Capital Typically a revival programme entails provision of additional capital. This may be required for modernisation and repair of plant and machinery, for purchase of balancing equipment, for sustaining a new marketing drive, and for enhanced working capital needed to support a higher level of operations. The additional capital has to be provided on concessional terms, at least for the initial years, so that the financial burden on the unit is not high.

Divestment and Disposal The revival programme may involve divestment of unprofitable plants and operations and disposal of slow moving and obsolete stocks to improve liquidity.

Reformulation of Product–Market Strategy Many a business failure can be traced to an ill-conceived product–market strategy. For reviving a sick unit, its product–market strategy may have to be imaginatively reformulated to improve the prospects of its successful recovery.

---

[4] If the viability study indicates that the unit is "better dead than alive", steps must be taken to liquidate it expeditiously.

Modernisation of Plant and Machinery In order to improve manufacturing efficiency, plant and machinery may have to be modernised, renovated, and repaired. This may be essential for attaining certain cost standards and quality norms for competing effectively in the market place.

Reduction in Manpower Generally, sick firms tend to be over-staffed. The revival programme must seek to reduce superfluous manpower. Often a 'golden handshake' involving paying a significant retrenchment compensation is a better proposition than carrying redundant manpower on the payroll of the unit.

Strict Control Over Costs A profitable organisation can afford wastefulness and laxity in its expenditures. A tottering firm, seeking to regain its health and vigour, has to exercise strict control over its costs, particularly over its discretionary expenses.

Streamlining of Operations Manufacturing, purchasing, and selling operations have to be meticulously examined so that they can be streamlined. Value engineering, standardisation, simplification, cost-benefit analysis, and other approaches should be exploited fully to improve the efficiency of the operations.

Improvement in Managerial Systems The managerial systems in the unit must be strengthened. In this exercise greater attention may have to be paid to the following: environmental monitoring, organisational structure, responsibility accounting, management information systems, and budgetary control.

Workers' Participation During the revival phase, the dedication, commitment, and support of workers is indispensable and meaningful workers' participation and involvement goes a long way in ensuring this.

Change in Management A change in management may be necessary where the present management is dishonest and/or incompetent. It has been observed that a new chief executive, who is competent, committed, and upright can often bring about dramatic results. The classic example of this phenomenon was the dramatic turnaround of Chrysler Corporation under the stewardship of Lee Iacocca.

17.9 PRIVATISATION

Since the 1950s, governments in many developing countries, including India, relied on the public sector to accelerate development and achieve a more equitable regional dispersal of industries. In several countries, the public sector attained "commanding heights" of the economy.

From the late 1970s, however, serious concerns have been raised about the effectiveness and efficiency of public enterprises. As a result, a number of countries have taken steps in the direction of privatisation which essentially involves transfer of ownership (generally represented by equity shares), partial or total, of public enterprises from the government to individuals and non – government institutions. It may also be referred to as "people-isation" or "de-governmentisation" or "marketisation".

Rationale for Privatisation

The privatisation programmes of various countries have been motivated primarily by one or more of the following objectives:

- Improvement in efficiency
- Generation of resources
- Promotion of popular capitalism

Improvement in Efficiency It is generally argued that the private sector has a comparative advantage over the public sector in terms of efficiency. The right to profit in the private sector provides a strong incentive to be efficient. Owner-managers will strive for higher productivity and lower costs, as these get translated into extra profits. Even in firms where ownership and management are practically separated, the capital market and the threat of takeover prods managers to be more efficient. The sources of efficiency gains are as follows:

- *Autonomy* Distanced from political interference and bureaucratic control, the enterprise enjoys greater autonomy. This means more flexibility in investment, financing, and operating decisions.
- *Accountability* Private shareholders tend to be more demanding. Hence the management has to assume higher responsibility for performance.
- *Employee Pride* Typically, as part of privatisation, employees too acquire a stake in ownership. This leads to a greater identification with the enterprise and stronger commitment to excel.

Generation of Resources Governments in most of the countries are struggling to keep budgetary deficits within reasonable limits. This is true of developed countries as well as developing countries. Privatisation seems to be a very convenient way of raising resources for reducing fiscal deficits. Many governments may not find privatisation ideologically very palatable, yet they find it very appealing as a practical device to cope with fiscal problems.

Promotion of Popular Capitalism Privatisation invariably broadens the base of equity shareholders and promotes popular capitalism. Apart from the contribution it makes to the deepening of the capital market it can be politically very appealing. In the United Kingdom, for example, the privatisation programme received an unexpectedly enthusiastic response from investors. As one financial commentator said: "It was a policy with almost everything going for it as if by a process of alchemy the dull metal of Britain's unloved public sector was being transformed into pure gold".

Indian Experiment and What Needs to be Done

The first attempt in the direction of disinvestment was made by the Government of India in 1991-92 when it sold equity shares of about 30 public sector undertakings mainly to public sector mutual funds and realised over ₹3,000 crores. Enthused by this experience, the government planned to step up its privatisation programme. However, a variety of factors, most important being the lack of political will, marred this initiative. The sporadic disinvestment that occurred between 1992 and 1999 has been an apology for privatisation. It was done in a very *ad hoc* manner and driven mainly by the desire to generate resources and reduce budgetary deficit.

While a determined attempt has been made from 2001 and companies like CMC, BALCO, VSNL and IPCL have been privatised, a great deal of internal opposition within the NDA government slowed the process. The UPA government which came into power in 2004, with the support of the Left Front, could not make any progress, thanks to the stiff opposition of the Left Front. On its return to power in 2009, the UPA government has set in motion the disinvestment initiatives. This is being pushed further by the NDA government that has come to power in 2014. Hopefully, the necessary political will emerge to execute a more meaningful and comprehensive privatisation programme aimed primarily at achieving efficiency gains and ensuring a fair price to the government.

SUMMARY

- Mergers, takeovers, divestitures, spinoffs, leveraged buyouts, and so on, collectively referred to as corporate restructuring, have become a major force on the financial and economic landscape all over the world.
- A merger (referred to as amalgamation in the legal parlance) represents a combination of two or more companies into one company. The principal economic rationale of a merger is that the value of the merged entity is expected to be greater than the sum of the independent values of the merging entities.
- With the step-up in corporate restructuring activity, purchase and sale of divisions or plants are becoming commonplace. Typically, when a division is purchased, the acquiring company takes over the assets of that division along with its accompanying liabilities. Three approaches are commonly used for valuing a business or a division thereof: adjusted book value approach, direct comparison approach, and discounted cash flow approach.
- A takeover generally involves the acquisition of a block of equity capital of a company which enables the acquirer to exercise control over the affairs of the company. While there is considerable controversy about takeovers in the popular literature, scientific evidence seems to indicate that corporate takeovers generate positive gains, that target firm shareholders benefit, and that bidding firm shareholders do not lose.
- More often than not, acquisitions do not produce the anticipated gains. Acquisitions seem to be plagued by five sins: straying too far afield, striving for bigness, leaping without looking, overpaying, and failing to integrate well.
- Business alliances such as joint ventures, strategic alliances, equity partnerships, licensing, franchising alliances, and network alliances have grown significantly. In many situations, well-designed business alliances are viable alternatives to mergers and acquisitions.
- Portfolio restructuring essentially involves modifying the business portfolio through divestitures and demergers. A divestiture involves the sale of a division or plant or unit of one firm to another. A demerger results in the transfer of one or more of a company's undertakings to another company. The company whose undertaking is transferred is called the demerged company and the company to which the undertaking is transferred is referred to as the resulting

company. Divestitures and demergers are motivated by reverse synergy or 'anergy'. This means that the value of the parts is greater than the whole. In simple arithmetic, it implies that 5 – 3 = 3!

- Financial restructuring involves a significant change in the financial structure of the firm and/or the pattern of ownership and control. Financial restructuring is done in a variety of ways. The more common ones are: going public, debt-equity swap, and leveraged buyout. Most of the partnership firms and private limited companies that have attained some size and stature have a compulsion to go public. When a firm finds it difficult to service its existing debt, it may explore the possibility of converting debt into equity. Such a conversion is referred to as a debt-equity swap. A leveraged buyout involves a transfer of ownership consummated mainly with debt. Generally, a leveraged buyout involves an acquisition of a division or unit of a company; occasionally, it entails the purchase of an entire company.
- Industrial sickness in India has been a cause of great concern to the government, financial institutions, banks, enterpreneurs, employees, and others. When an industrial unit is identified as sick, a viability study should be conducted to assess whether the unit can be rehabilitated and a suitable plan for rehabilitation has to be drawn up.
- Privatisation involves transfer of ownership (generally represented by equity shares), partial or total, of public enterprises from the government to individuals and non-governmental institutions. The privatisation programmes of various countries have been motivated by a desire to improve efficiency, generate resources, and promote popular capitalism.

International Finance

18

So far, we were concerned mainly with the financial aspects of doing business domestically. Many firms in India, however, export, import, borrow in foreign currency loans, and invest abroad. International involvement of Indian firms is increasing and this trend is expected to continue as India forges stronger linkages with the world economy.

While the principles of finance discussed in this book are equally applicable to a firm with international linkages, as a manager in such a firm, you need to understand certain special features of international finance. Multiple currencies, euromarkets, different tax regimes, and barriers to financial flows are the distinguishing features of international finance.

The field of international finance has witnessed explosive growth and dynamic changes in recent decades. This has been stimulated by a variety of forces: (a) The change in the international monetary system from a fairly predictable system of exchange to a flexible and volatile system of exchange. (b) Emergence of new institutions and markets and a greater need for international financial intermediation. (c) A greater integration of the global financial system.

This chapter discusses the basics of international finance. It is organised into nine sections as follows:

- World monetary system
- Foreign exchange market
- Multinational corporations
- Raising foreign currency finance
- International capital budgeting
- Financing and insuring exports
- Documents in international trade

- Foreign exchange exposure
- Management of foreign exchange exposure

18.1 WORLD MONETARY SYSTEM

In order to understand the present world monetary system, it is helpful to look at the developments during the last few decades. From the end of the second World War until February 1973, the adjustable peg exchange rate system, administered by the International Monetary Fund, prevailed. Under this system, the U.S. dollar which was linked to gold ($35 per ounce) served as the anchor currency. Other currencies were expressed in terms of the dollar and, through this standard, exchange rates between currencies were established. A special feature of this system was that close control was exercised over the exchange rates between various currencies and the dollar – a fluctuation of ± 1 percent was allowed around the fixed exchange rate.

Present System of Floating Exchange Rates

In 1973, the U.S. dollar was delinked from gold. Put differently, it was allowed to "float". This brought about a dramatic change in the international monetary system. The system of fixed exchange rates, where devaluations and revaluations occurred only very rarely, gave way to a system of floating exchange rates.

There are basically two types of floating rates: (a) free floating rates and (b) managed floating rates. The developed countries (like the U.S., Japan, U.K., and so on), in general, permit their currencies to float freely. The exchange rates for the currencies of these countries are determined by the forces of demand and supply in the foreign exchange market. Put differently, their currencies find their own levels without government intervention.

The developing countries, on the other hand, try to manage the exchange rates of their currencies to some extent. Essentially, they allow their currencies to fluctuate freely within certain bounds which are periodically revised. The purpose of such intervention is to avoid volatile fluctuations which may be destablishing.

18.2 MULTINATIONAL CORPORATIONS (MNCs)

A multinational, or global, corporation is a firm that operates in an integrated fashion in a number of countries. Companies "go global" for various reasons.

Trade Barriers Confronted with restrictions to export its products to foreign markets, a firm may set up production facilities in foreign countries to circumvent trade barriers.

Imperfect Labour Markets Due to immigration barriers, labour mobility is limited. So firms locate their plants or facilities in countries that offer labour cost advantage.

Intangible Assets Companies often possess special intangible assets like superior R & D capabilities, marketing savvy, brand equity, and managerial talent. So they invest in foreign countries to leverage these competitive advantages.

Vertical Integration Companies invest in countries to enjoy the benefits of vertical integration. While the majority of vertical foreign direct investments are *backward* to secure supplies of raw materials (oil, mineral deposits, and forest produce), some are *forward* as they involve an industry using the MNC's outputs.

Product Life Cycle According to Raymond Vernon, it is advantageous for a firm to set up production base in foreign countries when the product has reached the stage of maturity.

Diversificaiton By geographically diversifying their production base and markets, firms can reduce the risk of adverse economic developments in a single country.

Shareholder Diversification If there are restrictions to cross-border portfolio diversification, firms can provide their shareholders the benefits of indirect diversification by investing in foreign countries.

18.3 FOREIGN EXCHANGE MARKET

The foreign exchange market is the market where one currency is traded for another. This market has witnessed phenomenal growth in recent years and has emerged as the largest financial market.

Exchange Rate Quotations

An exchange rate represents the relationship between two currencies. There are two ways in which the exchange rate is quoted. In a direct quote, the exchange rate for a foreign currency is quoted in terms of the number of units of local currency that are equal to a unit of the foreign currency. For example, when we say that the exchange rate of a dollar is ₹68 we have a direct quote for the dollar. In an indirect quote, the exchange rate for a foreign currency is expressed in terms of the number of units of foreign currency that are equal to a unit of the local currency. For example, when we say $1.47 is equal to ₹100, we have an indirect quote for the dollar.

Till August 1993, the inter-bank foreign exchange market in India used the system of indirect quotes. Since then, it has adopted direct quotes so that exchange rates are now quoted as number of rupees per unit (or per 100 units in some cases) of a foreign currency. In the foreign exchange market, a **spot rate** refers to the rate applicable to transactions in which settlement (i.e delivery) is two business days after the date of transaction. Forward transactions are also possible in which the rate is fixed today, but the settlement is at some specified date in the future. Such rates are called **forward rates**.

They are often quoted in terms of premia or discounts over the spot rate. If the one month forward rate of dollar is quoting at a premium of say 21 paise over the spot rate of say ₹68.26, it means that the one-month forward rate is ₹68.47. Note that, if the dollar is at a forward premium, it means that the rupee is at a forward discount.

Exhibit 18.1 shows illustrative exchange rates. To understand the numbers given in Exhibit 18.1, note the following:

- A *spot rate* is the rate applicable to a transaction in which settlement is done in two business days after the date of transaction. A *forward rate* is a rate that is fixed today but the settlement takes place at some specified date in future. Banks normally quote forward rates for maturities in whole calendar months—such as 1, 2, 3, and 6 months—but will tailor a forward deal to suit the customer's requirements.
- A TT (telegraphic transfer) rate applies to transaction in which the bank receives or pays foreign currency without any document handling. A bill rate applies when the bank also handles import or export documents or collect bills.
- A forex dealer (such as a bank) offers a two-ways quotation. If a bank quotes ₹66.09/₹66.21 per US dollar, it means that the bank is willing to buy a US dollar for ₹66.09 and sell a US dollar for ₹66.21. The buying rate is called the 'bid rate' and the selling rate the 'offer rate'. In Exhibit 18.1 bid rates are shown under the EXPORT columns and ask rates are shown under the IMPORT columns.

EXHIBIT 18.1 *Exchange Rates*

Indicative on Monday January 21,2019								
IMPORT (Buy)					*EXPORT (Selling)*			
Spot	*1 month*	*3 months*	*6 months*	*Currency*	*Spot*	*1 month*	*3 months*	*6 months*
0.8798	0.8773	0.8729	0.8661	Euro	0.8796	0.8797	0.8772	0.873
0.777	0.7758	0.7735	0.77	Pound Sterling	0.7767	0.7769	0.7757	0.7735
109.6021	109.3101	108.7809	107.9615	Japanese Yen*	109.6246	109.5939	109.3076	108.7971
0.9978	0.9946	0.9892	0.9803	Swiss Frac	0.9978	0.9976	0.9946	0.9893
1.3596	1.3585	1.3565	1.353	Singapore Dollar	1.3599	1.3595	1.3588	1.357
71.34	71.62	72.10	72.82	Indian Rupees	71.2450	71.51	71.99	72.72

Source: State Bank of India, Chennai (as reproduced in Business Line dated 22-1-2019) *(100 units)

International Foreign Exchange Market

The foreign exchange market is the largest financial market in the world. The daily turnover in this market in December 2016 was estimated to be 5.1 trillions. The important features of this market are as follows:

- The foreign exchange market is primarily an over the counter market. This means that transactions take place through telephones, telexes, or the Reuter monitor, and not on the trading floor of an exchange.
- The principal "market-makers" [1] in the foreign exchange market are the major international banks. In recent years, large multinational companies have also become important players in the foreign exchange market.
- Speculative transactions account for more than 95 percent of the turnover on the foreign exchange market. Irrespective of how one looks at speculation, it cannot be gainsaid that if the turnover is not large, the foreign exchange market would be patchy and discontinuous.
- Extending from Tokyo and Sydney in the East to New York and San Francisco in the West, the international foreign exchange market spans almost all the time zones. It is virtually a 24-hour market.

Foreign Exchange Market in India

The foreign exchange market in India is very small. Its important features are as follows:

- The key participants in this market are the Reserve Bank of India, banks, and business undertakings.
- The Indian foreign exchange market is a somewhat controlled market in which the Reserve Bank of India tries to moderate day to day volatility.
- Business undertakings in India can participate in the foreign exchange market in India only to the extent that they need cover for exchange exposure arising from a merchant transaction or a foreign currency borrowing. This means that they cannot resort to speculative transactions.
- The present exchange control regulations permit banks to have a net overbought or oversold position in a foreign currency subject to limits notified by the RBI from time to time.

---

[1] As against a broker who transacts on behalf of his clients, a market maker deals for his own account.

18.4 RAISING FOREIGN CURRENCY FINANCE

The major sources available to an Indian firm for raising foreign currency finance are:

- Foreign currency term loans from financial institutions
- Export credit schemes
- External commercial borrowings
- Euroissues
- Issues in foreign domestic markets

Foreign Currency Term Loans from Financial Institutions

Financial institutions provide foreign currency term loans for meeting the foreign currency expenditures towards import of plant, machinery, and equipment and also towards payment of foreign technical knowhow fees. The periodical liability for interest and principal remains in the currency/currencies of the loans and is translated into rupees at the then prevailing rate of exchange for making payments to the financial institution.

Export Credit Schemes

Export credit agencies have been established by the governments of major industrialised countries for financing exports of capital goods and related technical services. These agencies follow certain consensus guidelines for supporting exports under a convention known as the Berne Union. As per these guidelines, the interest rate applicable for export credits to Indian companies for various maturities are regulated. Two kinds of export credit are provided: buyer's credit and supplier's credit.

Buyer's Credit Under this arrangement, credit is provided directly to the Indian buyer for purchase of capital goods and/or technical services from the overseas exporter. The buyer's credit facility operates as follows:

- The overseas exporter and the Indian buyer negotiate a contract.
- An application for the buyer's credit facility is made to the export credit agency of the exporter's country along with relevant details (like the types of goods/services to be exported, approximate value of the contract, terms of payments, schedule of projected shipment of goods or provision of services, percentage of financing required, etc).
- The buyer's credit facility is approved by the export credit agency of the exporter's country.

- A loan agreement delineating the terms and conditions of the buyer's credit is negotiated between the overseas exporter's bank, the Indian borrower, and where applicable, the Indian guarantor.

Supplier's Credit This is a credit provided to the overseas exporters so that they can make available medium-term finance to Indian importers. The supplier's credit facility operates as follows:

- The overseas exporter notifies his bank and the export credit agency of a potential order from an Indian buyer who requires medium-term finance.
- The export credit agency communicates to the bank its willingness to provide the facility.
- The terms of the facility are incorporated in the contract between the overseas exporter and the Indian buyer.

External Commercial Borrowings

Subject to certain terms and conditions, the Government of India permits Indian firms to resort to external commercial borrowings for the import of plant and machinery. The key steps involved in raising such borrowings are as follows:

1. Secure the permission of the Capital Goods Committee/Projects Approval Board.
2. Obtain an offer from a bank.
3. Get the approval of the Department of Economic Affairs (DEA), Ministry of Finance, for the offer.
4. Arrange for the documentation of the loan.
5. Secure the approval of the Reserve Bank of India.
6. Deposit a copy of the loan document with the DEA.
7. Draw the loan.

Features of Euro-currency Loans

A eurocurrency is simply a deposit of currency in a bank outside the country of the currency. For example, a eurodollar deposit is a dollar deposit in a bank outside the United States. Likewise, a euroyen deposit is a yen deposit in a bank outside Japan. How do eurocurrency deposits arise? This may be explained with an example. Suppose an American oil company buys oil from a Sheik in the Middle East and pays $10 million drawn on the Chase Manhattan Bank and the Sheik deposits the cheque in his account with a Swiss bank. The dollar deposit, placed outside the

United States, the country of the dollar currency, is a eurodollar deposit. The Swiss bank can use this deposit for granting eurodollar loans.

The main features of eurocurrency loans, which represent the principal form of external commercial borrowings, are as follows:

Syndication Eurocurrency loans are often syndicated loans, wherein a group of lenders, particularly banks, participate jointly in the process of lending under a single loan agreement. The syndicate of lenders is represented by the lead bank. The borrower is required to pay a syndication fee, which is a front-end payment, usually ranging between 1/2 percent and 2 percent, to the lead bank. This represents the management fees payable to the lead bank, participation fee to other banks, and other charges.

Floating Rate The rate of interest on eurocurrency loans is a floating rate. It is usually linked to LIBOR (London Interbank Offered Rate) or SIBOR (Singapore Interbank Offered Rate). The spread over the LIBOR or SIBOR rate is mainly a function of the credit worthiness of the borrower and size of the loan. Power Finance Corporation, for example, obtained a eurodollar loan of US $ 75 million in 1997, at an interest rate of 50 basis points (0.5 percent) above the LIBOR. While the rate is determined at the beginning of each interest period, the interest is payable at the end of each period.

Interest Period The interest period may be 3, 6, 9, or 12 months in duration. It is largely left to the option of the borrower.

Currency Option The borrower often enjoys the multi-currency option which enables it to denominate the interest and principal in the new currency opted for. This option is exercisable at the end of each interest period.

Repayment and Prepayment The eurocurrency loan may be repayable in installments or by way of a bullet repayment. The borrower may pre-pay the loan after giving due notice to the lead bank. When pre-payment is done, some premium is payable. The lender may also reserve the right to recall the outstanding loan under certain circumstances.

Euroissues

Till about the mid- 1980s, India's external debt was mostly public debt from multilateral institutions like the World Bank, the International Monetary Fund, and the Asian Development Bank. Since then, Indian corporates resorted to commercial borrowings. The bulk of it was in the form of syndicated/eurodollars loans. When the foreign exchange crisis hit the economy in 1990, India's credit rating plunged below the investment grade and all external funding avenues were closed. This situation continued till 1992.

Following the economic liberalisation, Indian companies started exploring the market again. Unlike the earlier period when syndicated credit was the predominant form of raising external finance, companies began looking at bonds and euroequities collectively referred to as "Euroissues". The two principal mechanisms used by Indian companies are **Depository Receipts** mechanism and **Euroconvertible Issues**. The former represents indirect equity investment, while the latter is debt with an option to convert it into equity.

In the depository receipts mechanism, the shares issued by a firm are held by a depository, usually a large international bank, who receives dividends, reports etc. and issues claims against these shares. These claims are called depository receipts with each receipt being a claim on a specified number of shares. The underlying shares are called **depository shares**. The depository receipts are denominated in a convertible currency- usually the U.S. dollar. The depository receipts may be listed and traded on major stock exchanges. This way, the issuing firm avoids listing fees and onerous disclosure and reporting requirements which would be obligatory if it were to be directly listed on the stock exchange abroad. Global Depository Receipts (GDRs), which can be used to tap multiple-markets with a single instrument have been the most popular instrument used by Indian firms. Holders of depository receipts can convert them into the underlying shares by surrendering the depository receipts to the depository.

A company planning a GDR issue must obtain the approval from the Ministry of Finance as well as the FIPB (Foreign Investment Promotion Board) since GDR issues are deemed to be foreign direct investment. The government periodically issues guidelines regulating GDR issues. These guidelines set out the criteria a potential issuer must satisfy and the permissible uses of the funds raised. The custodian is required to be an Indian institution.

A few issuers have also exploited the bond route. Most of these have been euroconvertible issues. During the initial flurry of enthusiasm about Indian paper, companies have been able to raise funds on very attractive terms via this route.

Issues in Foreign Domestic Markets

Apart from euroissues which are made in the euromarket (a market which falls outside the regulatory purview of national regulatory authorities), Indian firms can also issue bonds and equities in the domestic capital market of a foreign country. Reliance Industries Limited, for example, issued bonds in the U.S. domestic capital market. Such bonds are referred to as Yankee bonds. (Incidentally, bonds issued in the U.K domestic market are called Bulldog bonds and bonds issued in Japanese domestic market are called Samurai bonds). In recent years, Indian companies like Infosys Technologies and ICICI have successfully tapped the U.S. equity market by issuing American Depository Shares (ADSs). Like GDRs, ADSs represent claims on a specific number of shares. The principal difference between the two is that the GDRs are issued in the euromarket whereas ADSs are issued in the U.S. domestic capital market.

18.5 INTERNATIONAL CAPITAL BUDGETING

India Pharma Limited, an India - based multinational company, is evaluating an overseas investment proposal. India Pharma's exports of pharmaceuticals products have increased to such an extent that it is considering a project to build a plant in the U.S. The project will entail an initial outlay of $100 million and is expected to generate the following cash flows over its four year life.

Year	*Cash flow (in million)*
1	$ 30
2	$ 40
3	$ 50
4	$ 60

The current spot exchange rate is ₹65 per U.S.dollar, the risk-free rate in India is 8 percent and the risk- free rate in the U.S. is 6 percent – these are rates observed in the financial markets.

India Pharma's required rupee return on a project of this kind is 15 percent. Should India Pharma undertake this project? The answer, of course, depends on the NPV of the project. How is the NPV of such a project calculated? There are two basic ways of doing this:

Home Currency Approach	*Foreign Currency Approach*
• Convert all the dollar cash flows into rupees (use forecasted exchange rates)	• Calculate the NPV in dollars (use the dollar discount rate)

- Calculate the NPV in rupees (using the rupee discount rate)
- Convert the dollar NPV into rupees (use the spot exchange rate)

Home Currency Approach

To apply the home currency approach we have to come up with the forecasted exchange rates. An important international parity relationship says that the expected spot exchange rate at time *t* is:

$$S^e_t = S_o\left(\frac{1+r_h}{1+r_f}\right)^t$$

where S^e_t is the expected spot exchange rate at time *t*, S_o is the current spot exchange rate, r_h is the nominal risk free rate in home currency, and r_f is the nominal risk-free interest rate in foreign currency

In our example, S_o = ₹65, r_h = 8 percent and r_f = 2 percent. Hence the forecasted spot exchange rates are as follows:

Year	*Forecasted spot exchange rates*		
1	₹65 $(1.08/1.02)^1$	=	₹68.82
2	₹65 $(1.08/1.02)^2$	=	₹72.87
3	₹65$(1.08/1.02)^3$	=	₹77.16
4	₹65 $(1.08/1.02)^4$	=	₹81.70

Using these forecasted spot exchange rates along with the current spot rate of ₹65, we can convert the dollar cash flows into rupees.

Year	(1) Cash flow in dollar (million)	(2) Expected exchange rate	(3) Cash flow in rupees (million)(1) × (2)
0	100	₹65.00	– ₹6500
1	30	68.82	2064.6
2	40	72.87	2914.8
3	50	77.16	3858.0
4	60	81.70	4902.0

Given a rupee discount rate of 15 percent, the NPV in rupees is:

$$\text{NPV} = -6500 + \frac{2064.6}{(1.15)} + \frac{2914.8}{(1.15)^2} + \frac{3858.0}{(1.15)^3} + \frac{4902.0}{(1.15)^4}$$

$$= ₹2839 \text{ million}$$

Foreign Currency Approach

To apply the foreign currency approach we have to come up with a risk-adjusted dollar discount rate corresponding to the risk –adjusted rupee discount rate of 15 percent. To do this we have to first find the risk-premium implicit in 15 percent:

(1 + Risk-free rupee rate) (1+ Risk premium) = (1 + Risk – adjusted rupee rate)

(1 + 0.08) (1+ Risk premium) = (1 + 0.15)

Hence

$$(1+\text{ Risk premium}) = \frac{(1.15)}{(1.08)} = 1.0648$$

Applying the above risk premium to the risk free dollar rate of 2 percent, we find that the risk-adjusted dollar rate is:

(1 + Risk adjusted dollar rate) = (1.02) (1.0648) = (1.0861)

Given the dollar cash flows, the NPV in dollars works out to:

$$\text{NPV} = -100 + \frac{30}{(1.0861)} + \frac{40}{(1.0861)^2} + \frac{50}{(1.0861)^3} + \frac{60}{(1.0861)^4}$$

$$= \$\ 43.677 \text{ million}$$

Since the spot exchange rate is ₹65 per dollar, the rupee NPV of the project is:

$$\text{NPV} = 43.677 \times ₹65 = ₹2839 \text{ million}$$

Expectedly, this is the same as the rupee NPV we obtained earlier using the home currency approach.

Unremitted Cash Flows

In our previous example, we assumed that the post-tax cash flows from the foreign investments could be freely remitted to the parent firm. In reality, there may be substantial differences between the cash flows generated by a foreign project and the amounts that can be remitted to the parent firm because many governments put restrictions on remittances. Funds that cannot be currently remitted are referred to as blocked funds.

Risk-Premium on Foreign Investment

In our discussion so far we assumed that the risk-premium on the foreign investment will be the same as the risk-premium on a similar domestic investment.

Foreign investments generally involve higher risk which arises from factors like change in currency value, discriminatory treatment of a foreign company, and threat of expropriation. Risk stemming from fluctuations in exchange rate looms constantly on the horizon of foreign investment. In addition, a foreign investment is subject to discriminatory treatment and selective control in various forms, motivated mainly by political considerations. Finally, the threat of expropriation without adequate compensation may exist, particularly in countries where radical nationalistic sentiments are strong.

In view of the higher risk associated with foreign investment, a firm contemplating foreign investment would naturally expect a higher rate of return. Put differently, the discount rate applicable to foreign investment may be higher than the discount rate applicable to domestic investment.

A higher-than normal required rate of return by multinational corporations is often viewed unfavourably by the critics of multinational companies. They hurl accusations of 'profiteering' even when the multinational company may simply be following the sound financial practice of asking for a rate of return commensurate with the risks characterising the project.

Can there be situations where the demand for higher returns by a multinational company be unreasonable? Yes, when the multinational company invests in several different economies and enjoys the benefit of risk reduction arising from portfolio diversification. In such a case, it may be possible to reduce the overall risk of the firm's portfolio of investments even while accepting a project which individually is highly risky. Of course, this depends on the existence of low or negative correlations between the project under consideration and the other projects within the firm's portfolio of investments.

18.6 FINANCING AND INSURING EXPORTS

Commercial banks and EXIM bank provide export finance and Export Credit Guarantee Corporation provides insurance to exports.

Commercial Bank Finance

Commercial banks, the major source of export finance in India, provide finance before shipment of goods (pre-shipment finance) as well as after shipment of goods (post-shipment finance).

- *Pre-shipment Finance* The pre-shipment finance, typically is in the form of packing credit facility. Packing credit is bank advance provided to an exporter for purpose of buying/manufacturing/

packing/shipping goods to foreign buyers. An exporter with a firm export order placed with him by a foreign buyer or with an irrevocable letter of credit opened in his favour can approach a bank for packing credit. Packing credit, a short-term credit, is normally required to be liquidated within 360 days by negotiation of export bills or receipt of proceeds for exports. There are three broad types of packing credit: (i) clean packing credit, (ii) packing credit against hypothecation of goods, and (iii) packing credit against pledge of goods.

- *Post-shipment Finance* The finance provided after the shipment may be in the following forms: (i) purchase/discounting of documentary export bills and (ii) advance against export bills sent for collection. A commercial bank may purchase export bills payable at sight or discount usance bills covering confirmed sales and supported by relevant documents like the bill of lading, post-parcel receipts, etc. Or, a commercial bank may provide finance by way of advance against export bills forwarded through it for collection.

EXIM Bank Finance

The EXIM Bank provides finance to exporters in several ways:

- Direct financing of exporters
- Financing of export of technology and consultancy services
- Pre-shipment credit
- Overseas buyer's credit
- Refinance of export credit
- Export bill discounting

Forfaiting[2]

In recent years forfaiting has emerged as a popular method of financing export receivables. Basically, forfaiting refers to non-recourse discounting of medium term (1 year to 5 years) export receivables. In a forfaiting transaction, the exporter surrenders, without recourse to him, his rights to claim for payment of goods delivered to an importer, in return for immediate cash payment from the forfaiter. As a result, the exporter is able to convert a credit sale into a cash sale with no recourse to him. Under this arrangement the export receivables are usually guaranteed by the importer's bank (referred to as the 'avalling' bank).

[2] This section has been contributed by Dr. K. Sriram.

The exporter is required to pay a fee to the forfaiter for the forfaiting transaction. The fee has three components:

- **Commitment Fee:** This represents the fee payable to the forfaiter for securing its commitment to execute a specific forfaiting transaction at a firm discount rate within a specific time.
- **Discount Fee:** This reflects the interest cost payable by the exporter for the entire period of credit. This fee is based on the relevant market rate of interest as reflected by the prevailing LIBOR for the credit period and currency involved, plus a premium for the country risk and credit risk assumed by the forfaiter. This fee is deducted from the amount paid to the exporter against the discounted promissory notes or bills of exchange.
- **Documentation Fee:** This covers expenses involved in documentation and legal work.

In the Indian context the Exim Bank acts as a facilitator for facilitating the forfaiting transaction and charges a service fee for this purpose. Also, the RBI requires the fee levied by the forfaiter to be transferred to the overseas buyer. Put differently, the exporter must finalise the export contract in a manner, which ensures that the amount received in foreign exchange by the exporter after payment of the forfaiter's fee is equivalent to the price which he would obtain if goods were sold on cash payment terms.

From the exporter's standpoint the key advantages of forfaiting are as follows:

- It provides finance up to 100 percent of the export value as compared to 80-85 percent financing available from conventional export credit schemes.
- It obviates the need for export credit insurance.
- It provides fixed rate finance. The exporter is protected from the interest and exchange rate risks arising from deferred export credit.
- It relieves the exporter of credit administration and collection problems
- It does not impact the exporter's borrowing limits from banks. Thus forfaiting serves as an additional source of finance.

Insuring Exports

The Export Credit Guarantee Corporation (ECGC, hereafter), a Government of India undertaking, provides insurance to Indian exporters of goods and services, against the risk of non-payment for exports. Under the ECGC credit insurance policy, the exporter is assured that ECGC will pay if the overseas buyer fails to pay for the goods and services exported. ECGC, bearing the main brunt or risk, pays the exporter 90 percent of his loss on account of commercial and political risks subject to certain terms and conditions.

Under the Comprehensive Risks Policy, popularly referred to as the standard policy of ECGC, the exporter is covered for both political and commercial risks. The exporter may, however, insure himself against political risks alone, if he so desires. Insurance cover is provided from the date of shipment. Where goods are manufactured in accordance with buyer's specifications and which cannot be easily sold to others, insurance cover may be provided from the date of contract. In addition to the standard policy, ECGC offers a variety of other policies and schemes.

18.7 DOCUMENTS IN INTERNATIONAL TRADE

In comparison with domestic trade, international trade presents special problems: (i) Sellers in international trade are not able to assess the creditworthiness of their buyers as reliably and thoroughly as sellers in domestic trade. (ii) Transportation of goods is slower and less certain, and communication less efficient and more time-consuming. (iii) Legal settlement processes are complicated, tardy, and expensive. In order to cope with these problems, international trade relies considerably on three major documents/instruments: trade draft, bill of lading, and letter of credit.

Trade Draft

The international trade draft, also referred to as bill of exchange, is a written order by the exporter (the drawer) asking the importer (the drawee) to pay a specified amount of money at a certain time. The draft may be a sight draft (which is payable on presentation) or a time draft (which is payable a certain number of days after presentation)

The important features of the draft are: (i) It is an unconditional written order signed by the drawer. (ii) It specifies the exact amount of money to be paid and the time when it is payable. Once the drawee (or his banker) accepts the draft, he acknowledges his obligation. The draft then becomes a trade acceptance. If it is accepted by the banker, it becomes a banker's acceptance. In this case, the bank assumes responsibility for payment. Banker's acceptances generally are marketable.

Bill of Lading

A bill of lading is a document of shipping employed when the exporter transports goods to the importer. It serves several functions: (i) It is a document of title to goods. (ii) It is a receipt given by the transporter to the owner mentioning the receipt of specified goods. (iii) It is a contract that binds the transporter to deliver the goods to a specified party at a certain destination.

The bill of lading is released to the importer only when the payment is made (when the bill of lading is accompanied by a sight draft), or when the obligation is acknowledged (when the bill of lading is accompanied by a time draft).

Letter of Credit

A letter of credit is issued by a bank on behalf of the importer. As per this document, the bank agrees to honour the draft drawn on the importer provided certain conditions are satisfied. Through the letter of credit arrangement, the credit of the importer is substituted with the credit of bank. Hence, it virtually eliminates the risk of the exporter when he sells to an unknown importer in a foreign country. This arrangement is further reinforced if the letter of credit is confirmed by a bank in the exporter's country.

18.8 FOREIGN EXCHANGE EXPOSURE

With the advent of floating exchange rates in 1973, fluctuations in exchange rates have created foreign exposure. Firms which have cross-border transactions (such as exports, imports, foreign investment, foreign borrowings and lendings) have a direct exposure, and firms which have no cross-border transactions are likely to have indirect exposure as their customers, suppliers, and competitors may be exposed.

Foreign exchange exposure can be classified into three broad categories:

- Transaction exposure
- Translation exposure
- Operating exposure

Of these, the first and the third together are sometimes called "cash flow exposures" while the second is referred to as "accounting exposure" or "balance sheet exposure". The reasons for this will become clear below.

Transaction Exposure

Transaction exposure stems from transactions that give rise to known contractually determined future foreign-currency denominated cash inflows or outflows. Cross-border trade, borrowings and lendings in foreign currencies, and the local purchases and sales of foreign subsidiaries are examples of such transactions. If exchange rates change between now and when these transactions settle, the value of the associated foreign currency cash flows changes, resulting in currency gains and losses. For example, if an Indian exporter has a receivable of $100,000 due three months hence and if in the meanwhile the dollar depreciates relative to the rupee, a cash loss occurs. Conversely, if the dollar appreciates relative to the rupee, a cash gain occurs. In the case of a payable, the outcome is of an opposite kind: a depreciation of the dollar relative to the rupee results in a gain, whereas an appreciation of the dollar relative to the rupee results in a loss.

In the books of accounts, the foreign currency amount is expressed in the reporting currency by applying the exchange rate prevailing on the transaction date. If an item is settled during the current account period, it is revalued at the rate prevailing on the settlement day. This may result in loss or gain.

At each balance sheet date, foreign currency monetary items are reported using the exchange rate on the balance sheet date, non-monetary items carried at historical cost are reported using the exchange rate on the transaction date, and non-monetary items carried at fair value are reported using the exchange rate that existed when the fair values were determined. Exchange differences arising from either settlement or restatement of monetary items on the balance sheet date should be recognised as income or expense in the period in which they arise.

When a forward exchange contract is entered into as a hedge, the premium or discount arising at the inception of the contract should be amortised as expense or income over the life of the contract.

Translation Exposure

Translation exposure, also called accounting exposure, stems from the need to convert the financial statements of foreign operations from foreign currencies to domestic currency for purposes of reporting and consolidation. If there is a change in exchange rate since the previous reporting period, the translation or restatement of foreign-currency denominated assets, liabilities, revenues, and expenses will result in foreign exchange gains or losses. Translation gains/losses do no involve cash flows as they are purely paper gains/losses, except when they have some tax implications.

Indian accounting standards require consolidation of the accounts of foreign subsidiaries or branches with those of the parent firm in india. The method used for translating foreign currency statements depends on the nature of relationship between the parent and the foreign operations. From this point of view, foreign operations are classified into two categories.

- *Integral Foreign Operations:* An integral operation carries out business as if it is an extension of the operations of the parent. For example, the foreign operation may just sell goods imported from the parent and remit the proceeds of the same to its parent.
- *Independent Foreign Operations:* An independent or non-integral foreign operation is run independently, as if it is a separate enterprise. It is also referred to as a foreign entity.

The financial statements of an integral foreign operation are translated using the rules that we discussed under transaction exposure.

The assets and liabilities, both monetary and non-monetary, of the non-integral foreign operation are translated at the rates prevailing on the balance sheet date. The profit and loss items of such operations are translated at the exchange rates prevailing on the date of the transactions. All the resulting exchange differences are accumulated in a foreign currency translation reserve which is reflected under Reserves and Surplus.

The Income Tax Act requires that foreign currency liabilities are "marked to market" at the exchange rate prevailing on the date of casting the balance sheet. If the foreign currency liability increases (decreases) on account of such revaluation, the value of the fixed asset which is financed by the foreign currency borrowing is correspondingly increased (decreased). Depreciation is admissible on such revalued assets.

Operating Exposure

Operating exposure, like transaction exposure, involves an actual or potential gain or loss. While the latter is specific to a transaction, the former, much broader in nature, relates to an entire investment. The essence of operating exposure is that exchange rate changes significantly alter the costs of a firm's inputs and the prices of its outputs and thereby influence its competitive position substantially. Two examples may be given to explain this concept.

- Volkswagen had a highly successful export market for its 'Beetle' model in the U.S. before 1970. With the breakdown of the Bretton Woods system of fixed exchange rates, the Deutschemark appreciated significantly against the dollar. Since Volkswagen's expenses were mainly in Deutschemark and its revenues in dollars, it raised the dollar price of the cars in the U.S. However, in a highly price-sensitive U.S. market, such an action caused a sharp decrease in sales volume—from 600,000 vehicles in 1968 to 200,000 in 1976. (Incidentally, Volkswagen's 1973 losses were the highest, as of that year, suffered by any company anywhere in the world.)
- In the wake of the East Asian crisis in 1997, currencies of several East Asian countries fell sharply. This made exports from these countries very competitive in advanced markets. As a consequence, gems and jewellery exports from India suffered competitive disadvantage vis-à-vis their rivals from South East Asia.

18.9 MANAGEMENT OF FOREIGN EXCHANGE EXPOSURE

Management of Transaction Exposure

Transaction exposure arises on account of imports, exports, and foreign currency borrowings. To cope with such exposure, inter alia, firms commonly use forward market contracts and financial swaps (interest rate swaps and currency swaps).

Forward Market Contracts In a forward market hedge, a net liability (asset) position is covered by an asset (liability) in the forward market. To illustrate the mechanism of the forward market hedge, consider the case of an Indian firm, which has a liability of $100,000 payable in 60 days to an American supplier on account of credit purchases. The firm may employ the following steps to cover its liability position:

Step 1 Enter into a forward contract to purchase $100,000 in 60 days from a foreign exchange dealer. The 60-day forward contract rate is, say, ₹66.90 per dollar.

Step 2 On the sixtieth day pay the dealer ₹6,690,000 ($100,000 × ₹66.90), collect $100,000, and pay the same to the American supplier.

By using such a mechanism, the Indian firm can eliminate the exchange risk in dollars because of its asset position in the forward dollars. To cover a net asset position in the foreign currency, a reverse process has to be followed. To illustrate this process, consider an Indian firm which is expecting a payment of $100,000 due in 60 days, on account of a credit sale, from an American customer. The firm can take the following steps to cover its asset position.

Step 1 Enter into a forward contract with a foreign exchange dealer to sell $100,000 in 60 days. The 60 day forward rate is, say, ₹66.85.

Step 2 On the sixtieth day collect $100,000 from the American customer, deliver the same to the dealer, and collect ₹6,685,000.

The forward market hedge is a relatively simple and convenient arrangement. It merely involves getting a forward quotation from a foreign exchange dealer and advising him to do the needful. Of course, the dealer will charge a commission for performing the transaction.

Financial Swaps A financial swap basically involves an exchange of one set of financial flows for another. Widely used internationally, financial swaps have in recent years attracted the attention of firms in India. The two most important financial swaps are the interest rate swap and the currency swap.

An **interest rate swap** is a transaction involving an exchange of one stream of interest obligations for another. Typically, it results in an exchange of fixed rate interest payments for floating rate interest payments. Occasionally, it involves an exchange of one stream of floating rate interest payments for another.

The principal features of an interest rate swap are:

- It effectively translates a floating rate borrowing into a fixed rate borrowing and vice versa. The net interest differential is paid or received, as the case may be, as and when due.
- There is no exchange of principal repayment obligations.
- It is structured as a separate contract, distinct from the underlying loan agreement.
- It is applicable to new as well as existing borrowings.
- It is treated as an off-the-balance sheet transaction.

In a **currency swap**, both the principal and interest in one currency are swapped for principal and interest in another currency. On maturity, the principal amounts are swapped back. Thus, a currency swap involves: (a) an exchange of principal amounts today, (b) an exchange of interest payments during the period of the loans, and (c) a re-exchange of principal amounts at the time of maturity.

Some Suggestions While managing its foreign exchange exposure, a firm must bear in mind the following guidelines:

- *Be Selective* Foreign exchange risk is like a double-edged sword– while it can entail losses, it can also produce gains. Hence it may not be necessary or desirable to eliminate all foreign exchange rate risk. Further, even when the exchange rate risk is sought to be eliminated, the cost of doing so must be borne in mind. On balance, it appears that while it may be desirable to eliminate a portion of the exchange rate risk, it may not be worthwhile to eliminate the whole of it. Put differently, the firm must be selective.
- *Seek More than One Quotation* Exchange rates tend to differ across banks depending on their currency positions and other factors. Hence, a firm must seek quotations from at least two banks before concluding a deal with any one of them. (Note that banks generally quote indicative rates in the morning and firm rates only at the time of business.)
- *Choose a Proper Mix of Currencies and Interest Rates* For a foreign currency loan, the currency mix as well as the interest rate mix are important. In general, it is advisable to go for a mix of currencies rather than a single currency. Companies which had exposure only to the U.S. dollar in the early 1980s and to the Japanese yen in the late 1980s suffered grievously. It seems to make sense for an Indian firm to structure its foreign currency liability in such a way that about one half of it is in the U.S. dollar and the rest in other currencies.

  In addition to choosing the currency mix, the borrower has to decide about the interest rate mix (the mix between fixed and floating interest rates). Interest rate forecasting, in general, is an uncertain and unreliable exercise, particularly over a period of 5 to 7 years. So, it is desirable to spread risk by choosing a mix of fixed and floating interest rate. Thanks to the possibilities of financial swaps, the borrower can choose the desired liability structure, in terms of currencies as well as interest rates.
- *Establish Rapport with the Banker* The treasurer of a firm may not be able to manage its foreign exchange risks efficiently without the help of the corporate dealer in his bank, who has a good understanding of the firm's foreign exchange risk exposure. So, it is essential for the firm's treasurer to establish a good rapport with the corporate dealer in the bank and to disclose to him the positions he wants to cover on a continuing basis. Without such rapport and confidence, the firm may not benefit from the expertise, resources, and facilities of the bank.

- *Act Swiftly* Given the volatility of the foreign exchange market, prompt action is required. So, the corporate treasurer must be expeditious in his decision making. Further, to facilitate swift action, he may give standing instructions to the corporate dealer in his bank for covering certain exposures or meeting certain contingencies.

Management of Operating Exposure

Transaction exposure is short-term in nature and well-identified. Operating exposure, on the other hand, is long-term in nature and can scarcely be identified with precision. So, the instruments of financial hedging (forwards, swaps, and so on) which are helpful in hedging short-term, well-identified transaction exposure are not of much help in hedging operating exposure.

Managing operating exposure calls for designing the firm's marketing, production, and financing strategy to protect the firm's earning power in the wake of exchange rate fluctuations. The important levers for managing operating exposure are briefly described below.

Product Strategy A firm may introduce new products and expand its product line after its home currency depreciates. Conversely, after its home currency appreciates, a firm may re-orient its product line so that it caters to market segments which are more quality-conscious and less price-sensitive.

Pricing Strategy When faced with currency volatility, should a firm emphasise market share or profit margin? Economies of scale and price elasticity of demand are the key factors that drive the pricing strategy. If significant economies of scale exist or price elasticity of demand is high, it makes sense to hold prices down, expand demand, and lower unit cost of production. If economies of scale are insignificant or if price elasticity of demand is low, it may be profitable to charge higher prices.

Plant Location A firm may locate its production to countries whose currencies have depreciated in real terms to lessen the adverse impact of exchange rate variation.

Sourcing A firm may source its inputs in countries where it sells its products to achieve a better match between currency footprints of revenues and costs. Multinational giants such as Toyota, Honda, GM, and IBM manage their operating exposure through a better matching of currency footprints.

Product Cycle In a world of volatile exchange rates, a firm can get a competitive edge by reducing the time it takes to bring new products to market. A shorter product cycle compresses the adjustment period following a significant exchange rate change.

Liability Structure Suppose an Indian firm derives a good portion of its revenues from exports to the U.S. It would do well to hold a portion of its liabilities denominated in the U.S. dollar. This way it can achieve a certain match between its earnings and debt servicing burden.

SUMMARY

- Multiple currencies, euromarkets, differential taxation, and barriers to financial flows are the distinguishing features of international finance. Of these, the multiple currency factor, and the attendant issue of exchange rates, has received considerable attention in recent years.
- An exchange rate represents the relationship between two currencies. Presently, the system of direct quotes is used in India in which the exchange rates are quoted as number of rupees per unit (or per 100 units in some cases) of foreign currency.
- In the foreign exchange market a spot rate refers to the rate applicable to transactions in which settlement (i.e. delivery) is two business days after the date of transaction.
- Forward transaction is also possible in which the rate is fixed today but the settlement is at some specified date in the future. Such rates are called forward rates.
- Forward rates will in general be different from spot rates. With the direct system of quotations, the foreign currency is said to be at forward premium (discount) when the forward rate is greater than (smaller than) the spot rate.
- The foreign exchange market is the largest financial market in the world. It is primarily an over-the-counter market.
- The major sources available to an Indian firm for raising foreign currency finance are: foreign currency term loans from financial institutions, export credit schemes, external commercial borrowings, euroissues, and foreign domestic issues.
- Financial institutions provide foreign currency term loans for certain purposes. The periodical liability for interest and principal remains in the currency/currencies of the loan/s and is translated into rupees at the prevailing rate of exchange.

- Export credit agencies have been established by the governments of major industrialised countries. Two kinds of export credit are provided: buyer's credit and supplier's credit.
- Subject to certain terms and conditions, the Government of India permits Indian firms to resort to external commercial borrowing.
- Many Indian companies are raising funds by way of Euroissues and foreign domestic issues. The two principal mechanisms used by Indian companies are the Depository Receipts mechanism and Euroconvertible Issues. The former represents indirect equity investment while the latter is debt with an option to convert it into equity.
- Commercial banks and EXIM Bank provide export finance and Export Credit Guarantee Corporation provides insurance to exports.
- In comparison with domestic trade, international trade, presents special problems. In order to cope with these problems, international trade relies considerably on three major documents/instruments: trade draft, bill of lading, and letter of credit.
- There are three broad types of foreign exchange exposure: transaction exposure, translation exposure, and economic exposure.
- Transaction exposure arises when a company has a payable or receivable denominated in a foreign currency and a change in the exchange rate can alter the amount of local currency received or paid. Forward market hedge and financial swaps are the tools commonly employed to manage transaction exposure.
- The two most commonly used devices for managing foreign exchange exposure in India are forward market contracts and financial swaps (interest rate swaps and currency swaps).
- The essence of operating exposure is that exchange rate changes significantly alter the costs of a firms' inputs and the prices of its output and thereby influence its competitive position substantially. Managing operating exposure calls for designing the firm's marketing, production, and financing strategy to protect the firm's earning power in the wake of exchange rate fluctuations.

Value-based Management 19

The idea that the primary responsibility of corporate management is to increase shareholder value has gained widespread acceptance in the United States in the past three decades or so. With the globalisation of capital markets, intensification of competition, and massive privatisation initiatives, shareholder value creation is gaining the attention of executives all over the world, including India. The interest in value creation has been stimulated by several developments:

- Institutional investors, who traditionally were passive investors, have begun exerting influence on corporate managements to create value for shareholders.
- Many leading companies, which have accorded value creation a central place in their corporate planning, serve as role model for others.
- The market for corporate control has made value destroyers more vulnerable to raiders.
- Business press is emphasising shareholder value creation in performance rating exercises.
- Greater attention is being paid to link top management compensation to shareholder returns.

To help firms create value for shareholders, value based management (VBM) systems have been developed. VBM is a generic term for a set of tools helpful in managing a firm's operations for enhancing shareholder value. VBM is a relatively recent innovation in financial practice. Many regard it as one of the most important developments in corporate management. VBM represents a synthesis of various disciplines like finance, strategy, accounting, and organisational behaviour.

This chapter discusses various facets of VBM. It is organised into four sections as follows:

- Methods and key premises of VBM
- Measure of value creation : MVA
- Drivers of value creation
- Economic value added

19.1 METHODS AND KEY PREMISES OF VBM

Several methods have been used in VBM. The three principal methods of VBM are:

- The free cash flow method proposed by Mckinsey and LEK/Alcar group.
- The economic value added / market value added (EVA/MVA) method pioneered by Stern Stewart and Company.
- The cash flow return on investment/cash value added (CFROI/CVA) method developed by BCG and Holt Value Associates.

Common Premises

Though these methods look outwardly different, the basic premises underlying them are the same. They are as follows:

- The value of any company (or its individual strategies and investments) is equal to the present value of the future cash flows the company is expected to produce.
- Conventional accounting earnings are not a sufficient indicator of value creation because they are not the same as cash flow, they do not reflect risk, they do not include an opportunity cost of capital, they do not consider time value of money, and they are not calculated the same way by all firms because of variations in accounting policy.
- For managing shareholder value, firms should use metrics that are linked to value creation and employ them consistently in all facets of financial management.
- A well designed performance measurement and incentive compensation system is essential to motivate employees to focus their attention on creating shareholder value.

Key Difference

The key difference between these methods relates to VBM metrics. For example, the LEK/Alcar method uses shareholder value added, the Stern

Stewart method emphasises EVA and MVA, and the BCG method focuses on CFROI and CVA.

Each camp argues that its measures are the best and cites supporting evidence for the same. It is difficult to objectively assess the validity of these claims.

While the different methods to VBM have their own fan clubs, the EVA/MVA method seems to have received more attention and gained more popularity. Our discussion of VBM in this chapter will also be in terms of EVA and MVA.

19.2 MEASURE OF VALUE CREATION: MVA

To determine whether management has created or destroyed value, the market value of the firm's capital (both equity and debt capital) may be compared to the capital invested by shareholders and lenders (the capital employed in the firm). The difference between the market value of capital and capital employed is called the *market value added* or, simply, MVA.

$$\text{Market value added (MVA)} = \text{Market value of capital} - \text{Capital employed}$$

A positive MVA implies that value has been created; a negative MVA means that value has been destroyed.

MVA measures creation or destruction of value at a given point in time. If you want to measure the value created or destroyed during a period of time, look at the change in MVA during that period.

Computing MVA

To compute the MVA, you should know the market value of the firm's equity and debt capital as well as the amount of capital invested by shareholders and debtholders. Let us look at how these are estimated.

Market Value of Capital For a firm whose equity and debt securities are publicly traded, the market value of capital can be obtained from the financial market. If a firm's securities are not publicly traded, financial market information is not available for estimating MVA. In such a case, the MVA can be estimated if someone makes an offer to buy the firm.

Consider Metachem Limited, a pharmaceutical company set up in 20X0. As on March 31, 20X5, Metachem had debt with a market value of ₹200 million. The firm had 20 million shares outstanding that were trading at ₹35 a share. The market value of its equity (its market capitalisation) was ₹700 million. The market value of capital was ₹900 million (₹200 million of debt plus ₹700 million of equity).

Capital Employed The amount of capital employed by the firm can be derived from the balance sheet and the accompanying notes. Debt capital includes all forms of borrowings and other obligations like financial leases which are equivalent to debt obligations. Estimating the amount of equity capital is not so straight forward. To get a handle over the amount of equity capital employed in the firm, you have to add to the book value of equity reported in the balance sheet several items such as research and development expenses, amortisation of goodwill, deferred tax provision, and allowance for bad debt. These items, arbitrarily classified as expenses, lower reported profits and retained earnings. As a consequence, the equity account in the balance sheet is understated.

Exhibit 19.1 presents two versions of Metachem's balance sheets as on March 31, 20X4 and 20X5. The first balance sheet , the **unadjusted balance sheet**, reports sources of funds (or capital employed) and application of funds (or invested capital) according to standard accounting conventions. The second balance sheet, the **adjusted balance sheet**, adds to book value of shareholders' funds (equity) and application of funds (invested capital) a few items that accounting conventions exclude. Loan funds (debt capital) as on 31 March, 20X5 (₹200 million), however, are the same in both types of balance sheets.

Notice that two adjustments have been made to the book value of shareholders' funds (equity) to get the adjusted shareholders' funds. These relate to amortisation of goodwill and research and development expenses. According to standard accounting conventions, these items are arbitrarily regarded as expenses. Consequently, reported profits, retained earnings, and shareholders' funds (equity) are understated. Hence adjustments are needed.

Properties of MVA

The importance of MVA stems from the following properties.

MVA Increases When the Firm Undertakes Positive NPV projects Remember that the net present value (NPV) of a project is:

$$\text{NPV} = \underset{\text{from the project}}{\text{Present value of cash inflows}} - \underset{\text{in the project}}{\text{Capital employed}}$$

Now look at the definition of MVA:

MVA = Market value of capital – Capital employed

EXHIBIT 19.1 ***Metachem's Balance Sheets as on March 31, 20X4 and 20X5***

Unadjusted Balance Sheet		*March 31, 20X4*			*March 31, 20X5*
Sources of Funds					
1. Shareholders' funds			550			600
2. Loan funds			200			200
Total			750			800
Application of Funds						
1. Net fixed assets			475			510
Property, plant and machinery (net)		400			460	
Goodwill (net)		75			50	
Gross value	125			125		
Accumulated amortisation	(50)			(75)		
2. Net current assets			275			290
Total			750			800

Adjusted Balance Sheet	*March 31 20X4*		*March 31 20X5*	
Sources of Funds				
1. Adjusted shareholders' funds		640		725
Book value of shareholders' funds	550		600	
Accumulated goodwill amortisation	50		75	
Capitalised R&D	40		50	
2. Loan funds		200		200
Total		840		925
Application of Funds				
1. Net fixed assets		565		635
Property, plant, and equipment (net)	400		460	
Gross goodwill	125		125	
Capitalised R&D	40		50	
2. Net current assets		275		290
Total		840		925

In the MVA definition (a) the market value of capital is equal to the expected cash inflows from all the investment projects, past and present and (b) the capital employed is the capital employed in all the investment projects, past and present.

Thus, conceptually NPV and MVA are similar. The contribution of an investment project to a firm's MVA is equal to the NPV of that project.

Maximising MVA Is Consistent with Maximising Shareholder Value Shareholder value creation is represented by the difference between the market value of the firm's equity and the equity capital invested by shareholders. The former reflects the value imputed by the financial market on the equity of the firm and the latter reflects the actual amount of money contributed by equity shareholders by way of capital and retained earnings.

MVA, on the other hand, is the difference between the market value of total capital and the total capital employed. MVA can be expressed as follows:

$$\text{MVA} = \text{Equity MVA} + \text{Debt MVA}$$

Equity MVA is the difference between the market value of equity and the adjusted book value of equity and debt MVA is the difference between the market value of debt and the book value of debt.

Debt MVA may differ from zero mainly because of interest rate change or credit rating change. If interest rates decline after the firm has issued debt securities, the market value of debt exceeds the book value of debt and vice versa. If credit rating declines after the firm has issued debt, the market value of debt is less than the book value of debt and vice versa.

If debt MVA differs from zero only on account of a change in interest rates, then, for a given level of interest rates, maximising MVA is equivalent to maximising equity MVA.

19.3 DRIVERS OF VALUE CREATION

There are three key drivers of value creation:

- The profitability of the firm, measured by its after-tax return on invested capital (ROIC).
- The weighted average cost of capital (WACC) of the firm.
- The growth rate of the firm.

The after-tax ROIC (see Chapter 2) is defined as:

$$\text{ROIC} = \frac{\text{PBIT}(1 - \text{Tax rate})}{\text{Invested capital}} = \frac{\text{NOPAT}}{\text{Invested capital}}$$

where PBIT is profit before interest and tax, NOPAT is net operating profit after tax [it is equal to PBIT (1 – Tax rate)], and invested capital is the sum of net fixed assets and net current assets.

The weighted average cost of capital or WACC is:

$$\text{WACC} = \left(\begin{matrix}\text{Cost of} \\ \text{equity}\end{matrix} \times \begin{matrix}\text{Proportion of} \\ \text{equity capital}\end{matrix}\right)\left(\begin{matrix}\text{Post tax cost} \\ \text{of debt}\end{matrix} \times \begin{matrix}\text{Proportion of} \\ \text{debt capital}\end{matrix}\right)$$

To illustrate the calculation of ROIC and WACC, let us look at the adjusted balance sheet, given in Exhibit 19.1 and the adjusted profit and loss account, given in Exhibit 19.2.

Based on the figures in these exhibits, Metachem's post-tax return for 20X5 on invested capital is:

$$\text{ROIC} = \frac{200(1 - 0.30)}{925} = 15.1\%$$

EXHIBIT 19.2 ***Metachem's Profit and Loss Account for 20X5***

Figures in millions of rupees

Unadjusted		*Adjusted*	
Sales	990	Sales	990
Cost of goods sold	520	Cost of goods sold	520
Selling, general, and administration expenses	200	Selling, general and administration expenses	200
Depreciation expense	50	Depreciation expense	50
R&D expenses	30	Amortisation of R&D expense	20
Goodwill amortisation	25		
Profit before interest and tax	165	Profit before interest and tax	200
Interest expenses	25	Interest expense	25
Profit before tax	140	Profit before tax	175
Tax (30%)	42	Tax	42
Profit after tax	98	Profit after tax	133

Metachem's estimated cost of equity is 15 percent and its pre-tax cost of debt is 12.5 percent. The market value of its equity and debt are ₹700 million and ₹200 million respectively. Thus, Metachem's WACC is:

$$\text{WACC} = 15\% \times \frac{700}{900} + 12.5\% \,(1 - 0.30) \times \frac{200}{900}$$
$$= 11.67 + 1.94 = 13.61\%$$

How MVA is Related to the Basic Drivers

To understand how ROIC, WACC, and growth rate interact to create value, let us examine the case of a firm that is expected to grow at a constant annual rate forever.[1] In this case, the MVA is given by the following formula:

$$\text{MVA} = \frac{(\text{ROIC} - \text{WACC}) \times \text{Invested capital}}{\text{WACC} - \text{Constant growth rate}}$$

[1] For expositional convenience we have assumed a constant growth rate. Note that the conclusions drawn from the formula are valid in general.

In this formula, the constant growth rate must be less than the WACC. Two important conclusions may be drawn from the above formula.

1. Value is created when the expected return spread (ROIC – WACC) is positive; value is destroyed when the expected return spread (ROIC – WACC) is negative; value is neither created nor destroyed when the expected return spread (ROIC – WACC) is nil. Bear in mind that it is the entire future stream of expected return spreads, and not the historical return spread, that drives value creation.
2. Growth *per se* does not create value. Growth is value-creating only when the expected return spread is positive (ROIC > WACC); growth is value-destroying when the expected return spread is negative (ROIC < WACC); growth is value-neutral when the expected return spread is nil (ROIC = WACC).

Delving Deeper into the Drivers of Value Creation

To delve deeper into the drivers of value creation, you can decompose the firm's expected ROIC into its fundamental components as follows:

$$\text{ROIC} = \frac{\text{PBIT}}{\text{Sales}} \times \frac{\text{Sales}}{\text{Invested capital}} \times (1 - \text{Tax rate})$$

Thus, the ROIC of a firm can be increased through a combination of the following actions:

- The *operating profit margin* (PBIT/Sales) is improved.
- The *capital turnover* (Sales/Invested capital) is increased.
- The *effective tax rate* is reduced.

The drivers of value creation, viz., return on invested capital, weighted average cost of capital, invested capital and growth rate, are summarised in Exhibit 19.3.

19.4 ECONOMIC VALUE ADDED

Recall that for a firm that is expected to grow at a constant annual rate, MVA is equal to:

$$\frac{(\text{ROIC} - \text{WACC}) \times \text{Invested capital}}{\text{WACC} - \text{Growth rate}}$$

The numerator of this ratio is referred to as economic value added (EVA). EVA is essentially the surplus left after making an appropriate charge for the capital employed in the business. It may

EXHIBIT 19.3 ***The Drivers of Value Creation***

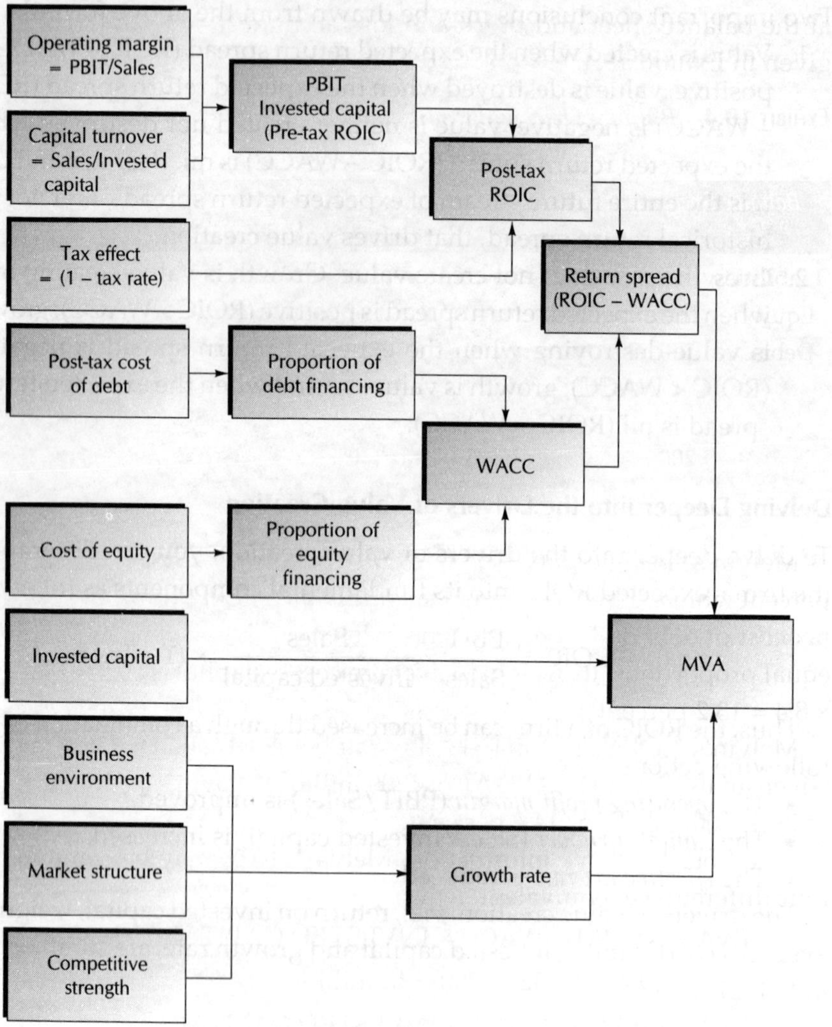

be calculated in any one the following, apparently different but essentially equivalent, ways:

$$\text{EVA} = \text{NOPAT} - \text{WACC} \times \text{INVESTED CAPITAL}$$

$$\text{EVA} = (\text{ROIC} - \text{WACC}) \times \text{INVESTED CAPITAL}$$

$$\text{EVA} = [\text{PAT} + \text{INT}\ (1 - \text{TAX RATE})] - \text{WACC} \times \text{INVESTED CAPITAL}$$

$$\text{EVA} = \text{PAT} - \text{COST OF EQUITY} \times \text{EQUITY}$$

To illustrate the calculation of EVA using the above formulae let us look at the balance sheet and profit and loss account of Melvin Corporation given in Exhibit 19.4.

EXHIBIT 19.4 ***Balance Sheet and Profit and Loss Account of Melvin Corporation***

₹ in million

Balance Sheet as on 31.-3-20X0				*Profit and Loss Statement for the Year Ending on 31.03.20X0*	
Liabilities		Assets		Net sales	300
Equity	100	Fixed assets	140	Cost of goods sold	258
Debt	100	Net current assets	60	PBIT	42
				Interest	12
				PBT	30
	200		200	Tax (30%)	9
				PAT	21

Melvin's cost of equity is 18 percent. The interest rate on its debt is 12 percent which, given a marginal tax rate of 30 percent, translates to a post tax cost of debt of 8.4 percent. Since Melvin employs debt and equity in equal proportions, its weighted average cost of capital is : $0.5 \times 18.0 + 0.5 \times 8.4 = 13.2$ percent.

Melvin's NOPAT is: PBIT (1 – Tax rate) = 42(1 – 0.3) = ₹29.4 million. Given an INVESTED CAPITAL of ₹200 million, Melvin's ROIC works out to 29.4/200 = 0.147 or 14.7 per cent.

Based on the above information, Melvin's EVA may be computed in four different, yet equivalent, ways:

$$\text{EVA} = \text{NOPAT} - \text{WACC} \times \text{INVESTED CAPITAL}$$
$$= 29.4 - (0.132) \times 200 = ₹3 \text{ million}$$

$$\text{EVA} = (\text{ROIC} - \text{WACC}) \times \text{INVESTED CAPITAL}$$
$$= (0.147 - 0.132) \times 200 = ₹3 \text{ million}$$

$$\text{EVA} = [\text{PAT} + \text{INT}(1 - 0.3)] - \text{WACC} \times \text{INVESTED CAPITAL}$$
$$= [21 + 12(1 - 0.3)] - 0.132 \times 200 = ₹3 \text{ million}$$

$$\text{EVA} = \text{PAT} - \text{COST OF EQUITY} \times \text{EQUITY}$$
$$= 21 - 0.18 \times 100 = ₹3 \text{ million}$$

While MVA is a stock measure, EVA is a flow measure. Hence EVA is eminently suitable as a periodic performance measure.

EVA as the Basis of an Integrated Financial Management System

The financial management system refers to financial measures, policies, methods, and procedures that guide the strategy and operations of a firm. It subsumes such things as setting financial goals, developing long-term strategic plans and short term profit plans, making capital investment and disinvestment decisions, measuring operating performance, determining incentive compensation, and communicating with investors. Companies often do not do these things in a unified, systematic, and cohesive manner. Corporate financial goals are defined in terms of earnings per share and return on net worth; individual lines of business are assessed in terms of return on assets; capital investment is analysed in terms of discounted cash flow; acquisitions are judged on the basis of contribution to earnings growth; departments are evaluated with reference to budgeted cost or profit figures; incentive compensation schemes are based on arbitrarily determined targets; and investor communication is primarily in terms of earnings per share and dividend policy.

It appears that a typical financial management system is hardly a system. As Al Ehrbar says : "Rather, it's a hodgepodge of rules, guidelines, and procedures that employs an array of frequently contradictory measures and objectives, that fosters confusion and conflict within an organization, that focuses on performance variables that bear little relation to the value of a business and often leads smart managers to do dumb things."[2] In many companies an obsolete financial management system confounds the search for value. These deficiencies call for an entirely different approach to financial management and the EVA financial management system seems to be an answer.

The EVA financial management system is based on the premise that EVA provides a single, unified, and accurate measure of performance. It links well forward looking valuation and capital budgeting analysis with actual performance measurement. For these reasons and more, EVA may be used for goal setting and business planning, performance evaluation, bonus determination, investor communication, capital budgeting, and valuation.

EVA is an excellent bedrock on which an integrated financial management system can be constructed, as it has the following features or characteristics.

---

[2] Al Ehrbar, *EVA: The Real Key to Creating Wealth*, New York: John Wiley & Sons, 1998.

- It is a performance measure that ties directly, theoretically as well as empirically, to shareholder wealth creation.
- It converts accounting information into economic reality that is readily grasped by non-financial managers. It is a simple yet effective way of teaching business literacy to everyone.
- It serves as a guide to every decision from strategic planning to capital budgeting to acquisitions to operating decisions.
- As the basis for incentive compensation, it truly aligns the interest of managers with that of shareholders and makes managers think and act like owners.
- It is an effective tool for investor communication.
- It serves as an anchor for an internal system of corporate governance that motivates everyone to work co-operatively and enthusiastically to achieve the best attainable performance.

SUMMARY

- With the globalisation of capital markets, intensification of competition, and massive privatisation initiatives, shareholder value creation is gaining the attention of executives all over the world, including India.
- To help firms create value for shareholders, value based management (VBM) systems have been developed. VBM is a generic term for a set of tools helpful in managing a firm's operation for enhancing shareholder value.
- Market value added (MVA), which represents the difference between market value of capital and capital employed, is a widely used measure of value creation.
- MVA depends on return on invested capital (ROIC), weighted average cost of capital (WACC), growth rate, and invested capital. The relationship between these factors and MVA is:

$$\text{MVA} = \frac{(\text{ROIC} - \text{WACC}) \times \text{Invested capital}}{\text{WACC} - \text{Constant growth rate}}$$

- Economic value added (EVA) is essentially the surplus left after making an appropriate charge for the capital employed in the business. It may be defined as follows:

$$\text{EVA} = (\text{ROIC} - \text{WACC}) \times \text{INVESTED CAPITAL}$$

- While MVA is a stock measure, EVA is a flow measure. Hence EVA is eminently suitable as a periodic performance measure.
- The EVA financial management system is based on the premise that EVA provides a single, unified, and accurate measure of performance.

Business Performance Measurement

20

The performance measurement system of a firm has a strong influence on the behaviour of its people. As Robert W Hall says: "Performance measurement is the basis of every system in a company: cost systems, planning systems, capital budgeting systems, personnel assignments, promotions, reorganizations, budget allocations – the mechanisms, built up over years, by which everything runs." In a similar vein, Robert Kaplan and David Norton argue: "An organisation's measurement system strongly affects the behaviour of people both inside and outside the organisation. If companies are to survive and prosper in information age competition, they must use measurement and management systems derived from their strategies and capabilities."

In an interesting 1991 HBR paper titled "The Performance Measurement Manifesto", R.G. Eccles argued that" within the next five years, every company will have to redesign how it measures its business performance". The heightened interest in business performance measurement since the early 1990s suggests that he was substantially right.

This chapter discusses various aspects of performance measurement. It is organised into five sections as follows:

- Performance measures
- Balanced scorecard
- Divisional performance measurement
- Designing an effective performance measurement system
- Performance measurement: some examples

20.1 PERFORMANCE MEASURES

Companies use a wide range of performance measures, some financial, some non-financial:

Financial Measures

The commonly employed measures of financial performance are:

- Return on capital employed
- Return on investment
- Return on equity
- Return on sales
- Profit before depreciation interest and tax
- Profit before interest and tax
- Profit after tax
- Net operating profit after tax
- Cash flow
- Free cash flow
- Economic value added
- Earnings per share
- Dividend yield
- Total shareholder return

Non-Financial Measures

Performance measurement sometimes relies heavily on financial measures. An excessive emphasis on financial measures in a business is like an obsession with the score card while playing cricket (or any other game). The score in a game, like the financial results in a business, reflects the outcome of past performance. While it is important to know the score it must be recognised that the success in a game or business calls for paying considerable attention to the steps required for competing effectively in the game or the marketplace. Just as a cricket player must focus on batting, bowling, and fielding, a company must concentrate on activities like product development, manufacturing, marketing, and customer service. Well-conceived performance measures in these areas are essential for monitoring improvements required for maintaining competitive edge.

Recognising the importance of non-financial measures, firms use a variety of such measures. A representative list is given below:

- Customer satisfaction index
- Customer returns
- Market share
- New product introduction
- On-time delivery

- Manufacturing cycle time
- Defects percentage
- Throughput
- Employee productivity index
- Patents obtained

20.2 BALANCED SCORECARD

Most companies have a performance measurement system that includes financial measures as well as non-financial measures. Financial measures are used primarily by senior managers to monitor the performance of the firm as a whole and its business units or divisions; non-financial measures are employed mainly by operating managers to control short-term operations. Till recently, not much effort was made to combine financial and non-financial measures in an integrated measurement framework. The balanced scorecard approach pioneered by Robert Kaplan, David Norton and others seeks to develop an integrated performance measurement system.

Distinctive Features

The proponents of the balanced scorecard approach claim that it has the following distinctive features:

1. The balanced scorecard is strategy driven. It is a mechanism for implementing the strategy of a business unit into a comprehensive system of performance measurement and management. As Robert Kaplan and David Norton say: "The balanced scorecard is more than a tactical or an operational measurement system. Innovative companies are using the score-card as a strategic management system to manage their strategy over the long run. They are using the measurement focus of the scorecard to accomplish critical management processes."
2. The balanced scorecard covers four important perspectives in a business viz., financial, customer, internal business, and learning and growth. The key issues relating to these perspectives are as follows:

Perspective	**Key Issue**
Financial	Is the company attractive to share holders?
Customer	Does the company provide value to its customers?

Internal business	What must the company excel at?
Innovation and learning	Is the company improving and innovating continually?

Robert Kaplan and David Norton believe that these four perspectives are fairly robust for a wide range of businesses. An illustrative balanced scorecard, provided by Kaplan and Norton for a company they refer to as Electronic Circuits Inc (ECI), is shown in Exhibit 20.1.

3. The balanced scorecard represents a linked series of objectives and measures. The linkages capture cause effect relationships obtaining in a business. As Robert Kaplan and David Norton say: "The multiple measures on a properly constructed balanced scorecard should consist of a series of objectives and measures that are both consistent and mutually reinforcing. The linkages should incorporate both cause and effect relationships and mixtures of outcome measures and performance drivers." Exhibit 20.2 shows how the important measures under the four perspectives are linked in a cause—effect relationship.

EXHIBIT 20.1 ***An Illustrative Balanced Scorecard***

Financial Perspective		**Customer Perspective**	
Goals	*Measures*	*Goals*	*Measures*
Survive	Cash flow	New products	Per cent of sales from new products
Succeed	Quarterly sales growth and operating income by division		Per cent of sales from proprietary products
Prosper	Increased market share and ROE	Responsive supply	On time delivery (defined by customer)
		Preferred supplier	Share of key accounts purchases
			Ranking by key accounts
		Customer partnership	Number of cooperative engineering efforts

(Contd.)

EXHIBIT 20.1 ***(Contd.)***

Internal Business Perspective		**Innovation and Learning Perspective**	
Goals	*Measures*	*Goals*	*Measures*
Technology capability	Manufacturing geometry vs. competition	Technology leadership	Time to develop next generation
Manufacturing excellence	Cycle time/unit cost yield	Manufacturing learning	Process time to maturity
		Product focus	Percentage of products that equals 80% sales
Design productivity	Silicon efficiency Engineering efficiency	Time to market	New product introduction
New product introduction	Actual introduction schedule vs. plan		

EXHIBIT 20.2 ***Key Measures and Cause Effect Relationship***

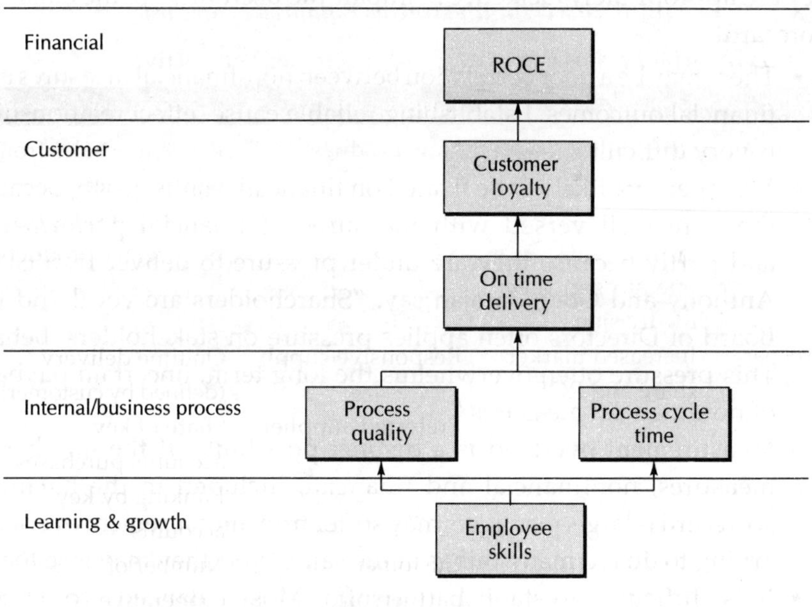

Pros and Cons

The proponents of balanced scorecard believe that it is a very useful tool for the following reasons:

- It focuses managerial attention on a handful of measures that are critical to a company's substantial success.
- It pulls together in a relatively simple management report the key elements of the competitive agenda of a company.
- It guards a company against sub-optimisation, as the managers are forced to look at all the measures together.

The balanced scorecard seems to have caught the fancy of the business and consulting world. Why? The reasons appear to be:

- It is an idea whose time has arrived. Dissatisfaction with traditional measurement systems combined with the need to cope with an increasingly complex world has created a great market opportunity.
- It has been well packaged and astutely marketed.
- It is simple in appearance but has potential depth. Managers can immediately understand it and can explore the concept in greater detail.

The balanced scorecard approach appears to be a definite improvement in performance measurement. However, the following problems, unless they are appropriately tackled, can impair the usefulness of the balanced scorecard.

- There may be a poor correlation between non-financial measures and financial outcomes. Establishing reliable cause- effect relationships is very difficult.
- Managers are likely to be fixated on financial results, partly because they are well versed with measures of financial performance and partly because they are under pressure to deliver results. As Anthony and Govindarajan say: "Shareholders are vocal and the Board of Directors often applies pressure on stakeholders' behalf. This pressure often overwhelms the long term, uncertain payback of nonfinancial measures."
- Measurement overload is a distinct possibility. If the number of measures, nonfinancial and financial, included in the balanced scorecard is large, managers may suffer from measurement overload. Trying to do too many things at the same time, they may lose focus.
- It is difficult to establish tradeoffs. Most balanced scorecards, for understandable reasons, do not assign weights to different measures. This leads to difficulty in specifying trade–offs between financial and non financial measures.

- The supplier perspective has been ignored. In these days of outsourcing and growing business interdependencies, specially in manufacturing, the supplier perspective is important. Indeed many organisations have modified the balanced scorecard to include supplier perspective.

20.3 DIVISIONAL PERFORMANCE MEASUREMENT

Most multi-business and multi-location firms are organised into divisions. A division has been defined as "a company unit headed by a person fully responsible for the profitability of its operations, including planning, production, financial and accounting activities, and who usually, although not always, has his own sales force"[1]. In a divisionalised business, the divisional head enjoys the authority to determine how the operations under his control are to be carried out. More important, he determines to a great extent what operations are to be carried out. The essence of divisionalisation is delegated profit responsibility.

Functional Organisation vs. Divisional Organisation

To compare divisional organisation with functional organisation, let us look at an organisation chart for a representative of each type. Exhibit 20.3 shows the organisation chart, in a somewhat abbreviated form, of a functionally organised firm. The company manufactures two broad types of products, consumer products and industrial products, in three different locations. These products are marketed all over the country in several different markets. No department has the exclusive responsibility for any product or for any market.

Turn now to Exhibit 20.4 which shows, in a summary form, the organisation chart of a divisionally organised firm. The company is organised into four divisions, which are fairly autonomous. Each divisional vice-president has freedom over the production and marketing operations of his division and is accountable to the top management for the profitability of his division.

---

[1] Divisional Financial Executives, *Studies in Business Policy*. No.10, New York: National Industrial Conference Board, 1961

EXHIBIT 20.3 ***Functional Organisation***

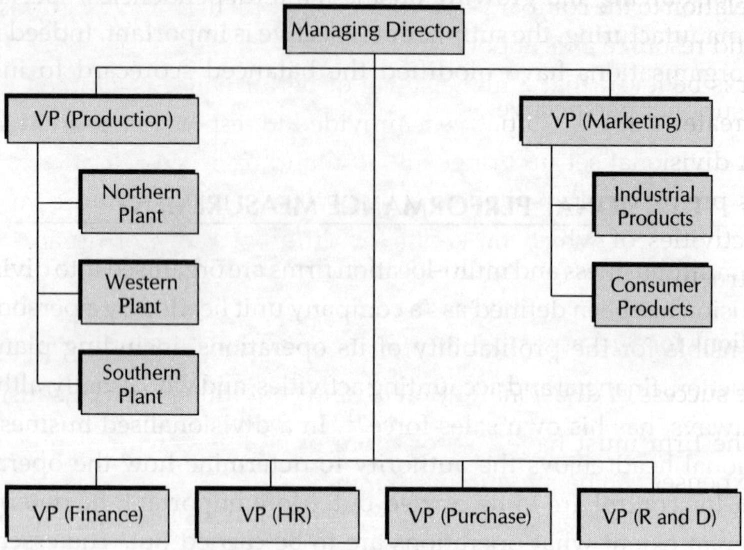

EXHIBIT 20.4 ***Divisional Organisation***

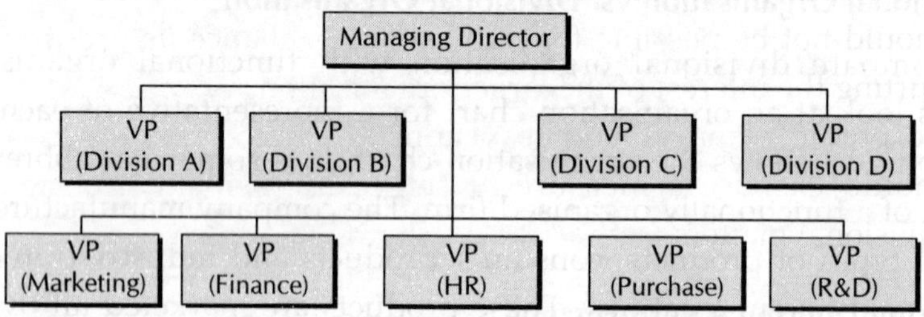

Reasons for Divisionalisation

Many large, diversified organisations tend to resort to divisionalisation. Why? The reasons seem to be:

- Entrusted with profit responsibility a manager makes rational trade-offs between revenues and costs. Without decentralised profit responsibilities, it becomes necessary to exercise control over his day to day decisions. Divisional operations provide an excellent training ground for grooming top management personnel.
- When a manager is given operational autonomy his performance can be measured more accurately.

- Information about the profit performance of various divisions in relation to the company as a whole is helpful in strategy formulation and resource allocation.
- It is believed that a higher level of performance is attained when greater scope for initiative is provided to responsible individuals.
- A divisional set up brings about a kind of decentralisation which is pre-eminently suited to a highly diversified firm, the various activities of which may call for different types of organisation structures.

Conditions for Success

For the success of divisionalisation certain conditions must be satisfied.

- The firm must have two or more units for which revenues and expenses can be measured separately.
- Each division should be sufficiently independent of other divisions with respect to production and marketing activities in order to make its separate profit responsibility meaningful.
- The relations between the divisions should be so regulated that it should not be possible for a division to enhance its profits while hurting the interest of the larger organisation.
- Corporate management, respecting the autonomy of divisions, should exercise a measure of self-restraint in interfering with divisional matters.

Measuring Divisional Performance

The measures that are commonly employed to judge the financial performance of an organisation or a sub- unit thereof are: return on investment, residual income, and return on sales.

To illustrate these measures, let us look at an example. Bharat Cola Corporation owns and operates aerated drinks bottling plants in Mumbai, New Delhi, and Bangalore. Exhibit 20.5 summarises the data for each of the three units for the year 20X0. Presently, Bharat Cola Corporation does not allocate loan funds to the three units.

EXHIBIT 20.5 ***Financial Data for Bharat Cola Corporation for 20X0***

(₹ in million)

	Mumbai (1)	*New Delhi (2)*	*Bangalore (3)*	*Total (4) = 1 + 2 + 3*
Revenues	300	250	150	700
Variable costs	70	60	30	160
Fixed costs	150	130	80	360
Operating profit	80	60	40	180
Interest				60
Profit before tax				120
Tax				40
Profit after tax				80
Current assets	200	100	80	380
Fixed assets	300	200	120	620
Total assets	500	300	200	1000
Current liabilities	40	30	30	100
Loan funds				400
Shareholders' funds				500

Given the data for Bharat Cola Corporation, let us look at the measures employed to judge financial performance.

Return on Investment Return on investment (ROI) is the ratio of income to investment. It is popularly measured as:

$$\text{Return on investment} = \frac{\text{Operating profit}}{\text{Total assets}}$$

The ROI for the three units of Bharat Cola Corporation is calculated below:

Unit	*Operating Profit*	/	*Total Assets*	=	*ROI*
Mumbai	80	/	500	=	16%
New Delhi	60	/	300	=	20%
Bangalore	40	/	200	=	20%

Residual Income Residual income is the income left after providing a capital charge on the investment made. Operationally, it may be measured as:

Residual income = Operating profit – (Required rate of return) (Total assets)

Assuming a required rate of return of 18 per cent, the residual income for the three units of Bharat Cola Corporation is calculated as follows:

Unit	*Operating Profit* –	*Required Rate of Return*	×	*Investment*	=	*Residual Income*
Mumbai	80	– 0.18	x	500	=	–10
New Delhi	60	– 0.18	x	300	=	6
Bangalore	40	– 0.18	x	200	=	4

Return on Sales A commonly used financial measure, the return on sales (ROS) reflects the relationship between income and sales. Operationally, it is defined as:

$$\text{Return on sales} = \frac{\text{Oprating profit}}{\text{Revenues (Sales)}}$$

The ROS for the three units of Bharat Cola Corporation is calculated as follows:

Unit	*Operating Profit*	/	*Revenues (Sales)*	=	*Return on Sales*
Mumbai	80	/	300	=	26.7%
New Delhi	60	/	250	=	24.0%
Bangalore	40	/	150	=	26.7%

Exhibit 20.6 summarises the financial measures for the various units of Bharat Cola Corporation for 20X0.

EXHIBIT 20.6 ***Financial Measures for the Various Units of Bharat Cola Corporation for 20X0***

	Return on Investment	*Residual Income*	*Return on Sales*
Mumbai	16%	–10	26.7%
New Delhi	20%	6	24.0%
Bangalore	20%	4	26.7%

20.4 DESIGNING AN EFFECTIVE PERFORMANCE MEASUREMENT SYSTEM

A logical approach to managing for value links shareholder value targets, through corporate objectives and strategies, to a performance scorecard. Exhibit 20.7 shows these linkages.

Competent managers translate the sometimes confusing mantra of shareholder value into corporate objectives that are easy to understand. For example, the objectives at General Electric are to achieve a revenue growth rate which is 2 to 3 times the growth rate of the U.S. GDP, a net profit margin of 10 percent, and a return on capital employed of 20 percent.

EXHIBIT 20.7 ***Designing Performance Measurement***

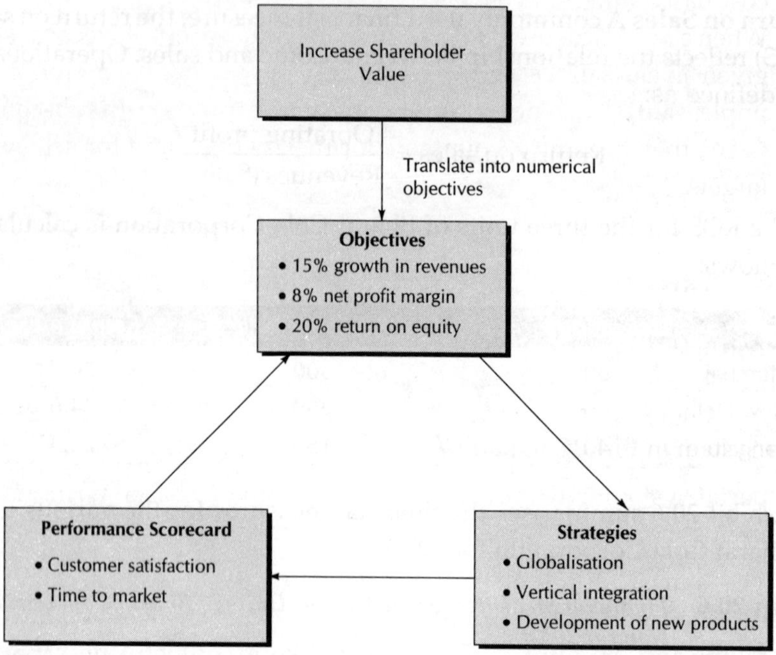

Right objectives are just the starting point. Nothing will happen unless they are backed by the right strategies that energise the organisation. So the company must choose specific strategies such as globalisation, new product offerings, strategic alliances, process cost reduction, outsourcing, and so on.

Strategies by themselves are not enough. They have to be operationalised through an effective performance measurement system. Since what gets measured gets managed, many executives are surprised to find what good measures can do, once in place.

In designing an effective performance measurement bear in mind the following:

1. As a rule of thumb, seven to eight processes and result objectives provide the basic framework on which to build a company's measures.
2. The corporate performance scorecard should consist of a series of measure pairs: measures which are both leading and lagging; measures which reflect both internal (people) and external (customers, competitors, and suppliers) concerns; measures which are both quantitative and qualitative; and measures which are both cost-based and non-cost based.
3. When a new measurement system is introduced, employees must be given a year's grace during which they are can freely communicate unpleasant occurrence without any fear of retribution. In subsequent years, they become accountable for their actions and for achieving targets.

20.5 PERFORMANCE MEASUREMENT: SOME EXAMPLES

It is instructive to look at some performance measurement systems in practice.

Parta System in Birla Companies

The 'parta' system is widely used in Birla companies as a performance measurement and control system. Its salient features are as follows:

- The 'parta' represents the commitment of the unit in charge to the chairman of the company or the group. It is arrived at after taking into account various factors like manufacturing capacity, operational efficiency, consumption norms, market situation, supply of materials, and labour productivity.
- The performance of the unit in-charge is regularly monitored (on a daily, weekly, or monthly basis) on a daily basis by the group chairman on key variables like:
  - Quantity produced
  - Value of production
  - Sales
  - Material consumption
  - Fuel efficiency
  - Material cost
  - Variable conversion cost
  - Contribution
  - Fixed costs

- Profit
- Cash flow

- The rewards to the unit in-charge are linked to the extent to which the 'parta' commitment is fulfilled.

Tata Business Excellence Model

Patterned after the Balridge Award, the Tata Business Excellence Model, adopted by the business house of Tata in India, evaluates the performance of Tata companies along seven criteria. The criteria and the points assigned to them are as follows:

1. Leadership		125
• Organisational leadership	85	
• Social responsibility and citizenship	40	
2. Strategic Planning		85
• Strategy development	40	
• Strategic deployment	45	
3. Customer and Market Focus		85
• Customer and market knowledge	40	
• Customer relationship and satisfaction	45	
4. Information and Analysis		85
• Measurement and analysis of organisational performance	45	
• Information management	40	
5. Human Resources Focus		85
• Work systems	35	
• Employee education, training, and development	25	
• Employee well being and satisfaction	25	
6. Process Management		85
• Products and service processes	45	
• Business processes	25	
• Support processes	15	
7. Business Results		450
• Customer focused results	125	
• Financial and market results	125	

- Human resources results 75
- Organisational effectiveness results 125

GE System

The performance measurement system in General Electric, arguably the most successful conglomerate in the world, focuses on eight broad areas listed below (along with key measure/s used).

1. Profitability
   - Residual income
2. Productivity
   - Labour productivity
3. Market position
   - Market share in appropriately defined market category
4. Product leadership
   - Percentage of products that are superior, equal, or inferior to competitors
5. Personnel development
   - Proportion of employees whose performance is considered to be (a) improving, (b) unchanged, or (c) deteriorating.
   - Ratio of promoted/promotable employee.
   - Proportion of satisfied/dissatisfied employees.
6. Employee attitudes
   - Turnover rates, absenteeism, and accidents
7. Public responsibility
   - Compliance with regulations
   - Survey of suppliers, customers, and so on
8. Balance between short and long-range goals.

SUMMARY

- The performance measurement system of a firm has a strong influence on the behaviour of its people.
- Companies use a wide range of performance measures, some financial, some non-financial.
- The balanced scorecard approach pioneered by Robert Kaplan, David Norton and others seeks to develop an integrated performance measurement system.

- The balanced scorecard is strategy driven. It covers four important perspectives in a business, namely, financial, customer, internal business, and learning and growth.
- The balanced scorecard represents a neat series of objectives and measures. The linkages capture the cause-effect relationships obtaining in the business.
- Most multi-business and multi-location firms are organised into divisions. In a divisionalised business, the divisional head enjoys the authority to determine how the operations under his control are to be carried out.
- The measures that are commonly used to judge the financial performance of a division are: return on investment, residual income, and return on sales.
- A logical approach to managing for value links shareholder value targets, through corporate objectives and strategies, to a performance scorecard.

Corporate Valuation 21

The primary objective of management is to maximise the value of a firm. For this, the managers need a tool for estimating the effects of alternative strategies on firm value. This tool is the corporate valuation model. This chapter discusses the enterprise DCF model which is the most important model for corporate valuation; in addition, it looks at other approaches to corporate valuation. This model draws on a number of concepts and tools such as financial statements, cash flows, financial projections, present value, and cost of capital which have been discussed at length in the previous chapters.

Value maximisation is the central theme in financial management. Owners of corporate securities will hold the management responsible if they fail to enhance value. Hence all senior managers must understand what determines value and how to measure it. While valuation was regarded as an abstruse academic subject in the past, it is of considerable importance to managers now.

In the wake of economic liberalisation, companies are relying more on the capital market, acquisitions and restructuring are becoming commonplace, strategic alliances are gaining popularity, employee stock option plans are proliferating, and regulatory bodies are struggling with tariff determination. In these exercises a crucial issue arises that how the value of a company or a division should be appraised?

The goal of such an appraisal is essentially to estimate a fair market value of a company. So, at the outset, we must clarify what is meant by "fair market value" and what is meant by "a company". The most widely accepted definition of fair market value was laid down by the Internal Revenue Service of the U.S. It defined fair market value as "the price at which the property would change hands between a willing buyer and a willing seller when the former is not under any compulsion to buy and the latter is not under any compulsion to sell, both parties having reasonable knowledge of relevant facts." When the asset being appraised is "a company", the property which the buyer and the seller are trading consists of the claims of all the investors of the company. This chapter discusses the following approaches to corporate valuation:

- Adjusted book value approach
- Direct comparison approach
- Discounted cash flow approach

21.1 ADJUSTED BOOK VALUE APPROACH

The simplest approach to valuing a firm is to rely on the information found on its balance sheet. There are two equivalent ways of using the balance sheet information to appraise the value of a firm. First, the book values of investor claims may be summed up directly. Second, the assets of the firm may be totaled and, from this total, non-investor claims (like accounts payable and provisions) may be deducted. To illustrate this approach, let us look at an example. Exhibit 21.1 presents the balance sheet of Horizon Limited as on March 31, 20X1. From the balance sheet, the value of the firm can be calculated using the investor claim approach or the asset-liabilities approach as illustrated in Exhibit 21.2.

EXHIBIT 21.1 ***Balance Sheet of Horizon Limited as on March 31, 20X1***

(₹ in crore)

Liabilities		*Assets*	
Share capital	**15.00**	Fixed assets (net)	**33.00**
Equity	15.00	Gross block	59.00
Preference	-	Accumulated depreciation	26.00
Reserves and surplus	**11.20**	Investments	**1.50**
Secured loans	**14.30**		
Term loans	7.00	Current assets, loans, and advances	**23.40**
Debentures	7.30		
Unsecured loans	**6.90**	Cash and bank	1.00
Bank credit	2.50	Debtors	11.40
Inter-corporate loans	4.40	Inventories	10.50
		Pre-paid expenses	0.50
Current liabilities and provisions	**10.50**	Miscellaneous expenditures and losses	-
	57.90		57.90

EXHIBIT 21.2 ***Balance Sheet Valuation***

(₹ in crore)

Investor Claims Approach		*Asset-Liabilities Approach*	
Share capital	15.00	Total assets	57.90
Reserves and surplus	11.20	Less: Current	
Secured loans	14.30	liabilities and provisions	10.50
Unsecured loans	6.90		
	47.40		47.40

The accuracy of the book value approach depends on how well the net book values of the assets reflect their fair market values. There are three reasons why book values may diverge from market values:

- Inflation drives a wedge between the book value of an asset and its current value. The book value of an asset is its historical cost less depreciation. Hence it does not consider inflation which is definitely a factor influencing the market value.
- Thanks to technological changes, some assets become obsolete and worthless even before they are fully depreciated in the books.
- Organisational capital, a very valuable asset, is not shown on the balance sheet. It is the value created by bringing together employees, customers, suppliers, and managers in a mutually beneficial and productive relationship. An important characteristic of organisational capital is that it cannot be easily separated from the firm as a going entity.

Adjusting Book Value to Reflect Replacement Cost

Though an asset's earning power may not be related to its book value, especially if the asset is old, it is likely to be related to its current replacement cost. Hence, net book values may be substituted by current replacement costs. The various assets are valued as follows:

Cash Cash is cash. Hence there is no problem in valuing it. Indeed, it is gratifying to have an asset which is so simple to value.

Debtors Generally debtors are valued at their face value. If the quality of debtors is doubtful, prudence calls for making an allowance for likely bad debts.

Inventories Inventories may be classified into three categories: raw materials, work-in-process, and finished goods. Raw materials may be valued at their most recent cost of acquisition. Work-in-process may be approached from the cost point of view (cost of raw materials plus the cost of processing) or from the selling price point of view (selling price of the final product fewer expenses to be incurred in translating work-in-process into sales). Finished goods inventory is generally appraised by determining the sale price realisable in the ordinary course of business less expenses to be incurred in packaging, handling, transporting, selling, and collection of receivables.

Other Current Assets Other current assets like deposits, prepaid expenses, and accruals are valued at their book value.

Fixed Tangible Assets Fixed tangible assets consist mainly of land, buildings and civil works, and plant and machinery. Land is valued as if it is vacant and available for sale. Buildings and civil works may be valued at replacement cost less physical depreciation and deterioration.

The value of plant and machinery may be appraised at the market price of similar (used) assets plus the cost of transportation and installation.

Non-operating Assets Assets not required for meeting the operating requirements of the business are referred to as non-operating assets. The more commonly found non-operating assets are financial securities, excess land, and unused buildings. These assets are valued at their fair market value.

Adjusting Book Values to Reflect Liquidation Value

The most direct approach for approximating the fair market value of the assets on the balance sheet of a firm is to find out what they would fetch if the firm was liquidated immediately. If there is an active secondary market for the assets, liquidation values equal secondary market prices. However, active secondary markets do not exist for many business assets. In such cases, the appraiser must try to estimate the hypothetical price at which the assets may be sold.

The principal weakness of the liquidation value approach is that it ignores organisational capital. Instead of valuing the firm as a going concern, it values it as a collection of assets to be sold individually. This approach makes sense only for a firm that is worth more dead than alive.

The Bottom Line

The unadjusted book value approach makes sense only in rare cases, such as the appraisal of regulated industries. The adjusted book value approach (replacement cost approach or liquidation value approach) makes sense for firms which derive their value mainly from owning tangible resources. Even such situations are not common because most firms have valuable organisational capital. Thus, in most real life situations, the book value approach has limited applicability.

21.2 DIRECT COMPARISON APPROACH

Common sense and economic logic tell us that similar assets should sell at similar prices. Based on this principle, one can value an asset by looking at the price at which a comparable asset has changed hands between a reasonably informed buyer and a reasonably informed seller. This approach, referred to as the direct comparison approach, is commonly applied in real estate. If there are two identical or near-identical apartments and one of them sells for ₹12 million, the appraised value of the other apartment is also ₹12 million.

Differences in scale, however, make it difficult to find directly comparable properties. If the apartment next to yours measures 3,000 square feet and is sold for ₹15 million, you cannot appraise your apartment which measures 2,000 square feet also for ₹15 million. To solve the scale problem you may first determine the price per square foot of the apartment next to yours and apply it to the size of your apartment. In this case the price per square foot works out to ₹5000. When you apply this rate to your apartment which measures 2,000 square feet, you get an appraised value of ₹10.0 million.

Essentially, the direct comparison approach is reflected in a simple formula:

$$V_T = x_T \frac{V_c}{x_c}$$

where V_T is the appraised value of the target firm (or asset), x_T is the observed variable for the target firm that supposedly drives value, V_c is the observed value of the comparable firm, and x_c is the observed variable for the comparable company.

Steps in Applying the Direct Comparison Approach

Operationally, a top-down procedure may be followed in applying the direct comparison approach. This involves the following steps:

- Analyse the economy
- Analyse the industry
- Analyse the subject company

- Select comparable companies
- Analyse subject and comparable companies
- Analyse multiples
- Value the subject company

Analyse the Economy The first step in the comparable company approach is to analyse the economy. An analysis of the economy provides the basis for assessing the prospects of various industries and evaluating individual companies within an industry. Such an analysis calls for, *inter alia*, examining the following factors and forecasting their growth rates: gross national product, industrial production, agricultural output, inflation, interest rates, balance of payment, exchange rate, and government budget (as well as its composition).

Analyse the Industry The second step in the comparable company approach is to analyse the industry to which the subject company belongs. This analysis should focus on the following:

- The relationship of the industry to the economy as a whole
- The stage in which the industry is in its life cycle
- The profit potential of the industry
- The nature of regulation applicable to the industry
- The relative competitive advantages in procurement of raw materials, production costs, marketing and distribution arrangements, and technological resources

Analyse the Subject Company The third step is to carry out an in-depth analysis of the competitive and financial position of the subject company. The key aspects to be covered in this examination are as follows:

- Product portfolio and market segments covered by the firm
- Availability and cost of inputs
- Technological and production capability
- Market image, distribution reach, and customer loyalty
- Product differentiation and economic cost position
- Managerial competence and drive
- Quality of human resources
- Competitive dynamics
- Liquidity, leverage, and access to funds
- Turnover, margins, and return on investment

Select Comparable Companies After the subject company is studied, the next step is to select companies which are similar to the subject company in terms of the lines of business, nature of markets served, scale of operation, and so on. Often, it is hard to find truly comparable companies because companies are engaged in a variety of businesses, serve different market segments, and have varying capacities. Hence, in practice, the analyst has to make do with companies which are comparable in some ways. He should make every effort to look carefully at 10–15 companies in the same industry and select at least 3–4 which come 'as close as possible' to the subject company. Understandably, a good deal of subjective judgment is involved in this process.

Analyse the Financial Aspects of the Subject and Comparable Companies Once the comparable companies are selected, the historical financial statements (balance sheets and income statements) of the subject and comparable companies must be analysed to identify similarities and differences and make adjustments so that they are put on a comparable basis. Adjustments may be required for differences in inventory valuation methods, for intangible assets, for off-balance sheet items, and so on. The purpose of these adjustments is to normalise the financial statements.

Choose the Observable Financial Variable For the direct comparison approach to provide a reliable estimate of value, the ratio of the value indicator to the observed financial variable, V/x, must not vary widely for the comparable firms and the target firm. Since the variability of V/x depends considerably on the choice of V and x, the two variables must be selected with care.

The financial variables that are likely to produce a constant V/x ratio are those that are closely associated with the value of the firm. Since the value of a firm is ultimately based on the cash generated for its investors, financial variables like earnings and cash flow are the obvious choices for x. In addition, financial variables such as sales and net worth which indirectly measure earning power are also possible candidates.

The value indicator must be consistent with the financial variable chosen. If a gross financial variable like PBDIT (profit before depreciation interest and tax) is chosen, then it should be matched with total firm value. On the other hand, if the appraiser uses a financial variable like equity earnings, it should be matched with equity value and not the total firm value. In such a case the estimated value of equity must be added to the estimated value of other investor claims (debt and preferred stock) which are separately assessed to calculate the total value of the firm.

The ratios or multiples that are commonly used in the direct comparison method are as follows:

- Firm value to sales
- Firm value to book value of assets
- Firm value to PBIDT
- Firm value to PBIT
- Equity value to equity earnings (Price-earnings multiple)
- Equity value to net worth (Market-book ratio)

Value the Subject Company The final step in this process is to decide where the subject company fits in relation to the comparable companies. This is essentially a judgmental exercise. Once this is done, appropriate multiples may be applied to the financial numbers (sales, EBITDA, and so on) of the subject company to estimate its value. If several bases are employed, the several value estimates may be averaged (for this purpose a simple arithmetic average or a weighted arithmetic average may be employed).

Illustration

The following financial information is available for company D, a pharmaceutical company,

- Earnings before interest, taxes, depreciation and amortisation ₹400 million
- Book value of assets ₹1,000 million
- Sales ₹2500 million

Based on an evaluation of several pharmaceutical companies, companies A, B, and C have been found to be comparable to company D. The financial information for these companies are given below.

	A	B	C
EBITDA*	280	360	480
Book value of assets*	800	1000	1400
Sales*	1600	2000	3200
Enterprise value* (EV)	2000	3500	4200
EV/EBITDA	7.1	9.7	8.8
EV/Book value	2.5	3.5	3.0
EV/Sales	1.25	1.75	1.31

* In million rupees

Taking into account the characteristics of company D vis-à-vis companies A, B, and C, the following multiples appear reasonable for company D:

EV/EBITDA = 8.5 EV/Book value = 3.0 EV/Sales = 1.44

Applying these multiples to the financial numbers of company D, gives the following value estimates:

1. EV = 8.5 × EBITDA = 8.5 × 400 = ₹3400 million
2. EV = 3.0 × BV = 3.0 × 1,000 = ₹3000 million
3. EV = 1.44 × Sales = 1.44 × 2500 = ₹3600 million

A simple arithmetic average of the three value estimates is:

(3,400 + 3,000 + 3,600)/3 = ₹3333 million

Bottom Line

The direct comparison approach is very popular because it relies on multiples that are easy to relate to and can be obtained easily and quickly. They are particularly useful when several comparable companies are traded and, on average, the market prices them accurately.

However, multiples are amenable to misuse and manipulation. Since no two firms are likely to be identical in terms of risk and growth, the key determinants of multiples, the choice of "comparable" companies is subjective. Hence, the appraiser can choose a group of firms that confirm his biases about the target firm's value. While the potential for subjective bias exists with the DCF approach as well, the appraiser there has to be much more explicit about his assumptions and has lesser scope to hide his biases in unstated assumptions.

There is another problem with the direct comparison approach. The multiples used in this approach reflect the valuation errors (overvaluation or undervaluation) of the market. Thus, if software companies in general are overvalued, applying the average price-earnings multiple of listed software companies to determine the value of an unlisted company may lead to overvaluation. In contrast, the DCF approach is grounded on firm-specific cash flows and growth rates and hence is likely to be less affected by market valuation errors.

21.3 DISCOUNTED CASH FLOW APPROACH

Traditionally, the adjusted book value approach and the direct comparison approach were used more commonly. From the early 1990s, however, the discounted cash flow approach has received greater attention, emphasis, and acceptance. This is mainly because of its conceptual superiority and its strong endorsement by leading consultancy organisations.

Valuing a firm using the discounted cash flow approach is conceptually identical to valuing a capital project using the present value method. However, there are two important differences:

- While a capital project is deemed to have a finite life, a firm is considered as an entity that has an indefinite life. This means that when we value a capital project we define its economic life and impute a salvage value to the assets of the project at the end of its economic life; however, for a firm we don't define an economic life and impute a salvage value to its assets at the end of such a period.
- A capital project is typically valued as a 'one-off' investment. We do not ordinarily look at the follow on investments on the assumption that these will be evaluated separately as and when they crystallise. A firm, however, is viewed as a growing entity and for valuing a firm we take into account all the investments in fixed assets and net working capital that are expected to be made over time to sustain the growth of the firm.

To sum up, valuing a firm using discounted cash flow approach calls for forecasting cash flows over an indefinite period of time, for an entity that is expected to grow. This is indeed a daunting proposition. To tackle this task, in practice, the value of the firm is separated into two time periods:

Value of the firm = Present value of cash flow during the explicit forecast period + Present value of cash flow after the explicit forecast period

During the explicit forecast period, which is often a period of 5 to 15 years, the firm is expected to evolve rather rapidly and hence a great deal of effort is expended to forecast its cash flow on an annual basis. At the end of the explicit forecast period, the firm is expected to reach a "steady state" and hence a simplified procedure is used to estimate its continuing value.

Procedure for Calculating Discounted Cash Flow Value

The discounted cash flow approach to business valuation involves three basic steps:

Step 1 Define the present value of the free cash flow during the explicit forecast period

The free cash flow (FCF) is the cash flow generated after providing for additional investments required for operations. It is the cash available for distribution to investors. It is generally defined from the perspective of total investor claims on the firm. It is expressed as:

Net operating profit adjusted for taxes (NOPAT) – Net investment

NOPAT = Profit before interest and tax (1 – tax rate)

Net investment = Gross investment in fixed assets and current assets – Depreciation

The time horizon (*H*) for defining the free cash flow is selected in such a way that beyond the horizon period the growth rate of free cash flow is constant. Thus, if after say six years, the growth rate of free cash flow is expected to be constant, say 8 percent, the time horizon for defining the free cash flow will be 6 years.

The present value of the FCF during the explicit forecast period is:

$$\text{PV (ECF)} = \frac{\text{FCF}_1}{(1+r)} + \frac{\text{FCF}_2}{(1+r)^2} + \cdots + \frac{\text{FCF}_H}{(1+r)^H}$$

The discount rate, *r*, must reflect the opportunity cost of capital.

Step 2 Establish the horizon value of the firm and discount it to the present time

The horizon value (V_H) of the firm refers to the value placed on it on the horizon date, which is simply the terminal point of the horizon period (the explicit forecast period) used for defining the free cash flow. Since the free cash flow is expected to grow at a constant rate beyond the horizon period, the horizon value is equal to:

$$V_H = \frac{\text{FCF}_{H+1}}{r-g}$$

The present value of the horizon value is:

$$\frac{V_H}{(1+r)^H}$$

Step 3 Add the present value of free cash flow during the explicit forecast period and the horizon value to get the value of the firm

The value of the firm, V_0 is simply:

$$V_0 = \underbrace{\frac{\text{FCF}_1}{(1+r)} + \frac{\text{FCF}_2}{(1+r)^2} + \cdots + \frac{\text{FCF}_H}{(1+r)^H}}_{\text{PV (free cash flow)}} + \underbrace{\frac{V_H}{(1+r)^H}}_{\text{PV (horizon value)}}$$

Illustration

The DCF method may be illustrated with the help of an example. Global Limited is interested in acquiring the foods division of Regional Company.

The forecast of free cash flow for the proposed purchase, as developed by Global Limited, is shown in Exhibit 21.3. It is based on the following assumptions: (i) the growth rate in assets and revenue will be 20 percent for the first three years, 12 percent for the next two years, and 8 percent thereafter, and (ii) the ratio of NOPAT to net assets would be 0.12. The opportunity cost of capital is 11 percent. Looking at Exhibit 21.3 we find that after six years the free cash flow is expected to grow at a constant rate of 8 percent. So, we set the horizon period at six years.

21.3 FREE CASH FLOW

(₹ in million)

Year	1	2	3	4	5	6	7
Asset value(Beg)	50.00	60.00	72.00	86.40	96.77	108.38	117.05
NOPAT	6.00	7.20	8.64	10.37	11.61	13.00	14.05
Net investment	10.00	12.00	14.40	10.37	11.61	8.67	9.36
FCF	(4.00)	(4.80)	(5.76)	-	-	4.33	4.69
Growth rate (%)	20	20	20	12	12	8	8

$$\text{PV (FCF)} = \frac{-4.00}{(1.11)} + \frac{-4.80}{(1.11)^2} + \frac{-5.76}{(1.11)^4} + \frac{0}{(1.11)^4} + \frac{0}{(1.11)^5} + \frac{4.33}{(1.11)^6}$$

$$= ₹9.40 \text{ million}$$

The horizon value at the end of six years, applying the constant growth model, is:

$$V_H = \frac{\text{FCF}_{H+1}}{r-g} = \frac{4.69}{0.11-0.08} = ₹156.33 \text{ million}$$

The present value of V_H is:

$$\frac{156.33}{(1.11)^6} = ₹83.58 \text{ million}$$

Adding the present value of free cash flow and the present value of horizon value, gives the value of acquisition:

$$V_0 = -9.40 + 83.58 = ₹74.18 \text{ million}$$

SUMMARY

- The IRS of the US has defined **fair market value** as "the price at which the property would change hands between a willing buyer and willing seller when the former is not under any compulsion to buy and the latter is not under any compulsion to sell, both the parties having reasonable knowledge of relevant facts".

- There are three broad approaches to appraising the value of a company: Adjusted book value approach, Direct comparison approach, and Discounted cash flow approach.
- The simplest approach to valuing a company is to rely on the information found on its balance sheet, adjusted for replacement cost or liquidation value.
- When the securities of a firm are publicly traded, its value can be obtained by merely adding the market value of all its outstanding securities. This approach is called the **stock and debt approach** to valuation.
- The **direct comparison approach** involves valuing a company on the basis of how similar companies are valued in the market place.
- The **discounted cash flow** approach to valuation involves five steps: (a) Analysing historical performance, (b) Forecasting cash flows, (c) Establishing the cost of capital, (d) Determining the continuing value at the end of the explicit forecast period, and (e) Calculating the firm value and interpreting results.

Risk Management: Basics of Financial Engineering

22

Since the early 1970s financial prices have become more volatile. This has had a detrimental impact on a number of firms which were ill prepared for unexpected price shifts.

Initially firms responded to volatility in financial prices—interest rates, exchange rates, commodity prices, and equity prices—by resorting to forecasting; however, forecasters in general flunked. This is not surprising because in efficient markets, and financial markets, are characterised by a high degree of efficiency, price changes tend to be random. This means that there is no way to accurately predict future prices.

Since forecasting did not address the problem of financial price risk, firms looked for other methods. The financial market responded to this need by developing a range of risk management products like forwards, futures, swaps, and options. Many firms now use financial derivatives to manage currency, interest rate, and commodity price risks.

This chapter is organised into six sections:

- Managing financial risk
- Hedging with forward contracts
- Hedging with futures contracts
- Hedging with swap contracts
- Hedging with option contracts
- Hedging with insurance

22.1 MANAGING FINANCIAL RISK

The increase in the volatility of prices and rates may or may not be a matter of concern to a firm, depending on the nature of its operations and financing. For example, interest rate fluctuations matter a great deal for a commercial bank but hardly have any impact on a fast moving consumer goods (FMCG) company. Likewise, exchange rate fluctuations are a great concern for a predominantly export-oriented company but are of much less concern to a firm with little or no international activity.

Risk Profile The risk profile is a basic tool for measuring a firm's exposure to financial risk. It is a graph showing the relationship between changes in the price of some good or service and changes in the value of the firm. Constructing a risk profile is analogous to performing a sensitivity analysis.

To illustrate, consider an oil company that produces large quantities of oil. Because oil prices tend to fluctuate a lot, the oil company wishes to understand its exposure to oil price fluctuations, that is, its risk profile with respect to oil prices. To do this, it plots changes in the value of the firm (*DV*) versus unanticipated changes in oil prices (DP_{oil}). Exhibit 22.1 shows the result.

Exhibit 22.1 ***Risk Profile for an Oil Producer***

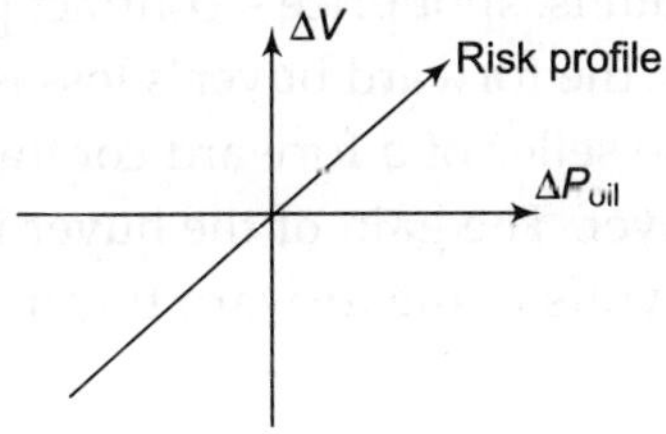

The risk profile in Exhibit 22.1 suggests two things: first, because the line slopes upward, the value of the firm increases when oil price increases; second, the slope is fairly steep, implying that the firm has a significant exposure to oil price fluctuation. So it may be worthwhile to take measures to reduce that exposure.

22.2 HEDGING WITH FORWARD CONTRACTS

Forward contracts are perhaps the oldest and simplest tools for managing financial risk. A forward contract represents an agreement between two parties to exchange an asset for cash at a predetermined future date called the settlement date for a price that is specified today. For example, if you agree on January 1 to buy 100 bales of cotton on July 1 at a price of ₹800 per bale from a cotton dealer, you have entered into a forward contract with the cotton dealer. As per this contract, on July 1 you will have to pay ₹80, 000 and the cotton dealer will have to supply 100 bales. According to this agreement, you have bought forward cotton or you are long forward cotton, whereas the cotton dealer has sold forward cotton or is short forward cotton. No money or cotton changes hand when the deal is signed. The forward contract only specifies the terms of a transaction that would occur in future.

Note that the terms "buy" and "sell" have a somewhat different meaning here. It is helpful to think in terms of a:

- *Short position* which commits the seller to deliver an item at the contracted price on maturity.
- *Long position* which commits the buyer to purchase an item at the contracted price on maturity.

The forward buyer is obliged to purchase the underlying instrument at the contract price or enter into an offsetting transaction.

The Payoff Profile What are the payoffs to the forward buyer and forward seller? When the spot price in future exceeds the contract price, the forward buyer's gain is: spot price – contract price.

If it is the other way, the forward buyer's loss is: contract price – spot price. The payoff to the seller of a forward contract is the mirror image of the payoff to the buyer. The gain of the buyer is the loss of the seller and vice versa. The payoffs to the forward buyer and forward seller are shown in Exhibit 22.2

EXHIBIT 22.2 ***Payoff Profiles for a Forward Contract***

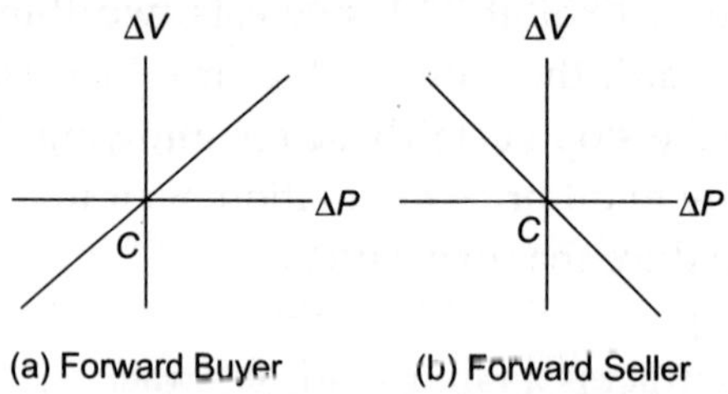

Hedging with Forward Contracts To illustrate how forward contracts can be used for hedging, let us consider the case of a power company that uses oil as fuel. Assuming that the tariff that this company can charge cannot be adjusted quickly, a sudden change in the price of oil is a source of risk. The risk profile for this company, an oil buyer, is depicted in Exhibit 22.3(a).

What should this company do to cope with its oil price risk?—It should buy a forward contract. If it does so, its exposure to unexpected changes in oil prices will be eliminated. The result is shown in Exhibit 22.3(b).

EXHIBIT 22.3 ***Hedging with a Forward Contract***

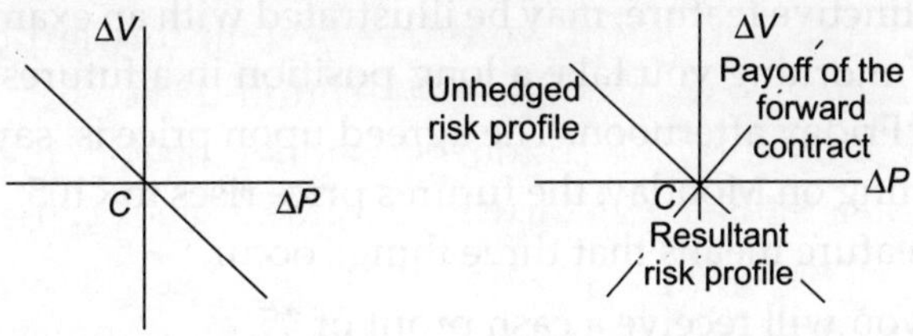

(a) The unhedged risk profile (b) The hedged risk profile

A Caveat Exhibit 22.3 shows that the forward contract reduces the power company's net exposure of oil price fluctuations to zero. If the oil price rises, the damage from the higher price is offset by the gains on the forward contract. However, if the oil price falls, the benefit from the lower price is offset by the losses on the forward contract. Bear in mind that price fluctuation can be good or bad, depending on the nature of its movement. A forward contract protects against the risk of an adverse price change, but it also eliminates the potential gain from a favourable price change. Is it possible to hedge against adverse price change, while preserving the potential gains from a favourable price change?—Yes, it is and we describe this how in a later section.

Credit Risk At the time a forward contract is initiated, no money changes hand. Because it is simply an agreement to transact in the future, there is no upfront cost. However, since a forward contract entails future obligations, it carries credit risk. On the settlement date, the party on the losing side of the contract has an incentive to renege on the agreement.

22.3 HEDGING WITH FUTURES CONTRACTS

A futures contract is a standardised forward contract. The key differences between forwards and futures are as follows:

- A forward contract is a tailor-made contract.
- While there is no secondary market for forward contracts, futures contracts are traded on organised exchanges.
- Forward contracts usually end with deliveries, whereas futures contracts are cash settled.
- Usually no collateral is required for a forward contract. In a futures contract, however, a margin is required.
- Forward contracts are settled on the maturity date whereas futures contracts are 'marked to market' on a daily basis. This means that profits and losses on futures contracts are settled daily.

The marking-to-market feature of futures contract, which is perhaps its most distinctive feature, may be illustrated with an example: Suppose on Monday morning you take a long position in a futures contract that matures on Friday afternoon. The agreed upon price is, say, ₹100. At the close of trading on Monday, the futures price rises to ₹105. The marking-to-market feature means that three things occur.

- First, you will receive a cash profit of ₹5.
- Second, the existing futures contract with a price of ₹100 is cancelled.
- Third, you will receive a new futures contract at ₹105.

The marking-to-market feature implies that the futures contracts are settled every day. Put differently, a futures contract is converted into a sequence of one-day forward contracts.

Futures and the Exchanges Where They Are Traded Broadly there are two types of futures: commodity futures and financial futures. A commodity futures is a futures contract in a commodity like cocoa or aluminum; a financial futures is a futures contract in a financial instrument like treasury bill, currency, or stock index. Exhibit 22.4 lists some illustrative commodity futures and financial futures and the exchanges in India where they are traded.

EXHIBIT 22.4 ***Commodity Futures and Financial Futures in India***

Commodity Futures	*Exchange*	*Financial Futures*	*Exchange*
Aluminum	MCX, NCDEX	BSE Sensex	BSE
Cashew	NCDEX	Nifty	NSE
Gold	MCX, NCDEX	NSE Bond Futures	NSE
Coffee	NMCE, NCDEX	USDINR	NSE
Sugar	MCX, NCDEX, NMCE		

MCX: Multi Commodity Exchange of India Limited
NCDEX: National Commodity and Derivatives Exchange Limited
NMCE: National Multi Commodity Exchange of India Limited
BSE: Mumbai Stock Exchange
NSE: National Stock Exchange

Futures and Hedging Suppose a coffee plantation firm expects a harvest of 1,000 tons of coffee three months from now. If the firm is bothered by the uncertainty of future price, it can sell a futures contract for 1,000 tons. Such a simple hedge eliminates the risk of price fluctuation. Exhibit 22.5 shows how the futures contract neutralises the inherent risk associated with price volatility.

EXHIBIT 22.5 ***Hedging with Futures***

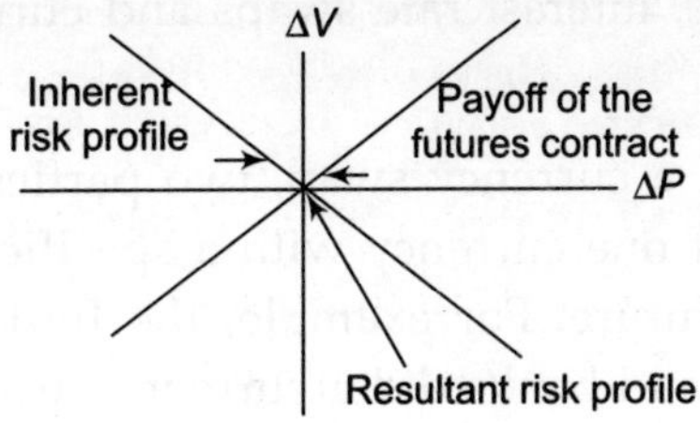

The type of futures contract a firm wants may not be available. For example, a soybean oil producer may not be able to get soybean oil futures contracts. In such a case, it may have to make do with some surrogate. It may perhaps substitute groundnut oil futures for soybean oil futures if the soybean oil and groundnut oil prices tend to move in unison. Such a substitution is referred to as a **cross-hedge**.

When a firm resorts to cross-hedging it must take into account how the relative prices move. In the above case, for example, it should know the relationship between the movements of the soybean oil prices and groundnut oil prices. Suppose it finds that the following regression relationship holds:

Percent change in soybean oil price = 0.9 Percent change in the price of groundnut oil.

Hence, the soybean oil producer must sell 0.9 units of groundnut oil futures for every unit of soybean oil to be sold.

Thanks to their unique contractual features, futures provide several advantages over other hedging devices:

- There is no need for an initial cash flow, except the margin money.
- It is easy to take a short position in futures as it is to take a long position.
- It is easy to close a futures contract by on offsetting trade.
- The wide range of commodities and financial instruments on which futures contract are available exceeds anything available in other markets.

22.4 HEDGING WITH SWAP CONTRACTS

A swap contract is an agreement between two parties to exchange one set of cash flows for another. In essence, it is a portfolio of forward contracts. While a forward contract involves one exchange at a specific future date, a swap contract entails multiple exchanges over a period of time.

In principle, a swap contract can be tailored to exchange just about anything. In practice, interest rate swaps and currency swaps are the most popular.

Currency Swaps In a currency swap, two parties agree to exchange a specific amount of one currency with a specific amount of another at certain dates in future. For example, the Indian Railway Finance Corporation (IRFC) and banks did a currency swap. Under this swap, banks would pay USD 80 million to IRFC in 5 equal annual installments of USD 16 million each and in return IRFC would pay banks the rupee equivalent in installments at a predetermined conversion rate. IRFC needed USD 80 million to repay a Eurocurrency loan.

Interest Rate Swaps An *interest rate swap* is a transaction involving an exchange of one stream of interest obligations for another. Typically, it results in an exchange of fixed rate interest payments for floating rate interest payments. Occasionally, it involves an exchange of one stream of floating rate interest payments for another.

The principal features of an interest rate swap are:

- It effectively translates a floating rate borrowing into a fixed rate borrowing and vice versa. The net interest differential is paid or received, as the case may be.
- There is no exchange of principal repayment obligations.
- It is structured as a separate contract distinct from the underlying loan agreement.
- It is applicable to new as well as existing borrowings.
- It is treated as an off-the-balance sheet transaction.

Interest rate swaps and currency swaps may be combined. A company may obtain floating rate financing in a particular currency and swap with a fixed rate financing in another currency.

Commodity Swaps A commodity swap is a contract to exchange a specified quantity of a commodity at a specified price at fixed times in future. For example, an oil user needs 100,000 barrels every quarter. It can enter into a swap contract with an oil producer to supply the quantity it requires at a specified price over the next 2 years.

Swap Dealers Unlike futures contracts, swap contracts are not standardised contracts that are traded on an organised exchange. Hence, a firm interested in a swap agreement typically contacts a swap dealer (commercial banks are the dominant swap dealers) to take the other side of the swap agreement. The swap dealer in turn will try to enter into an offsetting transaction with some other party or dealer. Otherwise, the swap dealer may cover its exposure using futures contracts.

Interest Rate Swap An example for a better understanding of swap contracts and the role played by the swap dealer, let us consider a floating-for-fixed interest rate swap.

Suppose Company P can borrow at a floating rate equal to LIBOR plus 1 percent or at a fixed rate of 8 percent, whereas Company Q can borrow at a floating rate of LIBOR plus 2.5 percent or at a fixed rate of 8.75 percent. Company P wants a fixed rate loan while Company Q wants a floating rate loan.

Company P contacts a swap dealer who asks the company to borrow at a floating rate of LIBOR plus 1 percent. The swap dealer agrees to cover the floating interest obligation of Company P and asks Company P to pay a fixed rate of, say, 7.75 percent in return. As a result, Company P swaps a floating interest obligation into a fixed interest obligation.

Company Q too contacts the swap dealer. The swap dealer advises company Q to borrow at a fixed rate of 8.75 percent. The swap dealer agrees to cover the fixed interest obligation of Company Q and asks Company Q to pay a floating rate of, say, LIBOR plus 2.25 percent. As a result Company Q swaps a fixed rate obligation into floating rate obligation.

Exhibit 22.6 shows the transactions involved in the interest rate swap. The net effect of the transactions is as follows: (a) Company P gets a fixed rate loan of 7.75 percent which is cheaper than the 8.00 percent loan that it can get on its own, (b) Company Q gets a floating rate loan at LIBOR plus 2.25 percent which is cheaper than the LIBOR plus 2.50 percent loan that it can get on its own, (c) The swap dealer earns a net margin of 0.25 percent.

EXHIBIT 22.6 *Interest Rate Swap*

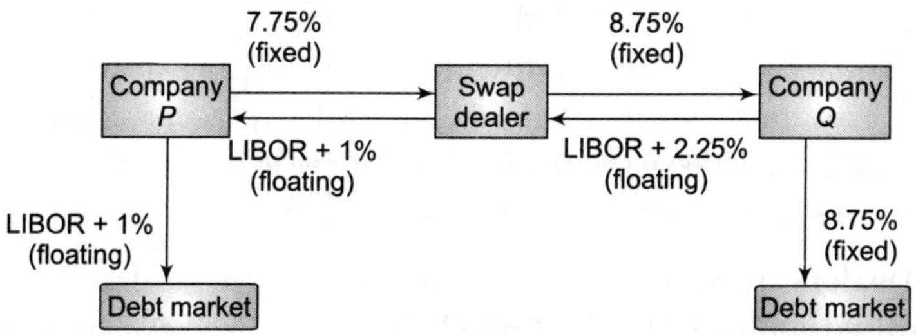

22.5 HEDGING WITH OPTION CONTRACTS

An option contract is an agreement under which the seller (or writer) of the option grants the buyer (or holder) the right, but not the obligation, to buy or sell (depending on whether it is a call option or a put option) some asset at a predetermined price during a specified period. Clearly, the buyer (or holder) of an option has to pay a premium to enjoy the right.

Thus, there are two key differences between a forward contract and an option contract:

- In a forward contract, both parties are obligated to transact in future. In an option contract the transaction occurs only if the buyer (or holder) of the option chooses to exercise it.
- When a forward contract is created no money changes hand. On the other hand when an option contract is created, the buyer of the option contract pays option premium to the seller of the option.

Ignoring the premium paid by the buyer of the option, which is non-refundable, the payoff profiles are as follows.

Option Payoffs Profiles Exhibit 22.7 depicts the payoffs profiles for call and put options. The horizontal axis shows the difference between the value of the asset and the exercise price of the option; the vertical axis shows the payoffs from the options. Exhibit 22.7(a) shows the payoff profile of a call option from the buyer's point of view; Exhibit 22.7(b) shows the payoff profile of call option from the seller's point of view. Since a call option is a zero-sum game, the seller's payoff profile is exactly the mirror image of the buyer's.

EXHIBIT 22.7 ***Payoffs Profiles for Call and Put Options***

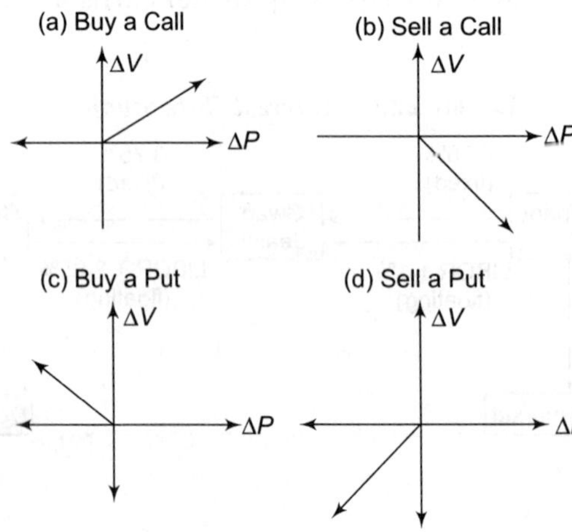

Exhibit 22.7(c) shows the payoff profile for the buyer of a put option. Remember that a put option gives its buyer the right to sell an asset at the strike price. Hence if the value of the asset falls below the strike price the buyer profits because the seller of the put option is obliged to pay the strike price. Exhibit 22.7(d) shows the payoff profile for the seller of a put option.

Hedging with Options Suppose a firm has a risk profile of the kind shown in Exhibit 22.8(a). What should it do if it wishes to use options to hedge against adverse price movements? Looking at the payoffs in Exhibit 22.8, it appears that buying a put option suits this firm. If it does, its net exposure changes as shown in Exhibit 22.8(b). By buying the put option, the firm eliminates the "downside" risk while retaining the "upside" potential. Put differently, the put option serves like an insurance policy. Of course, like any insurance it costs money because the firm has to pay the option premium.

EXHIBIT 22.8 ***Hedging with Options***

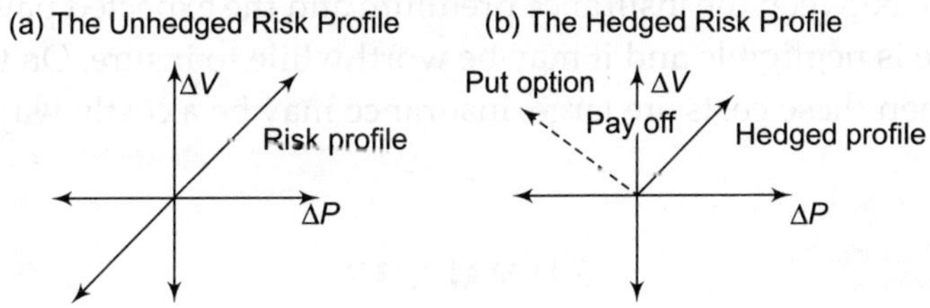

22.6 HEDGING WITH INSURANCE

Most business firms buy insurance against a variety of risks: the risk of plant destruction in a fire, the risk of liabilities arising from legal suits, the risk of losing key person, and so on.

When a firm buys insurance, it pays premium to shift the risk to the insurance company. Is it worthwhile to do so? The answer depends on how the advantages offered by the insurance company compare with the disadvantages suffered by it. The main advantages offered by an insurance company are:

- It can price risks reasonably accurately as it has considerable experience in insuring similar risks.
- It can provide low-cost claims administration service, thanks to specialisation and economies of scale.

- It has expertise in providing advice on measures to reduce risks and may lower premia to clients that follow its advice.
- It can pool risks by holding a large, diversified pool of assets.

As against the above advantages, an insurance company may suffer from the following disadvantages which can increase the cost of insurance.

- Like any other business, an insurance company incurs administrative costs.
- It faces the problem of **adverse selection**. If the insurance company cannot distinguish between 'good' and 'bad' risks, its portfolio is likely to be dominated by bad risks. After all, a bad risk firm has a greater incentive to buy insurance.
- It is exposed to the problem of **moral hazard**. This is the risk that the insured parties, comforted by the insurance cover, tend to behave negligently. Isn't it true that if you have a comprehensive insurance policy for your car you become somewhat careless in driving?

When the above costs are small, the 'loading fee' which represents the difference between the insurance premium and the expected payoff from insurance is negligible and it may be worthwhile to insure. On the other hand, when these costs are large, insurance may be a costly way to shed risk.

SUMMARY

- Since the early 1970s financial prices, i.e., interest rates, exchange rates, commodity prices, and equity prices, have become more volatile.
- The financial market responded to business needs for managing risk by developing a range of risk management products like forwards, swaps, and options. Many firms now use financial derivatives to tailor their exposures to currency, interest rate, and commodity price risks.
- A **forward contract** is an agreement between two parties to exchange an asset for cash at a predetermined future date for a price specified today. A **futures** is a standardised forward contract. Broadly there are two types of futures: **commodity futures** and **financial futures.**
- A **swap contract** is an agreement between two parties to exchange one set of cash flows for another. In essence, it is a portfolio of forward contracts.

- In principle, a swap contract can be tailored to exchange just about everything. In practice currency swaps and interest rate swaps are quite popular.
- In a **currency swap**, two parties agree to exchange a specific amount of one currency with a specific amount of another at certain dates in future.
- An **interest rate swap** is a transaction involving an exchange of one stream of interest for another. Typically, it results in an exchange of fixed rate interest payments for floating rate interest payments.
- A **commodity swap** is a contract to exchange a specified quantity of a commodity at a specified price at fixed times in future.
- An **option contract** is an agreement under which the seller (or writer) of the option grants the buyer (or holder) the right, but not the obligation, to buy or sell (depending on whether it is a call option or put option) some assets at a predetermined price during a specified period.
- When a firm buys **insurance**, it pays premium to shift the risk to the insurance company.

Macroeconomics: A Primer[1]

23

Macroeconomics is the study of an entire economy. Its goal is to understand, explain, and predict the behaviour of a nation's economy and its interactions with the global economy. The primary concerns of macroeconomics can be said to be:

- Why do levels of economic activity fluctuate in a cyclical fashion? What are the causes of persistent high unemployment?
- How do we explain fluctuations in inflation rates? What causes sustained bouts of high inflation?
- What factors determine long term economic growth of a nation? Why do some countries grow faster than others? Why does poverty persist in some parts of the world?
- How can governments moderate the short-term fluctuations and promote long term growth?

Theoretical foundations of macroeconomics are provided by microeconomic analysis of decisions of individual households and firms. Macroeconomics focuses on aggregate outcomes of these individual decisions and studies the behaviour of aggregate variables such as Gross National Product, aggregate investment and saving, total employment, wholesale and consumer price indices, money supply and bank credit, and key financial variables like interest rates and exchange rates. It then goes on to formulate policy prescriptions to achieve the goals of high employment, low inflation, and rapid economic growth.

23.1 HOW BIG IS THE ECONOMY?

It is said that the United States is the biggest economy in the world. Some estimates indicate that India may rank as the 7th largest economy.

[1]Contributed by Dr. P. G. Apte.

How does one measure the size of an economy? We measure the level of economic activity and hence the size of an economy by the volume of goods and services produced during a specified period of time. But since we cannot add tons of steel to litres of milk, we must convert everything to a common denominator. The most acceptable such common denominator is money. We can add monetary values of the millions of different goods and services produced. Gross Domestic Product (GDP) and Gross National Product (GNP) are two such rupee-denominated measures of the level of economic activity. To avoid double counting, only final goods and services are included. In one of its versions, GDP is the market value of all final goods and services produced in an economy during a specified interval of time, usually a year, irrespective of who owns the productive assets or provides productive services such as labour—domestic residents or foreigners.

What are "final" goods and services? Those that do not enter as inputs in the production of something else. Thus raw materials, intermediate goods, and other inputs in production like fuels and electric power are left out. Bread sold to households is included but the wheat flour that goes into it is not; value of a car is included but not like steel, plastics, and aluminum that go into its manufacture.

Why are intermediate inputs excluded? The answer is that the market value of the final product includes the value of all the inputs that have gone into it—a loaf of bread priced at say ₹10 includes the value of the flour it contains and the market price—say ₹5 lakhs—of a car includes the value of all the inputs that go into it. Including them again would be double counting.

What about machinery, equipment, and other capital items? Aren't they used as inputs in production processes? Should they therefore be left out? The answer is while they are indeed used to produce something else, this happens over time and unlike raw materials their entire value does not get incorporated in the value of the product being produced in a single period. In the year in which they are produced, they are counted as part of final outputs as investment in fixed capital.

What about steel or cement or any other intermediate that is produced in a year but is not used up? It gets added to the year-end inventory—investment in working capital—and would have to be included in GDP calculations. Does the sale of an existing house add to GDP? Only to the extent that a real estate agent's services might have been used in the transaction. What about transactions in financial assets such as Mr. X selling Infosys shares to Ms. Y? Once again, the only item to enter GDP will be the brokers' commission. What about services provided by the government such as police force, justice system, and so on? These are not bought and sold in the market and hence have no market valuation; but they are "produced" like any other services provided by the private sector and certainly contribute to a people's well-being and hence must be included in GDP. The convention is to value them simply at their "cost of production" i.e. we include in GDP all the expenditure of the government on current goods and services. To paraphrase, include all the goods and services which have not been used up as inputs into the production of something else during the period under consideration.

There is an alternative approach to measuring GDP which focuses on income generation. The most obvious valuation of a final product e.g. a loaf of bread is its market price. It consists of the cost of all intermediate inputs (wheat flour, butter, electricity, fuels, etc.) used in its manufacture plus value added which consists of wages and salaries, interest, rents ,and profits. In economics these items of value added are known as "factor payments". Labour, capital, and land are called "factors of production" and value added consists of payments for the services of these "factors". Now take a step back. We can break up the cost of intermediates like wheat flour into:

(1) The cost of raw materials that are used in their manufacture (e.g. wheat in wheat flour)
(2) Value added in their production.

Let us go back further one step and repeat the process. Ultimately, the market price of the loaf of bread is composed of a series of factor payments—value added in its production, plus value added in the production of wheat flour, plus value added in production of wheat, etc. Hence the output of final goods and services can be valued at their market prices or at all the factor payments made at all stages in the production chain. Now note that these factor payments are nothing but incomes earned by the suppliers of factor services – salaries, wages, interest, dividends, rents and so forth. We can thus define GDP as the total of all the incomes or "factor payments" generated in domestic production. Keep in mind that

(1) we must include value added at all stages and
(2) even if a portion of the value added is not paid out to the suppliers of factor services e.g. retained profits, it must be included in GDP.

Notional deductions like depreciation allowances which companies make while calculating taxable profits must be added back. What about income taxes? Companies pay taxes on profits, individuals pay taxes on the incomes they earn, and so forth. These are mere transfers from income earners to government and must be left out. Conversely, items like pensions paid to retired employees must not be included because they are not payments for services rendered during the period of accounting; they are transfer payments for past services. In other words, in computing GDP using the income approach, incomes before taxes and other such deductions paid as compensation for current factor services must be included.

Will these two valuations—at market prices and at "factor cost" — be always identical? The answer is yes provided there are no "indirect taxes"—taxes like excise duties, sales taxes, and so forth. In the presence of such taxes they differ. To understand this, remember that an excise duty paid by the manufacturer of any product gets included in its market price and hence in the valuation of final goods and services at their market price. But it does not represent a factor payment at any stage of the production process. Consequently, in the presence of such taxes and duties, valuation at market prices will exceed valuation at factor cost. Conversely, if the government pays subsidies to some producers, GDP at market prices will fall short of GDP at factor cost.

GNP is a related but slightly different concept. Here the focus is on incomes accruing to residents of a country. Some of the factor payments arising in domestic production are made to non-residents. Examples of these are dividends paid to foreign shareholders of domestic companies, interest paid to foreign creditors, and so forth. These must be deducted from GDP; conversely, domestic residents may earn incomes—dividends, interest, salaries—by rendering services to foreign producers. These must be added to GDP. GNP is thus arrived at by adding to GDP an item which has the rather cumbersome designation "Net factor incomes from abroad". As a measure of the level of economic activity, GDP is preferred to GNP.

Net Domestic Product (NDP) and Net National Product (NNP) are obtained by deducting depreciation allowances from GDP and GNP respectively. NNP at factor cost is sometimes referred to as National Income.

The international comparisons and rankings of GDP are done by converting the GDPs of various countries from their respective currencies into a common currency such as the US dollar using the market or other appropriate exchange rate.

Real and Nominal GDP and GNP—Which Prices to Use?

Valuing a collection of goods and services in monetary terms gets around the problem of adding apples and oranges but poses another problem. Which market prices should be used? Market prices vary over time and a given collection of goods and services would have significantly different value at two different points in time. A deceptively simple answer to this question would be use the prices prevailing at the time valuation is done. Recall that GDP and GNP are used as a measure of economic activity. As we will discuss further, per capita GDP is widely used as a measure of living standards. Obviously, this would be justified if these concepts measure in some sense the physical volume of goods and services available in an economy. Money provides a convenient unit of account so that apples and oranges can be added up. However monetary valuations can be quite misleading. Consider a firm that manufactures and markets apple jam and mango pickle. Suppose during 2016 it produced 5 lakh kilograms of apple jam and 3 lakh kilograms of mango pickle. At market prices of ₹95 per kilogram of apple jam and ₹60 per kilogram of mango pickle the rupee value of its output was ₹6.55 crores. During 2017, the apple crop in some parts of the country was affected by bad weather and the company could produce only 4 lakh kilograms of apple jam and 3 lakh kilograms of mango pickle. However, the price of apple jam had shot up to ₹125 per kilo while the price of mango pickle had gone up to ₹63. The value of output of the firm in 2017 measured with 2017 prices thus increased to ₹6.89 crores, apparently an increase of a little over 5% when the physical quantum of production had actually gone down. If 2016 prices are used, the value would have been ₹5.60 crores. While the nominal output went up "real" output declined. What is true of a firm is true of an economy. We must find some way of separating the change in physical quantum of production from the change in monetary value which can be attributed only to changes in prices. National income statisticians solve this problem by using two different sets of prices to do the valuation. The nominal GDP or GDP at current prices for a particular year is measured using that year's prices; real or constant price GDP is measured using a fixed set of prices usually the prices ruling in a specified base year. Obviously, the choice of the base year is discretionary. In practice, it is updated every ten years or so. To assess the performance of the economy it is the real GDP that matters.

Rich and Poor Nations

The World Bank classifies countries into: "Low Income", "Middle Income" and "High Income". The low income countries are often referred to as the "Third World". The question we face is how do we measure richness of a country?

The accepted measure of standard of living of a nation is Per Capita GDP. It is simply GDP divided by the population. By this measure the World Bank reported Burundi to be the poorest country with per capita GDP of $277 per annum in 2015 and Luxembourg to be the richest with $101,450 followed by Switzerland with per capita GDP of $80,945. In the same year, India had a per capita GDP of $1,598. Can one say that a typical Swiss citizen is about 51 times as well of as an average Indian? In analyzing such data two caveats should be kept in mind.

(1) Inter-country comparisons of per capita GDP measured in a common currency can be quite misleading.

(2) Market exchange rates do not reflect the differences in purchasing powers of different currencies in their own countries.

For example a haircut in New York might cost 15–20 dollars whereas the price of a haircut in Mumbai converted into dollars at the market exchange rate would be no more than a dollar or two. One needs a correction to take account of these "relative price differences". The correction is unlikely to change the relative ranking of countries but will correct extreme distortions which the raw figures tend to project. Also, it has been argued quite convincingly that a higher per capita GDP need not imply a higher "quality of life".

Over time, changes in living standards are captured by changes in per capita real GDP. This is obtained by subtracting the population growth rate from the growth rate of real GDP.

23.2 COMPONENTS OF GDP—THE DEMAND SIDE OF THE ECONOMY

Gross Domestic Product consists of outputs of all final goods and services. How are these used? The largest component is accounted for by private household consumption—food, clothing, fuels and power, travel, personal services, durables and so forth. This is captured in private consumption expenditure. Next comes investment. This consists of both additions to fixed assets—plant, equipment and structures—as well as net increase in inventories of all kinds. The third component is government use of current goods and services captured in government expenditure on the same. A part of the domestic output is exported to foreign countries. But then we must also account for the fact that private spending, investment spending and government expenditure may also consist of some imported items which must be taken out. Thus we can visualize the following sources-and-uses identity:

GDP (Y) = Private Consumption (C) + Investment (I) + Government Expenditure (G) + Exports (X) – Imports (M)

Keep in mind that this is just an accounting identity—value of goods and services available from domestic production and imports must equal the value of goods and services used up for various purposes including net additions to inventories. We do not know yet what determines the volume of goods and services produced during a year. For that we must investigate determinants of spending decisions—C, I, G and X—on the one hand and production decisions of producers on the other. In a market economy, demand and supply determine the volume of output and its price.

Determinants of Aggregate Spending

Let us begin with the largest component of aggregate demand. Household consumption behaviour has been studied extensively both in the aggregate as well as at the level of individual households. The most important influence on the household spending decision is its current and past income levels, in particular what is known as "personal disposable income (PDI)" i.e. income that actually ends up in the hands of households after all the statutory deductions like income taxes. Every hundred rupees increase in income leads to approximately seventy-five-rupee increase in consumption expenditure for the economy as a whole though this proportion differs between different income groups. Spending volumes are also positively affected by accumulated wealth. Finally, real returns to saving may also have some impact, e.g. high interest rates paid on deposits and debentures, attractive returns to investment in stocks etc. would probably induce households to spend less and save more. However, empirically this last factor has not been found to be very significant.

Determinants of investment spending have been inquired into both by economists and corporate finance specialists. The widely accepted theory of investment behaviour postulates that investment by corporations depends primarily on expected changes in output, after-tax real cost of capital, and availability of funds. Expectations of changes in output may be based partly on past changes in output. After-tax cost of capital is determined by interest rates and factors like investment tax credits, depreciation allowances and expected inflation. Availability of funds, in particular sufficient retained earnings, appears to be an important factor even in the absence of capital rationing. Investment responds positively to expectations of increase in output and negatively to increases in cost of capital.

Government expenditure is largely a policy variable. It responds partly to economic conditions and is partly influenced by non-economic factors. When the economy is depressed, the government may deliberately increase its expenditure on goods and services to provide a stimulus to economic activity. Conversely, when the economy is overheated, discretionary expenditure may be curtailed though some items of mandatory expenditure such as salaries cannot be easily contracted.

A country's exports will generally depend upon two major factors. The levels of economic activity and incomes in countries to which it exports would be the dominant consideration. If income levels in its foreign markets are high, a country's exports would boom. The second factor would be the price its foreign consumers face in their respective currencies relative to the prices of its competitors. This would depend partly on the exchange rate. In the case of "small" countries exports are often treated as exogenous i.e. unaffected by economic conditions at home.

By the same token, a country's imports would depend upon its own income level and the exchange rate. For many developing countries, the price factor may not be very important; imports are then an increasing function of domestic economic activity.

To summarize, demand for goods and services depends partly upon past, current and expected future income, policy variables like interest rate and public spending and exogenous factors like income in the rest of the world.

At any given time, aggregate demand would respond positively to decrease in the price of output and vice versa. Over time, growth in the economy would increase demand for output at each price level. Events which affect consumer and investor sentiment adversely such as a stock market crash would reduce demand at each price level.

This aggregate demand together with supply side factors determine the equilibrium level of income and prices. We now turn to a brief examination of the supply side of the economy.

23.3 PRODUCTION, COSTS AND AGGREGATE SUPPLY

Firms make output decisions based on market price and their cost of production. The latter is determined by the technology employed and the prices of inputs like labour, capital and materials used in production. Existing capacity also constrains the maximum possible output that can be produced.

Extending the same logic to the entire economy, we can say that the aggregate supply of goods and services would depend upon the "price" and some measure of cost of production. At the aggregate level, we think in terms of the price level, wages and some index of material costs. Supply shocks like weather and oil prices would also impinge on the behaviour of aggregate supply. Given the technology, the stock of capital equipment and prices of variable inputs like labour and materials, aggregate supply would respond positively to increase in the price level till capacity output is reached.

An increase in wages, material prices, or an adverse supply shock like bad weather would reduce the supply of output at any price level. Conversely, reduction in input costs or a favourable supply shock would increase the supply of output at every price level.

In the short run, the main determinant of aggregate supply is the behaviour of wages. Wage determination in a market economy has two components. Given expectations about future inflation, workers will try to protect their real wages by demanding nominal wage increases at least equal to the expected inflation. In addition, there is the influence of conditions in the labour market. In an economy which is working at or beyond full capacity, labour markets are very tight and workers can demand increases in real wages i.e. nominal wage increases beyond expected inflation. Conversely, in a recession with high unemployment, workers would tone down their wage demands and perhaps even accept a cut in real wages.

In the short run, the behaviour of the aggregate price level is determined by changes in variable costs viz. labour and material costs. If wage increases are highly sensitive to prevailing unemployment rates, increase in aggregate supply can be brought about only by a sharp increase in price level—the aggregate supply curve is steep. If material prices increases, the curve shifts up causing higher prices at all levels of output.

In an economy like India's where a large fraction of the labour force is employed in the so-called unorganised sector with virtually no unionisation and collective bargaining, the wage-employment relationship and its influence on the aggregate supply behaviour is limited. Aggregate supply is more sensitive to other shocks such as increases in material prices and weather factors.

In the long run, supply behaviour is largely determined by changes in productive capacity brought about by investment, productivity increases and technological changes.

Putting it together

An economic equilibrium in a market economy is characterized by equality of supply and demand. At the aggregate level, GDP and the price level are determined by the interaction of aggregate supply and aggregate demand. Shifts in either, caused by policy actions and exogenous shocks would lead to changes in output or the price level or both. If the economy is in a recession, an increase in demand would lead largely to an increase in output with little or no increase in prices. Conversely, if the economy is operating near capacity, increased demand would cause a spurt in prices; if the demand pressure persists, it would give rise to persistent inflation. An adverse supply shock would lead to a contraction of GDP and a rise in price level. If wage increases tend to outrun productivity improvements or if material prices show a persistent upward trend, once again inflation would be the outcome.

The dynamics of wages and inflation is closely related to formation of expectations, credibility of policy makers and the level of unemployment. If workers experience time and again that their real wages suffer erosion because actual inflation always outruns the expected inflation built into their wage agreements, it would feed into their subsequent wage demands and result in an inflationary spiral. This effect would be strengthened if the economy is currently operating near full employment. Of course this linkage is much stronger in developed economies with organized labour markets and strong unions.

23.4 MACROECONOMIC POLICY

A market economy left to itself will often produce an equilibrium which the government in a democratic society may not find acceptable. It may be characterized by high levels of unemployment or a high rate of inflation; the distribution of income may be very lopsided; balance of payments may show a large deficit and so forth. Dynamically, the economy may show undesirable features such large fluctuations in income and employment or low rates of long term growth. Most democratic governments regard it as their duty to design and implement macroeconomic policies which will mitigate if not eliminate some of the undesirable consequences of operation of the market mechanism.

Macroeconomic policies are of two types. Fiscal policies pertain to the volume and structure of public revenue and expenditure and government borrowing. Monetary policies refer to control of money supply, credit and interest rates. In addition, exchange rate policy may also be looked upon as an instrument of macroeconomic policy.

In addition, the government attempts to influence the economy by means of other policy instruments. Tariffs and quotas on foreign trade are employed to serve a number of objectives including protection of domestic industry. Government may also directly intervene in the economy by means of administrative controls on production, prices, consumption and investment. Some sectors of economic activity may be reserved for public sector or government may be an important player in them along with the private sector.

Our discussion of economic policy here is confined to traditional fiscal and monetary policies.

Fiscal Policy

Governments collect taxes and other revenues such as various fees, user charges for services provided, dividends and interest on its investments in public enterprises and so forth. Part of the money is spent on current expenses of running the country—salaries of government employees, travel, communications, etc.—while the rest may be devoted to investments in physical and social infrastructure. If the expenditure exceeds the revenue, the government must borrow either from the central bank or the "market" including external sources. By altering the aggregate volume and composition of its revenues and expenditure and the size and source of its borrowings the government can exercise a significant influence on the economy.

Changing the tax structure and tax rates can have important incentive-disincentive effects. High levels of income and profit taxes for instance may have adverse effects on the incentives to work and invest and may also lead to widespread tax evasion and other distortions. Excise and sales taxes affect relative prices of different goods and services and hence consumption and production patterns. If the government is unable to control its current expenditure it may have to curtail investments in infrastructure or resort to excessive borrowing both of which have undesirable long term consequences.

In the past, governments have used tax expenditure policies to moderate cyclical fluctuations in economic activity. Public expenditures are increased when the economy shows signs of sliding into a recession and cut back when a boom is in the offing. Alternatively or concurrently, taxes may be lowered to encourage private spending when the economy is weak and raised when the economy is strong. The size of the budget deficit is regarded as a measure of fiscal stimulus. The so called "fiscal deficit" is the difference between government's current revenues and its total expenditure— current plus capital. It indicates the amount of borrowing government must resort to. The size of the fiscal deficit in relation to GDP has become an important policy parameter with the government attempting to bring it down to about 3% of GDP.

Excessive fiscal deficits can lead to accelerating inflation and can potentially crowd out private investment by preempting a large chunk of savings. In particular, if rising fiscal deficits are on account of increases in current government expenditure, it is a matter of grave concern since it implies reduction in total investment with undesirable consequences for future growth of the economy.

The distinction between government borrowing from the central bank and from the "market" is an important one. The former, as we will see below leads to an expansion of the money supply which in turn may cause faster price inflation. The latter drives up the interest rates. In terms of its long term effects both can give rise to undesirable consequences.

Fiscal policy, in particular tax structure and public investments also have significant implications for the long term growth potential of the economy.

Monetary Policy

The responsibility for the control of money supply, bank credit, and interest rates lies with the central bank of the country viz. the Reserve Bank of India.

The money in circulation with the public consists of currency and coin issued by the central bank plus deposits with banks and some other depository institutions. Depending upon which deposits are being included, we get different monetary aggregates which are termed M1, M2, M3 and so forth. M3 is the so called "broad money" and includes demand and fixed deposits along with currency and coin. Bank credit is also a measure of liquidity in the economy since banks' ability to extend credit depends upon their ability to mobilise deposits and the cash reserves they have to maintain against these deposits. The stock of currency together with the reserves maintained by the banking system with the central bank constitute the monetary base or "high powered money". Changes in this are magnified and lead to changes in the total money stock or bank credit.

The central bank can use a variety of policy instruments to regulate the volume and cost of credit in the economy. It can lower or raise the cash reserve ratio (CRR) within specified limits to make it easier or more difficult for banks to extend credit. By engaging in open market purchases or sales of securities from its portfolio it can inject or suck out reserves enabling banks to expand or contract credit as also lowering or raising the cost of credit. It can use the discount rate—the rate it charges banks for refinancing facility – and discretionary limits on refinancing facilities to influence the volume of bank credit. At times it can impose administrative controls to alter the volume and sectoral composition of outstanding bank credit. Lately, the Reserve Bank of India has more or less dispensed with such administrative controls on credit and interest rates and has been relying more on open market operations and the market mechanism.

The RBI has adopted inflation control as the primary objective of monetary policy. From time to time it also deploys the policy tools under its control to address other targets such as exchange rate and employment. Often, these objectives can conflict with each other. Thus massive capital inflows into the economy which is already awash with liquidity pose a dilemma for the central bank. If the central bank does nothing, the exchange rate would appreciate which may hurt exports; if it intervenes and buys foreign exchange to prevent this, it would have to inject additional liquidity into the system. At such times, it must trade off one target against another.

The degree of autonomy enjoyed by the central bank is an important determinant of its ability to conduct effective monetary policy and achieve credibility with financial markets. If it has to play second fiddle to the Finance ministry and accommodate government's borrowing requirements irrespective of the resulting impact on money supply, interest rates and inflation, it loses its ability to conduct effective monetary policy. Similarly, excessive reliance on opaque administrative control mechanisms reduces its credibility with financial markets and makes it difficult to implement anti-inflationary policies or appropriate exchange rate policies. In recent years, there has been a gradual move towards granting more and more operational independence to the RBI.

SUMMARY

- Macroeconomics focuses on aggregate variables such as Gross National Product, aggregate investment and saving, total employment, wholesale and consumer price indices, money supply and bank credit and key financial variables like interest rates and exchange rates.
- Gross Domestic Product (GDP) and Gross National Product (GNP) are two widely used measures of the level of economic activity.
- Per capita GDP is widely used as a measure of living standards. The World Bank classifies countries into: "Low Income", "Middle Income" and "High Income". The low income countries are often referred to as the "Third World".
- GDP consists of output of all the final goods and services. GDP can be expressed as follows:

  GDP (Y) = Private Consumption (C) + Investment (I) + Government Expenditure (G) + Exports (X) – Imports (M)
- The most important influence on the household spending is "personal disposable income (PDI)". Investment spending by corporates depends primarily on expected changes in output, after-tax real cost of capital, and availability of funds. Government expenditure is largely a policy variable. It responds partly to economic conditions and is partly influenced by non-economic factors. Exports of a country depend upon the level of economic activity in countries to which it exports and the exchange rate. A country's imports would depend upon its own income level and the exchange rate.
- The two most important macroeconomic policies are fiscal policy and monetary policy. Fiscal policy pertains to the volume and structure of public revenue and expenditure and government borrowing. Monetary policy is concerned with the control of money supply, credit, and interest rates.

Appendix A

TABLE A.1 *Future Value Factor FV (r, n) = $(1 + r)^n$*

Period n	1%	2%	3%	4%	5%	6%	7%	8%	9%	10%	11%	12%	13%
0	1.000	1.000	1.000	1.000	1.000	1.000	1.000	1.000	1.000	1.000	1.000	1.000	1.000
1	1.010	1.020	1.030	1.040	1.050	1.060	1.070	1.080	1.090	1.100	1.110	1.120	1.130
2	1.020	1.040	1.061	1.082	1.102	1.124	1.145	1.166	1.188	1.210	1.232	1.254	1.277
3	1.030	1.061	1.093	1.125	1.158	1.191	1.225	1.260	1.295	1.331	1.368	1.405	1.443
4	1.041	1.082	1.126	1.170	1.216	1.262	1.311	1.360	1.412	1.464	1.518	1.574	1.630
5	1.051	1.104	1.159	1.217	1.276	1.338	1.403	1.469	1.539	1.611	1.685	1.762	1.842
6	1.062	1.126	1.194	1.265	1.340	1.419	1.501	1.587	1.677	1.772	1.870	1.974	2.082
7	1.072	1.149	1.230	1.316	1.407	1.504	1.606	1.714	1.828	1.949	2.076	2.211	2.353
8	1.083	1.172	1.267	1.369	1.477	1.594	1.718	1.851	1.993	2.144	2.305	2.476	2.658
9	1.094	1.195	1.305	1.423	1.551	1.689	1.838	1.999	2.172	2.358	2.558	2.773	3.004
10	1.105	1.219	1.344	1.480	1.629	1.791	1.967	2.159	2.367	2.594	2.839	3.106	3.395
11	1.116	1.243	1.384	1.539	1.710	1.898	2.105	2.332	2.580	2.853	3.152	3.479	3.836
12	1.127	1.268	1.426	1.601	1.796	2.012	2.252	2.518	2.813	3.138	3.498	3.896	4.335
13	1.138	1.294	1.469	1.665	1.886	2.133	2.410	2.720	3.066	3.452	3.883	4.363	4.898
14	1.149	1.319	1.513	1.732	1.980	2.261	2.579	2.937	3.342	3.797	4.310	4.887	5.535
15	1.161	1.346	1.558	1.801	2.079	2.397	2.759	3.172	3.642	4.177	4.785	5.474	6.254
16	1.173	1.373	1.605	1.873	2.183	2.540	2.952	3.426	3.970	4.595	5.311	6.130	7.067
17	1.184	1.400	1.653	1.948	2.292	2.693	3.159	3.700	4.328	5.054	5.895	6.866	7.986
18	1.196	1.428	1.702	2.026	2.407	2.854	3.380	3.996	4.717	5.560	6.544	7.690	9.024
19	1.208	1.457	1.754	2.107	2.527	3.026	3.617	4.316	5.142	6.116	7.263	8.613	10.197
20	1.220	1.486	1.806	2.191	2.653	3.207	3.870	4.661	5.604	6.728	8.062	9.646	11.523
25	1.282	1.641	2.094	2.666	3.386	4.292	5.427	6.848	8.623	10.835	13.585	17.000	21.231
30	1.348	1.811	2.427	3.243	4.322	5.743	7.612	10.063	13.268	17.449	22.892	29.960	39.116

(Contd.)

TABLE A.1 (Contd)

Period n	14%	15%	16%	17%	18%	19%	20%	24%	28%	32%	36%	40%
0	1.000	1.000	1.000	1.000	1.000	1.000	1.000	1.000	1.000	1.000	1.000	1.000
1	1.140	1.150	1.160	1.170	1.180	1.190	1.200	1.240	1.280	1.320	1.360	1.400
2	1.300	1.322	1.346	1.369	1.392	1.416	1.440	1.538	1.638	1.742	1.850	1.960
3	1.482	1.521	1.561	1.602	1.643	1.685	1.728	1.907	2.097	2.300	2.515	2.744
4	1.689	1.749	1.811	1.874	1.939	2.005	2.074	2.364	2.684	3.036	3.421	3.842
5	1.925	2.011	2.100	2.192	2.288	2.386	2.488	2.392	3.436	4.007	4.653	5.378
6	2.195	2.313	2.436	2.565	2.700	2.840	2.986	3.635	4.398	5.290	6.328	7.530
7	2.502	2.660	2.826	3.001	3.185	3.379	3.583	4.508	5.629	6.983	8.605	10.541
8	2.853	3.059	3.278	3.511	3.759	4.021	4.300	5.590	7.206	9.217	11.703	14.758
9	3.252	3.518	3.803	4.108	4.435	4.785	5.160	6.931	9.223	12.166	15.917	20.661
10	3.707	4.046	4.411	4.807	5.234	5.695	6.192	8.549	11.806	16.060	21.647	28.925
11	4.226	4.652	5.117	5.624	6.176	6.777	7.430	10.657	15.112	21.199	29.439	40.496
12	4.818	5.350	5.936	6.580	7.288	8.064	8.916	13.215	19.343	27.983	40.037	56.694
13	5.492	6.153	5.886	7.699	8.599	9.596	10.699	16.386	24.759	36.937	54.451	79.372
14	6.261	7.076	7.988	9.007	10.147	11.420	12.839	20.319	31.961	48.757	74.053	111.120
15	7.138	8.137	9.266	10.539	11.974	13.590	15.407	25.196	40.565	64.359	100.712	155.568
16	8.137	9.358	10.748	12.330	14.129	16.172	18.488	31.243	51.923	84.954	136.969	217.795
17	9.276	10.761	12.468	14.426	16.672	19.244	22.186	38.741	66.461	112.139	186.278	304.914
18	10.575	12.375	14.463	16.879	19.673	22.901	26.623	48.039	85.071	148.023	253.388	426.879
19	12.056	14.263	16.777	19.748	23.214	27.252	31.948	59.568	108.890	195.391	344.540	597.630
20	13.743	16.367	19.461	23.106	27.393	32.429	38.338	73.864	139.380	257.916	468.574	836.683
25	26.462	32.919	40.374	50.658	62.669	77.388	95.396	216.542	478.905	1033.590	2180.081	4499.880
30	50.950	66.212	85.850	111.065	143.371	184.675	237.376	634.820	1645.504	4142.075	10143.019	24201.432

TABLE A.2 *Future Value Interest Factor for an Annuity FVA (r, n)* $= \frac{(1+r)^n - 1}{r}$

Period n	1%	2%	3%	4%	5%	6%	7%	8%	9%	10%	11%	12%	13%
1	1.000	1.000	1.000	1.000	1.000	1.000	1.000	1.000	1.000	1.000	1.000	1.000	1.000
2	2.010	2.020	2.030	2.040	2.050	2.060	2.070	2.080	2.090	2.100	2.110	2.120	2.130
3	3.030	3.060	3.091	3.122	3.152	3.184	3.215	3.246	3.278	3.310	3.342	3.374	3.407
4	4.060	4.122	4.184	4.246	4.310	4.375	4.440	4.506	4.573	4.641	4.710	4.779	4.850
5	5.101	5.204	5.309	5.416	5.526	5.637	5.751	5.867	5.985	6.105	6.228	6.353	6.480
6	6.152	6.308	6.468	6.633	6.802	6.975	7.153	7.336	7.523	7.716	7.913	8.115	8.323
7	7.214	7.434	7.662	7.898	8.142	8.394	8.654	8.923	9.200	9.487	9.783	10.089	10.405
8	8.286	8.583	8.892	9.214	9.549	9.897	10.260	10.637	11.028	11.436	11.859	12.300	12.757
9	9.369	9.755	10.159	10.583	11.027	11.491	11.978	12.488	13.021	13.579	14.164	14.776	15.416
10	10.462	10.950	11.464	12.006	12.578	13.181	13.816	14.487	15.193	15.937	16.722	17.549	18.420
11	11.567	12.169	12.808	13.486	14.207	14.972	15.784	16.645	17.560	18.531	19.561	20.655	21.814
12	12.683	13.412	14.192	15.026	15.917	16.870	17.888	18.977	20.141	21.384	22.713	24.133	25.650
13	13.809	14.680	15.618	16.627	17.713	18.882	20.141	21.495	22.953	24.523	26.212	28.029	29.985
14	14.947	15.974	17.086	18.292	19.599	21.015	22.550	24.215	26.019	27.975	30.095	32.393	34.883
15	16.097	17.293	18.599	20.024	21.579	23.276	25.129	27.152	29.361	31.772	34.405	37.280	40.417
16	17.258	18.639	20.157	21.825	23.657	25.673	27.888	30.324	33.003	35.950	39.190	42.753	46.672
17	18.430	20.012	21.762	23.698	25.840	28.813	30.840	33.750	36.974	40.545	44.501	48.884	53.739
18	19.615	21.412	23.414	25.645	28.132	30.906	33.999	37.450	41.301	45.599	50.396	55.750	61.725
19	20.811	22.841	25.117	27.671	30.539	33.760	37.379	41.446	46.018	51.159	56.939	63.440	70.749
20	22.019	24.297	26.870	29.778	33.066	36.786	40.995	45.762	51.160	57.275	64.203	72.052	80.947
25	28.243	32.030	36.459	41.646	47.727	54.865	63.249	73.106	84.701	98.347	114.413	133.334	155.620
30	34.785	40.568	47.575	56.805	66.439	79.058	94.461	113.283	136.308	164.494	199.021	241.333	293.199

(Contd.)

TABLE A.2 (Contd)

Period n	14%	15%	16%	17%	18%	19%	20%	24%	28%	32%	36%	40%
1	1.000	1.000	1.000	1.000	1.000	1.000	1.000	1.000	1.000	1.000	1.000	1.000
2	2.140	2.150	2.160	2.170	2.180	2.190	2.200	2.240	2.280	2.320	2.360	2.400
3	3.440	3.473	3.506	3.539	3.572	3.606	3.640	3.778	3.918	4.062	4.210	4.360
4	4.921	4.993	5.066	5.141	5.215	5.291	5.368	5.684	6.016	6.362	6.725	7.104
5	6.610	6.742	6.877	7.014	7.154	7.297	7.442	8.048	8.700	9.398	10.146	10.946
6	8.536	8.754	8.977	9.207	9.442	9.683	9.930	10.980	12.136	13.406	14.799	16.324
7	10.730	11.067	11.414	11.772	12.142	12.523	12.916	14.615	16.534	18.696	21.126	23.853
8	13.233	13.727	14.240	14.773	15.327	15.902	16.499	19.123	22.163	25.678	29.732	34.395
9	16.085	16.786	17.518	18.285	19.086	19.923	20.799	24.712	29.369	34.895	41.435	49.153
10	19.337	20.304	21.321	22.393	23.521	24.709	25.959	31.643	38.592	47.062	57.352	69.814
11	23.044	24.349	25.733	27.200	28.755	30.404	32.150	40.238	50.399	63.122	78.998	98.739
12	27.271	29.002	30.850	32.824	34.931	37.180	39.580	50.985	65.510	84.320	108.437	139.235
13	32.089	34.352	36.786	39.404	42.219	45.244	48.497	64.110	84.853	112.303	148.475	195.929
14	37.518	40.505	43.672	47.103	50.818	54.841	59.196	80.496	109.612	149.240	202.926	275.300
15	43.842	47.580	51.660	56.110	60.965	66.261	72.035	100.815	141.303	197.997	276.979	386.420
16	50.980	55.717	60.925	66.649	72.939	79.850	87.442	126.011	181.868	262.356	377.692	541.988
17	59.118	65.075	71.673	78.979	87.068	96.022	105.931	157.253	233.791	347.310	514.661	759.784
18	68.394	75.836	84.141	93.406	103.740	115.266	128.117	195.994	300.252	459.449	700.939	1064.697
19	78.969	88.212	98.603	110.285	123.414	138.166	154.740	244.033	385.323	607.472	954.277	1491.576
20	91.025	102.440	115.380	130.033	146.628	165.418	186.688	303.601	494.213	802.863	1298.817	2089.206
25	181.871	212.793	249.214	292.105	342.603	402.042	471.981	898.092	1706.803	3226.844	6053.004	11247.199
30	356.787	434.745	530 321	647.439	790.948	966.712	1181.882	2640.916	5873.231	12940.859	28172.276	60501.081

Table A.3 *Present Value Factor PV (r, n) = $(1 + r)^{-n}$*

Period n	1%	2%	3%	4%	5%	6%	7%	8%	9%	10%	11%	12%	13%
0	1.000	1.000	1.000	1.000	1.000	1.000	1.000	1.000	1.000	1.000	1.000	1.000	1.000
1	0.990	0.980	0.971	0.962	0.952	0.943	0.935	0.926	0.917	0.909	0.901	0.893	0.885
2	0.980	0.961	0.943	0.925	0.907	0.890	0.873	0.857	0.842	0.826	0.812	0.797	0.783
3	0.971	0.924	0.915	0.889	0.864	0.840	0.816	0.794	0.772	0.751	0.731	0.712	0.693
4	0.961	0.924	0.889	0.855	0.823	0.792	0.763	0.735	0.708	0.683	0.659	0.636	0.613
5	0.951	0.906	0.863	0.822	0.784	0.747	0.713	0.681	0.650	0.621	0.593	0.567	0.543
6	0.942	0.888	0.838	0.790	0.746	0.705	0.666	0.630	0.596	0.564	0.535	0.507	0.480
7	0.933	0.871	0.813	0.760	0.711	0.665	0.623	0.583	0.547	0.513	0.482	0.452	0.425
8	0.923	0.853	0.789	0.731	0.677	0.627	0.582	0.540	0.502	0.467	0.434	0.404	0.376
9	0.914	0.837	0.766	0.703	0.645	0.592	0.544	0.500	0.460	0.424	0.391	0.361	0.333
10	0.905	0.820	0.744	0.676	0.614	0.558	0.508	0.463	0.422	0.386	0.352	0.322	0.295
11	0.896	0.804	0.722	0.650	0.585	0.527	0.475	0.429	0.388	0.350	0.317	0.287	0.261
12	0.887	0.788	0.701	0.625	0.557	0.497	0.444	0.397	0.356	0.319	0.286	0.257	0.231
13	0.879	0.773	0.681	0.601	0.530	0.469	0.415	0.368	0.326	0.290	0.258	0.229	0.204
14	0.870	0.758	0.661	0.577	0.505	0.442	0.388	0.340	0.299	0.263	0.232	0.205	0.181
15	0.861	0.743	0.642	0.555	0.481	0.417	0.362	0.315	0.275	0.239	0.209	0.183	0.160
16	0.853	0.728	0.623	0.534	0.458	0.394	0.339	0.292	0.252	0.218	0.188	0.163	0.141
17	0.844	0.714	0.605	0.513	0.436	0.377	0.311	0.270	0.231	0.198	0.170	0.146	0.125
18	0.836	0.700	0.587	0.494	0.416	0.350	0.296	0.250	0.212	0.180	0.153	0.130	0.111
19	0.828	0.686	0.570	0.475	0.396	0.331	0.276	0.232	0.194	0.164	0.138	0.116	0.098
20	0.820	0.673	0.554	0.456	0.377	0.312	0.258	0.215	0.178	0.149	0.124	0.104	0.087
25	0.780	0.610	0.478	0.375	0.295	0.233	0.184	0.146	0.116	0.092	0.074	0.059	0.047
30	0.742	0.552	0.412	0.308	0.231	0.174	0.131	0.099	0.075	0.057	0.044	0.033	0.026

(Contd.)

Table A.3 (Contd)

Period n	14%	15%	16%	17%	18%	19%	20%	24%	28%	32%	36%	40%
0	1.000	1.000	1.000	1.000	1.000	1.000	1.000	1.000	1.000	1.000	1.000	1.000
1	0.877	0.870	0.862	0.855	0.847	0.840	0.833	0.806	0.781	0.758	0.735	0.714
2	0.769	0.756	0.743	0.731	0.718	0.706	0.694	0.650	0.610	0.574	0.541	0.510
3	0.675	0.658	0.641	0.624	0.609	0.593	0.579	0.524	0.477	0.435	0.398	0.364
4	0.592	0.572	0.552	0.534	0.516	0.499	0.482	0.423	0.373	0.329	0.292	0.260
5	0.519	0.497	0.476	0.456	0.437	0.419	0.402	0.341	0.291	0.250	0.215	0.186
6	0.456	0.432	0.410	0.390	0.370	0.352	0.335	0.275	0.227	0.189	0.158	0.133
7	0.400	0.376	0.354	0.333	0.314	0.296	0.279	0.222	0.178	0.143	0.116	0.095
8	0.351	0.327	0.305	0.285	0.266	0.249	0.233	0.179	0.139	0.108	0.085	0.068
9	0.308	0.284	0.263	0.243	0.226	0.209	0.194	0.144	0.108	0.082	0.063	0.048
10	0.270	0.247	0.227	0.208	0.191	0.176	0.162	0.116	0.085	0.062	0.046	0.035
11	0.237	0.215	0.195	0.178	0.162	0.148	0.135	0.094	0.066	0.047	0.034	0.025
12	0.208	0.187	0.168	0.152	0.137	0.124	0.112	0.076	0.052	0.036	0.025	0.618
13	0.182	0.163	0.145	0.130	0.116	0.104	0.093	0.061	0.040	0.027	0.018	0.013
14	0.160	0.141	0.125	0.111	0.099	0.088	0.078	0.049	0.032	0.021	0.014	0.009
15	0.140	0.123	0.108	0.095	0.084	0.074	0.065	0.040	0.025	0.016	0.010	0.006
16	0.123	0.107	0.093	0.081	0.071	0.062	0.054	0.032	0.019	0.012	0.007	0.005
17	0.108	0.093	0.080	0.069	0.060	0.052	0.045	0.026	0.015	0.009	0.005	0.003
18	0.095	0.081	0.069	0.059	0.051	0.044	0.038	0.021	0.012	0.007	0.004	0.002
19	0.083	0.070	0.060	0.051	0.043	0.037	0.031	0.017	0.009	0.005	0.003	0.002
20	0.073	0.061	0.051	0.043	0.037	0.031	0.026	0.014	0.007	0.004	0.002	0.001
25	0.038	0.030	0.024	0.020	0.016	0.013	0.010	0.005	0.002	0.001	0.000	0.000
30	0.020	0.015	0.012	0.009	0.007	0.005	0.004	0.002	0.001	0.000	0.000	0.000

Table A.4 *Present Value Factor for an Annuity PVA (r, n) =* $\frac{1-1/(1+r)^n}{r}$

Period n	1%	2%	3%	4%	5%	6%	7%	8%	9%	10%	11%	12%	13%
0	1.000	1.000	1.000	1.000	1.000	1.000	1.000	1.000	1.000	1.000	1.000	1.000	1.000
1	0.990	0.980	0.971	0.962	0.952	0.943	0.935	0.926	0.917	0.909	0.901	0.893	0.885
2	1.970	1.942	1.913	1.886	1.859	1.833	1.808	1.783	1.759	1.736	1.713	1.690	1.668
3	2.941	2.884	2.829	2.775	2.723	2.673	2.624	2.577	2.531	2.487	2.444	2.402	2.361
4	3.902	3.808	3.717	3.630	3.546	3.465	3.387	3.312	3.240	3.170	3.102	3.037	2.974
5	4.853	4.713	4.580	4.452	4.329	4.212	4.100	3.993	3.890	3.791	3.696	3.605	3.517
6	5.795	5.601	5.417	5.242	5.076	4.917	4.766	4.623	4.486	4.355	4.231	4.111	3.998
7	6.728	6.472	6.230	6.002	5.786	5.582	5.389	5.206	5.033	4.868	4.712	4.564	4.423
8	7.652	7.325	7.020	6.733	6.463	6.210	5.971	5.747	5.535	5.335	5.146	4.968	4.799
9	8.566	8.162	7.786	7.435	7.108	6.802	6.515	6.247	5.995	5.759	5.537	5.328	5.132
10	9.471	8.983	8.530	8.111	7.722	7.360	7.024	6.710	6.418	6.145	5.889	5.650	5.426
11	10.368	9.787	9.253	8.760	8.306	7.887	7.499	7.139	6.805	6.495	6.207	5.938	5.687
12	11.255	10.575	9.945	9.385	8.863	8.384	7.943	7.536	7.161	6.814	6.492	6.194	5.918
13	12.134	11.348	10.635	9.986	9.394	8.853	8.358	7.904	7.487	7.103	6.750	6.424	6.122
14	13.004	12.106	11.296	10.563	9.899	9.295	8.745	8.244	7.786	7.367	6.982	6.628	6.302
15	13.865	12.849	11.938	11.118	10.380	9.712	9.108	8.559	8.060	7.606	7.191	6.811	6.462
16	14.718	13.578	12.561	11.652	10.838	10.106	9.447	8.851	8.312	7.824	7.379	6.974	6.604
17	15.562	14.292	13.166	12.166	11.274	10.477	9.763	9.122	8.544	8.022	7.549	7.120	6.729
18	16.398	14.992	13.754	12.659	11.690	10.828	10.059	9.372	8.756	8.201	7.702	7.250	6.840
19	17.226	15.678	14.324	13.134	12.085	11.158	10.336	9.604	8.950	8.365	7.839	7.366	6.938
20	18.046	16.351	14.877	13.590	12.462	11.470	10.594	9.818	9.128	8.514	7.963	7.469	7.025
25	22.023	19.523	17.413	15.622	14.094	12.783	11.654	10.675	9.823	9.077	8.422	7.843	7.330
30	25.808	22.397	19.600	17.292	15.373	13.765	12.409	11.258	10.274	9.427	8.694	8.055	7.496

(Contd.)

TABLE A.4 (Contd)

Period n	14%	15%	16%	17%	18%	19%	20%	24%	28%	32%	36%	40%
0	1.000	1.000	1.000	1.000	1.000	1.000	1.000	1.000	1.000	1.000	1.000	1.000
1	0.877	0.870	0.862	0.855	0.847	0.840	0.833	0.806	0.781	0.758	0.735	0.714
2	1.647	1.626	1.605	1.585	1.566	1.547	1.528	1.457	1.392	1.332	1.276	1.224
3	2.322	2.283	2.246	2.210	2.174	2.140	2.106	1.981	1.868	1.766	1.674	1.589
4	2.914	2.855	2.798	2.743	2.690	2.639	2.589	2.404	2.241	2.096	1.966	1.849
5	3.433	3.352	3.274	3.199	3.127	3.058	2.991	2.745	2.532	2.345	2.181	2.035
6	3.889	3.784	3.685	3.589	3.498	3.410	3.326	3.020	2.759	2.534	2.339	2.168
7	4.288	4.160	4.039	3.922	3.812	3.706	3.605	3.242	2.937	2.678	2.455	2.263
8	4.639	4.487	4.344	4.207	4.078	3.954	3.837	3.421	3.076	2.786	2.540	2.331
9	4.946	4.772	4.607	4.451	4.303	4.163	4.031	3.566	3.184	2.868	2.603	2.379
10	5.216	5.019	4.883	4.659	4.494	4.339	4.193	3.682	3.269	2.930	2.650	2.414
11	5.453	5.234	5.029	4.836	4.656	4.486	4.327	3.776	3.335	2.978	2.683	2.438
12	5.660	5.421	5.197	4.988	4.793	4.611	4.439	3.851	3.387	3.013	2.708	2.456
13	5.842	5.583	5.342	5.118	4.910	4.715	4.533	3.912	3.427	3.040	2.727	2.469
14	6.002	5.724	5.468	5.229	5.008	4.802	4.611	3.962	3.459	3.061	2.740	2.478
15	6.142	5.847	5.575	5.324	5.092	4.876	4.675	4.001	3.483	3.076	2.750	2.484
16	6.265	5.954	5.669	5.405	5.162	4.938	4.730	4.033	3.503	3.088	2.758	2.489
17	6.373	6.047	5.749	5.475	5.222	4.990	4.775	4.059	3.518	3.097	2.763	2.492
18	6.647	6.128	5.818	5.534	5.273	5.033	4.812	4.080	3.529	3.104	2.767	2.494
19	6.550	6.198	5.877	5.584	5.316	5.970	4.844	4.097	3.539	3.109	2.770	2.496
20	6.623	6.259	5.929	5.628	5.353	5.101	4.870	4.110	3.546	3.113	2.772	2.497
25	6.873	6.464	6.097	5.766	5.467	5.195	4.948	4.147	3.564	3.122	2.776	2.499
30	7.003	6.566	6.177	5.829	5.517	5.235	4.979	4.160	3.569	3.124	2.778	2.500

APPENDIX

B

Depreciation

Although depreciation is an important item on the profit and loss account, its nature is often not properly understood by non-finance managers.

This note clarifies what depreciation is, explains the manner in which the depreciation schedule is prepared, presents information on the methods and rates of depreciation under the Companies Act and the Income Tax Act, and dispels some of the myths surrounding depreciation.

Nature of Depreciation

A fixed asset is used over a number of accounting periods. So it is necessary to allocate its costs to various accounting periods that benefit from its use. Such an allocation is called depreciation. Accountants normally allocate the cost of an asset over its useful life using a well-defined procedure.

Depreciation Schedule

Three steps are involved in calculating the depreciation schedule.

- Determine the *depreciable base*.
- Estimate the *useful life* of the asset
- Choose the *depreciation* method

Depreciable Base The depreciable base is the cost of the asset less its residual value.

The *cost of the asset* is equal to:

List price, less discount

+

Taxes

+

Insurance, freight, and handling

+

Installation charges

+

Interest during the construction period

The *residual value* (or salvage value) is the amount expected from the disposal of the asset after its useful life. Since it may not be much or difficult to estimate, it may be put at 5 per cent or so of the original cost or even completely ignored.

Useful Life The useful life of an asset is the period over which it is expected to be used. Often it is less than the physical life of the asset because of factors such as technological obsolescence, fall in demand, and legal restrictions. Estimating the useful life is largely a matter of managerial judgment.

Depreciation Method There are several methods of depreciation. The two most commonly used depreciation methods in India are the straight line method and the written down value method.

Under the *straight line* method the depreciable amount of the asset is allocated equally over the useful life of the asset. To illustrate, assume that a car costs ₹500,000 and is expected to fetch a salvage of ₹80,000 after a useful life of 6 years. The annual depreciation charge is:

$$\frac{\text{Cost} - \text{Salvage value}}{\text{Useful life}} = \frac{₹500{,}000 - ₹80{,}000}{6} = ₹70{,}000$$

The depreciation schedule of the car under the straight line method would be as follows:

Year	*Original cost*	*Depreciation*	*Accumulated depreciation*	*Book value at year-ends*
1	₹500,000	₹70,000	₹70,000	₹430,000
2	500,000	70,000	140,000	360,000
3	500,000	70,000	210,000	290,000
4	500,000	70,000	280,000	220,000
5	500,000	70,000	350,000	150,000
6	500,000	70,000	420,000	80,000

Under the *written down value* method, the depreciation charge for an accounting period is equal to a fixed percentage of the book value at the beginning of the period. To illustrate, assume that the cost of an asset is ₹100,000 and the depreciation rate applicable to it under the *written down method* is 40 per cent. The depreciation schedule for the asset will be as follows:

Year	Original cost	Depreciation	Accumulated depreciation	Book value at year-ends
1	100,000	40,000	40,000	60,000
2	100,000	24,000	64,000	36,000
3	100,000	14,400	78,400	21,600
4	100,000	8,640	87,040	12,960
5	100,000	5,184	92,224	7,776

Depreciation for Company Law and Income Tax Purposes

Unlike most other countries, the methods and rates for depreciation are prescribed by law in India.

Depreciation under the Companies Act The Companies Act requires that a company that intends to pay dividend must provide depreciation in accordance with Schedule XIV of the Act. This schedule gives the rates under the straight line method and the written down value method for various classes of assets. For assets used in multiple shifts, extra depreciation has to be provided. The key rates presently are as follows:

	Straight Line Method	*Written Down Value*
Building (other than factory Buildings)	1.58%	4.87%
Factory buildings	3.17%	9.50%
Other	31.67%	63.16%
Furniture & Fittings	9.50%	25.89%
Plant & Machinery (Gen)	6.33%	18.10%

Note that the above rates are the legal *minimum* rates for determining divisible profit.[1] The purpose of the Companies Act is to protect the creditors. It tries to ensure that companies do not overstate profits to pay large dividends to the detriment of creditors.

Depreciation for Income Tax Purposes For income tax purposes, tax payers have no choice but to follow the written down value method. The rates permitted for various assets presently are as follows:

Buildings	:	5%
Plant and machinery	:	15%
Vehicles on hire	:	30%

[1]A company may choose to use higher rates.

Computers	:	60%
Pollution control equipment	:	100%

There is no concept of higher depreciation for multiple shift under the Income Tax Act. Note that the rates prescribed under the Income Tax Act are the *maximum rates* that a company can claim whereas the rates prescribed under the Companies Act are the *minimum rates* that a company must charge.

Myths Surrounding Depreciation

The nature of depreciation is often misunderstood and users of financial statements seem to have wrong notions about it. The following are the common myths surrounding depreciation.

- Depreciation is a source of cash
- Depreciation provides funds for replacement
- Depreciation is a valuation process

Depreciation is a Source of Cash To get the cash profit from operations, depreciation is added to profit. So, there is an impression that depreciation is a source of cash. This is a completely wrong notion.

Depreciation, as we have learnt, is nothing but the allocation of the cost of an asset over its useful life. Being an expense, it reduces profit. However, since it is a non-cash charge, it is added to profit to arrive at cash profit. Put differently, what is subtracted initially is later added back. As a result the net impact is zero. This point may be clarified by the example below.

		Case A	*Case B*
1	Revenues	1,000	1,000
2	Costs, other than Depreciation	600	600
3	Depreciation	200	100
4	Profit	200	300
5	Cash profit: (4) + (3)	400	400

From the above example it is clear that whether the depreciation expense is ₹200 or ₹100, the cash profit remains at 400. In general, irrespective of what the depreciation charge is, the cash profit remains unchanged.

Depreciation Provides Funds for Replacement Some people believe that accumulated depreciation represents cash set aside for replacement of assets. This is not true. Accumulated depreciation is simply the portion of the cost of an asset that has already been written off, nothing more nothing less.

Depreciation is a Valuation Exercise Financial statements are not meant to reflect the market values of fixed assets. Even if the market value of some asset (say building) increases, it is depreciated in the books according to a well-defined method (straight line method or written down value method or whatever). Remember that depreciation is the allocation of the cost of an asset over its useful life and not an exercise meant to reflect the fluctuating market value of the asset.

Index

CFM-MHE Series in Finance

Honorary Consulting Editor: Dr. Prasanna Chandra

The CFM-MHE Series in Finance, a joint initiative of the Centre for Financial Management and McGraw Hill Education (India), seeks to synthesise the findings of financial research with the concerns of practitioners. The aim of the books in this series is to convey the important developments in the theory and practice of finance in a rigorous, but relatively non-technical manner for the benefit of: (a) finance practitioners and (b) students of MBA.

Titles in the Series

- *Behavioural Finance* — **Prasanna Chandra**
- *Financial Management: Theory and Practice, 9/e* — **Prasanna Chandra**
- *Projects: Planning, Analysis, Selection, Financing, Implementation, and Review, 8/e* — **Prasanna Chandra**
- *Finance Sense: Finance for Non-finance Executives, 5/e* — **Prasanna Chandra**
- *Investment Analysis and Portfolio Management, 5/e* — **Prasanna Chandra**
- *Corporate Valuation: A Guide to Analysts, Managers, and Investors* — **Prasanna Chandra**
- *Strategic Financial Management: Managing for Value Creation* — **Prasanna Chandra**
- *International Finance: A Business Perspective, 2/e* — **Prakash G Apte**
- *Investment Banking: Concepts, Analyses and Cases, 2/e* — **Pratap G Subramanyam**
- *Macroeconomic Policy Environment, 2/e* — **Shyamal Roy**

CFM Quarterly in Finance

Centre for Financial Management brings out an e-journal called *CFM Quarterly in Finance* edited by Dr. Prasanna Chandra.

Written in a relatively non-technical manner, *CFM Quarterly in Finance* has three sections. The first section, the principal section, carries short articles and cases to discuss important ideas, concepts, and state-of-the-art practices in the broad fields of finance and investments. The second section carries snippets that provide useful insights. Finally, the third section provides some wit and wisdom.

CFM Quarterly in Finance is designed for two categories of readers: finance educators and finance practitioners. Finance educators will find the material useful to enrich the courses taught by them. Finance practitioners will get valuable insights and perspectives to handle their professional challenges.

You can access the *CFM Quarterly in Finance* at www.cfm-india.com

Online Executive Education Programme

FINANCE FOR MANAGERS

Managing for Value Creation

Centre for Financial Management Offers an Online Executive Education Progamme. Finance for Managers : Managing for Value Creation

For details visit www.cfm-india.com